*Volume Two*

# PHARISEE
## AMONG
# PHILISTINES

Judge Matthew P. Deady, late 1880s.

*The Diary of*
*Judge Matthew P. Deady*
*1871-1892*

# PHARISEE  AMONG PHILISTINES

*Edited and with Introduction by*
MALCOLM CLARK, JR.

*Oregon Historical Society*
*Portland, Oregon*

Published by the Oregon Historical Society
with the aid of the Western Imprints Fund
and the Northwest Area (Hill) Foundation

LC 74–75363
SBN 87595–046–9
Designed by Corinna Campbell Cioeta
Printed in U.S.A.
Kingsport Press, Inc.
Kingsport, Tennessee

# CONTENTS

# ILLUSTRATIONS

# ILLUSTRATIONS

# PHARISEE
## AMONG
# PHILISTINES

## Menu.

Blue point oysters.

**Potage.**
Cousommé à la Princesse.
Créme d' artichaut à la Victoria.

**Hors d'oeuvre.**
Cramosqui de gibier à la Russe.
Faisans.
Basse rayée à la Borgia.
Carpe du Rhin à la Régence.

**Relevé,**
Filet de bœuf à la Luculus sauce Madère.

**Entrées.**
Suprême de Cailles en demi-deuil.
Terrapine à la Maryland.
Sorbet Tortoni, paté de foie gras en
Belle- vue Sur Socle.

**Roti.**
Canvass back Duck.
Laitues, céleri, tomates mayonnaise.

**Légumes.**
Tomates farcies à la Duxelle
Céleri à l'espagnole, petits pois à la Française.
Haricots verts, asperges en branches.

**Entremets.**
Croute de Savarin à L'ananas.
Gelée à l'orange Rubannée.
Glaces variées.
Fruit dessert.
Ramquin au fromage.
Café.

Saturday, January 14th 1882.

*Wormley*

When the Deadys visited the East, 1881–82, Supreme Court Justice Stephen J. Field gave a dinner for them. Those who signed the menu were Field, Supreme Court Chief Justice M. R. Waite, Justices Stanley Matthews, John M. Harlan, Samuel F. Miller, W. B. Woods and J. P. Bradley. Senators George Pendleton, L. F. Grover, James H. Slater and ex-Senator A. A. Sargent were there, with Sallie H. Swearingen, Isabelle McCreary and Oregon Congressman M. C. George.

# 1881

*January 1 (Sat)* Made 30 calls in a carriage. . . . I did not make half as many as usual—touching only the highest peaks in the social range, or those in whom I felt a special interest.

The sleet and rain froze upon the trees and wires so that upon [last] Thursday night & Friday many of them broke down. The ice on the telephone and telegraph wires was about an inch in diameter. Corbetts beautiful elms were badly injured. The maples, on account of the limbs being more upright fared better. Had a letter from Judge Pratt on Xmas eve written at Milan. Sent him a letter and Xmas *Oregonian* next day. The Xmas & New Year editions of the *Oregonian* were very fine this year, both being double numbers, and the first containing [two of] my opins . . .

*8 (Sat)* Sunday (Jan 2) . . . Trinity as usual. Called to see old Mr Steel in the afternoon.[1] Found him quite sick and not expected to live. Called at Col [Dudley] Evans new house also. Found them comfortably fixed but Mrs E was in bed from the effects of a miscarriage. During the week sat in the C C & D C courts, nothing of importance. Monday & Tuesday engaged on my accounts and paying bills. Paid L & T $250 on the note. . . . Thursday purchased a Steinway upright piano E style 1 from Barstch for $475 payable without interest in 6 months, the instrument warranted for 5 years and kept in tune for 1. For the first 2 nights after we got it Paul played until 12 oclock—it is a great comfort in the house. . . .

Purchased *Endymion* and have been reading it the latter part of the week. It is very readable, even fascinating—full of action well sketched pictures and pithy, sententious and sometimes cynical sayings. Every plebian scrub in this country thinks he is bound to sneer at it because it was written by a Tory Earl.[2] . . .

*15 (Sat)* . . . Lectured on Friday before the medical class. Thursday went around with the subscription for the debt of Trinity Parish and got $130, did the same thing this afternoon and got $95, in all $842. . . .

Glanced over Lawson on contracts by common carriers in restriction of their liability . . . and think well of its tone. It . . . quotes three of my cases frequently—the *Pacific,* the *California* & the *Oriflamme.* . . .

*29 (Sat)* Sunday, Jan 16 . . . at Trinity as usual. Mrs D went out with Henders to school and service and came back feeling so badly at leaving him there against his will that we determined then and there to let him stay with us until Monday morning and during the week I had a talk with Prof Hill on the subject and he agreed to throw off $20 for the term on his board on account of his absence on Saturday & Sunday. . . .

. . . Saturday obtained subscriptions to debt of the Parish for $60. Called at the Hall in the evening. Had a full and free talk with the Misses Rodney about their relations with the Couch family. They feel very keenly the slight put upon Clementine and the school by the employment of Edith Yarn[d]ley to give music lessons to Eva Lewis and Lucy Wilson. I tried to put the matter on more pleasant grounds . . . But it was not much use. I am very sorry for them for they have neglected and slighted others for these [things] in times gone by and they know it and feel it.

Sunday, Jan 23. Attended . . . Trinity. Went to Reeds to luncheon which was elegant and excellent—if he does owe me $40 which he borrowed on Nov 10 and promised to pay in 10 days certain. Poor fellow I suppose he hasn't got it. I don't know how they manage to live as they do. Henders and I commenced our Sunday afternoon walks after nearly 2 years intermission, this being his first whole Sunday home from school in that time. Went to Dodds for a little while, then up to the end of the horse railway and in it down to the Clarendon, and back afoot. . . . The week has been cold until this morning which is as balmy as spring. Schulze got a dispatch this week . . . from Villard, that my stock & bonds in the Or Im Co ($10,000) had been sold at .65 cts, [$1.65] making the gain in the operation deducting the advance on purchase, of about $6300. The dispatch also advised that V had sent his check for the amount to me[A]. . .

*February 5 (Sat)* Sunday (Jan 30) . . . Trinity as usual. Put $1 in the plate for Dom Missions, not much, but all I could spare. Lewis put in $10 and Flanders $5 and all the rest were content with their usual Sunday contribution. . . . Was quite indisposed on Monday and Tuesday with sore throat and inflammation of the head, besides aching all over. Took a prescription for bilious attack from Dr Strong and got better except my throat which is still sore with an occasional cough. . . . On Wednesday evening attended a whist party at Laidlaws, and played whist with Good, Mrs Holt Wilson & Mrs Col Gillespie—the latter for a partner. We were badly beaten for want of cards, but it was a pleasant game. It was a pleasant party and the refreshments were elegant. Friday afternoon lectured before the medical class and had Dr Brown in the audience.

*12 (Sat)* . . . Tuesday [the] 8 received H Villards check to Schulze endorsed to me for $6413.33, the net proceeds of the sale of $10,000 worth of the stock of the Or[egon] Im[provement] Co purchased on Dec 1, 1880 at par and sold on Jan 21 at 165 deducting 52 days interest at 6% on the investment $86.67 and deposited same Feb 9, when it was selling at 191. Wednesday Henders broke out with Scarlet Fever and was brought in from the Gram School. He could not be kept at the boarding house on account of the children and so Mrs Deady and he went to the G S Hospital. I called to see them Thursday evening. They were very comfortably fixed, but I am very sorry that Mrs D may have to stay there 3 or 4 weeks and Henders lose that time from school.

*19 (Sat)* Sunday (Feb 13) . . . Went from church with Mrs Glisan and took lunch and then to the Hospital to see Mrs D & H B—a hard and slavish walk through the slush and snow. Found them both comfortable. . . .

. . . Went to hear Dr Lindsley on Evolution at the Cong church on Monday evening. Did very well but it took him an hour and half to do so. Took Miss Rodney with me. Very small but select audience. Thursday evening went with Mrs & Capt Ellicott & Miss C Rodney to hear [John] Owen[s] in "Our Boys."[3] It was excellent. The week has been cold with more or less snow on the ground. Mrs Deady came back from the hospital on Friday afternoon looking very well. Left H B there doing well. Today he sent me a drawing of his room, which is excellent. . . .

*26 (Sat)* Sunday (Feb 20) . . . Dined at Dr Wilsons where I met Mr [Alexander] Guthrie[4] of Balfo[u]r, Guthrie of Liverpool—a pleasant quiet gentleman. Monday evening delivered my lecture on Law & Lawyers at the Congregational church, to a very fair audience—the best, committee said, of the four. I was very well satisfied with my lecture and pretty well satisfied with the delivery.

. . . after the lecture, went with Paul to a Musicale at the Lewis' given to Mr Guthrie. An elegant affair, and some good music . . .

. . . Wrote to Villard thanking him for his kindness in the matter of my $10,000 investment in the Or Im Co stock and particularly for the delicate and considerate way in which he did it in writing to our medium (S) that he did not wish me to consider myself under any obligation to him on account of the matter. Mrs Deady was out to the Hospital yesterday to see Henders. He is doing well and begins to want to get out. Sent me a very pretty drawing of a cabin and fence. . . . Today, is Mrs Ds 46 birthday. I gave her a silver comb, cost $8.50. Spent the evening at Edward Failings where we had tableaus and presents in honor of Lucy F[ailing]s birthday—tomorrow. . . .

*March 5 (Sat)* . . . Got letters from Judge Pratt today at London and photos of Gladstone et ux, Beaconsfield and [John] Bright. The latter looks like a well-to-do-tradesman, and B[eaconsfield] like a Jew drummer. G is a very fine looking man. Got a nice Blarney letter from Ben Stark the other day in which he said that Senator Anthony[5] in a speech made in defense of the suffrage laws of Rhode Island had quoted one of my decisions on the subject. . . .

*19 (Sat)* . . . Have spent some time examining property with a view of purchasing a piece for a home in the Couch addition. Got a long pleasant letter from [Charles] Lancaster night before last in which he announces the existence of a baby 7 months old, also a letter from Judge [John] Burnett of Corvallis enclosing 2 very handsome cabinet Photos of Erskine & Curran[6] as he says, though there is nothing upon them to indicate who they are or when and/or where they were taken. [Milton] Smith returned this week from his trip to Salem where he went for examination, and was admitted to the bar of the C C & D C, yesterday and today. Today received from a Mr McKinney of Arkansas volume 1 of the *Or Spectator*, the first paper published on the Pacific coast, containing 26 numbers and issued between Feb 1846 & Jan 1847 for the Library for which I paid $100. . . .

*26 (Sat)* Sunday (Mar 20) Attended M prayer and S S as usual. In the afternoon walked to St Vincents Hospital and called on Bishop Blanchet. Had a pleasant hour with the old man. He is getting feeble. Called at Dr Wilsons on Mrs Burns on my way back. It was the first time I had seen her since she became a mother, and I was impressed with the tempus fugit, when I remembered her as a little prattling girl, and now she was a mother in Israel. She looked large, but very well and seemed to be glad to see me. Called also on Mrs Wilbur at the Clarendon on her way home from the east. She has been sick and looks old, but is cheerful. Father Wilbur looks as well as when I first saw him nearly 30 years ago. . . .

Monday sat in the C C and heard argument upon the motion to modify the injunction in the city of Portland v Oregonian Ry Co. Wrote and delivered opinion on Wednesday allowing the company to lay and operate track and side tracks on the public levee, so called, during the pendancy of the suit, it giving bond to remove same when ordered in the sum of $5000. Tuesday sent by express $1500 in gold to John Henderson to loan in Mrs Ds name $1100 of the same being hers and $400 H B Ds. . . .

Wednesday and Thursday [*Mar 22 & 23*] heard evidence and argument on an application to enjoin the building of the Wallamet Bridge. An interesting case. Friday & today busily engaged in considering it. On Monday bargained with A[tkinson] & W[akefield] for the north ½ of Block 174 in Couchs addition, in front of Lewis' residence for $3500, and on Tuesday did the same with Gillette for the north ½ Block 128 in Caruthers addition for $2500, for Mrs Deady.[7] Read some in the magazines, and attended evening prayer some afternoons, but have been very busy this week. Tuesday deposited $25 to the credit of H B D for his 12 birthday. . . .

*April 2 (Sat)* . . . Monday finished opin in bridge case and delivered it in the C C sustaining the plaintiffs right to a preliminary injunction upon the ground that the bridge with the draw contemplated was an obstruction to navigation contrary to . . . the act of Feb 14, 1859 admitting Or into the Union, and declaring the navigable waters thereof free and common highways. The court was full and the east Portlanders were vexed. In consideration that Sawyer would sit in the Circuit Court in a short time, I delayed the issue of a formal injunction until he would be present and made an Order restraining the defendant as prayed in the meantime. . . . Thursday evening got a letter from Gen Lane, written by his son Lafayette I suppose and signed by him, stating that his end was drawing nigh and bidding me good bye. It was a very kind and complimentary letter and touched me to the heart. I wrote him in reply the same evening and shall visit him next week if he lives. Friday settled my accounts for the quarter amounting to $634 and paid today $250 on the Ladd note. On Monday March 28 paid $3500 for the north ½ of Block 174 in Couchs addition for Mrs Deady. Hope to build a home upon it some day for our old age. Settled with Prof Hill today for H B D, having concluded that we would not send him back the rest of this term. Charged me for three weeks, $19.50 together with back dues on German and drawing and books made the amount $35. Paid $45 at the Hospital for him and his mother also . . . Had a nice letter from Villard dated March 17 in reply to mine acknowledging receipt of the proceeds of my Im Co stock. Got a copy of Lanmans *Biographical Annals* from Washington for the Library, in which I find myself handsomely noticed.[8]

*9 (Sat)* . . . Thursday went to Roseburg and spent a couple of hours with Gen

Lane in the evening. He is passing away but cheerfully and may last a month yet.
. . . Sawyer arrived yesterday evening and today he and I went up the west side road to McMinnville and back. The day has been cloudy and damp, but the country looked well.

*16 (Sat)* . . . Sat in the C C during the week with Sawyer . . . Called at the Hall on Thursday evening where I met Bishop [John] Paddock[9] and his daughter—a bright chatty maiden to whom I took a fancy. . . . Hirsch paid me $250 on the share of the appropriation received by Fleischner for referee fees. He brought $300 but I only took $250 the sum to which I was entitled.

Today . . . delivered opinion in the Bridge case sustaining the injunction. Sawyer took the Bull by the horns and said that in his judgment a bridge ought not to be erected in this harbor. The poor bridgites went away sad. . . .

*30 (Sat)* Sunday (Ap 17) Easter Day. Attended a Sunday School service at 10 oclock where the scholars decorated a cross and made their offerings amounting to $155 or more. The church was beautifully decorated. The music in the morning was noisy and jerky and altogether out of taste. The church was crowded so that many persons could not get seats and the same in the evening. . . .

. . . Friday [*April 22*] Mrs D went to Yamhill and I followed on Saturday. Staid at Johns until Monday when Harvey took us to Amity and we took the train for Nesmiths where we staid all night and came home the next day. It rained all the time nearly that we were gone. Henderson enjoyed himself hugely with his gun. Killed some birds, a squirrel and a rabbit. John has a nice home and is in a way to be well fixed. Nesmiths were very agreeable—particularly Velina & Hattie. Mrs N was not at home. Nesmith had just returned from burying Joe Lane, and read me the outline of his address on the occasion which was very warm and laudatory. I wanted to ask him if he was not glad that he did not have Lane committed to the Bastil[l]e in 1862 for treason as he proposed to Bush but thought it would be mean.[10]

On our return from Nesmiths we fell in with Mother Sc[h]olastica, a Benedictine nun from Minnesota.[11] She was born in Cologne and came to the U S when she was 4 years old. She is a Prioress of the order and is only 34 years old. She taught 13 years in succession and is a very pleasant woman.

Friday, April 29. Mrs Bishop Paddock died this morning at 5 oclock at the Hall of typho-pneumonia, and will be buried at Vancouver on Monday next. She reached here about the middle of the month from Brooklyn and has been sick ever since her arrival. In fact was taken sick crossing the plains. It is a very sad affair and a mournful beginning of the Bishops life in his new diocese. . . .

Today, went to Reedville, to attend a sale of fancy stock—horses, cattle and sheep.[12] Went out on a special train at 8:30 A M and came back on the regular train that passed down at 2 P M. . . . Ladd was there in his portable chair taking a/c of sales with as much earnest[ness] and anxiety as if his future depended on the result. The sale of horses amounted to over $6000. The sheep and cattle were still to sell; a few of the former had been sold for from $22½ to $15 per head—Leicesters. . . .

*May 14 (Sat)* . . . Went to the Negro minstrels this afternoon. Humbug as usual.

Four showy courtesans sat in front of me and stomped their feet when their favorites said or sang. Thursday was my 57 birthday. It passed off quietly. Mrs D gave me a china porridge bowl. Tempus fugit. Attended a meeting of the Medical Faculty in the evening. . . .

*21 (Sat)*. . . Tuesday organized the Grand Jury 21 strong . . . and they remained in session until Friday finding only two indictments—but one of them against Watkinds for illegal voting upon the same charge as the former indictment was held insufficient. On Friday Mallory got a letter from the Atty Genl stating that an application had been made for Watkinds pardon supported by an elaborate argument from Grover from which he got the impression that Watkinds was technically guilty but ought not to be prosecuted, and advised Mallory to dismiss the case unless he thought it ought to be prosecuted.[13] M instead of continuing the case and reporting the facts to the Dept, weakened and dismissed the case. He wants to be reappointed and wants Grovers vote for confirmation.

. . . Attended organ concert with Mrs D at the Methodist church last night to celebrate the setting up of a pipe organ in that once place of primitive worship. The old Wesleyans must have turned over in their graves at the profane amusement. . . .

*28 (Sat)*. . . May 24, Tuesday, attended the B B society dinner on the Queens birthday. Sat on the left of the chairman, Donald Macleay and proposed the toast—The British Empire, in a speech of five minutes which I drafted and committed during the afternoon—the first time I ever did such a thing in my life. Got home towards 4 P M. Had a good dinner and a very pleasant time, about 75 persons present. The proceedings with my speech, Major [A F] Sears[14] and Col McCrackens are in this mornings *Oregonian*. They look and read quite well. Had a letter from Field yesterday saying that he had procured Mrs Deady a pass to go east and would me also if I would come with her. A welcome rain on Wednesday morning and cool cloudy weather since. Paul has been at the office this week. Goes on one crutch now. [*He had sprained his ankle two weeks earlier*]. . . . Henderson commenced going to dancing school last Saturday and went again today—2 bits a lesson.

*June 4 (Sat)*. . . [Tuesday, May 31] was decoration day and H B marched in the procession on horseback. Wednesday the jury came in the C C and commenced the trial of U S v Doig.[15] Concluded the argument Thursday evening at 10 oclock—Tom Strong showed well for the defense. Charged the jury at ½ past 9 Friday morning, 1¼ hours, verdict of not guilty, with a special finding that he was guilty of misconduct &c in grounding the vessel on Sand Island.

. . . Wednesday evening attended a dancing party with Mrs [D] at [John] Goodfellows.[16] Paul was there but did not dance on account of his ankle. I danced . . . We (Mrs D and I) came home immediately after supper—were the first to leave for the first time in our lives. Are they getting shorter?. . . .

*5 (Sun)*. . . Trinity as usual. Bishop Paddock preached. The chancel was full of clergymen attending the convocation. In the afternoon the Sunday school children of Trinity, St Stephens, St David and St Matthews had a service at which Bishops Morris, Paddock and Rev John Sel[l]wood and Plummer made short and stirring addresses. The singing of the children was good and hearty and the house was full of them. In the evening there was a missionary meeting. . . .

*18 (Sat)*. . . Got a letter Thursday evening . . . from Justice [S F] Miller of the S[upreme] C[ourt] dated June 10 at Denver in reply to one from myself to him complimenting him on his decision in the Kilbourn case. He asks me to come to Washington, which I hope to do. Wrote a paragraph or article last night which appeared in this mornings *Oregonian* on the "Morning Drum-Beat" in reply to another article in the *Daily Statesman* of the 14 inst from the pen of D W C[raig][17] in which he pays my Queens dinner speech a very high compliment, which I with some hesitation and mental blushing reproduced in my article. Appointed Paul crier of the courts to take effect from the first of the month during which time he had actually performed the duties of the office. He will clothe himself—take care of himself, except his board and lodging and washing which I will continue to pay while he is a student. . . .

*July 2 (Sat)*. . . Thursday June 24 the 29 anniversary of my marriage passed over without notice, Mrs D being away. [*She was visiting the Hardings.*] Saturday went up on the morning train to Gervais where I was met by Mr Harding and Henderson who drove me over to the farm. Staid there until Monday morning when Dan Harding & Henderson drove Mrs D & I to Gervais where we took the cars and came home in time for court. Had a very pleasant visit to Hardings. Ella looked well and was very kind and agreeable. Had some long pleasant chats with Ben, in his study and rambling about the place. Ate blackberries growing over the remains of the old Rivet cabin, probably built in 1830 and stood in the ruins of its pretentious successor built in 1850. He was a Canadian Frenchman who came to the country in an early day, probably with Hunt in 1812.[18] We left H B at Hardings. He is perfectly infatuated with farming and ploughs and harrows like a man. . . .

. . . Got a letter from Judge Field Thursday with a pass to New York and back, and I suppose now we will go east in the latter part of Sept to be gone until Jan 1882. Senator Grover called on Thursday evening. He looks very well and talks cheerfully. Paul was taken down with a bad sore throat on Wednesday and has been in bed ever since, but is better now. Thursday Mrs D and I attended a musical at Cy Dolphs where we heard some very good music and met some agreeable people. Mrs D[olph] read a piece of Negro dialect most admirably. . . .

This morning before 10 a dispatch came from the east that President Garfield was shot and killed, and later that his wounds were not mortal. What is this country coming to? Reaping the reward of our harboring and encouraging the assassins and outlaws of Europe.[19] Paid the quarters bills yesterday, amount to over $600 and there remains $275 on the piano which will clean us to the bed rock.

*9 (Sat)* . . . The Fourth—Monday—was a beautiful day. I was at work until 12 when I went up to the Plaza where I met Mrs D and C & L Rodney and saw portion of the procession counter march on third street. Heard portions of H Y Thompsons address of welcome, McCrackens reading of the Declaration, and Whites hifalutin poem. The Oration I did not stay to hear, but it read well and concluded

with the same quotation from Bayard Taylors "Centennial Poem" that my Roseburg oration did. I was not in the procession because I was not specially invited
and did not care to go under the general invitation to "Federal officers" including
the tide waiters. . . . Made a contract this morning with [C H] Marvin to paint,
paper and kalsomine house inside for $220 payable when I get the money. . . .
Judge Williams, Hill, Thompson & Durham have formed a law partnership here
and at the Dalles—they ought to incorporate, if for no other reason to shorten
the name. [Henry] Hewett called yesterday and I talked with him about the right
of Andrus to a seat in the council. Nicklin[20] called during the week on Wednesday
or Tuesday and I had a long talk with him on the same subject in which I advised
him that Andrus had no right to a seat in the council. Canvassers called on me
and asked my opinion on the propriety of comparing the certificate of the judges
from the third ward with the tally sheet of that ward. I told them if the tally sheet
was returned by the judges and appeared to be a part of the whole book, they
should regard it as such and correct any apparent errors upon the face of the
certificate by comparison with it.

*16 (Sat)* . . . Friday Mrs D and I went to Eugene. I to attend a meeting of the
board of Regents and she on her way to Bettys. She got a cinder in her eye on
the way up which pained her very severely. Dr Sharpless took it out after we got
to Eugene and she soon got over it. . . . Had a meeting of the Regents yesterday
afternoon and evening. Increased the teachers salaries 10 percentum all round
and provided that the salary of Mrs Spiller and Mr Straub[21] should be increased
to $1500 each if the income of the school sufficient. Had a good deal of plain
talk with Pres Johnson. Directed that $40 retained by the executive committee
out of Gatchs salary be paid. Left Mrs D at Dr. Gearys this morning where we
staid last night. She will go over to Bettys today. Reached here (my chambers)
at 5 P M . . . The country looked beautiful between here and Eugene, though
I have the impression that the acreage sown to wheat is less than I have seen
it. . . .

*23 (Sat)* . . . Have been alone all the week. Mrs D at Murchs and H B and Paul
at Hardings. . . . Took Alice Strong to the N M Theatre last evening to hear the
Mendelssohn Quintet of stringed instruments and Miss Marie Nellini vocalist.[22]
The most delicious and unexceptionable musical entertainment I ever attended,
I think. The first violin and the violin-cello were wonderful. . . .

*24 (Sun)* Attended . . . Trinity. John McCracken read the service in the morning
as far as the close of the litany when he became unwell and called to me to take
his place which I did and finished the service. Was a little embarrassed at being
jumped up so suddenly. . . .

*August 1 (Mon)* . . . Sat in the court until Saturday. Nothing of interest, except
on Wednesday I made a decree in the case of the Aurora community agt the
representatives of the Bethel community dividing the property and then dividing
that of the former among the members thereof.[23] Examined the case Monday &
Tuesday and wrote the decree from an outline furnished me by Effinger at my
request. Saturday Mrs D, H B & I went to Bushs. . . . Went to Methodist church
in Salem at Sunday with Estelle Bush and heard a good sermon from a young

preacher called Dennison. The congregation was thin and looked lean. The glory has departed from Salem—particularly the Methodist part of it. . . . Got a telegram today from Villard wanting to know the amount of the indebtedness on the University expressing a desire to help discharge it. Answered him, about $7000, $4000 of which was about to be enforced against the building by execution. A subscription of $2500 or even $1000 from him would be a good investment. . . .

*6 (Sat)*. . . Got a telegram on Tuesday (Aug 2) making a donation of $7000 to pay indebtedness of University building. I have ascertained since I telegraphed him that the amount is $8000 instead of $7000, but it is too late to correct the mistake in such matter as this. Drew my draft on him for the amount payable to the First N B on yesterday and prepared a little paragraph including Villards letter for publication which appeared in this mornings *Oregonian* & *Standard* with kindly editorial comment.

On Thursday evening . . . went down to the Kalama boat. Paul was bound to Clatsop . . . and Mrs D & H B to Capt Ellicotts camp at Port Orchard, on the Sound. On Friday evening went upon an excursion on the *Bob Lincoln* on the Wallamet as the guest of Major & Mrs Price of the U S Engineers to meet Gen and Mrs [Nelson A] Miles.[24] . . . Went to Milwaukee and down to Springville and back by 10 P M. Was a very pleasant affair and Mrs Price did well as Hostess & Commodore. Miles is a plain sensible man. His wife is a Sherman and knows it. . . .

Got a package of letters from Nesmith on the 4th written in 1859–1866—among which were 2 of my own, one from San Fran at the time Scott came there and the other from Washington. They read well and are entertaining if I do say it.[25] . . .

*13 (Sat)* . . . Got a note from Mrs Victor about the Park blocks in Lownsdales part of Portland, which I answered today. . . .

*27 (Sat)* . . . Thursday [Aug 18] . . . went on board the *Hayward* in the evening for Tacoma. Col Stevens of Washington, son-in-law of Col Baker called during the day. Found him and family aboard the *Hayward* for Olympia. He is a fine looking man and an excellent conversationalist. Believes in Shepherd, Dorsey, Mitchel[l] *et id omne genus*.[26] In the afternoon on Friday Capt Ellicott took me off the *Otter* in his steam launch in the bay of Seattle and we reached his camp in Port Orchard bay 15 miles from Seattle about 8 oclock where I met Mrs D & H B and was welcome. Took a box of fruit to Mrs E and a pretty pap spoon to the baby. Saturday rode over to Miss Babbitts school across the bay. She is a Holyoke graduate and teaches a district school and lives there by herself at a salary of $75 per month. The scholars are mostly half breeds and come to school in canoes or by water. She is a very bright pleasant person and a Jersey woman.

Sunday [Aug 21] Mrs D, H B & I came to Seattle in the Launch. Walked over the town to the University. . . . Left at 6 on the *Otter* for Tacoma where we spent a comfortable night, and had a good breakfast. Came home on Monday. . . .

. . . Rained hard yesterday and 2 near flashes of lightning, and is drizzling today. What is this country coming to. Engaged rooms today on the *Columbia* for the 20 proximo for San Francisco.

*September 10 (Sat)* Sunday August 28. Attended morning prayer at Trinity. Mr Sel[l]wood Sen. officiated. He had a sermon on the mystery of godliness, which in its modes of thought was a century behind the age. . . .

Friday [September 2] went to Eugene to attend a meeting of the Regents and came home on Saturday. Staid all night with Prof Condon and enjoyed his botanical and geological talk very much. He gave me some cones taken from the Picea amabalis and nobolis found in the Cascade Mts near the Columbia[27]. . . Passed a resolution of thanks to Mr Villard for his donation to the University at the Regents meeting. Called at the Hall Saturday evening and met the ladies on their return from the seaside. Presented my cones, and had a pleasant evening. . . .

. . . Tuesday evening [last] called at Ladds with Mrs D and saw Nells new baby. A handsome product and they are all very proud of it. I had not been there since New Year.

*17 (Sat)* . . . Paid the quarters bills today $558.47 and $100 on H Bs school bill of $152½ for Trinity term at the G S and have $232.57 left in bank for my trip east. Effinger called yesterday and said the people of Aurora wanted to make me a present to signify their obligation to me for my speedy action on their partition suit. Told him I wouldn't take money, despised a gold headed cane, and had a good watch. Concluded to give me a silver pitcher I believe. Rained today lightly. Ellicott telegraphed yesterday that Mrs E not able to go east. We are very sorry but not much disappointed.

*18 (Sun)* . . . Dined at Alices, called on Ollie & Frank and said Good-by. Same at the Hall. Miss Lydia gave me a letter to her sister Mrs McKim. . . . Kearney made Mrs D a present of $100 for expenses on her journey and me $150 for hotel bill in Washington. This was clever and opportune.

*19 (Mon)* Day cool and cloudy. Sat in the C C and D C, approved the accounts of officers. Executed with Mrs D a power of attorney to John Catlin and she and I executed separate wills giving our property to each other for life, remainder to the children in equal parts, and deposited them with Catlin.

4 oclock P M. Have about closed up my business, and will leave for the steamer about 6 this evening with Paul and Mrs Deady. Have $40 in my wallet and exchange on the east as follows—San Fran $100, Chicago $100 and New York $450, which includes my salary to the end of this month. I leave nothing due behind me of any moment—not to exceed $25 in all, and this would have been paid if presented. I shall now bid adieu to these rooms where I have so long worked and on the whole enjoyed myself until probably the middle of January next.

[*Beginning with the entry for October 2, Deady kept an account of his trip in two small separate books. In his regular diary, however, under date of February 8, 1882, he outlined the journey to San Francisco and overland to Chicago, which the Deadys reached on October 2. That entry is placed here to maintain the chronology.*]

Mrs Deady and I left Portland on the Steamship *Columbia* at 7 P M on Sept 19 (Monday). We went over the bar Tuesday morning, having heard of Garfields death at Astoria just before sailing. We reached S Fran on the morning of Thursday 22 and went to the Palace. On Sunday the 24 Judge Sawyer drove us to the

Park and Cliff House . . . Monday was the day of the Garfield obsequies. The procession was a very grand one—probably the largest ever seen in S Fran. I acted as one of the Pall bearers, walking on the right hand side of the catafalque, just behind Gen Rosencranz [*Rosecrans*][28] and in front of Judge Hoffman, being second from the front. About 1 oclock I dropped out of the procession and went to the Palace where I met Villard and S G Reed who had just arrived on their way to Oregon. At 2 oclock we got away and went over the bay to the depot of the Central Pacific . . . the boat was loaded to the guards with people returning from S Fran, where they had gone to witness the procession. Here we soon found our way to the sleeping car in which we had sec 8 where we were very politely received by a most urbane porter—an old colored man named Joseph Harnod from Baltimore.

As we sat down in this quiet elegant place, I felt almost as if I was in fairy land. Got a lunch basket at Sacramento that evening. The basket was excellent, but the filling only so so and very dear.

*27 (Tue)* Stopped for breakfast at Reno and dinner at Humboldt, of which latter we partook. This place by a little irrigation has been made a green oasis in the desert waste, truly.

*28 (Wed)* Took breakfast at Ogden where we met eastern people and cooking or at least from the eastern end of the road. Among other things got good corn bread. Here we left the train and went down to Salt Lake and put up at the Walker House. Mr Dooley, manager of Wells Fargo & Cos bank drove us about the city for 3 or 4 hours.[29] We visited the Tabernacle and were shown the great organ and the wonderful acoustic properties of the building, by which you can hear a pin fall distinctly from one end to the other. Examined the new stone temple in course of construction, which is one of the wonders of the age. The country for many miles back of Ogden and from there to S L city is very picturesque. The Wasatch mountains rising abruptly on the one hand and the rich plain sloping from their base to the Lake on the other. Whatever else may be said of this Mormon community, I agree with the writer who says that at least "It is an evangel of order, sobriety and industry."

*29 (Thu)* Returned to Ogden in the morning and took § 8 on car Woodstock for Omaha. A furious snowstorm as we passed through Weber and Echo Canyon. . . .

*30 (Fri)* Stopped for dinner at Sherman [*Summit, Wyo.*] highest point on the road where the sons of Oakes Ames are breaking up a huge rock to construct the pedestal of a monument to their father.

*October 1 (Sat)* Stopped for breakfast at Grand Island where I camped on my way to Oregon in June 1849, nearly 31 years before. Reached Council Bluffs in the afternoon, and took the Ch Bur & Quincy train to Chicago, on sleeping car § 9. Dined on the Hotel car Windsor—a pleasant contrast to the eating on the road. Had Blue point oysters on the ½ shell.

Sunday, October 2. Crossed the Mississippi at Burlington about daylight. Breakfasted on the car. Reached Chicago and went to the Grand Pacific in time for dinner.

[*Continued from Books A & B*]

Arrived here at 3 P M from the west and stopped at the Grand Pacific, Room 149, 2 floor . . . corner of Clark & Jackson Sts.

*3 (Mon)* Judge [Lyman] Trumbull, Gov Bross, Ex Senator [James] Doolittle, Mr [Charles] Bonney . . . and Agnes Knott, called. Went with Trumbull to the U S court rooms where I met Judges Drummond and Blodgett[30] and sat with them from 12 to 1 while they were hearing a patent case concerning cannery of meat. . . .

Gov Bross took us in his carriage to the Industrial exhibition after dinner. Some good paintings and many people. The exhibitions of wheat very poor as compared with Or. . . .

*4 (Tue)* Came in raining, but cleared off in the afternoon. Called at the office of the *Legal News*. Saw Judge [James] Bradwell and examined the establishment. The Madam not in. B took me to the Public library. Met Mr Poole librarian.[31] Plenty of books but comparatively few papers. . . .

Agnes called and took lunch. Bross called and drove us to the Water Works and Lincoln Park. Agnes accompanied us and we set her down in the park not far from her home. The water works are wonderful and the Park is beautiful, and altogether the ride was a very pleasant one. Met a Mrs & Miss Stephens at dinner of N Y.[32] They seem to know Mrs W[illiams] very well and to have a very low opinion of her. . . .

Went to Haverley theatre in the evening and saw [John] McCullough in "Lear."[33] A beautiful building, an interesting audience and some superb acting. Weather turned cool.

*5 (Wed)* Visited Agnes at Mrs Morgans . . . Went in the cars and had a pleasant ride there and back. Met Mrs Morgan & Mrs Goode 2 sisters who were Emma & Anne Hawkins and made my sister Elizas house a sort of home in 1859 when I was there. Two plain, sensible English women. Agnes has found a good home with them since her mothers death.

Went to Gov Bross' to lunch at one, where we met Jessie B[ross], now Mrs [Henry Demarest] Lloyd, and her husband . . .[34]

Had a very pleasant time. Jessie greeted me as kindly as ever but gave me her cheek instead of her lip. From there we went to the U S Court room . . . I sat on the Bench and Mrs D sat on the platform at the side of the Bench with Mrs Stephens & Miss Stephens—the former is the author of a series of novels including *The Golden Brick*. . . .

*6 (Thu)* . . . Mrs Deady & Agnes were out shopping in the morning . . . [I] Went with Agnes & Mrs D on the cars to the south Park and then in the Charabanc down the Boulevard and around the Park. A beautiful drive and lovely scene. We travelled 13 miles, were gone about 3 hours and it cost us just 90 cents. [At] ½ past 5 went to dinner at Gen [C P] Buckinghams,[35] in his carriage, 3 miles north of the G P H[otel]. Agnes came also, they sent the Phaeton for her. . . . the Gen was not at home. Had a good family dinner and a very comfortable, characterful house without high ceilings. Agnes played after dinner and played beautifully. Left at ½ past 9 and came home on the Clarke st[reet] cars. . . .

*7 (Fri)* Mr Ed & Will Buckingham called for us at ½ past 9 and took us to their Steel works and the Rolling Mills. At the last place we saw iron ore made into

Bessemer steel rails. The place and the operation were wonderful and suggested the infernal regions. Called in at the Board of Trade on our return and saw the grain gamblers in a state of vociferous tumult, to the number of probably 1000.

Left Chicago on the Fort Wayne & Penn Ry at 20 min to 4 P M on Hotel car Viceroy in sec 5. Had a pleasant ride to N Y.

*8 (Sat)* Reached Pittsburg in the morning. The dirtiest place I ever saw. Crossed the Alleganies [*sic*] about noon, in the observation car. Going around the Horseshoe curve and the descent into the valley of the Juniatta [*sic*] on the eastern side was very fine. Our greatest altitude I was told was 3200 feet. Stopped at Harrisburg a few moments. The country between there and Lancaster is rich & beautiful. Reached Phil after dark and saw nothing of it. Got to the ferry at Jersey City at 10 oclock and to the Brevoort at 11 P M, where we took up our temporary residence in No 10 and enjoyed the luxury of a good bath and sweet sleep.

*9 (Sun)* N Y. Got up this morning at 9 and breakfasted at 10, on porridge, bread & butter & beefsteak with tea & coffee. Everything was of the best except the milk which was very thin. The day has come in cloudy and wet. Upon making up my a/c, I find it has cost us $207.36 from Portland to this place since Sept 19 independent of our railway transportation—nearly $11 a day. But this includes sleeping cars and the detour to Salt Lake. . . .

Went in the afternoon on the El Ry to old Trinity to evening prayer. Heard it sung by a choir of men and boys about 40 in number in very good style. The audience went and came during the performance and but few took any part in it except to follow the change of postures. The church and surroundings are grand and impressive. A young preacher gave us a very good sermon on Joseph and his brethren as indicating the evil effects of parental partiality and fraternal jealousy. . . .

*10 (Mon)* The day came in cool and clear. In the forenoon went to High Bridge over the Ha[a]rlem—the aqueduct of the Crotan Waterworks—on the El Ry and back. Travelled 10 miles & back in 2½ hours for 50 cents and spent near an hour on and about the Bridge.

. . . Moved into 99, an old room, at the head of the first stair but with a bath and water closet for $4. Preferred this to 11 without B or W C. . . .

*11 (Tue)* Benj Stark called in the morning alone and in the evening with his 2 daughters, Grace & Genevieve. He looks well and his tongue is as limber as ever. The girls are very genteel looking and I think the eldest one—Grace—is pretty. Corbett called and invited us to go [to] Booth-Barrett matinee on Friday for the Mich sufferers.[36] Walked with Mrs D out to Broadway and up to [Union] Square. The morning was cool and bright and the walk, the crowd and the shops were exhilarating.

At ½ past 2 got into Mr [Wm R] Travers Victoria, drawn by two handsome bays and driven by a liveried coachman, and went to the races at Jerome Park, a distance of 10 miles, where we saw two petty races by pampered ponies, and many nobby people. The drive through Central park in the morning was beautiful and on our return about 4 oclock it was perfectly gorgeous with elegant turn outs of all kinds and styles. Got home at ½ past 5 & felt that we had seen one of the wonders of the world. In the evening went to hear "The Professor" at Madison

Square Theatre with Col & Mrs Gillespie, and had a very pleasant time.[37] Sat up on my return reading a file of the *Oregonian* until ½ past one. . . .

*13 (Thu)* Went early this morning to Judge [J W] Gilberts[38] in Brooklyn via the elevated Ry & Fulton ferry, where Miss Gilbert took us in her carriage through the city, to St Peters Church, of which Bishop Paddock was formerly Rector, to Prospect Park, and Greenwood cemetery where she left us an account of an engagement and we took the Phaeton and drove through the cemetery for an hour, our driver giving us the history of the noted monuments. Thence we came home stopping at Fultons Market for oysters, which we found most excellent. Went through St Peters church and Rectory and found the beautiful and useful well combined. The Sunday school room is perfect in arrangement and contains accommodations for 700 scholars. . . .

In the evening went to [Edwin] Booths theatre on the corner of 6th Ave & 23 st and saw him in the role of Hamlet, and did not get home until 12 oclock. The house and the performance was grand and beautiful. . . .

*14 (Fri)* Called on Mr Joel B Erhardt, who married a niece of Hugh J Jewett, at the Equitable Building and he took me to the City Hall—the one built by Tweed— where I visited the supreme court . . . Called on Jewett, Pres of the Erie.[39] Got to be an old man. Was polite but quiet. Attended the matinee at Booths theatre and witnessed "Othello"—[Lawrence] Barrett in Othello and Booth in Iago with Mr & Mrs [Henry] Corbett and then dined with them at Delmonicos. The play was grand and Delmonicos was brilliant with about 250 well dressed loquacious people but the cuisine doesn't compare with the Brevoort.

*15 (Sat)* Mr Hugh J Jewett placed his carriage at our disposal and we visited the Metropolitan Museum of Art in the Central Park where we spent 3 hours in mingled wonder and delight examining the collection of statuary, paintings and ancient pottery, ivories &c. Had Col & Mrs Gillespie to dinner, which occupied us 3 hours and cost $9.50 including one bottle of wine $1.25. . . .

*16 (Sun)* . . . Went to Grace [Cathedral]. Invited into John L Belchers pew by a lady in it. One Hundred people standing in the vestibule & aisles until after the first lesson when they were seated in the vacant pews. Dr [Horatio] Potter preached but I could not see him, as one of the columns was directly between us. He made a handsome but discriminate reference to the late Dr [Josiah] Holland at the close of his sermon, which was predicated upon the gospel for the day.[40] We remained after the service and examined the church. It is a handsome edifice. Some of the windows are beautiful, especially the one to Joseph & Benjamin lately imported from Europe. There are 3 organs in the church—one in the chancel, one in the ceiling and one in the loft over the main entrance and all are played from one keyboard by means of electricity.

In the afternoon visited the lower end of town in company with Col Gillespie. Saw Bowling Green, The Battery & Castle Garden—the most interesting part of the city. Visited St Patricks Cathedral with Mrs D & the Gillespies, but the service was just closing as we entered. It is a handsome stone pile with an immense organ and a number of altars but meanly seated and filled with very common people. . . .

*17 (Mon)* . . . Rode to the Park with Max & Mrs Louis Goldsmith and heard "Lohengrin" at the Academy of Music in the evening with Max Goldsmith.[41] The singing was good and the pageant was splendid. . . .

*18 (Tue)* . . . Left N Y on 11 oclock train and reached N[ew] H[aven] at 1:10 P M running about 50 miles an hour. The day was sultry, but the country though poor and rocky interesting. Stopped at the New Haven Hotel Room 3. Called on Prof [T A] Thacher and wife and presented Clinton Days letter. We were kindly received and had a pleasant call. Two charming old people. Called on President [Noah] Porter and found him at his office in the Treasury building. Presented Prof Hills letter. He did not demonstrate much about it. Took us to Alumni Hall, and then put us in the hands of Superintendent Hotchkiss while he went to hear a recitation. We saw the library, Peabody Museum, & the school of art. Found Couch Flanders early and he took us to his room. Had him at supper with us. Montgomery called also. He is in the scientific dept. After supper, which was a capital meal, including oysters caught in the bay, and the only real good ones I have had since I have been in the country, Clarence Glisan came in and spent the evening with Couch [Flanders].[42] What a fine looking well behaved fellow he is. Had good *milk* also for supper, which I have not seen before since I left S Fran.

*19 (Wed)* Mrs Thacher called for us and took us to morning prayer at the college chapel at 8. Pres Porter read the lesson from the New Tes, made a prayer and the choir sang a hymn to the tune of the Litany hymn. A symbol on the wall above and to the right of the chancel consisting of Dux uL crossed by Rex eL so as to spell Dux Lux, Rex Lex.

There were probably 500 boys in the church, only one of whom was red headed so far as I saw. We sat in the gallery & Clarence Glisan came in to see us.

After prayer went to drive and took Prof Thacher with us. Drove ¾ of an hour and saw the lovliest places I ever saw. Then ascended to the top of a tall building by an elevator and had a grand view of New Haven and its surroundings including east & west rock and the Sound. Left for New London on the 10:40 train and reached there before 1. Saw a rocky picturesque country.

Col Stark met us at the depot and took us to his house where we met Miss Grace, Will & Ben—three & as genteel, well bred & interesting children, young men and woman, as I think I ever met, and sat down to an excellent dinner. Walked about the town with Stark and sat up until after 12 talking of old times and people.

*20 (Thu)* The day came in quite cool. Went out to drive with Col & Miss Stark and returned . . . after seeing all N[ew] L[ondon] including Fort Trumbull. After dinner Stark & I crossed over to Groton, and went up to the Groton monument and walked over the remains of Fort Griswold where a detachment of the English army under [Benedict] Arnold took the fort and put the garrison to the sword on September 6, 1781. From the height we had a fine prospect of New L and the harbor. . . .

Had a sing this evening. Grace played the piano & Will the violin and we all sang from the hymnal. This seems to me a model family—and if happiness does not dwell under this roof it is not easy found on earth.

Left New London at 20 min past 10, crossed the Thames on the Ry ferry, where we took the train. Stark accompanied us there. Stopped at Providence over an hour. Took a hack and drove over the place. Saw Spragues, the Poor House, the Friends School & the University and many nice, beautiful residences. The morning was lovely. Providence is one of the most interesting & picturesque places we have seen. Returning to the depot we took some oysters & beer, I did not fancy the former much. Immense affairs, clammy & tasteless. We had some alewives this morning roasted in the shell at Starks for breakfast, that were good.[43] . . .

Reached Boston about ½ past 3 and drove to the Brunswick where we were assigned to 109 third floor fronting on Boylston street with a bath—altogether a beautiful lodging and convenient. The House seems to be superbly appointed. . . .

22 (Sat) Visited the Boston Commons & Public Garden, and were better pleased than with any public grounds we have seen. Indeed the avenue on the north side of the Common lined with majestic elms and full of troops of handsome joyous boys & girls, called the Mall is the most picturesque promenade I ever saw.

Remained at home during the afternoon . . . Bishop [Benj] & Miss Paddock called. Pleasant people. She is plain while he is rather elegant and courtly. Mr Robert G Fitch & wife, editor of the *Boston Post* called also.[44]

Went to the Park theatre in the evening and saw Barrett as Cassius in "Julius Caesar." Brutus & Antony were well played, indeed the former at least divided the laurels with Cassius.

The theatre and the audience though very well indicated that we were in a provincial town and not a city like New York. . . .

23 (Sun) Went to Trinity church at ½ past 10 oclock—Phil[l]ip[s] Brookes church —just across the street from our hotel.[45] The building is a beautiful structure and contains a stone tracing of a window of St Botolphs church in England, that is probably 500 years old. It is about 8 ft high and 6 feet across, and appears to have been the top of a window—from the spring of the arch upward.

We had to wait at the door until the first prayers were over before we could be admitted but then were furnished with a good seat well up the middle aisle. The singing was plain and good, but weak in the base [*sic*]. Brookes is a very large fine looking man—reads rapidly with much animation and feeling, looking earnestly upward as if in extemporaneous prayer, but not very distinctly. He preached in a black gown a written sermon in the manner of an extemporaneous speaker. Text "Thou shalt love the Lord thy God with all thy mind." And his effort was to show that unless the intellect was engaged in the love of God or the observance of his religion that it was only partly done. The church is beautiful inside—the chancel very large, but contains no altar—only a table with space all around it. . . .

Judge [John] Lowell called and invited us to go out to his house in the country Chestnut Hill tomorrow evening for dinner and stay all night.[46] . . .

*24 (Mon)* Day came in raw and foggy—almost a rain. Kate Stevens called in the morning and we all proceeded to Bunker Hill Monument. When we reached there we found no Hill to speak of but plenty of monument—222 ft high.

Made the ascent, Mrs Deady stood it better than I thought she would. But the view did not repay us as it was obscured by the fog & Mist. Visited Faneuil Hall on our return and Quincy Market. . . . I was rather pleased with the Hall, some interesting paintings in it. Visited the Athen[a]eum. A charming place. Full of choice books, paintings and statuary. Called then at the U S court rooms . . . Miss Stevens[47] left us here and we went home, got lunch and visited the art museum which contains a good many paintings and casts of statues, but the former are not catalogued and we did not enjoy it as much as we expected. At 20 min after 5 Judge Lowell called and we went down to his place—Chestnut Hill—on the Boston & Albany train to spend the night as per previous invitation.

We reached the place in 20 min and were ushered into one of the most charming old country houses in the world. Met Mrs L a hearty fine looking Yankee woman with 3 charming daughters—Mary, Lucy and Susan and 2 sons, John a young lawyer and Arnold a splendid boy of 13. Another son, George, she told us was at Harvard. The dinner—a leg of mutton and a roast chicken that reminded you of Turkey etc was very palatable and satisfying, and the evening very pleasant. *25 (Tue)* Got breakfast by 8 and came to town by ½ past 8 after bidding our kind friends adieu, with whom we fell violently in love. Mary is a splendid girl. The mother is a model wife, mother & woman and the Judge is a dear good man with a head as clear as a bell.

Went to Harvard, crossing the Charles river Bridge at Charles St. The morning wore fine and the ride was pleasant. Called on Longfellow, fortified with a letter from Lowell, but we failed. The servant said he was not well and was confined to his room. We were disappointed. Still we were in the house and sat in the parlor where Washington lived when in command of the army. Further on we saw the tree under which he took command. Saw the law Library where we met the Librarian Mr Arnold & Prof [J C] Gray.[48] Heard the latter lecture on estates . . . I sat on the platform with him & Mrs D occupied a seat in the room. Between 50 & 60 students present. The lecture was quite elementary but clear and orderly. The quizzing was not severe and the answers only moderate. Visited Memorial Hall where we saw 600 students at lunch and many beautiful tablets in commemoration of the graduates who lost their lives during the war; also the Gymnasium, a handsome building cost $100,000, where there are many ingenious ways and devices for taking exercise without being guilty of any useful or vulgar labor.

Visited the Episcopal Theological School—a beautiful, stone and brick building with a Refectory and chapel of the same—the gift of the late Amos Lawrence. The chapel and Refectory are gems of architecture. We were shown about by a young Englishman—deacon & Student. But I am afraid that the missionaries that are made here will not be good for much off the line of the Railway.

Went then to Mt Auburn [Cemetery], and walked through. Ascended the tower about 70 feet high, situate on the summit of the Hill & had a beautiful view of Boston and the suburban surroundings. Visited the chapel where we saw 4 very handsome marble statues—full length—Winthrop, Otis, Story and the elder Adams. The cemetery is much smaller than Greenwood, but it is handsomer as a whole and more interesting—and in proportion to numbers has many more historic names. Greenwood is full of fine marble & stone but the people they commemmorate are rich nobodys who made money in some way. Got home at 20 min after 5 after busy and hard but interesting day. Mrs D is nearly given out, but she has stood it well.

*26 (Wed)* Mrs Deady very tired from Yesterdays exercise and I left her at home. Visited the U S C[ircuit] Court room . . . [Elisha] Bassett showed me the records of the old vice Admiralty court for Mass, as early I think as 1722—the record of a suit for seamans wages, in which there was a decree for "Pltf." Visited the State House with Bassett, called on Gov [John] Long. Found him a bright genial gentleman. Met [L A] Jones the author of *Jones on Mort[gage]s* in the State Library. The State House is well appointed and like every other public place in Boston is ornamented with statues and paintings. Went up to the top of the Equitable Building and had a splendid view of Boston and the harbor, as also Charleston, Chelsea and other once distinct suburbs but now essential parts of the city. . . . Came back and took Mrs Deady on to Washington st and down about the P O building and then up Winter to Tremont st, where she gave up trying to go to Dorchester Heights to see the [Oliver] Stevens, as Kate had not left her the number. I then called on Mr Fitch the editor the the *B Post* at the office where I spent a pleasant hour. He tells me that he has been on the paper 10 years and became the editor in chief only 6 months since. This evening went to the Music Hall and heard . . . the Great Organ and Mr John Stoddard lecture on Athens & Jerusalem and their environments with the aid of the Stereopticon.[49] The organ is majestic in appearance and grand in tone. The lecture with illustrations was rather interesting but it had a scrappy showman tone about it after all. Got in the wrong car and had a long walk home.

*27 (Thu)* Left Boston at 11 oclock on the Boston & N Y train in the drawing room car . . . to Albany. Reached Springfield at 1:40 P M and went to the Massasoit House. The day was beautiful and the ride was charming over a hilly rocky country, largely grown up in wood and brush. Had dinner at the M House at which I enjoyed the milk and pumpkin pie. Sent our cards to the Bowles and very soon Sam Bowles and his mother called and took us off to their comfortable old house and beautiful grounds on the hill.[50] There we met the two young daughters, Bessie & Ruth, the former being a lovely specimen of the antique in her dress and manner.

Mrs Bowles took us around the House and showed us the view from each one [of the rooms], and the places where poor Sam Bowles, her husband, used to sit and read and write and the room where he died. She was very sad in speaking of him and I became so also. It seemed too bad that I could not have visited Springfield in his lifetime as we often talked about.

After dinner Mr Bowles took us all to the theatre to hear Rossi in "Othello." We occupied the lower right hand box. The house was full—probably with 900 persons. The play was well rendered and Rossi was the most natural Othello I ever saw.[51] I think he was helped by the fact that he spoke his part in Italian—and it is so much more natural and in keeping with the situation to hear this foreign Blackamoor speaking in a foreign tongue than in English. Our dinner and room for the two hours we were at the M House cost us $3.

*28 (Fri)* Had a pleasant meeting of the family at the breakfast table this morning; and at ½ past 10 went to drive with Mr & Mrs Bowles and did not get back until ½ past 12. The view from the high plain above the Con[necticu]t river was delightful. In the distance on the summit of a range of hills and a little to the north of Mt Tom I made out the little town of Blandford[52] where the Boises or Boies come from. We visited the *Republican* office and I saw the first vol of the *Republican* published by Sam Bowles grandfather—the first No bearing date in Sept 1824, a few months after I was born. I read the short prospectus from which I gathered that Bowles was a Republican of that day & therefore not a Federalist.

After a lunch and a hearty but sad good bye we were driven by Mr Bowles to the depot and put on the cars for this place—Pittsfield—at 2 and reached here at 4:10 P M. Bessie promised me her picture in her antique dress and I promised her a Professor in the Oregon University when she got through college.

The country between here and Springfield is marked with strong contrasts of rocky, woody hills and pleasant vales—this one of the Hoosatonic [*sic*] being the largest and handsomest we have seen in the State. We walked out between 5 & 6 and saw a Rom Cath church in stone and a little beyond the Maplewood Institute for young ladies, a cluster of large wooden buildings painted white with green blinds. It reminded me of the Peckham "Institoot" in *Elsie Venner.* Many of the dwelling houses look like the houses in Salem, Or. Had tea in a low dining room. The waiters were girls and the meal was a breakfast rather than a tea. . . .

*29 (Sat)* Paid $2½ for supper and lodging. Rained in the night, and more or less all day. At 8 oclock A M the carriage came and took us to Mr [Ensign H] Kelloggs[53] house—a handsome old brick mansion back from the st and near the Park where we met Mrs K a very pleasant genteel old lady and her daughter, Carrie, a bright young lady of I suppose 25 summers. We soon sat down to an excellent breakfast including fried perch just from the pond. After running about the house awhile Mr K & daughter and Mrs D & I started for [a] drive in a handsome covered carriage. We were gone over 2 hours having visited Mr Ks farm . . . and a factory in which he is interested where all the parti-colored blankets are made for all the sleeping cars in the U S. When we got back we sat down to an elegant lunch which we washed down with a glass of good Cal champaigne, and then in the carriage to the train for Albany which we boarded 1:28, and got seats in the drawing room car.

Mr Kellog is a splendid specimen of a hard headed bighearted farmer lawyer and the house is just full of cozy corners and nice things. They were all very kind to us.

The ride to Albany was through a beautiful country apparently much more fertile than any we have seen since leaving N Y. We reached [Albany] at ½ past 3 and went to the Kenmore where we got room 41 with a bed and bath Room and board for both of us at $9 per day.

At 4 P M we started out to see the State House. Saw the Superintendent and got a guide. Visited the legislative rooms, the Court of Appeals room and the Gov Rooms. Called on Gov [Cornell].[54] Found him in the handsomest rooms in the building. He is a big headed strong looking man but somewhat coarse and common. Went into the third story and got a good view of the town towards the river. It is a wonderful building. Then took the cars and rode out west from the river about 3 miles and back to tea at 6 which was excellent.

*30 (Sun)*. . . Went to All Saints this morning and heard Bishop Doane.[55] Visited St Agnes School & the Hospital for children. Met a Sister Eliza who knew the Rodneys at St Marys, [in] Burlington and the Lady Superior, Sister Helen who knows Mrs and Julia Hill very well. Altogether it was a very pleasant visit. The boarders are about 100 in number and from all parts of the country. Wrote to Miss Lydia about St Agnes. Went to St Peters in the afternoon. A handsome church but a hum drum service and congregation. Walked, saw an old brick building on Pearl St, near this hotel that purports to have been erected in 1710, and as I heard of brick imported from Scotland—more likely Holland. . . .

*31 (Mon)* Left Albany at 10:20 A M for N Y on the Central seats 9 & 10 in the Mayflower—the first relation I ever had with this mythical craft. Cloudy & moist. Beautiful country. Got telegram at Fishkill from Gen Howard telling us [Lieut] Sladen[56] would meet us at the ferry at West Point, where we stopped off and were driven . . . to the Superintendents—Gen H. It commenced raining soon after we got there. Saw something of the place. Heard portions of recitations in Ordnance & International law. Saw Woodbridge Geary. He called. Mrs Howard looked very well and was very polite. Jamie [Howard] caught us as we were driving off and sent his love to Paul. We got away on the 5:52 P M train. Gen H drove us to the station and was very kind and cordial. Got to the Brevoort at ½ past 8 and found room 100 reserved for us. Got letters—one . . . from Col [Benj] MacKall that had gone to Portland and back here. It contained a pressing invitation to make his house our home while in Barnesville. Trip to Boston consumed 2 weeks & $157.81.

*November 1 (Tue)* Visited the Astor Library, also Mr Francis old book store. . . . [Got] a check for the October Salary, $294.84. Visited the Lennox library and saw the most interesting collection of paintings that I have seen. Got a catalogue. Made the acquaintance of the Librarian, Dr [Saml A] Allibone, the author of the *Dic of Authors* and formerly of Phil.[57] He is a charming old man. Showed [me] his Shakespearean collection commencing with the first folio of 1622 that once sold for 3000 pds. Called with Mrs Deady at L Goldsmiths. Spent an hour ½ and came away without being asked to take refreshments.

*2 (Wed)* Mr D[avid] D[udley] Field called in the morning, and engaged to entertain us on Saturday. . . .

Visited the rooms of the Historical Soc cor 2 Ave & 10 st where we were admitted on Mr Francis' letter. Saw an interesting collection of paintings and still more interesting collection of Egyptian antiquities including three mummies of the Bull of [Apis].

Thence we visited the Astor library and then home where I found a note from Jewett enclosing a pass on his road—the Erie—to Niag[a]ra and back. Got lunch and commenced to get ready to leave the H[otel] at 5:20 this evening.

At 5:20 started from Jersey City on the car Morning Star—one of Jim Fisks[58] elegant palaces on wheels, for Niag[a]ra, which we made at 10 oclock the next day, a distance of 447 miles.

*3 (Thu)* Took a carriage at 10 A M . . . and drove all about the falls until 15 min of 3 P M when we stopped at the Spenser house and took dinner. The day was a mixture of cloud & sunshine, it having rained the night before. The falls are grand and grow grander the more you see them. The tolls and charges are in proportion and are a disgrace to the country or countries that possess such a wonder. Our tolls and charges exclusive of hack hire were $7.80—the latter being $5. At 7:30 P M we got away on the car Clifton.

*4 (Fri)* We passed through a very picturesque country between Lackawaxen and Port Jervis on the Delaware river, where the swiftfooted Ry car was passing on one side of the river and the slow moving canal boat on the other. Reached the Brevoort at 2 P M where we found a letter from Stark rather congratulating us that we did not go Montreal. Washed & dressed and went to Tiffanys . . . where we saw a canary colored diamond from South Africa that weighs 125 carats and is valued at $100,000, Two Solitaire earrings valued at $12,000 and a necklace of 28 solitaires valued at $60,000 and a necklace of pearls just as they came from the oyster valued at $30,000. Mr Stockwell, to whom we had [a] card, is a member of the firm and showed us these jewels in his private room. Then he sent us through the building in charge of Mr Green where we saw such magnificent bronzes, marbles and beautiful porcelain and glassware. Bought a little plaque, with a young face on it painted by a German artist. Went to the Academy of Music where we heard an Italian Co play the "Barber of Seville." The acting was very good and the music only fair.

*5 (Sat)* Visited old Trinity and the graveyard. Mr Field sent us to Staten Island with a Mr Douglas of his office, where we had a charming drive of 2 hours in an open carriage and saw the Sailors Snug Harbor, besides many other pretty places. On our way back to the Battery we met 9 Steamships going to sea and 4 of them were bound to Europe.

Dined with Mr Field at 64 Park Avenue where we met Maj Wyckham of the English Army one of the forlorn hope that was knocked over at the first attack on the Redan [*at Sebastopol during the Crimean War*] and a pleasant gentleman. From there, after leaving Mrs D at our hotel, we drove to the Century club where met many agreeable and distinguished people and staid until ½ past one in the morning. This club at least is a place where money is a very secondary consideration.

*6 (Sun)* Went to Calvary church. Sat in Fields pew, & heard Bishop Whipple, the Apostle of the Western Indians, preach a rather effective sermon upon those who are gone to the rest of the saints among whom he particularly mentioned and eulogized Dr Washburn[59] the late Rector of the Parish. Called at Corbetts to say good bye but they were not in. Finished a letter which I commenced last evening to Ella H of 14 pages. Went to Castle Garden with Mrs D and saw about 1000 emigrants just arrived from all parts of the world, but principally from the north of Europe. Poor ignorant people they are but they have the raw material and in the next generation will be the governors of the country. But this constant and large alloy of the lowest grade of European population must have the effect to keep down the general standard of the population of the country.

Called at ½ past 8 at Mr John W Hamersleys . . . Spent a couple of hours in the basement in company with H and a Cornishman whom I met last night at the Century, but cannot recall his name, and Hs son-in-law Mr Pierre van Cortland de Puyster Field, a N Yorker, a graduate of Columbia College and a commission merchant—a college chum of Bishop Tuttle[60] who was also his tutor and whom he fondly calls Dan, whom I liked amazingly. Drank a glass of hot Scotch and talked poetry, classics &c. Saw a copy of the original publication of Popes *Essay on Man,* Commencing "Awake *Laetius*" instead of ["Awake my] St John." Then upstairs where I met Hs two daughters, Mrs Field & Miss H . . . together with Thorwalsdens Mercury, a splendid figure in the act of drawing his sword to kill Argos, and other beautiful marbles & Bronzes, and the most elegant and recherche rooms I ever saw. Got home at 11. H presented me a copy of his translation of Jacques Abbadies, dean of Killaloe, Ir[eland] *Chemical Change in the Eucharist,* with his preface—a superb book typographically speaking at least.

*7 (Mon)* Visited Mrs Stewarts city house and picture gallery with Mr [Albert] Bierstadt. Oh, what a handsome place. Saw 2 Messioniers [*sic*] one The Charge at Jena which cost $60,000 and the other an ordinary sized picture containing a man on horseback, and a beggar soliciting alms, that cost $16,000. Saw the original of Rosa Bonheurs Norman Horse Show, an immense affair. Saw many handsome marbles and bronzes also. Visited Bierstadts studio also. Saw a grand landscape of Southern Cal and striking pictures of the Yellowstone Geysers under way, and mountain sheep. Saw a head of a very large Moose with the fan-shaped horns. Called at Mrs Gillespies and said good bye. Found Mrs Corbett at the Hotel when we returned. Left at 15 min after 12 for ferry at foot of Liberty Street en route for Mauch Chunk. Paid bill at Brevoort for 7 days . . . $50.05; and also $105.94 for bills paid &c. On the car, just before starting, Mr Corbett came on and brought my mail . . . Came here [*Mauch Chunk*] in 4¼ hours. It is a wonderful ride up the Lehigh. Saw the Moravian school and church at Bethlehem. Mrs [Charles] Albright met us at the train and took us to her home, a great rambling pleasant old House.[61] Had a good plain supper of which one dish was fried potatoes, cooked the way Lucy used to do them. For after supper, say 6 oclock until 10 she has entertained with the most thrilling, touching wonderful stories of her own and husbands life in Kansas, in the war, and the Molly Maguires. Found upon examining my bill that the Brevoort had made a mistake in my favor of $75 by crediting me with $150 I left on deposit when we went to Boston, and forgetting or overlooking that I drew $75 of it when we went to Niag[a]ra. Wrote . . . this evening stating the fact or my understanding of it.

*8 (Tue)* The day was cloudy and wet. An election held in the state. The poll for this borough just across the street from Mrs Albrights. Mrs A took us out to drive awhile in the forenoon. Visited the prison and saw where 4 of the Molly Mcguires were hung and the gallows on which they swung. . . .

*9 (Wed)* Still showery. Drove to Weisport, saw the process of making emery wheels, and the well that Franklin dug during the Revolution. Drove on top of the mountain between Mahoning valley and the Lehigh and had a beautiful view. In the afternoon drove to Nesquehoning,[62] and visited the Room Run mine . . . going down in it 300 feet. The vein is on edge, is about 14 feet wide across and worked out horizontally about ¾ of a mile. The mine is 5 miles from Mauch Chunk, west. They take out about 600 tons in 24 hours. They use mules to draw the cars to the elevator some of which have been in the mine continuously for 12 years. Hugo Ronemus, the foreman of the mine, came here from Germany 25 years ago since which time he has been connected with the mine except when he was in the war as a soldier under Gen Albright. Mrs A gave me a cup and egg made of this coal, by one of the Mollies, for Gen A. It is a perfect beauty. Looks like a black diamond. . . .

Forgot to note that we visited the Episcopal Church yesterday in M C—a substantial stone structure very churchly in its design and appointments. A young gentleman named Blakeslee showed us through. A beautiful reredos of Caen stone has lately been erected in the church as a memorial to Judge [Asa] Packer by his children.[63] Mr P was Mr Bs uncle. P died in Easter week and the central idea of the work is the resurrection & the ascension. B said it was not known generally what it cost, and that it was estimated from $75 to 200 thousand.

*10 (Thu)* Went to Wilkesbarre on the 8 oclock train, Mrs A with us. The morning was lovely and the ride up the Lehigh and over the mountain to the Wyoming valley was very interesting. The valley is a gem set in the mts. Drove to the Hotel & had lunch. Met a Mr Shumaker [*sic*], former member of Congress from here, and an interesting & agreeable man.[64] He said the output of the Vall[e]y mines this year would be 10 millions of tons, worth $2 per ton at the breaker, and that the strata of coal under the valley ranged from 50 to 1500 feet below the surface, though none had been worked below 900 feet. Left for Phil on the 1:45 train. Mrs A left us at M[auch] C[hunk] and we thanked her for her kindness which seemed to know no bounds. Reached Phil at 5:45 and then came to the Hotel Lafayette a distance of nearly 4 miles by horse cars in about ¾ of an hour for 12 cents. Put in room 203 and had a good dinner for $1.45. . . .

*11 (Fri)* Day cold, bright & cloudy. Mrs Ferguson & sister Mrs [E B] Shapleigh called in the morning. Had a pleasant chat with the former. Mrs C took me in her cab to the Phil Library & Mrs D went with Mrs F to see about a dress. . . . Got a note in the morning from Mr John Welsh[65] with a card of self & wife, asking to be excused from calling on the ground of being an invalid and inviting us to dinner at 3½ oclock tomorrow. Mrs F & C also invited us to the house of the latter for tea tomorrow at 7. Concluded to accept both invitations. . . .

. . . Went to the Chestnut St opera with Mrs D and heard the Abbot[t] troupe in a comic English Opera called "The 2 Cavaliers." A ridiculous, silly thing with some good music and picturesque scenes in it. . . . Got a card of admission to the Union League . . .

*12 (Sat)* . . . The day has been warm and wet. Went . . . to the Common pleas court rooms . . . Peeped in Independence Hall. . . . Went to Mr John Welshs to dinner at 3½ oclock and arose at ½ past 5. An elegant dinner & service. . . . [*Among the guests was*] Gen [E F] Noyes,[66] late minister to Paris. . . .

At Mrs Welshs I saw a lovely marble—a female figure called Penitence. The company except Gen Noyes were all members of Mr Welshs family. Everything was elegant agreeable & kind. Mr Welsh invited us to drive in the park on Wednesday morning. Got my cap and Mrs Ds shoe buttoner by express from Mauch Chunk, where we had left them, with a note from Mrs A. . . .

*13 (Sun)* Went to St Clements . . . A handsome church, a devout congregation, mostly women, an intoned service, plain singing and a good sermon on Abraham and his faith. A large picture of the Crucifixion is placed over the altar, on which are candles. In front of the altar are 6 swinging lamps which were lighted when we went in at the close of the communion. The choir contained 50 men & boys in surplices led by a conductor who handled his baton with as much gusto and as if he was in front of the stage. Went from there to Germantown on the horse cars to Rev John Rodneys, where we met the Rev gentleman[67] and his wife, and the son and daughter. Dined with them, dinner good particularly the roast beef. Went to St Lukes church at 4 with . . . Miss Louisa R. A beautiful stone church, richly decorated. Cost without the ground $80,000. Choir of men and boys, good singers. The Rector Mr Vibbert in the chancel. The curate, a young deacon preached a good sermon on the duty of guarding against temptation.

After service were introduced to . . . [*some*] leading men in the parish and the Rector Mr Vibbert. Went back to Rodneys to tea and had a pleasant chat . . . until after 9 when we came home in the cars in about an hour. The old gentleman is 86 and while he is strait [*sic*] and comparatively easy in his motions, his mind is about gone. Mrs R is 81 but she is still bright & sweet. Her hearing she lost many years ago. . . . Miss Louisa is . . . an interesting clear headed woman. When her parents pass away as they must soon she ought to go to Oregon. Here she is wasting her worth on the desert air. . . .

*14 (Mon)* Went to the Ridgway branch of the Phil Lib with Mrs D. Saw the Rush room furniture and Library. A very handsome and well arranged building and an effective memorial to the Rushes—a more than a *rush* light.[68] Visited the stores on Chestnut between Broad & 13th. Purchased Mrs D a silver shawl pin at the celebrated Silversmiths—the Wilsons.

Went to Germantown at 2:30 P M by the P & R Ry. Mrs Ferguson met us at Shelton Ave depot with a carriage and drove us about until after 5—through Germantown, Chestnut Hill, Church & School Lane &c, in the course of which we saw many handsome suburban places, and country views, besides some quaint specimens of pre-Revolutionary architecture. We alighted from the carriage at Mr [Wilson] Lloyds,[69] Mrs Fs brother where we had an excellent dinner with the family . . . and a Miss Perkins from New England, now teaching in Miss Clements school in the neighborhood—a friend of Mrs Fergusons. She is a sweet dignified woman and opens up well after a little skirmishing. Mrs Lloyd is a very attractive worthy woman and so appear her children. We got home by 12, Mrs F accompanying us on the train as far as 9th & Green where we took the Horse cars and she went to Dr S[hapleighs]. By the way I rather liked Dr S. He agrees with me as to the mythical character of the *Mayflower* legend and insists that the Penn story of the treaty with the Indians is much the same.

[*Here*] found letters from Paul & H B . . . Henders closed with two heads, his own and his mothers kissing each other and the words Oh! how good. It was very cunning.

*15 (Thu)* Day cool and clear. Mrs F[erguson] called at ½ past 9 and we went to the Academy of art, where I staid until ½ past 12, Mrs D & F leaving a few minutes before 12 to attend the dressmaker. Admission 25 cts each. Mrs F presented us with two catalogues—the one of the permanent collection and the other of the works on exhibition for the fall of 1881. The collection of paintings is large and interesting—I think more so than any gallery in N Y. I was in the Academy in Nov 1859. It was then on Chestnut St I believe, and the principal works were the Battle of the Centaurs and The Martyrdom of John Hus. The latter is not there now but the former stands under the dome in the same relative position as in the old building. In the basement there is a school of art where students—principally girls, are copying the various cast[s] with which the rooms were filled. I stood a few moments by a young girl while she copied a nude female figure, an upright front view, with as much nonchalance as if she was making apple dumplings. . . .

. . . Mr [Thomas H] Montgomery called about 3 and took me to the Pen His Soc Rooms on Spruce St where I spent the hours until ½ past 5 in examining the collection of ancient manuscripts relating to the settlement of the colony. Ed Geary, Mr [A J] Giesy and Mr J L Wortman . . . called, all Oregon boys attending the medical schools here.[70]

After dinner we went with Mr Montgomery to Christ Church to hear the chimes rung on the Bells 8 in number. Met there the Rector . . . and sundry of the vestrymen whose names I do not recollect . . . Saw all the relics of the church and altogether had a very pleasant and interesting time. Got a letter from Mr Welsh this morning proposing to drive us to Fairmount Park in the morning. . . .

*16 (Wed)* At 10 oclock drove with Mr John Welsh & daughter . . . to the Park and Centennial buildings and returned about 2 P M. The day has been cold and clear and the ride was a very pleasant and interesting one. The Pompeiian Museum was very interesting and consist[s] of 34 views of the ruins taken by Photosculpture, presented by Mr Welsh to the Park. Went through the conservatory and Memorial Hall, and into the main building which is just being removed. In the afternoon walked down Chestnut St and looked into the shops, and visited Independence Hall. The stores are very fine here and elegant in appearance.

Went to Oliver Landreths, 1917 Spruce st, to dinner . . . Had a good dinner—a litte nicknacky—the style I suppose. Plenty of good wine—sherry & champagne. There must have been 15 or 20 persons at the table . . . Everybody was very polite to us and altogether it was very pleasant. Oh! I forgot to say that Miss Louisa Rodney was one of the guests and not the least of them by any means. Mrs Deady sat at Mr Landreths right and I at Mrs Ls right. Bishop & Mrs [W B]

Stevens called while we were out in the afternoon.[71] Got an introduction from Mr John Welsh to Girard College. . . .

I forgot to mention that at Mrs Landreths dinner I was accidentally placed on a chair about 4 inches higher than the rest of the company, which made me look like a son of Anak.[72]

*17 (Thu)* Went to Burlington [N J] on the Penn Ry. Miss Louisa Rodney accompanied us. We left the Hotel at 10 A M and got back before 5. It was a lovely ride . . . We visited Mr & Mrs McKim at St Marys [Hall], dined with them and boarders about 60 in number and had a good dinner. Saw the school and buildings, attended the Litany in the chapel at 12. Visited the parish church and graveyard that was once Bishop [George] Doanes cathedral church and saw his grave upon which there was a cross of fresh flowers.[73] Mr McKim told us that this was kept full of fresh flowers the year round, but by whom he did not know. We also visited the old Parish church erected early in the 18th century. Mrs McKim is very pleasant and much like the Rodneys—more particularly Miss Lydia. She also looks like Mrs Story—particularly about the mouth. He is a bright positive man—somewhat peculiar I imagine and in some respects—particularly personal appearance, suggests Mr Burton the former H[ead] M[aster] of the Grammar School.

All over the school and buildings we were reminded of the former residence of the Misses Rodney here. I sat in the chair in which Miss Rodney used to sit in her classroom. I saw their names in the catalogues—Miss Rodney having graduated in 1852 and Miss Lydia in 1854. I didn't see Miss Clems. The situation on the bank of the Delaware is lovely, and altogether is a very attractive place. I brought away some ivy from the Parish church and cedar from Bishop Doanes tomb. . . .

Mrs D is worn out and went to bed as soon as we got home. [I] Wrote letters . . . [Received note] from Mr Frederick Fraley inviting me to his "Saturday evening" Nov 19, 1881.[74] This was done at the suggestion of Mr Welsh I suppose as he said he was going to have it done.

*18 (Fri)* Left Mrs D at home today for the first time on the trip. Visited the Baldwin Locomotive works, office on Cor Broad & Spring Garden. Had a letter of introduction and was sent through. The Works cover 9 acres and employ between 3 and 4 thousand men. It is a busy hive. Saw a locomotive for the North[ern] Pacific. There were 28 of them on the floor of the finishing room. The noise in the boiler shop where hundreds of men were hammering on rivets was simply indescribable. Saw a trip hammer worked by steam that struck heavy or light under the direction of the boy who worked it, with as much ease and precision as a human being. Came home at 11 and found Mrs D on the lounge. She had been taken with a fainting fit while at the dressmakers. Mrs Ferguson called here and finding her out went there to see her and found her there and brought her home. She was laughing and talking and soon got over it. At 12 I went to the Social art club . . . where I had been introduced by Mr S Davis Page. Did not find him in. Was shown over the house by a servant in a very handsome livery. Got a lunch—tomato soup, tea & bread & butter, 35 cents. The servant took 5 cents at the door. Left my card for Davis [Page]. Went from there to the Academy of Natural Science and saw some enormous skeletons of whales, giraffes and an extinct species of lizard [*Hadrosaurus*] found in 1858 in a marl bed in N J. Altogether it must have been 25 ft long and the bones of its hind legs were at least 6 inches in diameter. There were also a great many geological specimens & stuffed birds which I did not stop to examine. Went thence to Girard college where I spent 2 hours.[75] Got on the roof of the main building and had a good birds eye view of Phil. Visited the kitchens, washrooms, dormitories, passed through the tunnel more than 100 yds in which the pipes are hung that convey the steam to warm the buildings. Went in the chapel—a perfect gem of a building, finished inside as [an] amphitheatre, and capable of holding 2000 persons. There are 47 acres enclosed within the walls of the college. There are over 800 boys in the Institution. Was in one of the schoolrooms where a young woman was teaching boys to read at $500 a year and live outside. It is a wonderful work. I understand that the income of endowment is now over $200,000.

Went to the Pen His Soc and made some memorandums of pamphlets on Oregon in their collection which we have not gotten. . . . Called at the Union L[eague] club and left my card for Col [Sam] Bell, clerk of the U S C[ircuit Court]. This has been a busy day with me, but I have seen a great deal.

Wrote to W D Stone, librarian, Penn His Soc . . . enclosing list of works on Or of which he is to send me copies if the Soc has duplicates of them.

*19 (Sat)* . . . Mrs Ferguson called before 10, and we all went to Girard College, where we met Pres Allen[76] and had an interesting visit. The best evidence I saw about the dormitories of the good order & discipline of the school was the excellent condition of the water closets. The buildings have cost $3 millions. They have over 800 boys now and are about to take 200 more. It is a grand charity and as the world is, a useful one. From there we proceeded to the Zoological Garden where we saw some "truly" wild beasts; thence back to the Academy of music which we were shown by the janitor . . . It is a fine building with a great depth of stage, and every Philadelphian knows that it is larger and he thinks finer than the A of M in N Y. Got to the Hotel soon after one and had luncheon. At ½ past 2 Mrs F left, with a conditional good bye upon which I made a feint of kissing her, over which we had a great laugh, she saying that no man had kissed her since her husband died but Bishop Morris. At 3 we took a carriage and called [at] Mrs Oliver Landreths. She was out and we left cards . . . It commenced to rain about 4 P M. Delivered cheque . . . to the Hotel Lafayette on a/c and directed the clerk to pay bill for Mrs Deadys dress when same came in not to exceed $150.

At 8 P M went to Mr Frederick Fraleys Saturday Club, 2017 Delancey Place, where I staid until 11. The company consisted of about 100 gentlemen, mostly over 50 and some evidently past three score and ten with a very few young fellows. Met John Welsh, Gen Noyes . . . Bishop Stevens who expressed regret at not having met me and had us in his house which I think was somewhat pro forma, Mr [Eli] Price, the oldest member of the bar and his son, a man I should judge of 50, [and] Dr [Wier] Mitchell who attended Ladd here. He sent his regards to

L. Mr [Mc]Kean of the *Ledger,* Col [A K] McClure of the *Times,* a strong robust looking man about ½ an inch taller than myself. We talked about his paper, I told him I took it every morning with my breakfast & it had agreed with me so far. Spoke of Scott & the *Oregonian,* the latter of which he admires. Also of Hipple whom he knows and appreciates. Said he was in the legislature or Congress with Hs partner John M Thompson in 1859 when the latter told him that his partner H had run away with assets of the concern and he must go home. Col Bell, clerk of the U S C C who was very agreeable and polite, Mr Dutile & his father in law, Mr [J P] Lippincott who took me to supper . . . Dr Townsend,[77] who . . . said that I reminded him so much of Michael Angelos Moses [and] Rev Dr Alsop, a young Epis clergyman of this place who has had a parish in Pittsburg some years. He knows Bishop Morris & Bonnell. Says M was a great precision[ist] here, but was glad to learn that he had grown out of that rut. That B was a man of some ability but no faculty for doing anything with his fellow men . . . The majority of the guests were successful business men, with a fair sprinkling of Judges, lawyers, editors &c&c to give it life and conversation. We stood up and talked in the double parlors downstairs until ½ past 9 when we repaired to the refreshment room upstairs, where there were oysters, raw, scalloped, fried & stewed, salads, ice cream and plenty of champagne which was drunk freely. Our host must have been 70. His son assisted him in receiving & entertaining the company. They were both very cordial & polite to me. . . .

Mrs Ds new silk gown came home from Homer, Colladay & Co last night. It looks lovely. Bill $150.

*20 (Sun)* At ½ past 10 Col Bell & wife called for us and took us to St Lukes Church, where we saw a well dressed and behaved congregation, and heard an energetic sermon from the Rector . . . a Scotsman, but owing to his dialect [I] could not tell what it was about. The choir consisted of boys in lay dress and they were in the organ loft over the entrance to the church. The architecture of the building belongs to the Greco-American style of 50 years ago and is thoroughly Pagan. There is even a colon[n]ade around the rear of the chancel and the "Holy Table." The Bells pressed us to go to dinner, but we declined. Upon our return we found Mr & Mrs Charles M Bache of Germantown in the parlor.[78] She is a sister of Capt Ellicott and he is in the coast survey. . . . They were urgent that we should pay them a visit of some days, but we had made our arrangements to go to Balt tomorrow. However, we compromised on dining with them tomorrow, which postpones our journey to Balt until Tuesday.

In the afternoon Mrs Ferguson called . . . and took us to the 4 oclock service at St Marks. This a grand stone church, pure Gothic, with a chime of bells and rich and beautiful windows. The service was intoned and sung. The choir consisted of 20 men and boys in gowns & surplices. The music was sweet but rather low & weak. The Rector, Mr Nicholson, made a 20 minute talk on the end of the church year, applying the gospel of the day so far as the apostles were directed to gather up the fragments that remained after the multitude were fed.

He is a tall, grave, spiritual fine looking man and very earnest & effective. He is from Balt—the son of a banker to which business he was originally bred.

. . . N.B. We have not been in a horse car today

*21 (Mon)* Purchased trunk for Mrs Ds dresses, cost $7 & strap, 75 cts. Also a pair of undressed Kid gloves for myself at Wanamakers $2.25. The salesman told me that there were 18000 [*sic*] persons employed in the place and that there would be 2000 at Xmas. Visited St Stephens chapel on 10th bet. Walnut & Market and saw the Burd monument—an effigy of himself sleeping on his tomb at the entrance of the church and the 2 daughters & son in a side room with the resurrection angel standing over them. Also a beautiful window to the Magees—Father & daughter.[79] The marbles are beautiful, very beautiful . . .

. . . at 2 oclock we started to Germantown to dine with the Baches . . . Got to dinner at Baches by 6 and had a good feed, moistened with some good sherry and champagne. The ice cream as usual in Phil was simply delicious. . . . Came in on the horse cars to Chestnut & 13 in about an hour. The Baches are people of a good deal of character and were very polite to us. Their daughter, Margaret, is a lovely aesthete. *She* looks like a ruling elder and so does he—but she the most so. . . .

*22 (Tue)* . . . Purchased tickets on the 11:45 train for Baltimore. Got away in a coupe for the Station at West Phil by 15 minutes after 11, but did not leave the station until 12. Got here at 4 somewhat behind time. A pleasant day. The sun shone mildly.

. . . Crossed the Susquehan[n]a on a bridge where 22 years ago I crossed it on the same journey on a ferry boat. Put up at the Mt Vernon room 11 on first floor $4 per day without bath. In our drive from the depot to the hotel saw many places that I recalled—among others Battle Monument and of course Washington Monument. Heard a deep toned solemn bell strike the hour of 4 which I recognized in a moment as the cathedral bell, to the sound of which I used to go to mass at 9 oclock and then to Sunday school at some distance from there. I wish I could remember the gentleman who was my teacher. He was a very genteel pleasant man and was very attentive to me. This was in 1835–6, about 46 years ago, but I was not mistaken in the sound of the bell. Got to Baltimore with $159. Mr & Mrs Leo Knott called in the evening.[80] Mrs D had retired and I saw them in the parlor. She appears to be an agreeable genteel woman. . . .

*23 (Wed)* Day came in rainy and continued so all day. Mr William B Willson, the husband of Mrs Ellicotts sister Nannie, called in the morning and invited us to dinner this evening. Later . . . Julia Tyson and her sister Mary Howard called and invited us to dinner tomorrow—thanksgiving.[81] We accepted, provided we were not engaged to Mrs Knott, of which I was in doubt. Wrote to Knott stating the case and he said he had expected us but would excuse us *this once*. Knott called in the afternoon and we talked it over and I do not think he was offended, and I hope his wife is not. I did not understand that it was an engagement, but that he would call this morning and then it would be settled . . .

Went to dinner at Mrs Willsons . . . Mrs Willson in voice and manner is a perfect copy of Mrs Ellicott, and the tout ensemble is very much like her, although particular features are different. Had an excellent dinner—the best terrapin soup yet—and delicious ice cream, wines sherry & claret. Both good. Willson & I sat at the table an hour after the ladies retired and discussed many topics over a bottle of claret. He is considerable of a man and very agreeable to me. . . . Mr Willson gave us an invitation to the Wednesday club on Thursday evening. Mr Knott sent me an invitation to the Maryland club.

*24 (Thu)* Mr Willson called in the morning and took us to Grace church, nearby, to morning prayer. The Rector . . . preached a sermon in which he touched on public affairs saying among things, that although it might not be well to carry politics into religion yet it was always well to carry religion into politics. A handsome stone Gothic building. The choir consists of men and women in their lay clothes and they are on the floor at the back of the church. Went from church to Mr Knotts . . .

Went to the Md club with Mr Knott where I drank some eggnog . . . and made the acquaintance of sundry persons whom I shall forget with all convenient dispatch. Went to a Thanksgiving dinner at Mrs Howards, Mrs Tysons mother at 5 oclock . . . The house is elegant and elegantly furnished, and the dinner was superb. It included canvas back [duck] which was simply delicious and the ices were beyond expression good. After dinner, about 10 we went to the Wednesday club, where we saw about 500 people of the upper crust of Baltimore, mostly women and heard the comedy of the 2 [*word illegible*] right well played and much applauded. . . .

*25 (Fri)* Purchased 2 tickets for "Traviata" at the Academy of Music on Monday night and 4 for "Macbeth" at the same place tonight. The first cost $5 and the latter $6. Called at Mr Knotts office, and invited him & wife to accompany us to "Macbeth." Then he took me to Joseph Stine & Son, tailors, 74 Fayette St, where I ordered a dress coat and vest of English cloth at $70. The day is cool and clear, with some ice in the streets. Stine said the thermometer was at 27° this morning at 7 oclock. So far I am not much pleased with Baltimore, and this morning I felt real homesick and would have given a good deal to have been set down in my chambers at Portland once more. . . .

At 3 oclock Mr Jesse Tyson called in an open carriage and drove us to his country place about 4 miles distant on a hill about 500 feet above Jones falls.[82] We drove through the Park making a circuit of 7 miles. The place is beautiful—a large handsome stone house in the midst of a handsome lawn, with good natural forest nearby. We went up the tower on to the roof and saw the country for miles around, including the bay. The suburbs—hill & vale of Baltimore are very fine and certainly nature has done more for her Park than any one we have seen. We sat down to dinner at ½ past 5. . . . The conversation was light, pleasant and brisk, and 25 minutes to 7 came round just as we were at the ices of one of the best dinners we have had, when we bade our kind friends good by and were driven to Mill Vale station, about 1 mile distant, and took the train for town. At Union depot we were met by Mr Knott who took us to his house whence we drove to the Academy of Music to hear Booth in "Macbeth," the seats for which I had purchased in the morning. The play was quite well put on. Macduff did his part well and so did lady Macbeth—only she was too little. I did not like Booths Macbeth. It wasn't natural and strong enough. Too much introspection and misery—in short too Hamlety. Got home at past 11 [dis]satisfied with Booth.

*26 (Sat)* Slept until 9 oclock. Mr Willson called in the morning and invited us to dinner tomorrow . . . At 11 got away and had a ramble about the city until 4 oclock. Went down Eutaw St to the corner of Pratt—the SW corner, and saw the old house where my grandfather and uncle kept a grocery store and where I worked with them sometime in 1834–5. It is now occupied as a stove store and appears to have been built in 1830. Thence we went down Eutaw to the west side to Bottle Alley now Dover St on the corner of which my grandfather lived until his death some 10 years afterwards and where my mother was married. Saw the window of the room in which I slept and the upstairs parlor where I saw my Aunt Eliza in her coffin November 1833, the first corpse I ever saw. The lower portion of the building is occupied as a carriage store and the upper part as a residence.

Went out to the western end of Baltimore St & looked at the surroundings from a high and vacant block where there was a redoubt during the war. Saw many handsome country places to the west and north of the city. Indeed I think the surroundings—environments—of Baltimore are much handsomer than those of any place we have seen. Came back Bal[t] St to Gay and walked through a German neighborhood where we stopped and had a plate of fried oysters and a glass of beer. Saw battle monument, the city hall, the U S building, Barnums Hotel, and then home. Mrs Willson called and repeated the invitation to dinner tomorrow. Knott called and asked me to go to the club tonight. Accepted.

Went to the club at 9 oclock. . . . Had a drink and a talk about the early days of Baltimore.

*27 (Sun)* The day has been a delightful one. Went to St Pauls church at 11. An unchurchly looking edifice outside built many years ago, but quite otherwise inside, though the dim religious light is a little too *dim*. The choir consisted of men and boys in surplices and sang well. The reading was good as also the sermon. The psalter was read and nothing was intoned except the ante communion service and that only slightly. Went to Mrs Willsons to dinner at ½ past one with the family and thence to the Roman Catholic cathedral where I showed Lucy the little side gallery I used to sit in at 9 oclock mass preparatory to going to Sunday school in 1834–5. There were no vespers but the church was quite full of people at their private devotions. . . . Went to the Presbyterian church . . . The inside of it is quite churchly, but the minister in his cutaway coat looked odd and incongruous. His name is Leftwich and he preached a very good sermon. The congregation bowed their heads in prayer and stood up to sing. The world moves and in the right direction. . . .

*28 (Mon)* After breakfast paid our bill at the Mt Vernon and sent our trunks to Mr A Leo Knott, where we expect to stay a few days. A[t] 10 oclock Mr King, the brother in law of Mrs Tyson, called for us and drove us to the John[s] Hopkins Hospital, where we were shown the buildings in the course of construction. The grounds include, I believe, 13 acres. No money or pains is being spared in the premises, and I could but think while there, that for many it would be better to be sick there than well elsewhere. From thence we drove to the Peabody Institute where we saw the handsomest library room we have seen yet and the best collection of casts including those of Rinehart, and also the ½ size copy in bronze of the G[h]iberti gates. . . . Dined at Knotts. Quartered on the third floor in a capacious and pleasant suite of apartments. In the evening went to the Academy of Music and heard [Etelka] Gerster in "Traviata."[83] She sings and acts well, but I don't like the plot or story. . . .

*29 (Tue)* Called at Judge [T J] Morris' in the morning as per invitation to go to the U S court rooms. Called at the Athen[a]eum club on the way for Judge [Hugh] Bond, whom I was introduced to. At the court room I was introduced to several lawyers . . . Sat in the C C an hour or so with Bond and Morris . . . In the afternoon rode out to the house of Mr Abel[l], Jr the son of the proprietor of the *Daily Sun* about 3½ miles north of the city to attend a fete given in honor of the 10th anniversary of his wedding. A good many persons present, but no ladies except those of the family . . . Met old Mr Abel[l], the founder of the *Sun,* a genial gentleman of [75] years of age. Had some terrapin and a glass of champagne and a chat with the ladies, when we left at ½ past 3 so as to be at home and fit for dinner at Mrs Knotts in the evening. Had a beautiful dinner here in the evening. Present Judges Morris & [Robt] Gilmor, Mr Brown[84] a lawyer of prominence and wife, Mr & Mrs Mitchell the latter being a Tyson and second cousin to Mrs Ellicott. Took Mrs M[itchell] to the table and she told me that Francis Barton Key was her uncle and that Mrs E had a love affair with a cousin before she married the Capt. The dinner was a success gastronomically and socially. Mrs D wore her new yellow satin de-leon gown for the first time, and looked well in it.

*30 (Wed)* Went to Stine & co and had my coat and vest fitted and made them promise to have them done by Saturday at one oclock so we can go to Washington on the 3 oclock train. . . . Had my measure taken for a pair of dress shoes at Thomas Cullans under Barnums Hotel, to cost $11 and be sent to Washington, with liberty to return them if they don't fit.

Called at the Athen[a]eum club a little after 2 as per appointment with Judge Morris where I met him and Judge Bond and spent 2 or 3 hours very pleasantly over an excellent lunch and a bottle of delicious wine. Bond is an easy, genial, good natured strong sensed man and quite dissipated all my prejudices against him. . . .

Called on Mayor Whyte, with Mr Knott in the afternoon. Found him a handsome genial gentleman. Enquired about Col Kelly and spoke well of him. They were in the Senate together. Thinks he was not aware of the real character of the "Gobble" dispatch that he signed and approved.[85]

*December 1 (Thu)* Called to see John White, my aunt Margarets youngest son and child at 83 Second St where I was told that he was at the Corn Exchange, 72 South st and there I found him in the throng around the boards containing the momentary quotations of the price of grain from the principal cities of the U S. He is very plain looking, but genteel and smart. This evening he and his wife called as per invitation. . . . Went to the Peabody Institute and heard a lecture on decorative art illustrated by a magic lantern. Was not much. Mr Knott was with me. We left Mrs K at St Ignatius Church and called for her as we came back. Went in—the priest and people were saying the Litany of Jesus, phrases of which—such as "Son of David, Tower of Ivory—pray for us" sounded natural although I hadn't heard them for 40 years. The church is handsome inside. The altar is particularly so, being enclosed on 3 sides in a colon[n]ade of white marble. The people as a general thing looked common and ignorant. . . .

*3 (Sat)* Went to Stine & Son . . . this morning and tried on my new dress coat and vest. Fit me beautifully. Paid for them—$60 for the coat & $10 for the vest and had them sent to Knotts. Got letter from Dr Crane at the Mt V[ernon] dated the 1st inst on the subject of a room in Washington. Telegraphed him to exercise his judgment. Replied that he had engaged one at Wormleys. Lunched at Knotts at 2. Porter from Mt V came and took our baggage and we left the Union depot for Washington at ½ past 3—just 20 minutes behind time in the express train and a parlor car. A delightful ride through an uncultivated and poor country. Went to Wormleys in Hotel Bus at 5 and got room 63—an excellent one on the first floor. Our baggage did not arrive for more than an hour and then the handle was pulled off the large trunk and one of the valises bruised. Had an excellent dinner elegantly served. At this point Dr Charles H Crane and Gen R MacFeely called and I have just spent a pleasant hour with them in the parlor.[86] The Dr has invited us to occupy his pew at St Johns tomorrow. . . .

*4 (Sun)* Dr & Mrs Crane called to take us to St Johns Church, one of the oldest in the country, where we heard an excellent sermon from Mr Leonard the Rector, a nephew of our Leonard of Portland. We slept late in the morning and did not get to breakfast until 10, but the breakfast was delicious. At 3:30 Dr Crane called for us to go to his house to dinner walking as we went around the White House and war & navy dept buildings. During the dinner Gen [Robt] Schen[c]k called and sat at the table with us—the gentleman of poker fame—We had an excellent dinner and pleasant company—the Drs son constituting the fourth. Came home at 7 in the Herdick.[87] I enjoyed talking over our old southern Oregon experiences with the Dr. He is very natural—seems very little changed, only a trifle more deliberate or as some people might say heavy or dignified.

At 8 P M called at Judge Fields . . . where I met Mrs F & the Judge and also Gen [W Mc] Dunn ex Judge Ad Gen.[88] The Fields had a rough time crossing the Atlantic—in a severe gale for a week. They were enthusiastic over their visit to the east—Constantinople and beyond.

*5 (Mon)* Went to the treasury this morning and saw 1st Comptroller [Wm] Lawrence about my salary for October and November. He put me in charge of one Dr Robinson and we followed the matter up from one room to another first on the first story and then on the third until within an hour we had the drafts and the cash on the latter one $285.40. Then we hurried off to the capitol. Went into the Supreme Court room, sent card to Judge Field and he sent Messenger with us to get us admitted to the gallery of the H of R which he did after some delay and hundreds had gone away or were standing outside unable to obtain admittance. We took Robinson with us in consideration of his aid in getting my treasury drafts on short notice. After seeing Mr [J W] Keifer elected speaker by the Republicans and hearing him return thanks in writing and seeing him sworn in by Pig-Iron Kell[e]y[89] we left and went to the senate chambers where we met Messrs Grover & Slater, our Senators and went through the senate chamber during a recess. It took 2 hours to call the roll and elect a speaker. Examined the rotunda cursorily, looked into the supreme court—Field was not there—and came home. Had my hair cut. Made arrangements about a room when we come back. Had a telegram from Mr Knott saying that he could not see the party through whom he expected to get us a pass to Wheeling. . . . Wrote to Judge Field thanking him for the good offices of his messenger in getting us seats in the gallery and expressing my regret that I did not get to the capitol in time to meet the Judges in their robing room before going on the bench.

6 (Tue) Paid our bill at Wormleys $7 per day for 3 days and incidentals arriving and departing making $25.40. Bought 2 tickets on the Baltimore & Ohio for Wheeling $10 each. Left on the 10:40 train on the parlor car as far as Cumberland for which we paid $1 each. This was a delightful ride. Had dinner at Cumberland 75 cts each, and a good one. There took the palace car to Grafton, 50 cts each. The daylight lasted so as to see the ascent of the mountain, but not much of the descent. Crossed it in the night twice in the fall of 1859. Reached Grafton at 8 oclock and were then transferred to a common car for Wheeling—100 miles distant which we reached at ½ past 12, where we went to the McLure house. It rained considerably between Grafton & Wheeling. Slept in the 3 story in a good bed but we were afraid to touch anything for the soot.

7 (Wed) Got a good breakfast at 9 oclock and then started out to see Mrs McCoy at [her home] . . . a short distance from the Hotel. Soon found the place—comparatively speaking a very genteel one—to find that she and her daughter Mrs Whittaker had just started to the Hotel to see us. We went in and waited. Pretty soon they came, glad to see us and looking well cared for. Mrs W sang for me and sang with great force and beauty. They wanted us to stay and spend the evening but want of time compelled us to say no so about 12 we said good by. Mrs W accompanied us to Mr Danl Pecks where we stopped a moment and saw the old gentleman and his wife, who were very glad to see us. He is well preserved though a little emaciated while she is looking very well indeed. He said he took great interest in my career. Got away from the Hotel at 5 min past 1 but at the depot we learned that the train which connected with the narrow gauge to St Clairsville did not leave until 3:50. So we deposited our luggage and walked about the old town for 2 hours. Saw the house on 4th St (now Chapline) above 12th (once Monroe) that my father built before 1830 and where I lived when a boy still in good condition and occupied . . . We reached here [St Clairsville] about ½ past 5. Wilson Kennon met us at the depot and escorted us to the Hotel—the National—the one I left when I went to Oregon in 1849. We sat down in the same parlor and had an excellent supper in the same old dining room and are lodged not in the old corner room where O J Swaney and I used to lodge, but in the next one south of it. Swaney, Dr [Henry] West, and Isaac Patterson called.[90] Swaney has grown immensely, but looks well. Kennon is stout, but looks well and West is the best looking man for 72 I have seen.

8 (Thu) After breakfast & after receiving some calls Mrs D and I walked out to

the west end of town . . . where we called on Ann Askew now Aunt Nin, and [*sic*] old maid Quaker friend of mine, who was as cheerful and genial as ever, and talked thee & thou to me in a way that reminded me of the days gone by—"the dear old days of Arcady." Called at Dr Wests as we came back where we met Tom Cowen (D D T C) and thence with him to the court house where there was an intermission for a few moments—Judge [Wm] Oakey coming down from the bench. We were introduced generally and had a pleasant time. Then we [went] down to the old Graveyard below the Methodist Church and saw Judge [Wm] Kennons grave.[91] He is lying beside his boy John[n]y who died in 1847, and oh! I am so sorry I did not get here in time to meet him before he died.

After dinner we went down to Mrs Kennons. Met Ruth Eaton there, who had called during our absence. Jane the colored servant, who was in the family when I first knew them in 1846, met us at the door and she looked so young I did not know her. The place looked very natural and well, but Mrs K was very sad, although she looked comparatively well. Ruth looked older than I thought she would and is quite stout. But she was very pleasant, cheerful and well dressed. In the evening we went to tea at Isaac Pattersons where we met Mrs Theisa Frint (nee Coulter) besides Mrs P & son & daughter and had plenty of good biscuits and fried oysters. After tea there came Ann Askew, Jane Edgerton, who went to school to me in 1845 with her sister Bathsheba—both Quakers. The latter is dead and the former has since been a teacher and now lives here on her own property. She told me that Sarah McMillan nee Norris is not dead as I have supposed for 20 years and that she visited her last summer at Salem where she is living as a widow. I am glad to hear that she is living but sorry to think that I have not known it for so long. If I had known it in time I would have gone to see her. Then came also a Miss Ryan whose parents I knew here long ago. She is a teacher in the public schools and is a very sweet pleasant woman, and Mrs [Tom] Cochran the daughter of Mrs Frint and the wife of the Probate Judge. We chatted away until after 9 oclock. Just before we left Judge [Robt] Chambers came in and we were introduced to him.[92] He is a very good looking and prepossessing person. I told him that I knew him through the Barnesville *Enterprise.*

Wilson Kennon told me this afternoon that the bar and my friends generally are going to give me a serenade and reception tomorrow night.

*9 (Fri)* Called with Mrs D on Jane Edgerton and her sister Ann and had a pleasant visit, also on Mrs [Wm] Kennon, jr & daughter & had a pleasant visit there. The daughter is quite interesting, also on the Frints—Theisa & John. He looks very well. Mrs Ryan a pleasant Irish woman who has lived here over 40 years, the mother of the Miss Ryan we met at Pattersons and at Mrs Cochrans. Then we walked to the east end of town and looked over the old John Thompson house where I used to visit his granddaughters . . . long, long ago.[93] Then we called at Mrs Judge Kennons and bade her good by. She took quite a fancy to Lucy. We both said we never expected to see one another again.

Mrs Troll, Emma Steenrod, called in the afternoon. She looked very well and seemed anxious to have us at her house but we cannot wait. Mrs Swaney, her sister Sara . . . called with her husband in the evening. She is very sad. Her daughter has just lost her husband and two children with dip[h]theria. In the course of the evening we had a reception in the parlors and were serenaded by the band. Judge Chambers made a handsome speech of welcome to us—alluding to Mrs Deady as "the charming lady," to which I replied briefly and tolerably well, paying a tribute by the way to the memory of Judge Kennon, which was well received. . . . I have since written the substance of what I said for publication in the *Gazette*.

Judge Oakey and nearly all the members of the bar were present . . . The whole affair was very pleasant and cordial.

*10 (Sat)* Started for Barnesville on the narrow gauge about 9. A beautiful frosty morning. The walk to the station was about ½ a mile. Wilson Kennon & Isaac Patterson walked down with us. The latter passed us over the road and the former together with Dr West accompanied us to the junction. Got off the B & O road at the Childrens Home, about 2 miles east of Barnesville, in pursuance of a pressing invitation from my old friend, Mr Joseph Green, Superintendent, where we met his wife, a bright Yankee woman and his daughter and helped eat an excellent turkey dinner. In the evening Green drove us to town and every step of the road was full of reminiscence to me. Put up at the Frazier House, kept by my old friend Thomas Frazier and his son. Col Mackall was there to meet us and insisted on taking us home with him, but we excused ourselves & promised to spend a night with him.[94] He went away disappointed but soon came back with his daughter, Mary Wheeler with whom I went to school at the Barnesville Academy 36 years ago and took us home with them, whether or not, to the old brick [house] in which they lived when I first came to Barnesville on February 14, 1841. We staid with them until Monday morning and were very kindly treated. We all went to the Methodist church in the morning [*Sunday*] where I met 2 or 3 persons whom I remembered and where I heard an unpolished Boanerges discourse earnestly and also sensibly upon the text—"Hitherto ye have asked nothing in my name &c." After dinner the relations gathered in. Met Ben Hager, with his wife Harriet nee Mackall, a bright sharp little woman who said she used to go to school at the Academy with me in 1845 when old Prof Smith ruled there, and that she usually sat next to me in the Grammar class and when she could not answer a question I usually told her. Met Mr Tom Frazier, the son of Whalen F who married Emma Mackall, and went to school to me 2½ miles northwest of St Clairsville in 1845–6. In the afternoon it commenced to snow and by night [was] 2 inches deep. In the afternoon called with Tom Frazier and Ben Hager on the latters father and drank a glass of sparkling Catawba made by the old gentleman from his own grapes for the amusement of his old age. In the evening the Col, Mary Wheeler and I went to Presbyterian church and heard Dr Wallace discourse quite elegantly . . .

*12 (Mon)* Called with Mrs D at the public school where I was introduced to the teachers & 500 scholars by the Hon John Kennon[95] and responded in a short address. K was quite enthusiastic over my career & return to Barnesville. From there we went to the Hotel where we remained all day receiving calls. In the evening the Mackalls came in again and bade us good by, except the Col who said he would see us at the train station in the morning. . . .

*13 (Tue)* Left Barnesville in the morning for Bellaire. Mr Frazier would not accept any compensation for our stay with him. Col Mackall, although over 84 years of age, was on hand to accompany us to the station. I forgot to say that on Sunday I visited the little old brick Methodist meeting house, now occupied by the Disciples [of Christ], and the old country graveyard nearby. When I lived in Barnesville—from 1841 to 1845—it was the only place of worship in the place and was the focus of the social and religious life of the neighborhood. We reached Bellaire by 10 oclock where we met William Meek and his wife who had come from Columbus the night before by appointment to meet us—he having refused for some reason to come to Barnesville; and also Cooke Kelly, the son of John & Rachel Kelly with whom I learned the Blacksmith trade in Barnesville.[96] We all went to the Globe Hotel and had dinner, then to the glass works where we saw tumblers made and glass cut with a copper wheel and emery & iron dust. Mrs Meek presented Mrs D with a pair of celery glasses and Mr Kelly me with an ink stand engraved with my initials, and the proprietor Mr Sheets presented me with ½ dozen claret glasses. Then we went to Mrs Kellys, and from there in a carriage to the window glass works in which Mr Kelly is interested and also a large nail works nearby where 6000 kegs of nails are made a week. The manufacture of the window glass is very interesting. After this Mrs Meek went up the river and Meek remained with us. We had supper at Mrs Kellys—a very good supper and a pleasant evening until about 8 oclock. Then I bade Rachel and her children . . . good by. She and they were evidently much pleased with our visit. Mrs D retired about 9 and Meek & I talked until ½ past 10. He is in comfortable circumstances and looks well and so does his wife. He was very glad to see me I know.

*14 (Wed)* Got off from Bellaire at 9:10 on the train for Washington in the sleeping car. It rained hard all night and rained more or less all day. Cooke Kelly was down to see us off. I like him very much. . . . Meek was there and we said good by—probably for the last time. Got to Wormleys at 10 oclock. It rained most of the way and the country through West Virginia looked desolate and forlorn. . . .

*15 (Thu)* . . . Went to the capitol at 10 oclock. Sent my card to Field in the Judges robing room, where I was introduced to the Judges and some distinguished lawyers who happened to be present, Mr [R B] Potter & [Richard] Merrick among others. The latter invited me to his house this evening to attend a meeting of lawyers and judges on the question of increasing the judiciary. Potter said he regretted that he did not know when we were in New York as he would like to have paid us some attention. . . . Called on our Senators. Grover was just going off to Baltimore on account of his sons illness, and Slater took me on the Senate floor as his *private secretary* pro tem where I met [Wade] Hampton, [B F] Jonas, [Richard] Coke, [Geo] Vest, [Eli] Saulsbury, and [T F] Bayard. Had quite a conversation with the latter. Met old [A G] Thurman[97] also, lingering about the chamber. When introduced to him I said I had a crow to pick with him, and he replied in an embarrassed manner yes, I know that but you ought to be able to take a joke, and got away as soon as he could. I alluded to his saying once in the Senate when Corbett was seeking to have certain half breeds in Oregon made citizens, after my decision in McKay v Campbell et [al] "Holy St Patrick, what a court"—Corbett did not understand the case and probably stated it awkwardly. . . .

Wrote to John J Valentine San Fran enclosing passes for self & wife over the Southern (Central) Pacific both ways in 188*1* signed Chas F Crocker[98] and charged to account of "Business" and one on the A T Santa Fe Ry from Kansas City to Deming [N M] in 188*1* and charged to account of W F & Cos Express with the request that he would send me similar ones for 1882 if convenient. The first was handed to me by Dudley Evans before leaving home and the second sent me at New York by Mr H B Parsons, W F & Cos agt there, and both came as I suppose by Valentine and therefore I returned them to him.

*16 (Fri)* Went to Richard T Merricks . . . last night to a reception given to the committee of the Bar Association and others interested in the question of relieving the supreme court of the press of business. Met all the judges of the supreme court . . . many lawyers, Senators & members of congress of distinction . . . They were a strong fine looking lot. Plenty of terrapin, whiskey and champagne. . . .

Went to the capitol this morning with Mrs Deady and made the ascent of the dome, she going no farther than the last great terrace. The day was beautiful and the view grand. Lunched at the H of R restaurant and was charged extravagantly for it. I forgot to say that we attended the Guiteau trial[99] in the morning from 10 to 12, I occupied a seat on the bench with Judge [W S] Cox, and Mrs D had a front seat next to the counsel for the Government. G was in fine feather and entertained the audience with his rasping remarks and singular speeches the most of the time. Only 2 witnesses were examined . . . When we came home found Barnesville *Enterprise* & Belmont *Chronicle* with accounts of our visit to those places and speeches of Judge Chambers and myself at the reception in St Clairsville. Sent copies of them to Paul, Lydia R and Kearney. . . .

*17 (Sat)* Visited the Navy Yard in the forenoon . . . Went on board the Monitor *Passaic* and had the construction and working of her turret thoroughly explained. Her turret was full of dents made by shot when she was aground at Charleston. Visited the Corcoran Art Gallery this afternoon and saw the original Greek Slave—a lovely piece of marble. I think the collection of paintings quantity and quality considered is about the best we have seen. . . .

*18 (Sun)* Sallie Swearingen called in Judge Fields carriage and took us to Epiphany church where we saw a large and respectable congregation, heard the service well read and sung and listened to an earnest sermon from the gospel of the day but which I failed to get en rapport with. Took a drive after church. . . . Went to St Augustines in the evening at 8—a colored Roman Catholic church where we heard a good soprano voice, saw some very edifying Negro devotion and heard the stupidest young white priest discourse on the sign of the cross and the origin and efficacy of confirmation I ever did hear. The church is large & handsome, but much in debt. . . .

*19 (Mon)* Miss Sallie Swearingen called in the morning and drove us to the White House where we were shown the rooms and the conservatory. . . . In the evening got a letter from Mrs Field enclosing one from Sec Blaine granting her request that Judge Field might bring us to his reception to his successor and the foreign legations, and saying the Judge would call for us at ½ past 10. We got ready and went and had a pleasant time. Met Gail Hamilton with whom I had a pleasant set to.[100] She is as ugly as original sin, but as bright as an angel and very agreeable. Frelinghuysen is the personification of dignity and gentility, but his wife is very plain and looks old & feeble. The Chinese & Japanese Embassy [sic] was there in full fig. . . . The President [Arthur] came alone about 11 and we were presented to him by Judge Field. Mrs D says that the back of his neck and shoulders look just as I used to. He is a very fine looking man rather strong than intellectual and very dignified and quiet in his manner. The refreshments were very palatable and included champagne. Blaine is a fine looking man. His wife is showy but rather masculine. . . .

20 (Tue) Met Miss Sallie S at the capitol, went through the libraries, the marble and Presidents room. Saw the supreme court open and then went to the Smithsonian where we spent a good deal of time over a lot of anthropological curiosities, so-called, a great portion of which is unmeaning trash. Called at the Ry station and saw the place where Garfield was shot & fell. . . . In the evening got an invitation to the reception of the Japanese minister through Judge Field saying he would call for us at ½ past 9 or thereabouts. We went and had a very pleasant time indeed. Mr Yoshida the minister and his little wife, dressed as Americans, received us kindly. . . . Saw some handsome young women with low necks and white shoulders, but the party like the one at Blaines last night was mostly married people. . . .

21 (Wed) Day came in misty and increased to rain. Called [at] . . . the Dep of Justice about Ladds claim as jury commissioner and got but little satisfaction on the subject. Attended the opening of the supreme court . . .

At 15 minutes to 3 Mrs D and I went calling in Mrs Fields carriage which she was kind enough to send us. We took James from the house as footman. The calling was little else than distributing our cards and might as well have been done by a messenger. . . .

22 (Thu) Went to Richmond on the 10:40 train. Rained all the way and the country looked gloomy and poor. Major Bolton met us at the depot with a carriage and took us to the Exchange Hotel, kept by a Mr Carrington to whom I found I had a letter of introduction from L Q Washington, sent me by Judge Field.[101] We were lodged . . . and took dinner. Bolton said he would liked to have taken us to his house but his wife was just confined and he could not. I went with him to the Westmoreland club in the evening . . . and staid until 12 oclock.

23 (Fri) The day came in clear and bright, and about 10 oclock Bolton came down with a hack and drove us about the town—out to the reservoir, through Hollywood cemetery—to the capitol—over Church Hill and to Libby Prison. We went through the capitol but did not see the parti-colored legislature which had adjourned the day before. The site is a handsome one, and the grounds and monuments make a very favorable impression. The cemetery is a very picturesque place. We visited the Colonial church on Church Hill and saw tombs that dated

as far back as 1789. The building is frame and is said to be constructed of material brought from England. It looks more like a farmhouse than a church and the surroundings appear neglected. We saw the outside of Libby prison and visited a tobacco factory where the work was performed by Negroes—the men making from $7 to 9 a week and the women from $3 to 5. . . .

Left Richmond for Washington in the 4:50 train at ½ past 5. Our bill at the Exchange for one day was $12.50 which all things considered was the highest price we have paid. The table was very good, and I enjoyed the corn dodgers and hoe cake very much—no corn bread like them. Met a Miss McCay on the sleeper who proved to be a pleasant companion.[102] Her father was once Pres of a college in Georgia and I believe also in South Carolina. He now lives in Baltimore. She was returning from Georgia. We did not get to Washington until about 11 when we should have been here by 9:50.

*24 (Sat)* Got up this morning at before 6 oclock and got down to 7th street wharf before 7 oclock to take the *Arrowsmith* for Leonardtown, but the boat was not there & no word when she would be, so we came back as we went. . . . About 5 oclock got word that the boat was in and would leave at 6. Asked the clerk to telephone when she would return. His answer was on Monday. So we went down and got aboard, and after waiting there for about 1½ hours for her to start we accidentally learned from Mr Stone the clerk that the boat only touched at Leonardtown and returned immediately and would not be in Leonardtown again until next Saturday. Thereupon we got ashore and came back to the Hotel. In conversation with Mr Stone I found that he used to know Mrs Stott very well and also knew her Uncle & Aunt—the Coombs—he said they were very old and were unable to come out, and that they would hardly appreciate our visit. We told him all about Mrs Stott and he promised to tell them that he had seen us. I also wrote a letter to them by the steamer explaining why we did not come.

*25 (Sun)* Xmas Day. Went to the church of the Epiphany and sat in Mr Justice Fields pew. A large congregation and good music—particularly the soprano. At ½ past 3 went to the same place to the S S service. The carols were well sung. More men at church here in proportion to members than in New York. The rage or blight of trade has possession of the latter. Went to Judge Fields to dinner. . . . [Met] Mrs McCreary, Mrs Fields sister besides the family.[103] Had an elegant dinner and a charming time. We had Xmas cards at our plate. I got Alfred Percival Graves lines on the Blarney castle. Mrs Deady "A warm greeting"—a girl with a muff in one hand and a red pep[p]er pod in the other. Mrs McCreary is one of the handsomest women I ever saw and equally fascinating. There was only a vacant seat between us at table and we chaffed and chatted aesthetics and the like quite briskly. Saw a sideboard and clock that the judge bought in Venice. Elegant piece—is of wood carving. He is going to New York on Friday but says he has arranged to have us call on the President with the Judges on New Years.

*26 (Mon)* Went to Mt Vernon by the 10 oclock boat . . . Got there about 12 and left at 2 and reached our hotel at 4. Went all over the house and grounds and visited the tombs. Probably 50 persons went down at the same time. We had a lunch in the old kitchen, which was poor at 50 cts apiece. Nature has done a great deal for the place and in Washingtons time it must have been comparatively grand property. The premises are pretty well preserved but there is an air of low keeping and decay about the place that gives it a mournful appearance.

Sent a letter to Mr Knott, Baltimore, with $11 enclosed for Thomas Cullan who made me a pair of shoes. Sent letter to Capt Blacke, the Steamer *Corcoran,* [*the Mt Vernon boat*] with $5 that I borrowed of him this morning because I went off and left my pocket book on my table in my room. Found a card from J W Drew when we came back.[104] Sent him a card and asked him to call this evening at ½ past 7.

*27 (Tue)* The day came in moist and warm. Cleared off before noon but continued warm—the thermometer marking 70 in the shade at 3 P M at Mrs Judge Fields. Sent papers *Herald* & *Capitol* to Paul—the latter containing a notice of the Yoshida reception and noticing our presence there . . . Mrs Deady was not well and remained in bed until evening. Went to the Capitol about 10 and went through the collection of books on Oregon in the Congressional Library—the librarian Mr Spofford, very kindly putting them at my disposal. I made notes of such as I thought we did not possess in the Portland Library and would like to. I found [for] what I have long searched—a copy of Greenhows original memoir on Oregon compiled under the direction of Sec Forsythe and published by the Senate on the motion of Linn of Mo made on Feb 10, 1840 in which our river is called the "Wallamet." Called on Mr Myrick [*Merrick*] and had a long and pleasant talk with him about juries and courts—the Surrat[t] case—both mother & son—he defended the latter and when I told him I had a lecture on the subject he proposed that I should deliver it before the law class of Georgetown College, which I may do. Called also on Judge Williams and McBride, saw the former and had a pleasant chat with him, but the latter is in Phil. Went to Mrs Gen [Frederick] Landers at the meeting of the literary society of which Garfield was President before he was President of the U S. Mrs Landers read, and read beautifully a paper written by Miss Mary Clemmer, but who was not there on account of the death of her father on the *Bluestocking.* The paper was brilliant and discursive and pleasant. After this Mr Spofford made some very sensible remarks upon woman in society and Gen Alvord made some commonplace remarks about a literary club that gathered about a Mrs Otis when he was a young man in Boston. The President [*of the society*] made some pertinent remarks about the influence an established society of repute had upon its members by giving them what he was pleased to style "an historic consciousness." After this there was general conversation [and] music . . . The refreshments were simple but ample—salad, roll sandwiches, coffee & lemonade. I went from Mrs Fields with her in her coupe and she sent me home in the same. Mrs Upton[105] invited us to dinner on Saturday and we accepted—could not help it. Called on Mr [M C] George last evening and found him very comfortably fixed. . . .

*28 (Wed)* Visited the State, War & Navy depts in company with Gen Crane . . . The room in the ordonance [*sic*] dept in which the Rebel flags and other curiosities are kept is interesting. Saw the famous trotter Patchen there, stuffed, of course.[106] The diplomatic room and library in the State dept are very handsome.

Saw a copy in plaster of the treaty made between the Athenians and Chalcideans in 445-6 B C. The original was not discovered I believe until 1875. The buildings are very handsome and full of all kinds and colors of people who live off the government. At 1 oclock I went to Judge Fields . . . Showed me a sketch of his life and analysis of his leading opinions by [J N] Pomeroy of the law school in S F and wanted me to look it over and tell him what I think of the propriety of publishing it. Returned me the copy of O'Mearas naturalization in the Sandwich Islands and some lithograph copies of the same. Talked at some length and with some feeling of the mean way the railway people of Cal had used him about the Democratic nomination in 1880. . . . Got a postal from Capt Ellicott today announcing his and his wifes arrival in Baltimore yesterday. Wrote him to come over and spend a day with us. . . .

*29 (Thu)* Day came in wet and it rained more or less all day. Went to the treasury building with Mrs D; visited the life-saving apparatus and had it explained to us by the most voluble mulatto I ever met. Called to see the state of Kearneys accounts and found that the disbursements for the jurors, witnesses, prisoners and miscellany had passed the auditors office and been sent to the 1st comptroller. Saw the chief clerk and he said he would take them up next week. Were in the vault where the bonds deposited by the national Banks are kept. Saw and handled those of the bank in Portland—$250,000. In the afternoon went with Gen Crane to the medical museum, kept in the old Ford theatre where Lincoln was shot. A tablet upon a building just opposite shows that he died there. Saw the place where he was shot and from which Booth leaped onto the stage shouting *Sic semper tyrannus.* Saw an immense collection of skeletons dug from the tumuli of the west and an immense number of the bones and organs of the body that had been affected by disease or wounds. A collection of calculi taken from bladders interested me very much. They had generally formed round some hard substance that had been thrust into the bladder. Saw some of the cervical vertebrae of Booth and the spinal cord, the portion through which the bullet passed from the effect of which he died. This evening called at Fields. . . . In the afternoon I examined a sketch of Fields life as a judge & legislator written by Pomeroy of the S F law school, and an accompanying analysis of many of his judicial opinions at his request with a view of getting my advice or rather opinion as to the propriety of publishing it. Pomeroy is a capital writer but he is a little out of plumb on the subject of the common law—thinks it a relic of barbarism. I marked several passages for correction or modification and took it up with me, but not finding him in I left it there. . . .

*30 (Fri)* The day came in clear and cool. Called at Justice Millers to see about accompanying the Judges of the S C to call on the President on New Years. He said come with them. Mr Ch Justice Waite called this evening and invited us to go with him. Am sorry the other arrangements prevented us accepting the invitation. Talked with Miller about the judiciary bills and found he favored [David] Davis' for an intermediate court of appeals in each circuit. . . . Miss Sallie S[wearingen] called at noon and had lunch with us and sat in the parlor for a couple of hours chatting pleasantly and pointing out the swells as they passed by or came in. I walked with her to . . . K street and round about there saw Ben Holladays house . . . Called at Mrs McC[reary]s in the evening. She was elegant in a loose dress or robe of white bunting. Drank a cup and heard her sing an English ballad and a French Song—the latter "Thy soul is immortal" by Alfred Musset, the former a love strain "Forever and forever"—by a woman whose name I forget. She told us an amusing story of an adventure or adventures she met in travelling in the Ry cars in France, and gave me the history and origin of Mrs [John W] Mackay, the bonanza queen. . . . The N Y *Times* is savage on Cyrus Field, Gould, Sage & Russel[l] concerning their alleged jobbery in elevated Ry stock.[107]

*31 (Sat)* The day has been bright and cool. Read my lecture over this morning for the law school. Went to the club and read the *Times* account of the stock jobbing of Gould, Sage, Russel[l] and Field in the elevated roads. Miss S called about 1 and said the carriage would be ready for us on Monday to attend the Presidents reception. . . .

# NOTES

1. George Steel, father of James and George A.; Steele in original.
2. Disraeli, Earl of Beaconsfield.
3. John E. Owens (1823–86), actor-manager, he specialized in comedy roles; "Our Boys," a popular domestic comedy.
4. Alexander Guthrie (1869–1913), San Francisco businessman; member firm of Balfour, Guthrie.
5. Henry B. Anthony (1815–84), Rhode Island journalist and politician; U. S. senator, 1858–84.
6. Both Baron Erskine and John P. Curran died before photography was discovered.
7. Hatch v Willamette Iron Bridge Co.; Deady issued an injunction against the building of a bridge at Morrison Street on the grounds that it would interfer with a navigable stream, and thus violate federal law. Deady's decision was reversed by the Supreme Court in 1888, by which time there were already two bridges across the river, both built because of a Supreme Court decision rendered in 1885 in a California case. Despite this decision, Deady refused to vacate his original injunction. Josiah L. Atkinson (1823–1902) and D. W. Wakefield (1836–1926), real estate agents. Carruthers in original.
8. Charles Lanman (1819–85), author and biographer.
9. John A. Paddock (1825–94), Episcopal clergyman; missionary bishop of Washington Territory and bishop of Olympia.
10. In 1860 Joseph Lane accepted the vice-presidential spot on the Southern Democrat ticket of John C. Breckinridge, and after Lincoln's election he continued to express strongly pro-Southern and pro-slavery views. By the time he reached Portland, in May, 1861, word had already spread that he was come prepared to lead a rebellion looking toward the establishment of a Pacific republic. Three years earlier he had been the most popular political figure in the Pacific Northwest, now he was repeatedly hanged in effigy as he traveled slowly south to his home near Roseburg. For some time after, excitable Unionists were demanding he be imprisoned, despite the fact that there was no evidence he was engaging in treasonable activities. But if Lane was inactive, he was for a long time unregenerated. Toward the end of the war he was planning to join Dr. Gwin's colony for Southern expatriates. The failure of Gwin's enterprise changed his mind about leaving the country. See Joseph Lane to Pat Malone, Feb. 25, 1865, and Lafayette Lane to Joseph Lane, April 22, 1865.
11. Mother Scholastica Kerst (1847–1911), Benedictine nun; Superior of St. Benedict's, 1880–89, she later—1892—founded the Benedictine Motherhouse at Duluth. For details of her visit to Oregon see Steckler's "The Founding of Mount Angel Abbey," *OHQ*, Vol. LXX (Dec. 1969), pp. 312–27.
12. Reedville, Washington County, was the site of Simeon G. Reed's stock farm, famous for its blooded animals.
13. W. H. Watkinds had pleaded guilty to assault on Sam Clarke and was fined. Having been convicted of a felony he was ineligible to vote, despite which, he tried. The present case resulted.
14. McLeay in original. Alfred F. Sears (1826–1911), Union soldier, engineer, writer and lecturer.

15. Thomas Doig, pilot of the *Great Republic,* which went aground on Sand Island, April 19, 1879.

16. John Goodfellow, manager of the Bank of B. C. and later a Seattle banker; died 1912.

17. In his decision in the Kilbourn case, Justice Miller denied the power of Congress to punish for contempt except in impeachment and other proceedings of a judicial nature. David W. Craig (1830–1916), journalist; associated with *Oregon Statesman,* 1863–66, 1880–93, and with a number of other Oregon papers.

18. Francois Rivet, Hudson's Bay Co. interpreter and early Wallamet Valley settler. Revit in original.

19. President Garfield was shot at the railroad depot, Washington, D. C., July 2, and died the following September 19, helped on his way by the incompetence of his medical attendants. His assassin, Charles J. Guiteau, was undeniably deranged.

20. Elwood Evans delivered the oration. A tidewaiter is a minor customs official assigned to watch the unloading of ships. W. H. Andrus, hotelman and saloonkeeper; 2nd ward councilman, 1875–79, 1880, 1883–86. T. L. Nicklin (1846–1908), dentist; 2nd ward councilman, 1880–82.

21. Abram Sharpless (1841–1920), military surgeon and Eugene physician. John Straub (c.1851–1933), then head of the primary department; later professor of classical languages.

22. The Mendelssohn Quintet Society of Boston was organized in 1849 and continued active until approximately 1895. Marie Nellini has not been identified.

23. After Dr. Keil's death in 1877 the Aurora Colony, which was already split by dissensions, its young people increasingly restive under the doctor's autocratic rule, determined to divide its land and other assets equally among the members. So ended a remarkable experiment. Charles Nordhoff wrote of Aurora in 1875 that in its 19 years of existence, "it has not had a criminal among its numbers; it has sent no man to jail; it has not had a lawsuit, neither among the members nor with outside people; it has not had an insane person, nor one blind or deaf or dumb; nor has there been any case of deformity. It has no poor; and the support of its own helpless persons is a part of its plan."

But he was forced to add that "the community has no library; that its members, so far as I could see, lack even the most common and moderate literary culture, aspiring to nothing further than the ability to read, write and cipher; that from the president down it is absolutely without intellectual life." From this last stricture he might have excepted the Aurora German band, which for a generation oomphaed strenuously before admiring Fourth of July gatherings up and down the Wallamet Valley. For additional, see Charles Nordhoff, *The Communistic Societies of the United States* (New York, 1961).

24. There was no Major Price in the Engineer Corps; the highest rank held by an officer of that name was that of 1st Lt. Philip M. Price. Nelson A. Miles (1829–1925), career soldier; appointed a first lieutenant at the beginning of the Civil War, he was given the rank of major-general of volunteers in 1865, after distinguishing himself repeatedly; after the war he re-enlisted and was commissioned a colonel in the regular army; served on the frontier until 1891; became commander-in-chief in 1895 and organized the invasion of Cuba. He retired, 1903, a lieutenant-general. Married Mary Hoyt Sherman.

25. Gen. Winfield Scott came west in 1859 to cool the growing dispute over title to the San Juan Islands. On October 18, 1859, Deady wrote to Nesmith: "Well, we arrived here on Sunday morning last about nine oclock. As we came in the heads we saw *The Golden Age* coming in from Panama. As she passed Fort point, a salute of sixteen guns were fired . . . We soon learned that Genl Scott was on board. San Francisco has been in a state of delirious excitement waiting his arrival for two days and nights . . . It was said that Genl Josh Haven (probably of New Haven) had slept in his Regimentals and spurs for two nights so as to be ready to muster the civic warriors of the city at a moments notice. To add to the agony the old Genl declined entirely to enter the procession until he had attended church. At last he got into the procession. I was upstairs in [Alex] Campbells office on Montgomery and saw him pass under the triumphal arch inscribed with Lundy's

Lane Cerro Gordo &c. As he passed under a wreath was let down over his neck with the aid of a block [and] tackle, and then there was shouting and huzzaing . . .

"I called at the Oriental and was introduced to him. He is a fine-looking specimen of the olden times and well worth seeing."

Joshua P. Haven was a prominent San Francisco insurance man and militia leader.

26. Robert J. Stevens, paymaster during Civil War; married Caroline C. Baker, daughter of Senator Edward D. Baker. Stephens in original. Alexander R. Shepherd (1836–1902), political boss of the District of Columbia and its governor, 1873–74; noted for unscrupulousness and financial irresponsibility. Stephen W. Dorsey (1842–1916), politician and businessman; while engaged in fraudulent railroad promotion in Arkansas he served in U. S. Senate, 1873–76; indicted in the Star Route frauds, 1881, he escaped conviction. The quotation from Horace should read: *et hoc genus omne.*

27. The Pacific silver fir and the noble fir, both now assigned to the genus Abies.

28. William S. Rosecrans (1819–98), soldier; after conducting a series of successful campaigns in Tennessee against Confederate Gen. Braxton Bragg, Rosecrans was badly defeated at Chickamauga and relieved of his command; Democratic congressman from California, 1881–85.

29. R. M. Dooley; Utah banker.

30. Lyman Trumbull (1813–96), Illinois jurist; as a senator, 1855–73, he was a strong supporter of Lincoln. James R. Doolittle (1815–97), New York and Wisconsin lawyer and politician; Republican senator from Wisconsin, 1857–69. Charles C. Bonney (1837–1903), lawyer, reformer, authority on international law. Thomas Drummond (1809–90), jurist; Illinois U. S. Circuit Court judge, 1869–84. Henry W. Blodgett (1821–1905), jurist; U. S. District Judge for Northern Illinois, 1869–92.

31. James B. Bradwell (1828–1907), lawyer and jurist. Myra Bradwell (1831–94), lawyer; founder and editor of the *Chicago Legal News.* William R. Poole (1821–94), librarian and historian; helped establish libraries at the naval academy and Cincinnati; librarian, Chicago Public Library, 1874–87; organized and headed Newberry Library, 1887–94.

32. Ann Sophia Stephens (1813–86), author and editor of several magazines; wrote the first Beadle dime novel.

33. John McCulloch (1832–1915), Irish-American actor-manager; played with Forrest, Barrett and others.

34. Henry Demarest Lloyd (1847–1903), lawyer and journalist; as a bitter opponent of trusts and monopolies, he became the first of the great "muck-rakers." Married Jessie Bross, 1873.

35. Catherinus P. Buckingham (1808–88), businessman and Union soldier; commanded troops at New York during anti-draft riots in 1863; built Chicago grain elevator; with his sons operated the Chicago Iron Works, of which he was president.

36. The benefit was given to help survivors of the great forest fire which swept across east central Michigan, August 31 to September 6, destroying more than one million acres of forest land, burning out 44 townships, and causing great loss of life.

37. William R. Travers (1819–87), New York attorney. Jerome Park race track, located not far from the present reservoir, was torn down in the 1890s to make way for an aqueduct. "The Professor" was the first of William H. Gillette's plays to be produced; he also played the title role.

38. Jasper W. Gilbert, New York lawyer and jurist; served as district attorney of Monroe County and as justice of the state supreme court.

39. Joel B. Erhardt, New York attorney and sometime U. S. marshal; died 1909. Erdhardt in original. Hugh J. Jewett (1817–98), Ohio lawyer and legislator.

40. John L. Belcher, New York merchant; died 1883. Horatio Potter (1802–87), Episcopal clergyman; bishop of New York, *post* 1854. Josiah G. Holland (1819–81), physician, author, and editor, successively, of *Scribner's* and *Century* magazines.

41. Max and Louis Goldsmith were partners in the Portland mercantile firm of L. Goldsmith & Co.

42. Thomas A. Thacher (1815–86), educator; taught at Yale *post* 1838. Thatcher in original. Clinton Day remains unidentified. Noah Porter (1811–92), Congregationalist clergyman and educator; president of Yale, 1871–86. Montgomery is probably Henry M., eldest son of J. B. Montgomery. For Couch Flanders and Clarence Glisan, see DP.

43. William Sprague (1830–1915), manufacturer; Republican senator, 1863–75. The inheritor of great wealth, he married Kate Chase (1840–99), daughter of Lincoln's secretary of the treasury. Sprague lost most of his means in the panic of 1873 and was divorced from his wife in 1882, after an exchange of domestic pleasantries. Alewives are a kind of herring, and seldom served in their shells.

44. Benjamin H. Paddock (1828–91), brother of Bishop John Paddock; bishop of Massachusetts, 1873–91; married Anna Sanger, 1863. Robert G. Fitch (1846–1915), journalist; began with Sam Bowles' *Springfield Republican,* was with *Boston Post,* 1872–86, served as fire commissioner and as an editorial writer for the *Boston Transcript.*

45. Phillips Brookes (1835–93), Episcopal clergyman; bishop of Massachusetts, 1891–93. Deady admired him greatly.

46. John Lowell (1824–97), Massachusetts jurist; judge of the federal district court, 1865–78, and of the circuit court, 1878–84.

47. Katie Stevens was staying with her father's brother, Oliver Stevens.

48. John C. Gray (1839–1915), educator; associated with Harvard Law School from 1869.

49. Elisha Basset was deputy clerk, U.S.C.C. John D. Long (1838–1915), lawyer and politician; governor of Massachusetts, 1880–82, congressman, 1883–89. Leonard A. Jones (1832–1909), jurist and legal authority. John L. Stoddard (1850–1931), writer and travel lecturer.

50. Samuel Bowles (1851–1915), the third of that name.

51. Ernesto Rossi (1827–96), Italian actor.

52. Blandford is, in fact, south-west of Mt. Tom.

53. Ensign H. Kellogg (1812–82), lawyer and businessman.

54. Alonzo B. Cornell (1832–1904), Western Union official; governor of New York, 1879–83. Lucy Deady thought him rude.

55. William C. Doane (1823–1913), Episcopal clergyman; Bishop of Albany, *post* 1869.

56. Joseph A. Sladen was for many years Gen. Howard's friend and aide-de-camp.

57. Charles S. Francis (1805–87), publisher and book dealer. Samuel A. Allibone (1816–89), lexicographer and librarian.

58. James Fisk (1834–72), financial manipulator. Fiske in original.

59. Henry B. Whipple (1822–1901), Episcopal clergyman and missionary; bishop of Minnesota, *post* 1859. Edward A. Washburn (1819–81), rector, St. Paul's Cathedral, from 1865.

60. John W. Hamersley (1808–89), lawyer and author. Pierre van Cortland de Puyster Field (1839–1918), New York merchant. Daniel S. Tuttle (1837–1923), Episcopal clergyman; missionary bishop of Montana, 1867–86.

61. Cornelia C. Stewart, widow of the famous New York merchant. Albert Bierstadt (1830–1902), painter; noted for his western scenes. Charles Albright (1830–80), Union soldier and corporation lawyer, which last fact fitted him particularly for helping prosecute the Mollie Maguires, the Irish terrorists seeking to organize the Pennsylvania coal fields. According to one account General Albright attended each session of the trials in full military regalia, complete with sword.

62. Nisquahoning in original.

63. Asa Packer (1805–79), Pennsylvania railroad builder, politician and philanthropist.

64. Lazarus D. Shoemaker (1819–93), lawyer; Republican congressman, 1871–75.

65. Wife of Elisha B. Shapleigh, Philadelphia physician. Chapleigh in original. John Welsh (1806–86), merchant and philanthropist.

66. Edward F. Noyes (1832–90), Ohio lawyer, Union soldier, and minister to France, 1877–81.

67. John Duval Rodney, apparently an uncle to the Rodney sisters.

68. Benjamin (1745 o.s.—1813) and James Rush (1786–1869), famous physicians, and Richard Rush (1780–1859), lawyer and diplomat.

69. Wilson Lloyd has not been definitely identified.

70. Thomas H. Montgomery; president of the American Fire Insurance Co. Andrew J. Giesy (1853–1933), physician. Jacob L. Wortman (died 1926), geologist.

71. Oliver Landreth was a member of a famous Philadelphia seed firm. William B. Stevens (1815–87), Episcopal clergyman, historian and physician; bishop of Pennsylvania, *post* 1865.

72. The sons of Anak; Biblical giants.

73. George W. Doane (1799–1859), Episcopal clergyman.

74. Frederick Fraley (1804–1901), Philadelphia merchant.

75. S. Davis Page (1840–1921), Philadelphia lawyer. Girard College, a school for fatherless boys, endowed in 1848 by Stephen Girard.

76. William H. Allen (1808–82), educator; president of Girard College, 1849–62, 1872–82.

77. Eli K. Price (1797–1884), lawyer and legal reformer. Silas Weir Mitchell (1829–1914), physician, pioneer neurologist and author. William V. McKean (Kean in original), chief editor of the *Public Ledger*. Alex K. McLure (1828–1909), lawyer, journalist and editor of the Philadelphia *Times*, 1873–1901. J. P. Lippincott (1813–86), founder of the publishing house which bears his name. There were several Dr. Townsends in Philadelphia at that time.

78. Charles M. Bache, member of a prominent Philadelphia family; connected with the Coast Survey.

79. The recumbent effigy of Edward Shippen Burd (Bird in original), and the Anna J. Magee Memorial reredos may still be seen at St. Stephen's Church.

80. A. Leo Knott (1829–1918), Baltimore lawyer and legislator; Eliza Deady Knott's brother-in-law.

81. William B. Willson (c.1845–1922), coffee and sugar importer and the owner of a famous clipper fleet. Julia Howard Tyson and Mary Howard, daughters of James Howard (1832–1910), Confederate veteran and agent of the Southern Express Co.; in 1884 elected adjutant-general of Maryland.

82. Jesse Tyson (c.1820–1906), president of the Baltimore Chrome Works and prominent Quaker; his home was called Cylburn.

83. William H. Rineheart (1825–74), sculptor. Etelka Gerster (1857–1920), Hungarian coloratura-soprano.

84. Thomas J. Morris (1837–1912), U. S. District Court judge. Hugh L. Bond (1828–93), jurist; judge of U. S. Circuit Court, 1870–93. Arunah S. Abell (1806–88), journalist; founded the *Sun* in 1837. He had three sons. Robert Gilmore (1833–1906), jurist; successively judge of the Maryland superior court and associate justice of the state supreme court. George W. Brown (1812–90), lawyer and jurist; mayor of Baltimore, 1872–88.

85. William P. Whyte (1824–1908), Baltimore lawyer and Democratic politician; U. S. senator on three occasions and mayor, 1881-83. The Gobble Dispatch was a coded message sent to Oregon during the Hayes-Tilden electoral dispute.

86. Charles H. Crane, military surgeon and assistant surgeon-general, U. S. army; served in Oregon prior to the Civil War, became surgeon-general in 1882, died a year later. Wormley's Hotel was operated by James Wormley (1819–84), Negro hotel and businessman; it was noted for its excellent accommodations and fine food. Robert Mac-Feely (died 1901), soldier; he had served in Oregon prior to the Civil War.

87. William A. Leonard (1848–1930), Episcopal clergyman and from 1889 Bishop of Ohio; a nephew of H. C. Leonard, partner, with Henry Green, in the firm of Leonard

and Green. Robert C. Schenck (1809–90), Ohio lawyer and Union soldier; congressman, 1843–51, 1863–71; minister to Great Britain, 1871–76, he was forced to resign because of his connection with a fraudulent mining promotion. A herdick was a horse-drawn bus.

88. William McK. Dunn (1814–87), lawyer and soldier; judge-advocate general, U. S. Army, 1875–81.

89. William Lawrence (1819–99), Ohio lawyer, editor and Republican congressman; 1st comptroller, 1880–85. Joseph W. Keifer (1836–1932), Ohio Republican congressman, 1877–85, 1905–11; he was not a successful speaker of the house. William D. Kelley (1814–90), Pennsylvania congressman; called Pig-Iron Kelley because of his insistence on a high protective tariff on that product.

90. Catherine McCoy, an old friend of Deady's from his early days in Ohio, and her daughter, Mary Ellen Whittaker. Wilson S. Kennon (1826–95), lawyer. Oliver J. Swaney, attorney. Henry West (1800–87), physician and druggist; and apparently not overly truthful about his age. Isaac Patterson (1821–87), businessman.

91. Ann Askew (c.1818–89). D. D. T. Cowen (1826–84), lawyer and banker. William Oakey was judge in Belmont County, 1877–82. William Kennon (1793–1881), lawyer and jurist; Democratic congressman, 1829–33 and 1835–37, he became a Republican at the time of the Civil War; died November 2, just over a month before the Deadys arrived in St. Clairsville.

92. Theisa Coulter Frint was one of the few among the residents of St. Clairsville to write Deady with some regularity. Jane Edgerton (1823–1915), school teacher and administrator. Sarah Norris McMillan had made a considerable impact on Deady in his salad days. Thomas Cochran, lawyer and jurist, married Ala Frint in 1873. Robert E. Chambers (1827–84), lawyer and jurist.

93. John Thompson, died 1852.

94. Thomas and Richard Frazier (or Frasier) had operated the Frazier House since 1862. Benjamin Mackall (1801–91), merchant; Barnesville's leading citizen.

95. John W. Kennon (1812–1903), Barnesville attorney.

96. Carolus Cooke Kelly, an official of the Union Window Glass Co., Bellaire. John Kelly (1809–71), blacksmith; Deady was apprenticed to him at 17. Rachel Judkins Kelly (c.1814–1904), widow of John Kelly and daughter of Dr. Carolus Judkins, Barnesville's first physician

97. Robert B. Potter (1829–97), New York attorney and Union soldier. Richard T. Merrick (1826–85), attorney; defended John Surratt in the Lincoln assassination trials. Wade Hampton (1818–1902), planter and Confederate cavalry leader; governor of South Carolina, 1876–78, senator, 1878–91. Benjamin F. Jonas (1834–1911), Louisiana senator, 1879–85. Richard Coke (1829–87), Texas lawyer and Confederate soldier; governor, 1874–78, senator, 1876–94. George G. Vest (1830–1904), Missouri lawyer and legislator; member of Confederate Congress, 1862–65, and U. S. senator, 1879–1903. Thomas F. Bayard (1828–98), Massachusetts lawyer and Democratic politician; U. S. senator, 1869–85; Secretary of State, 1885–89; minister to Great Britain, 1893–97. Allen G. Thurman (1813–95), Ohio lawyer and Democratic senator, 1867–79.

98. Charles F. Crocker, son of Charles Crocker of the Central Pacific and vice-president of Wells-Fargo.

99. Charles J. Guiteau, President Garfield's assassin, was tried before Walter S. Cox, associate justice of the U. S. Supreme Court. Guiteau continually interrupted the proceedings with outcries, exhortations and rambling speeches. He insisted that he was a public benefactor. He urged petitions be circulated in his behalf and expected to file several hundred thousand signatures with the court. In general he behaved after the fashion of the Chicago Seven. Judge Cox seems to have had greater patience than Judge Hoffman.

100. James G. Blaine (1830–93), lawyer and politician; Maine congressman and senator, Secretary of State, 1881 and 1889–92, and repeatedly a presidential hopeful. Gail Hamilton, the pseudonym of Mary A. Dodge (1833–96), journalist.

101. Bolton cannot be identified. Lucius Q. Washington, distantly related to our first

President, was chief clerk, and after April, 1862, acting assistant secretary of state for the Confederate Government.

102. Miss McCay was the daughter of Charles F. McCay (1810–89), South Carolina mathematician, banker and actuary, and president of South Carolina College, 1855–57.

103. For Belle Swearingen McCreary, see Field, DP.

104. Joseph P. Drew (died 1883), army paymaster; prior to the Civil War had been active in Oregon Democratic politics.

105. Jean Davenport Lander (1829–1904), widow of Frederick W. Lander (1821–62), soldier, explorer and engineer; prior to her marriage she had been a prominent actress. W. W. Upton was then 2nd comptroller of the Treasury. Mary Clemmer, author, 1839–84.

106. Patchen, named for George S. Patchen, a prominent turf man of the day.

107. Morrison R. Waite (1816–88), Ohio lawyer and jurist; chief justice of the United States, 1874–88. David Davis (1815–86), Illinois lawyer and jurist and politician; justice of the Supreme Court, 1862–77; U. S. senator, 1877–83. Marie Louise (Hungerford) Bryant; a widow at the time she married Mackay. Jay Gould (1836–92) and his associate Russell Sage (1816–1906) were contesting with Cyrus Field for control of New York's elevated railways. In the process both parties manipulated stocks, bought venal judges and mercilessly squeezed the small investor. Deady apparently believed Russell Sage to be two men, since no other Russell is named in the articles in question.

# APPENDIX A

### THE OREGON IMPROVEMENT COMPANY

The Oregon Improvement Company was organized by Villard late in 1880, its capital stock having a value of $5,000,000. Another $5,000,000 was acquired by floating an issue of 6% bonds. The company would eventually build and operate three small feeder lines, control the Pacific Steamship Company, and own the Newcastle and Franklin coal mines. It operated chiefly in western Washington and its collapse, in November of 1890, carried down with it the hopes of a number of flourishing communities.

Deady, of course, had not the funds available to buy $10,000 worth of stock, and indeed it is clear from the entry that he is uncertain whether it was stock or bonds which had been held in his name. The transaction amounted to a gift from Villard, who purchased as an insider and sold at a profit, and would have sustained any loss had there been one. Had the circumstances become known they would have raised eyebrows even in that day of sketchy legal ethics.

It may be said for Villard that he never sought any favors of Deady, and of Deady that he would never have granted favors, and it is not difficult to understand why the judge, always living on the edge of polite penury, was happy to accept what was the largest single sum he received in his entire lifetime.

Deady visited Roseburg in March, 1881, traveling by train. But the stage continued to link Oregon and California from that town south until the O&C was completed in 1887. Late 1870s view at Metropolitan hostelry. Roseburg engraving, 1880s, from the *West Shore.*

While in Roseburg, Deady visited Gen. Joseph Lane, Oregon's first territorial governor, whose "end was drawing nigh . . ."

Henry Villard, by this time active in Oregon railroad development.

When the Deadys went east in the fall of 1881, they visited Benjamin Stark and his family, reminiscing about "old times and people" in Oregon. Among Army figures they saw was then Assistant Surgeon General C. H. Crane, with whom Deady also "enjoyed talking over our old southern Oregon experiences." (Deady album.)

Beginning their journey east, the Deadys went to San Francisco on the OR&N Co.'s new *Columbia,* an 1880 arrival.

On this visit they stayed at the Palace Hotel.

At Salt Lake they toured the city. The still unfinished Mormon Temple and Tabernacle (begun in 1850s and 1860s, respectively) are at right. The Tabernacle has the domed roof.

id Dudley Field (Deady album). Both he
his brother, Justice Field, entertained the
dys while they were in the East.

St. Johns Church, Washington, D. C., "one of the oldest in the country
. . ." (Deady album.) They sat in General Crane's pew on Jan. 1, 1882, and
"called at the White House with the Justices of the Supreme Court" on Jan.
2. Mrs. Deady went in on the President's arm.

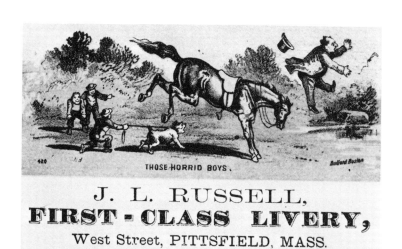

THOSE HORRID BOYS.

J. L. RUSSELL,
FIRST-CLASS LIVERY,
West Street, PITTSFIELD, MASS.

Dear Henderson. While
taking a ride at Pittsfield
yesterday with the Kelloggs
I found this card in the card
pocket of the carriage, and
said to myself, I'll keep
this and send it to H.B. and so
I have. I wrote Paul last night
Sunday oct 3d            Deady
Albany N.Y.

# 1882

*January 1 (Sun)* The day has been dry but cloudy & cold. Went to St Johns church. Sat in Gen Cranes pew and staid to communion. House overflowing full. About the usual proportion staid to communion—one-third. . . . Went over my lecture on Jury trial and fitted it to this place and to accompany the one on Law & Lawyers. . . .

*2 (Mon)* Day was bright and cool—indeed beautiful. Called at the White House with the Justices of the supreme court in Judge Fields carriage. Were presented to the President by Mr Justice Miller, who then took Mrs D on his arm and conducted her through the room. Received in the red room, then we went into the green room and from there to the east room. We met many people of distinction and saw more. Met the British minister, Mr [Sackville] West; the German minister wore his helmet, and the Turkish on[e] his Fez. We went at 15 minutes after 11 and came away about ½ past 12. The army & navy made a splendid display of gold lace and cord, and it looked as if none were left on the frontier *at all.* Mrs Deady went to Mrs Justice Harlans[1] to receive and I went with Judge Upton and Mr George to call. We started a little after one and kept at it until nearly 8 . . . [Got] pass for Mrs D and self from Kansas City to Deming over the A T Santa Fe road. . . .

*3 (Tue)* Day clear and cold. Went to the Treasury building and [talked with] Asst Sec [Henry] French on the subject of a clock for my court room and a chair for myself. He called in Major Power who has charge of the "Furniture" of pub buildings and I had a talk with him on the subject. He said I should have a chair such as I wanted, but about the clock he thought $275 a little high, and I don't know but it is. He showed me a list of the clocks and their prices furnished to the pub buildings and none was above $80 except N Y where $500 had been expended through the influence of Mr James when he was P M there. I am to see him again, when I hope to get $150 allowed for the clock. Found out that my salary account for December had not been started yet. called on Mr [S F] Philips the solicitor and had a talk with him about Ladds claim as Jury Comr and things in General. He is a very pleasant, sensible man, and so are his two daughters whom I met at his home yesterday. Called [on] Mrs Michler and found her kind and charming but full of grief at the loss of her husband—enjoying as our mutual friend Crane says—the luxury of woe. She goes no wheres except to church—the little one round the corner—St Pauls where Will Barker is Rector. She has lost flesh since she was in Oregon, her hair has regained its natural color and altogether I never saw her look so well. Gen Schenck & daughter and Com[m] Baldwin[2] called while I was there and others whom she did not admit. Her rooms are beautiful and full of pretty things. She gave me a delicious glass of eggnog. When I came home found Ellicott and George Brooke in the room. Had a pleasant [word] from them both. E went back to Baltimore and B to Alexandria. We go over to Baltimore in the morning to visit the Ellicotts and will return on Thursday. Delivered my lecture on "Trial by Jury" this evening before the law class of the Georgetown University. Mr Merrick & Hoffman, law librarian of Congress accompanied me to the place . . . and the latter introduced me. I occupied about an hour in its delivery and think I did pretty well. I had much applause and may compliments at the close. . . .

*4 (Wed)* Found a handsome notice of my lecture last night in this mornings *Post* and a respectful mention of it in the *Republican*. Mailed copies of the former to Paul . . . and the *Oregonian*. Went to Baltimore on the 9:40 train. It was a beautiful morning and we had a pleasant ride on the B & P road. Capt Ellicott met us at the depot with a carriage and drove us to Mrs Es uncle Jesses house . . . where we met Mrs E and the baby. . . .

*5 (Thu)* When we got up found about 3 inches of snow on the ground and more falling. . . . Ellicott went with me to Saxtons where I purchased a watch for Henderson—a stem winder in a nickel case for $12 and a silver chain for $4 and left it there to be regulated and brought over by Capt Ellicott. At ½ past 3 we said good bye—and it may be forever and came home on the B & O, reaching the hotel at 25 min to 5 and being an hour and ten minutes on the road.

Merrick and Hoffman called after dinner and owing to the inclemency of the evening it was agreed that the delivery of my lecture on Law & Lawyers should be postponed until Tuesday evening next. Called at [Congressman] Georges and read the papers. Upon our return from Baltimore found the N Y *Herald* and *Evening Star* of yesterday with very complimentary notices of my lecture on "Trial by Jury" . . .

*6 (Fri)* Day cloudy and cool. The snow remained on the ground. Went to the Treasury dept and worked my salary for December through, $294.80. Saw Mr Solicitor Philips on the subject of Ladds claim as Jury Comr and he thought it ought to be paid, but [*the chief*] clerk, Hodges persisted that it should not be, it was concluded that I should see the Atty Gen about the matter in the morning.

. . . We concluded today that we should start home on the 14th.

*7 (Sat)* Called on the Atty Gen, [*Mr Brewster*], this morning in relation to Ladds claim as Jury Comr.[3] Was introduced by the solicitor, Mr Philips. He promised me to take it up soon and pass upon it. . . .

*8 (Sun)* Day was warm and foggy. Went to the Presbyterian church and sat in Mr Justice Harlans pew. Mrs D was not very well and staid at home. The service was somewhat advanced for Presbyterian. It began with the congregation singing the doxology led by a conductor who stood on the platform with the preacher. Then the congregation still standing said after the minister the Apostles Creed, which was followed by the Gloria in Excelsus, the congregation singing under the direction of the conductor. Then the minister read the ten commandments and the summary of them taken from the sermon on the mount. After a hymn there was an extempore prayer by the minister concluding with the Lords prayer in which the congregation joined audibly. The sermon was an extraordinary piece of declamation, gesticulation and brusqueness with some excellent thoughts and sentiments often delivered in a very abrupt & forcible way. It was from the words of St Paul before Felix—"He reasoned of righteousness, temperance and the judgment to come." In the afternoon I called on Mrs Michler and she gave me her picture and an excellent glass of port. . . . We called at Adml [S P] Lees in the evening where we met Montgomery Blair,[4] with whom I had a chat. . . .

9 (Mon) Called on Gen Sherman this morning and asked him to send maps of his Georgia campaign to Wm T Meek of Martinsville, Ohio, and he ordered them sent. Had a passage of words at the Atty Gen office in the morning about Ladds claim as Jury Comr. Went to the capitol at ½ past 11. Went into the senate chamber where I met Gilfrey & Slater & Sen [J B] Beck.[5] The latter gave me some copies of the speeches in the debate on the question of the "inability of the President." Met Mrs D in the Rotunda at 12 as per appointment. Went in the Supreme court room and saw Associate Justice [Horace] Gray sworn in after his commission was read. . . . Saw Grover about the payment of my referees fee of $300 and told him if we had $150 of it we could get along. He promised to give it to me on Friday certain. . . .

This evening went to a party given by the Mexican minister Signor [sic] Zamaema & his wife with Judge Field. Went at 15 minutes to 10 and returned at 15 min after 12. A great crowd and a splendid show. . . . Saw Nellie Sartoris nee Grant. She was painted and dressed in the Sara[h] Bernhardt style and looked furious. The Sneads, mother and daughter were there as usual taking notes and faith they'll print them so they say.[6] The refreshments were good but the champagne was miserable. The House was beautifully illuminated outside with gas jets in cups and parti-colored. The host is a tall slender Yankee looking man with long iron gray locks and the hostess a plain plump little woman of the brunette order. . . . there was dancing at the party in the conservatory with Mexican Mts and scenes painted on the walls and a fountain of claret punch at one end of it. There were some lovely necks and shoulders in the dances.

10 (Tue) Went to the Patent office . . . Saw the room that constituted the National Gallery when I was here in 1846 and saw some of the things that I saw then—for instance, Franklins printing press, Washingtons camp chest and contents and the suit of clothes he wore when he resigned his commission at Annapolis—the small clothes or breeches being buckskin and the facing of the coat the same . . . Delivered my lecture on Law & Lawyers this evening to the law class. Dr [J P] Drew & Judge Williams were present. I was very hoarse and spoke with some difficulty. The cheers and congratulations were numerous and hearty at the end of it. . . .

11 (Wed) Went to the Atty Gens office in the morning. Saw him a few moments. Said nothing had been done about the nomination of the Dis Atty . . . Suffering from a very severe cold in the head and hoarseness. Called at Dr Cranes as I came home and he gave me some chloride of potash lozenges. . . . Called at Mr Justice

Harlans where we spent nearly 3 hours very pleasantly . . . Harlan and I adjourned to the study on the third floor where he administered some hot whiskey punch or punches to me for my cold—taking some of the medicine himself as a preventive. We discussed Williams et ux and Hipple somewhat, and the political situation generally. I think him an earnest, honest, bigheaded and bighearted man. His wife is a lovely specimen of a worthy Kentucky woman.

*12 (Thu)* Remained in bed on account of my cold until 12 oclock. . . . Walked out in the afternoon. Called on Judge [Noah] Swayne and Madame [Sarah] Dahlgren. Found the former in and spent 20 minutes with him in which he said that the best charity was personal kindness and Providence had furnished everyone an inexhaustible supply thereof. Mrs Dahlgren was not in. Field called in the evening and took me to Dr Buseys[7] on account of my throat who gave me a prescription and said I must stay in the House tomorrow . . .

*13 (Fri)* Dr Busey called in the morning and examined my chest and said nothing the matter with it, which I knew before. Directed me to finish my medicine and keep in the house. . . . Paul Schulze called and took dinner with us. The depreciation in Villards stock has made him feel poor. Gilfrey called and paid me $150 on account of L F Grover in part payment of $300 he owes me as referee.

*14 (Sat)* Went to the observatory with Mrs D . . . where we saw the big telescope and witnessed the operation of giving New York the time at 12 oclock. Were also introduced to Admiral [John] Ro[d]gers, who is in charge—an interesting old man. Went from there to Georgetown College and back on the cars, and enjoyed the trip. The new college building is of grey stone and makes a very fine appearance. . . . Field sent a note with the passes from N Y home extended to 1882. Wormley made examination and said that we took train for Harrisburg on Monday at 10 A M and there joined the train for which we have passes to Chicago. At ½ past 6 we left the Hotel with Judge Field in Grovers carriage, and got home at 15 minutes past 11. At the dinner there were Miss Swearingen, Mrs MacCreary, Judge Field, Chief Justice Waite, Mr Justice[s] Matthews, Harlan, Bradley, Miller, Woods, Senators [George] Pendleton,[8] Grover, Slater and ex Senator Sergeant, M C George and myself and Mrs Deady. The dinner was most excellent. I took Miss Swearingen in and sat on her right while Judge Field took Mrs D in and she sat on his right. The Ch J sat on Miss Ss left and Mrs MacCreary & Pendleton next below & just opposite to me, Mr J Bradley sat on my right and George next. Mrs D & I passed our menus around and we got on them the names of all the guests. On the whole it was the most delightful evening ever spent and I shall remember Judge Field for it with gratitude the longest day I live. Judge Matthews when he bade me good by said he never should reverse me but with regret. . . .

*15 (Sun)* . . . Got my Hotel bill and went through it. Reduced a charge of $10 for a coupe on New Years Day to take Mrs D to Justice Harlans and back from $10 to $5 and had the deductions on account of absence increased from $5 to $10, which left the amount including transportation to the depot in the morning $294.57—time 32¾ days. Wrote to Field good by and thanking him for his kindness . . .

Dr Drew called and said that he had examined Mallorys letter to the Atty

Genl on the Tompkins case[9] and the most objectionable features of it are the atrocious syntax and orthography. Has commenced raining again.

*16 (Mon)* Day came in warm and balmy, but a little cloudy. Got on the B & P train for Harrisburg at 10 A M fare $3.84 each and seats and sleeper 75 cts each. At Baltimore saw Capt Ellicott and Mrs Tyson who were at the depot to see us. After a brief but hearty greeting we bade them good by—perhaps forever, but I hope not. At Harrisburg got on the Penn fast train for Pittsburg at 15 min after 3, on passes, paying $2 for chairs. About 40 miles east of Pittsburg it began to snow and were detained from time to time by something ahead of us so that instead of getting to P between 10 & 11 P M did not get there until after 12.

*17 (Tue)* Left Pittsburg about ½ past 1 A M for Chicago on passes paying $5 for sec[tion] on sleeping car. Got to bed about 2 oclock and soon slept soundly. At 7 oclock the Porter called us to get up for breakfast, which we took at Crestline, Ohio—and a very good one it was for 75 cts each. Here telegraphed to Gen Buckingham that we were coming. Stopped for dinner at Ft Wayne. We made ours out of the remains of our lunch with some beer and boiled eggs added that I bought in town. Reached Chicago nearly on time, where Mr William Buckingham met us with a coupe and took us to his fathers house . . . [*On the cars*] from Pittsburg on there was ½ a score of bright, fast young commercial travellers, who spent their time in drinking beer and playing Sancho Pedro seven-up. . . .

*19 (Thu)* Drew my check for $100 on 1st N B Portland in favor of William Buckingham under my letter of credit thereon. This makes $250 I have drawn and I thought when I left home I would need at least $500. Left Gen Bs at 15 min to 12 in his coupe for the depot of the N W Ry Co. Forgot my Scotch cap that I had carried through our journey. Left at ½ past 12 for Council Bluffs. . . .

*20 (Fri)* Reached Council Bluffs 9:30 A M and left for Kan Cy on the C B, St Jo & K Cy Ry at 10 A M and reached the latter place between 5 & 6 P M . . . At Kansas City we went in to the waiting room where we waited with some hundreds of others until 10 when we got off for Deming on the A T & Santa Fe Ry. Here we bought a new lunch basket and lunch together with some periodicals. Found our baggage 40 pounds overweight (200 lbs) for which I had to pay $6. Our car was the El Paso and sec 6 and we got to bed as soon after starting as possible.

*21 (Sat)* Were called to Breakfast at Florence at 6 oclock—156 miles west of K C. But we did not get up and took our breakfast out of our basket about 8. The day came in clear and frosty with small patches of snow on the ground. Stopped for dinner at Larned and supper at Coolidge. Most of the day on the left bank of the Arkansas, the land occupied for grazing mostly. Read the *N[orth] A[merican] Rev[iew]* and *Harp[ers] Week[ly]*. 2 good articles in the former, "Do the spoils belong to the victor" and the remedy for railway troubles.

*22 (Sun)* Woke up before daylight and observed the Raton Mts which we were passing. About daylight passed through the tunnel—the line between Colorado & New Mex passing across it about the middle where the elevation is 7600 feet. Stopped for breakfast at Raton, a place at the western foot of these Mts. Weather clear and bright but cold and frosty. The general appearance of the country that of southern Cal. Sat on the rear of the car with Mrs Deady from the commencement of the ascent of the Glorietta Mts near a very striking and attractive peak called "Starvation rock" until we passed through the Apache cañon . . . This was a very interesting piece of road. Reached Lamy about 5 P M where the train stopped for supper and we changed off onto the Santa Fe train. About 6 we left for Santa Fe a distance of 18 miles due north, where we arrived in an hour and were driven to the Palace hotel and lodged in room 68.

*23 (Mon)* Got up early this morning, got breakfast and at 9 oclock drove about the town in an open carriage and saw what there was of it. Went into the old adobe church of San Miguel said to be 300 years old. The Christian brothers have a large modern school building adjoining and we went into the school rooms where the Brother was teaching about 25 urchins of from 6 to 10 years of age. He sent an American boy with us into the chapel as he called it. On a table under a placard hung on the wall giving the history of the church was a book for visitors to subscribe their names and gifts in. We complied with the request to the amount of 20 cts. We were set down at a curiosity shop on S[an] F[rancisco] street where we spent $6 in Indian pottery, baskets and a cactus stick for a cane. Called on Gov [L A] Sheldon & wife where we met Judge [Joseph] Bell, whom Arthur has just made one of the Judge[s] of the territory.[10] The Gov resides in an old adobe building called the Palace once occupied by the Spanish Gov. We saw the legislative chambers in the same building but unfortunately the solons were not in session until 2 P M. . . .

At ½ past 2 went to the depot and on board the train for Lamy. A pleasant ride and beautiful day—but the former cost 8 cts per mile. The train was on time at Lamy and we left there 15 min after 8 in the car Guaymas, sec 8. . . . Picked up a volume of Oscar Wildes poetry and among other things read "Charminides" —on the rape of a statue.

*24 (Tue)* Reached Deming about daylight after a good nights rest. Changed cars for the Southern Pacific where we got sec G in Palace car No 6 to Los Angeles at a cost of $13. Had breakfast on the car. A great flat dreary country about here. Left Deming at 8 A M the only passengers in the sleeper being ourselves. Got San Francisco papers here for the first time since we left home. Scarcely a word in them from Oregon except the sailing of the *Columbia* on the 20 and the list of passengers. Train stopped for dinner at Bowie. We lunched on board at 11 and dined the same at 5 P M. Passed over a monotonous country, but saw the Mesquite, the cactus in several forms and what I suppose is a palmetto or little palm. Read Suetonius—the lives of Galba, Vitellius, Otho and Trajan—What a beastly lot they were. The day was warm and cloudy. Train stopped for supper at Tuscon, [*sic*], where we had a walk . . .

*25 (Wed)* Rested pretty well last night. Crossed the Colorado, at Yuma, just before day. Saw it from the windows of our berth. The Porter said it rained hard between 1 & 4 oclock this morning. The day broke on the most desolate country I have ever seen. But the weather is delightful. Train stopped for breakfast at 5, N[ew] M[exico] and for dinner at Colton. We took our meals on the car and had a pot of hot coffee for breakfast or rather Mrs Deady had. Ate oranges for every meal from Kansas City. Since leaving Deming we got them from Cal. At Dos Palmos the country is over 200 [feet] below the level of the sea. Here we got some light porous stone that is found here, and at the first station this side we saw 4 large cactus plants in the yard. They were cylindrical in form, solid, with an open growth of spikes and fiber around the body. The largest one was not less than 4 feet high and 15 inches in diameter. At Colton we struck a settled country again. Met [C H] Lar[r]abee there who gushed over us in his usual style.[11] He showed us in the distance his 20 acres at the foot of the mountain where he is making an orange orchard and home as he says for Minnie and his grandchildren. He came up to Angeles with us and talked at a great rate. Reached Angeles about 5 and went to the Cosmopolitan Hotel and were lodged in room 18. The streets were still muddy from the rain of the day before—the first of the season. It is a pretty country between Colton and Angeles, but wants water and always will. The Sierra Madre mountain is very striking and handsome. Saw the old mission church at San Gabriel with the usual complement of dinner pot bells. There were Orange trees and vines scattered along the route but the most of them are back near the mountain. The sheep were dying for want of grass and L[arrabee] said the lambs of this winter were killed to save the ewes. Our Porter from Deming to Angeles was John Blackstone, the most obliging and attentive man we have found. I gave him a buzzard dollar with great pleasure.

*26 (Thu)* Had a poor dinner last evening and a like breakfast this morning, but a tolerable room and bed. The dispatches in the morning paper brought the welcome news that Guiteaus jury found him guilty after 6 minutes deliberation. About 9 we got in the street car and rode out to the Washington Garden—a distance of near 2 miles where we saw a very handsome Orang[e] orchard and bought $1 worth which we took from the trees—one bunch containing 19 oranges. The proprietor is named [D V] Waldron. His wife who waited upon us said they lived at the Dalles before they came here. They have 30 acres under cultivation in oranges, figs and walnuts, mostly oranges. They have been on the place 16 years and made a garden of it in fact. She gave Mrs D a couple of immense oranges, cut from a tree which she said grew from a seed brought from Mexico. Upon returning we took an open carriage and drove about for an hour or more and saw Angeles and its surroundings were very well. The old Mexican part of the town lying around the plaza is occupied mainly by [the] Chinaman. They will work and the Mexicans won't. The place seems to be occupied mainly by Jews Irishmen and Chinese. The street with the handsome residences belongs I am told to the first named. Wrote a note to Daisy Buckingham[12] enclosing some Orange leaves in place of the blossoms I promised her—the latter having been nipped by the late frost—the coldest Mrs Waldron said, had been known for 15 years. . . .

After dinner walked down to old Spanish church which the padre said was built in 1771. It contains a frescoe of a female martyr of the 3 century and once contained her bones taken from the Catacombs at Rome but now given up to the new Cathedral—at least so the priest told me, but whether he believed it or not I don't [k]no[w]. . . .

Got away from Los Angeles on sleeper 34 sec F at ½ past 5 and reached the Palace in S F about 3. Crossed the mountains in the night. Daylight at Fresno and from there on a beautiful country if it was only watered. Took breakfast at Merced. [J H] Butler met us at the ferry and we were as glad to see him as he us. Lodged in 372 at the Palace in parlor with bath at $4 per day. Found letters here . . . and many papers including a number of the *Evening Stars* of Washington with Morris' review of my lecture on Law & Lawyers and a pleasant note from him.[13] The article is kind and intelligent and I must thank him for it. . . . Took dinner in the restaurant and had a good one for $1.75. Went to the Cal Theatre to see "Michael Strogoff." A good deal of shooting and high talk and a liberal admixture of the naked ballet which shocked Mrs D and drew most of the crowd I imagine. We came away before the last act. . . .

*28 (Sat)* The day came in clear & cool. . . . Went to the steamship office and saw about my room on the steamer *Columbia* No 53 and berth for Butler No 2 in room 13. Called on [Wm] Alvord at the bank of Cal and at the P[acific] Club where I lunched with Judge Lake and saw Hoffman and many others. Called with Mrs D at Lakes this afternoon in a coupe. Saw Mrs Lake & Minnie and we all talked as fast as we could for ½ an hour—when we came home. . . .

*29 (Sun)* Got up early and down to breakfast by 8. Met Arnold and Reed in the office who had just arrived on the *Oregon* from Portland. Reed breakfasted with us. Took carriage for the steamer . . . It was a lovely morning and we got off about 11. We both went to bed and staid there most of the time until we crossed the bar which we did on Tuesday morning at 10 oclock with a strong swell.

*31 (Tue)* Got to St Helens bar about 7 oclock and were transferred to the *S G Reed* and got home about ½ past 11. Paul & Henderson were at the wharf to meet us. . . .

Will I ever go again? It may be.

[*Here the diary is resumed in the regular journal with remainder of the entry of Feb. 8*]

*February 8 (Wed)* . . . Closed up my accounts. Our trip east—4 months & 12 days cost us $1842.84 of which $424.12 was spent for clothing—$115 for myself and the bal for Mrs Deady, but our passes saved us about $525 expense.

Wrote to Justice Field and enclosed him the passes over the U P & C P road which we did not use, by reason of travelling the southern route. The weather has been delightful most of the time since our return. My taxes and assessments amount this year to $436.02. Saw Ladd on Tuesday and told him I wanted to overdraw my a/c for a few hundred dollars—not over seven—and asked him what terms. Oh, the same as ever he said. I drew about $300 over and paid all my bills. Friday saw Henry Failing and settled up with Bank for money received under its letter of credit of $1000 while in the east. Gave my note for $250 the amount I used payable in 3 months.

*18 (Sat)* Nothing special since the last entry. On Friday evening [Feb 10] Mrs D and I attended the play of "Claude Melnotte," given by some amateurs for the benefit of the G S Hospital. McCracken as Claude & Mrs Holt Wilson as Pauline. The audience was large and elegant, the orchestra was splendid but the play was only so so. Neither C nor P could be heard, and P instead of giving her lines as parts of a splendid piece of declamation, full of romantic and heroic thoughts, exhausted herself in pantomimic motions, gesticulations and postures of the Clara Morris school—mincing the thoughts and words without the least apparent appreciation of them. McCracken would have been well enough if he could have been heard. In the Sunday *Oregonian* following some writer criticized the bonnets of the ladies as being in the way and spoke of one lady who wore no bonnet and complimented her on the beauty of her hair. It was Mrs D. The play was repeated on Saturday night to a rather small audience, but in a much improved manner. . . .

. . . Nesmith called on Wednesday and dined with us on Thursday. He tells his stories as well as ever but living among those who only listen to him, he is getting to be a very poor listener. On Friday week Ben Harding returned from Colorado and lunched with us. He thinks Ella is better.[14] Left her with his uncle at Colorado springs. Mrs Deady had a letter from her on Thursday. I think she will get well and indeed I hope so.

Last night we attended the "Batchelors" party at Turn Halle. It was a beautiful affair. After 12 oclock the German occupied the floor. I danced the Lancers with Miss Eaton, Miss Lewis and Mrs Corbett and conversed with Mrs Gen Miles an hour or so during the German. The night was very cold—in fact I think the coldest of the season. The morning before was 24 below freezing.

*25 (Sat)* . . . Have been very busy during the week. On Shrove Tuesday evening went with Mrs Deady to Greens to a domino party. A very brilliant affair. Charles Ladd was a great success as a kind of comic female Wilde.[15] We came away at 12 when the young folk were just fairly into the German in the attic. On Thursday evening we went to Ladds to dinner. Met the Reeds (S G) and the Greens there. Mrs L did not say so when she invited us but I suppose the dinner was given to us—at least we occupied the positions at the right of the hostess and host and Mrs L took me in or I her as the case may be. The dinner and appointments were both elegant and excellent including the wine. Yesterday subscribed $5 to help build the German Methodist Episcopal church—but why German I don't know. . . .

*March 4 (Sat)* . . . [*On Sunday last*] [David] Hurst called to see me at my chambers. He thinks Mitchel[l]s engagement with Villard will prevent him from being a candidate for the Senate. . . . Judge Lord called on Tuesday evening and read me a project of an opinion on the question of the validity of the appointment of the judges Kelly, Boise & Prim under the act of 1878. We talked it over. I suggested that while the Legislature had power to provide for the election of the Justices of the S[upreme] C[ourt] and C[ircuit] C[ourt] in separate classes, that they couldn't do it otherwise, as by appointment, and they must therefore provide for doing it at the next general election thereafter and not otherwise. But his head is set that the passage of the act *created* the three offices of Justice of the S C and that the Gov could fill them until election, even without the provision in the act to that effect, under the Constitution, as existing vacancies. . . . Velina Nesmith called to see Mrs D yesterday and told her of her engagement with Mr [Wm] Molson.[16] I called at Vin Cooks to see her last evening and congratulated her.

She looked very well and happy. I told her so and attributed it to her being engaged. She said no, it was her "bangs"—something which I had not seen her wear before. He is about 22 years older than herself, but I hope he will make her a good husband. I am afraid he will overreach himself and fail in business. I have heard rumors that he had done so already. It has rained very hard portions of this week, sufficiently to make high water. This is Hendersons 13th birthday. He got up this morning by daylight and staid away until breakfast to avoid being "spanked" 13 times. His mother and I gave him a copy of the *Boys Own Annual* at $2½. Sunday was Mrs Deady 47 birthday, and it passed without notice. Thursday evening we were invited to a musicale at S G Reeds, but declined on account of Lent.

*11 (Sat)* Sunday (March 5) Attended M & E prayer at Trinity also S S. Commenced a class of boys including Henderson whom I want to give some attention to. . . . Sat in the C C & D C all the week. Had a jury in the former from Tuesday to Saturday. Tried an Indian from Berhings [*sic*] Bay, Alaska named Katatah for the murder of 2 white men in August 1880 named Maloney and Campini, for which he was found guilty on Tuesday. Monday morning Mrs D started to Spokane to see Edward and probably bring him home. Had a note from her Thursday evening saying that she was at Spokane and would not be home until this evening and maybe not until Tuesday. It depended upon her communication with Edward who was at the lake beyond. Wednesday evening we attended the wedding of Martin Winch[17] and Nellie Wygant at the Unitarian church and the reception at the house. It was rather a brilliant affair. I did not stay at the house only long enough to make my compliments to the bride & groom and Mr & Mrs Wygant. Thursday evening took a cold in my head suddenly which has been getting worse ever since, until today I have not been able to do anything but toast my feet over the register and doze over an old copy of *Gil Blas*. . . . [J F] Watson was qualified as District attorney on Monday and he and Mallory conducted the prosecutions during the week. He has a very good persuasive voice and candid manner that will go far with juries and perhaps courts. Have been reading Landors biography this week by [?Colvin]. It is interesting. An impractible man. I read his conversation with [*sic*] "Pericles and Aspasia" and Houghtons monograph on him with Miss L the season we were at Clatsop together. A pleasant memory.

*18 (Sat)* . . . Read *Gil Blas* at odd moments. Pretty well through it. Gil has just married Antonia and had a son born. What a dish of cock and bull stories it is with here and there a shrewd touch of human nature.

On yesterday I changed the day of Ka-tah-tahs execution from 31 of March to 28 with his consent so that the Indian witnesses from Alaska could see him swing. They leave on the 29. The prisoner wanted them and the interpreter Kostrometinoff[18] to remain and talk with him. Poor fellow! he seems anxious for the day to come. . . .

*25 (Sat)* . . . This morning we got the news of Longfellows death yesterday. It recalled his Bowdoin ode—"How beautiful is youth" &c. When his name is mentioned I always think of it. I would rather be the author of it than anything or *all* the things he wrote. Tuesday heard Dr [J M F] Browne lecture at the

Congregational church on the loves & lyrics of Robert Burns.[19] Took Miss Lydia with me. Pretty good.

*April 1 (Sat)*. . . Attended lecture on Monday evening [*Mar 27*] at the Congregational M H and heard Prof Skidmore on the mathematics of life.[20] The subject discussed was longevity and how to produce it—a good deal of bosh delivered ore rotundo. Took Miss Rodney.

Ka-ta-tah was hung on Tuesday and his body dissected at the medical school. I saw the mangled remains on the dissecting board on Friday when I lectured on Med Jur. No wonder that Doctors are atheists—materialists. . . . On Wednesday Mrs Deady sat for her picture, at [Joseph] Buchtels and I sat today.[21] Want some to send east. Settled my quarters bills today—Gave Kat-lan, an Indian chief from Sitka who was here as a witness in the Ka-ta-tah case, a writing stating that he had deserved the confidence of the court and officers while here. He and the other Indians got drunk last night I understand, but that is not a very serious matter for a Russian Siwash. He looked very penitent this morning. . . .

*8 (Sat)* . . . Attended church yesterday in the morning and evening at Trinity. Mr Plummers reading of the gospel in the morning was very slovenly—it was scandalous. . . . Got some of our pictures today. The best picture of Mrs D is very good and she will keep it. But the standing one she will sit for again tomorrow.

*15 (Sat)* . . . Monday evening [the 10th] attended a Parish meeting and made a report of the financial condition of the Parish. Same vestry elected except Effinger in whose place a Mr [C N] Scott was chosen by the votes of 6 persons to 5. I am sorry for it, but is too late to help it after the vote was counted. I spent a day in preparing this paper and when I went there, there was no one there to hear it. Thursday evening I attended a concert at the Masonic Hall given by the H[aydn] & H[andel] society by invitation of the society. The instrumental performance was pretty good but the vocal was poor except "Ding-Dong" from "the Chimes of Normandy," in which Miss Giffin sang the solo beautifully.[22] Mrs Deady *sat* for another standing picture on Tuesday; and last evening I mailed copies of hers (bust) and mine looking to the left [to friends in the East]. . . .

*22 (Sat)*.. . . Got draft for my March Salary on Wednesday $301.40. Republican convention met here on Thursday and made nominations and constructed platform on the same day. The candidate for Governor, [Zenas] Moody, was one of the famous packed Grand Jury in the U S District Court that refused to indict the bribers in 1873. He can be relied on to do anything which the exigencies of party politics may demand. . . . Old John Crawford[23] has been here today talking about an indictment against him in Linn co for perjury in swearing to his property returns to the assessor in Sept 1881. Taking the facts as they appear I think he ought not to be found guilty, but as the case stands the burden of explanation is upon him. He is gotten too rich for his neighborhood and is an easy mark for envy or malice. . . .

*29 (Sat)* . . . Sat in the C C & D C all the week. Tried Harper v John Adair[24] with a jury on Monday. A verdict was found against the deft for $7000, about $4000 of which was money borrowed and as good as embezzled some years ago and the rest interest. It looked ugly for Adair. He was not present and I suppose did not care to be. . . . Judge Sawyer arrived Wednesday afternoon . . . Today we visited Albina afoot—went down the river as far as the site of the dry dock and back—a distance of probably 6 miles and then lunched with me at the Poodle Dog and I bade him good by about ½ past 3. He returns on the *Columbia* at 12 tonight or rather sails at that hour. I have had a very pleasant time with him this visit. . . . Called at the G S late Thursday evening where there was a dancing party given by the scholars to the doves of St Helens. Henderson and I came away a little before 12 against his will. On the way home I suggested to him that considering his position and opportunity he did not look very high in the selection of his partners, when he informed me with great earnestness that he did not believe in anything of that kind—that a Judges son was no better than anybody elses son and that people didn't reverence Princes because they were better than others but because they were afraid of them and more of the same sort. Sent out more photos; have distributed 48 in all which makes ones friends very dear indeed. . . .

*May 6 (Sat)* . . . Walked out with Mrs D [Sunday] in the afternoon to see her property in front of Lewis' and then we went in and staid for dinner. . . . The day was a lovely one and the dinner and the company was very good. In the evening about 15 min to 11 we had quite an earthquake. Mrs D was asleep, but I was awake having just retired. There were two shakes—the last one was drawn out some seconds. The house shooked and rattled but nothing was thrown down or displaced. . . . On Wednesday evening attended the meeting of the Shakespeare club at Mr Arnolds and read Wolseys farewell to his greatness. . . . On the same day Mrs D & I called to see Velina Nesmith at Cooks and bid her good bye. She was privately married the same evening to Mr Molson, at the Chapel, against the wishes of her family, none of whom were present, and sailed for San Francisco that night. Poor girl! I felt sorry for her, and do still for I am afraid she has not done well—and she deserves to. . . .

*13 (Sat)* . . . [On Sunday] Walked with Henderson to St Vincents hospital w[h]ere we called on Bishop Blanchet. Found [him] looking very well but very feeble. . . . [During the week] Had some correspondence with Nesmith on the subject of Velinas marriage. He is furious at Molson, [Jonathan] Bourne[25] and Mrs Effinger. Sent me a copy of the letter he wrote M on May 1 in which he addressed him as "villain," and said all the mean things to him he could think of. I told him he would welcome the young truants home yet. He indignantly says no. . . .

. . . Went with Henderson to the German given to his dancing class by Mr Varney.[26] The Grand March was very handsome. About ½ past 9 I went to the concert with Mr & Mrs Corbett at New Market theatre where I staid until ½ past 10 when I returned to the Turne[r] Hall and saw the German out. Got Home at 12. Henderson did right well and enjoyed himself. He got up this morning at ½ past 4 to ride to Clackamas, but I kept him back until breakfast at 7. The Shakespeare club met at my chambers on Wednesday evening for McCracken. We had a pleasant evening. Plenty of refreshments. I read Belarius in scene 3 act 3 [of "Cymbeline"], and think I did tolerably well, and so and more Mc said.

. . . Yesterday was my 58 birthday. It passed without special notice. Mr [John] Cran gave me a handsome book and Paul a set of gold shirt studs. Two more cycles and I reach the three score—and then, well.

*20 (Sat)* . . . Wednesday evening attended the meeting of the Shakespeare club at Mrs Montgomerys. Not many there. Read Wolseys Farewell, Miss MacConnell being Cromwell.[27] Had a pleasant evening and ice cream. How Mrs M does enjoy her share of this world. . . .

*27 (Sat)* . . . Wednesday went to Seattle, Mr [John] Leary took me to his house. Got there at 11 and found a very pleasant lady and home. . . . Attended the commencement exercises of Washington University in the Presbyterian church and at the close delivered the Address, "Towns & Cities," which was very well received. . . . The Learys gave me a dinner at their house—an elegant and pleasant affair. Sat down at 6 and got up at 9 and chatted in the parlor until ½ past 10. There were about 15 persons present, among which were Mr & Mrs [Henry] Yesler the proprietors of the place—a very pleasant, attractive old couple, Mr & Mrs [J C] Haines and Judge [Thomas] Burke[28] & wife, two young lawyers and promising men. Mrs H is a little peculiar but somebody. . . . Got off at 4 oclock on the *Zephyr* at Friday morning for home, caught the train at Tacoma, and got here by 4 oclock. . . .

*June 3 (Sat)* . . . Making citizens more or less all the week for the election on Monday. . . .

*10 (Sat)* . . . Monday voted the Republican ticket mainly. Did not vote for Gov, Judge or State Senator. Everything has gone Republican in the State and the Chinese phobia which was to work wonders for the Democracy didn't affect 100 votes in the state.

Attended H Bs examinations at the Gram School during the week. He did pretty well—quite well. Attended the closing exercises last evening. Mr Hill made his report, Rev Mr Stevens made an address. Both sensible and to the point—particularly the former. Wednesday evening attended the last meeting of the Shakespearean club at Montgomerys. I read Birons speech on ladies in "Loves Labor Lost." McCracken and Miss MacConnell gave us the best of "Macbeth"—the former did remarkably well. We had refreshment of strawberries and ice cream. Thursday signed 11 diplomas for the graduates at the University that are to be on Thursday next.

Monday night the hot spell which lasted near a week came to a close with a copious rain and it has been cool and cloudy ever since. The river is nearly up to high water mark. It is over front st at Stark this morning I am told.

Subscribed this morning to Bancrofts *History of the Pacific States* $4½ a volume in cloth—probably 25 volumes.

*17 (Sat)* Sunday June 11. Attended S S and M prayer at Trinity as usual. Called with H B in the afternoon at Ladds and Stotts—the first time I have called at the former place on Sunday afternoon since Nells marriage. . . .

. . . Monday evening attended the [Julie] Rivé-King Concerts with Mrs D.[29] The piano playing was nothing but an exhibition of fingering—the singing was only tolerable. . . . Thursday went to Eugene to attend the annual meeting of the regents—Henry Failing went with me. . . . Heard the afternoon graduating exercises—four essays by the women graduates—all of them excellent, but strongly and uniformly marked in the delivery with Mrs Spillers elocution. The Regents met in the evening and remained in Session until ½ past 11 and met again in the morning at 8. We overhauled the by laws, salaries, work of chairs &c. There is a quar[r]el on hand between Profs Johnson & Condon and I suppose now it will have to take the course and let the fittest survive. . . .

*24 (Sat)* . . . Mr Justice Field arrived on Wednesday evening. Sat in the C C Thursday & Friday formally. Looks very well and appears to take great interest in my appointment as Circuit Judge. Drove yesterday with him in Mr Corbetts carriage to the New Cemetery. A beautiful drive and lovely place. Stopped at Dolphs as we came back and saw his house and the madam and drank a glass of champagne. Dined last evening with Field at Judge Williams, Mrs Deady and I. An excellent dinner and a pleasant evening. Field and I got a little warm over Napoleon. This morning we both apologized and laid it to the wine. . . . Dined at Col Kellys with Judge Field. Had a nice dinner and a pleasant evening . . . Field brought me home in his carriage and I bade him good bye. He went on board I suppose about 11, and in the meantime discussed the Presidency with some of his democratic friends at the Esmond.

*July 1 (Sat)* . . . Mrs [Clara] Foltz the Cal woman lawyer called this morning and I took her into court and gave her a seat on the Bench.[30] She is bright and tries to be a man but can't forget that she is a woman always. On going into court she thought she might have to take of[f] her hat (bonnet) so she look[ed] in my glass to see that her hair was all right and disposed of her curls to the best advantage. Attended a lawn party with Mrs D at Jones on Tuesday evening, given by Trinity guild for a new carpet. Cost me $2.50. Kearney furnished $11.50 of my stationery bill in money to buy what I wanted including stamps, and made me a present of $100 to buy a suit of clothes with.

*8 (Sat)* . . . on Tuesday the Fourth . . . I went to Vancouver with Henderson on the *Wide West* to see the Sham fight and attend the celebration. Netta Brooke and the boys [*the Brooke twins*] went with us. Stopped at Major [Sam] Cushings . . . Saw the fight from the balcony of Col [E D] Bakers house and enjoyed it very much. Then we went to the park and sat on the platform with Gen Miles and heard the speeches of [Nathaniel] Bloomfield[31] and Gen Morrow both very fair and the latter first rate. Drove up with Gen[s] M[iles] & M[orrow] to head quarters and had a glass of wine and then down to the river and home in the *Washington* by 15 min to 6 after a very pleasant day. . . .

*15 (Sat)* Sunday (July 9) Attended S S and M prayer at Trinity as usual. . . . Went to the Congregational meeting in the evening to hear our fellow boarder—Dr [Frederick] Marvin. He delivered a lecture on the Jews which was full of extravagant and partial statement and something slangy. His manner is very good. . . . Monday delivered opin in Chapmans case sustaining demurrer to bill or parts of it. Wrote the opinion to please Fred Holman attorney for the defendants. Might have decided it orally but it was his first case and it did him so much good to appear in print as attorney for the prevailing party. . . . [This evening] Mrs

Deady and H B went on the *Oregon* at 10. I accompanied them in the carriage to the Steamer, where we found Paul and the Whitneys and Mr [Gordon] Blanding[32]—all but P going down [to San Francisco]. About 11 I left and came home. The steamer was to sail at 12 . . .

*22 (Sat)* Sunday (July 16) Attended . . . Trinity as usual. Mr Boyd read the service in Mr Plummers absence. Found my class diminished to David Lewis, and disbanded it until Henderson and Wistar would be back in Sept. Dined at Brookes where I met Mrs [Annie] Hodges.[33] Brooke told a story about loaning H a new coat at Oregon City in early days when he was sparking Mrs H *nee* Abernathy and finding pomade on the shoulder of it when it was returned. It was well told but I think a little broader than Mrs H liked. . . .

Went to hear "Hazel Kirke" with Paul on Thursday evening and enjoyed it,[34] although I feel very sad in many parts of it, because it constantly brought to mind poor Edward. . . .

Paid or allowed R[oswell] L[amson] $50 for fees received by E N D and not accounted for. He thought the amount was near $80, and I am afraid it may have been. Poor fellow, what will become of him. Got a letter from H[enry] V[illard] suggesting that he would procure an endowment of the University equal to an income of $3000 if the Legislature would provide for the same amount annually. Sent it to Dr Geary for suggestions.

*29 (Sat)* . . . Got a letter from Mrs Deady last night, [dated] July 25. She had just returned from Monterey and was ready to start to Colorado when she felt so unwell that she did not think she would go. I am uneasy about her.

Last Saturday evening [*the 22nd*] I took Nettie Brooke to the circus and saw the best educated horses I ever saw. Paul and Reed came and the former took us to Aliskys for ice cream.

Yesterday Gov Thayer commuted Powers sentence to imprisonment for life, solely on the ground that many people have petitioned for it. A mistake which is at least as bad as a crime. This afternoon went with [Preston] Gillette[35] in his buggy to Mountain Park view [*Mountain View Park*]—the East donation on the mountain to the north of Balch creek—to look at some property he has for sale there. It was a lovely ride up the new road from Guilds Lake and back the Balch creek road. He gave me until Monday to say whether I would take a lot . . . containing 3 42/100 acres on the brow of the mountain looking north and east at $350.

*August 5 (Sat)* . . . Monday read the proof of my annual report as Pres of the Regents for the *Oregonian*, in which it was published next morning. I mailed about 20 copies far and near. . . . Have skimmed over "Don Juan" somewhat. I remembered it pretty well until I came to the sack of Ismail and thenceforward it was almost new to me. It is very slovenly and audacious. Got the deed for my lot in Mountain View Park from [M B] Rankin[36] today through Gillette and gave him my note for $350 payable in one year from date—Aug 1, 1882. Mrs Deady started for Colorado Springs on Sunday as per telegram received on Monday . . . Spoken to by Cohen for the Board of Trade about drafting pilot law. Told him I would for $250.

*12 (Sat)* Sunday (Aug 6) . . . Dined at Molsons. An excellent dinner and well served. Velina appears well. Had marrow bones and toast after soup. . . . Have been busy most of the time during the week preparing a set of rules for the Circuit Court. Got a letter on Thursday evening from Mrs D written at Colorado Springs on the 3 inst and the day after her arrival there. She does not give a flattering account of Ellas health—indeed she thinks her months if not days are numbered. But I hope she is unnecessarily alarmed. Tuesday evening went to the Masonic Hall to hear a lady read for the benefit of the Orphanage. Audience small and select. The reader rather excelled as an actor, but not much voice, and was very lachrymose.

Today Mr [Solis] Cohen called and said the pilot committee had agreed to ask me to prepare a pilot law and would pay me $250.[37] I accepted. Bush called on Thursday a little while and took Gen Hamilton and Nettie Brooke home with him. How the world goes round. Got a telegram from Crane . . . informing me of his confirmation on the 7 inst as Surgeon General, and wrote him my congratulations the same evening. Judge Delos Lake died at San Francisco this week . . . He will be missed in Cal and elsewhere. The generation that I know and that know me are passing away. Nesmith is here, and as anecdotal as ever.

*19 (Sat)* . . . On Wednesday evening went aboard the *Columbia* for Astoria. Got off in room 17 at 15 min past one Thursday morning and made Astoria at 7 A M. Got my breakfast on board at 8 and went ashore. Called on Mrs Stott and then on Mrs Morris at the upper town. Saw Miss Lydia and Clem and had a pleasant call and a very palatable luncheon. Got back to the steamship wharf about 2 P M and just as the *Oregon* was coming in from S F with Mrs D, Henderson and Ella Harding. Found the former very well, but Ella very poorly. Got to Portland at 11 leaving Astoria at 3, but did not get to the wharf and ashore before 12. . . .

Mrs Deadys expenses were $225 including $35 for shopping in San Francisco, and she was absent just 33 days and travelled about 5000 miles. Got Gardner Dorseys *Waterloo* this week and have read over 100 pages which brings me to the opening of the fight or rather a preliminary description of the ground. It is very interesting and instructive and makes mince meat of the mendacious memoirs of Napoleon and Thiers hifalutin amplification of them. The fighting at Quartre [*sic*] Bras and Ligny—particularly the latter. So far old Blucher is the hero of the drama. A wonderful man aged 73. Napoleons sun paled before him.

Walton of Eugene had a communication in the *Oregonian* of the 10th inst eulogizing me as a suitable person to be made Senator from Oregon; and Scott had a little editorial paragraph upon the subject to the effect that the idea was absurd—that such a man could not stoop to the honor and it was very doubtful if I would accept it. I know I ought not to and don't believe I would. Am to[o] poor to go to the senate and would leave it poorer still and without fortune or vocation and too old to begin anew.

Mr Preston, a son of John B Preston the first Sur Gen of Oregon, called on me yesterday with a letter from his uncle, Gov Trutch of Victoria. Introduced him to Paul this evening and today took him to the cupola and the Sur Gen office where he was shown his fathers letter book commencing with his first letter from Oregon to the Comr of the Gen L office [Justin] Butterfield, dated, Oregon City, May 5, 1851, and complaining of the high prices incident to the recent stampede to the Klamath mines. . . . Mr Harding called yesterday. . . .

*26 (Sat)*. . . Finished Dorseys *Waterloo* and found it a very instructive as well as an entertaining work. I knew comparatively nothing of the fight before. Old Blucher looms up wonderfully and the "Iron Duke" is not attractive but he was active and equal to the occasion.

Sat in the C C and D C during the week, nothing of importance done. Worked all week on draft of pilot law for the Board of Trade and have just finished it, but will probably have to make alterations and additions after consultation with the committee. Got a letter from Judge Sawyer last night in which he advises me to take the senatorship if I can get it and if not to resign the judgeship and make some money at the bar. Easier said than done. I am not likely to get the senatorship and don't want it, and am too old to go to the bar or rather have been absent from it too long. . . . Another friendly communication in the *Oregonian* of the 22 dated Benton Co and signed Pioneer speaking well of me for the Senate, but saying that my proper place is the supreme bench. Alfred Holman had a very well written and effective article on Mitchells methods as a lawyer as illustrated by his conduct in the case of the Balch children.[38] It was infamous. . . .

*September 16 (Sat)*. . . Went on the steamboat *S G Reed* on Friday evening [*Sept 1*] for Clatsop Beach, C J Reed with me, and reached Grimes on Saturday evening at 6 oclock. Went from Astoria to Seaside landing in the *Daisy* and from there to Grimes in [C A] McGuires waggon.[39] Sunday, Sept 3. A beautiful day, went in bathing in the surf—splendid.

Remained at Grimes until Wednesday morning the 13 inst when I came up in the Grimes waggon to Skipanon where I waited from 10 A M to 5 P M for the steamer *Sam* and then got Worth to take me to Astoria in a small boat. With the ash [*oars*] and the natural breeze we made the *Mt Queen* at 8 oclock where I took room "0" for Portland and reached home at ½ past 3 the next day—Thursday. Had a very pleasant time at Grimes. Bathed once a day in the surf for 10 days— two or three times in the rain, with a wind from the southwest soft and warm. . . .

. . . Called at the Hall this evening and met the Rodneys and the new teachers Miss Fullick, Dovine and Harrington. They don't "pretty" much but appear genteel and sensible.

*23 (Sat)* . . . Sat in the C C and D C during the week except W & Thur when I was at the State Fair. Fell in with Mrs D P Thompson, Misses Dekum, and Haley on the way up and rode with them on a platform car.[40] On the way Alfred Holman joined us. Took tea Wednesday evening with Hendricks and Dorris, members from Lane and prepared a memorial to the Assembly on Villards proposition to endow the University with $50,000 provided the Assembly gives it $5000 a year and left it with Dorris to present. Went to Bushs from there and staid all night. Met Carrie Ladd there and Asahel [N] Bush who has grown to be a fine looking young man—just returned from college. The fair amounted to nothing this year except as a collection of people—There were some good horses and cattle on exhibition but no fruits, grain or vegetables and scarcely any mechanical products. The racing was in the hands of a committee of jockeys and was conducted mainly for gambling purposes; and all about the grounds there were little dirty gambling devices in full blast. . . .

Mentioned at the dinner table that the Swedish Lutheran minister had called on me to see if he was compelled to pay $4 road tax on his poll, and when I told him I supposed he was, he said it was hard to do with a wife and six children and a salary of only $400 a year, whereupon we raised the sum for him, [C E] Wantland,[41] [C J] Reed, Marvin and myself giving him $1 apiece. I did not tell the minister that he had too many children for his salary but I was tempted to. Visited the mechanics fair in the evening with Mrs D and H B D. Between 3 & 5000 people present. The electric light was a success. But the crowd was the principal show.

*30 (Sat)* Sunday Sept 24. Attended . . . Trinity. Mr Plummer preached two remarkably good sermons—the wonder with me is how he comes by them. They are not borrowed and they are so superior to any of his mental manifestations out of the pulpit that he must be inspired. . . .

. . . Voting for senator has been going at Salem all week without result. Yesterday the Democrats voted for [Erastus] Shattuck. Today the opposition Rep may go over to him and elect him, which is what the Dem expect. It seems to be either that or Mitchell or no election. Have been reading Stanleys *Christian Institutions* this week.[42] Sometimes very interesting and sometimes very hazy. But it confirms an impression which has been growing in my mind for years—that the Church as an ecclesiastical institution is a growth and not a creation. . . .

*October 7 (Sat)* . . . Visited the Mechanics Fair [*on Saturday last*] . . . with H B D. Called at the Hall and took Wistar & Miss Rodney. The People in the electric light were a pleasant sight, but the mechanical part of it is slim. The cereal exhibition from the Immigration office of N P Ry Co is very fine.

. . . Tuesday I went up the O R & N Cos road 30 miles near Multnomah falls to the driving of the last spike. Quite a number present. On the way Dolph suggested that I might be called on to speak and I commenced to arrange some thoughts which I delivered after the ceremony of driving was concluded and Dolph replied. Both speeches were published in the Wednesday mornings papers—corrected and revised by the authors—though mine was published very near as delivered, I think. I had some compliments paid me on account of it. . . . Friday, Mrs Deady went up to Hardings to see Ella who is not better and may be worse.

Paul went to Salem on Monday evening to be [*sic*] apply for admission to the supreme court. Got a telegram from him on Wednesday saying—"Passed splendidly" and so I have heard from many sources. Came home last evening feeling very happy and so did I. . . . H B D commenced to board at the B S Gram School on Wednesday and the same day fell from the rings in the gymnasium and sprained his left fore arm and had to come home where he remained until Friday when he returned to school.

Have been reading Stanleys *Christian Institutions* this week with much interest generally, but with a feeling that with his knowledge of the subject I could have made it clearer and more interesting. . . . The senatorial election still hangs fire. Mitchell lost another vote yesterday—Smith of Tillamook. I don't think he can be elected, but he may prevent an election, in which case I suppose the Governor will appoint—*but who?* . . .

*14 (Sat)* . . . Mrs D came home from Hardings last evening, looking well. She said she left Ella very poorly indeed. Mr Saml Bowles called yesterday. He came up on the *Queen* in the morning. He looks very well. Took him to lunch with me at Mrs H[ill]s and into the cupola. Contention for senator still goes on at Salem, without result and with little variation in details. . . .

*21 (Sat)* . . . Sat in the C C & D C during the week. Grand Jury organized in the latter on Tuesday and discharged on Friday evening. . . . I appointed [Nathan] Sitton (Doc) of North Yamhill foreman. The last work in which we were engaged together before this was bear hunting in the coast mountains on the head waters of the Wilhelmina in September, 1850. Sitton shot a bear in the top of a branching fir as I came up the hill towards it and the first intimation I had of its presence was his saying "look out" and the crack of his rifle and the form of Bruin as he fell from the tree but a few steps from me and raised up on his hind feet and looked as big as the side of a house. I leveled my gun in an instant and shot him between the eyes. Charles Fendal[l] was of the party and upon reflection I believe it was him that shot the bear. The legislature adjourned last night at 10—electing Dolph Senator at the last moment by 51 votes on the [78th] ballot. It passed my pilot bill among other things to be thankful for, if they have not spoiled it in the process. Poor Mitchel[l], he has jumped high and fallen hard, and I rather think this is the last of him in Oregon.[43] . . .

Called with Saml Bowles at the Hall . . . [*this*] evening. After he left we went up to the corner of the block and heard some of the speeches at the reception at Dolphs—Williams and Hirsch. The evening was beautiful but the speeches were mournful.

*28 (Sat)* . . . Sat in the D C & C C during the week. As District Judge issued warrants for the arrest of George Moncour alias Ah Wah and Ah Kee, the cook and steward of the American ship *Patrician,* for being Chinese laborers unlawfully in the U S. Heard the cases on the 25th and decided them on Friday the 27, delivering a written opinion to the effect that they being members of the crew of a vessel bound to a foreign port they were not within the law and ordered their discharge. Opin in this mornings *Orego* and I suppose it will furnish a topic for tomorrows Sunday papers or rather its author will. . . .

Wednesday evening Mrs D and I dined at Lewis' where we met a Dr Smith[44] an old resident of Honolulu who is on his way to Washington to aid the Hawaiian Minister in getting a renewal of the sugar treaty with the Islands. A pleasant shrewd old Yankee I think. . . . Smith is neutralizing the Portland opposition to his treaty by proposing to aid in the establishment of a sugar refinery here. . . .

*November 4 (Sat)* . . . Friday evening I attended a meeting of *the* whist club at Molsons and was elected a member. I played partner with Brooks Trevett, Gen [O D] Greene[45] and Henry Failing and lost 33 points, but whether this is a reflection on myself or partners I will not say. At 12 oclock we sat down to a very substantial cold supper of which a roast turkey and a game pie were the principal elements. Got home tired and not much edified at ¼ past one. Playing whist as if it was the chief object of existence makes people stupid and uninteresting. . . . On or rather in June 1878 John Catlin paid the Scotch Bank as security for Edward $415.35. In June 1879 we gave them our Chickering piano, which was afterwards allowed on the debt at $200 and on March 1, 1881 I paid the balance in cash $215.35; and on Nov 1, 1882 I paid $75 as interest on the same, that is interest on the whole amount for one year and until the delivery of the piano and on $215.35 for 2 years and 9 months.

. . . Saml Bowles lunched with us on Tuesday and left for San Francisco on the Steamer in the evening. At his request I gave him Carey Johnsons statement to me of Mitchells attempt to buy him off with a retainer of $2000 from the Ry Co, which included also Sharps vote for M[itchell] as senator. He had it from Gibbs also more in extenso.

Whall[e]y made a brief sketch of myself for an Oregon publication, which he submitted to me and I ran over and corrected yesterday. He has promised to write my biography for Bancrofts "Oregon Biography.". . .

*12 (Sun)* . . . Hirsch called at my chambers in the afternoon and told me the inside of the late senatorial election. He says that he had it arranged once for enough democrats to absent themselves from the joint convention so that the vote which Mitchel[l] had—42 I believe—would elect him, but that the latter refused to take the office by less than 46 votes or a majority of all the members elect. . . .

*25 (Sat)* . . . Sat in the C C and the D C during the week. Finished the opinion on the On Yuen Hai Cos case and delivered it on Wednesday. It is set up but not published yet. Enjoined the collection of the road tax from the transient Chinese laborers. Finished Stephens life of Dean Swift—what a character.[46] Got about ⅔ through Bancrofts 1 volume of the Pacific States, a mass of well ordered facts and some very original and peculiar writing. . . .

Monday attended a meeting at L & Ts Bank to organize a Cemetery Association. Since upon an interview with Mr Edward Failing who was present and acted as clerk [I learned] that the By-laws which were adopted on Mr H W Corbetts report were not sufficient and have given some time to sketching another set. . . .

The weather has been pleasant this week but cloudy. Wrote to Villard enclosing copies of act to aid University and J[oint] R[esolution] respecting himself as per request of the Regents.

*December 2 (Sat)* . . . Wednesday we had a fright at the near prospect of Dr Strongs death. He was suffering from inflammation of the stomach and bowels and I suppose took an overdose of chloral. Sketched a set of By-laws during the week for the R V Cemetery Association and discussed and criticized them with Mr Edward Failing to whom I gave them for redraft. Friday I received 25 copies of Hodge & Galvins *Pen Pictures of representative men* for which I am taxed $25 and furnished with three pages of biography written by John W. Whalley and pruned and purged by myself. It is full of good average people and some great scallowags [*sic*] and petty rogues, all done up in the same high colors and utter disregard for "the blistering facts.". . .

*9 (Sat)* . . . Wednesday announced opinion of Sawyers in Dowell v Applegate, holding the deeds of 1867 valid but those of 1869 and 1871 invalid, because they were voluntary and left the grantor unable to pay the defaulcations which had then taken place on the second bond of 1866.

Read the first part of a very entertaining article in *Littel* on the Edgeworths. . . .

*16 (Sat)* . . . [*Sunday*] Called at Dr Strongs & James Holmans in the afternoon to see the sick. The Dr getting better and H dying slowly. . . . Tuesday evening we attended Lizzie Lewis' wedding. Went to the church before 8 took Ed & Ollie Failing with us, and from thence to the house and got home at 12. It rained hard all the evening but the affair was a very brilliant and pleasant one after all. I kissed the bride and she looked very sweet. Good is a lucky fellow and I hope he will deserve her.

Wednesday morning Mrs Deady went up to Hardings to see Ella whom we learned was very low. She got up but no train has run over the road since on account of high water. Got a telegram from her yesterday saying Ella would live some days she thought. Poor girl! I wish I could get away. I would go and see her. . . . Have read some chapters in Bancrofts P[acific] S[tates] this week. Poor Vasco Munez de Balboa has been judicially murdered by Gov Davilla not far from the South Sea (P[acific] O[cean]) that he discovered. Much rain has fallen during the week and the river is 17 feet above low water. Washouts on all the railways west and east and bridges carried off in every direction. Attended the Baptist festival last night and bought Lucy Failing a pretty willow cradle. Thence to the open rehearsal of the Orches Union at the Masonic Hall, where I heard the most entertaining musical performance I ever listened to in Oregon—and went up to the first floor in an elevator, the first I ever saw in Oregon outside of a warehouse, store or manufactory.

*23 (Sat)* . . . Had several letters from Mrs D during the week. She is still at Hardings and Ella is very low. On Tuesday attended Mrs Greens china wedding and contributed $3.35 to the purchase of a pair of Limogen vases for her. A splendid party . . . Paul went up to Hardings on Monday and came home on Tuesday. Did not go to the party [*at Greens*]. Felt very badly, poor fellow, about Ella. . . .

*29 (Sat)* . . . [*Last Sunday*] Got a telegram from Mrs D saying that Ella died Saturday evening at 7 P M and would be buried at 12 Sunday.

Monday, Paul went to Hardings to Ellas funeral. H B and I went to the Hall to breakfast and early service and staid until after the stripping of the Xmas tree. We were both remembered. . . .

Dined Xmas day at Brookes. H B with me. Most excellent dinner and pleasant time. Tuesday Mrs D and Paul came home and told us all about Ellas death and funeral. It was a sad story. Brought some of her things home with them—among others the picture which I gave her in S S on Xmas 187–. . . .

The weather has been very fine the most of the week. Xmas was a perfect day and this is another. Sunday school festival at Trinity on Thursday evening. We were present. Tolerable affair. Invited to party at Vancouver same evening. Declined on account of the recent death of James Holman & Ella Harding. Will make no calls on the New Year for the same reason. . . .

*30 (Sun)* Attended . . . Trinity as usual. Called at Dr Strongs, found the baby dead. . . .

# NOTES

1. John Marshall Harlan (1833–1911), Kentucky lawyer and jurist; associate justice of the supreme court, *post* 1877.

2. Thomas L. James (1831–1916), New York businessman, publisher and politician; New York postmaster, 1873–81; postmaster-general, 1881. General Michler died in 1881. Commander Charles H. Baldwin (1822–88), fought in Mexican and Civil wars.

3. Benjamin H. Brewster (1816–88), lawyer; attorney-general, 1881–84.

4. Samuel P. Lee (1812–97), distinguished Union naval officer; retired 1873. Montgomery Blair (1813–83), Missouri lawyer and politician; Lincoln's postmaster-general.

5. H. H. Gilfrey was secretary to the U. S. Senate. James B. Beck (1822–90), Kentucky senator, 1876–90.

6. Nellie Grant's first husband was Algernon Sartoris, a British officer. Mrs. Snead was a newspaperwoman who wrote under style of "Mrs. Grundy."

7. Noah H. Swayne (1804–84), Ohio lawyer and jurist; justice of the supreme court, 1862–81. Sarah Vinton Dahlgren (1825–98), author; widow of Rear-Admiral John A. B. Dahlgren. Dahlgreen in original. Samuel C. Busey, Washington, D. C. physician; graduate of the University of Pennsylvania Medical School, 1848.

8. John Rodgers (1812–82), explorer, Union naval officer. Stanley Matthews (1824–89), Ohio lawyer and jurist; justice of the Supreme Court, *post* 1881. William B. Woods (1824–87), Ohio lawyer and jurist; justice of the Supreme Court, *post* 1880. Judge George H. Pendleton (1825–89), Ohio lawyer, Democratic senator, 1879–85.

9. Mallory was still urging Tompkins' release.

10. Lionel A. Sheldon (1831–1917), Ohio lawyer and Union soldier; "carpetbag" governor of Louisiana, 1869–75; territorial governor of New Mexico. Joseph Bell; according to Bancroft, he was not appointed until 1885-6.

11. Charles H. Larrabee was destined to die in a railroad accident less than a year later.

12. Daisy Buckingham, daughter of Catherinus P. Buckingham.

13. M. F. Morris, Richard Merrick's law partner.

14. Ella Harding was dying of tuberculosis.

15. Charles Ladd (1867–1920), a son of W. S. Ladd.

16. David Hurst, Douglas County farmer. William M. Molson (1833–1913), businessman and brewer; member of the prominent family of Canadian brewers.

17. Martin Winch (1858–1915), prominent and highly-respected Portland businessman.

18. Castromitinoff in original.

19. Dr. James M. F. Browne; Irish-born physician.

20. J. H. Skidmore, Methodist minister; founded, 1872, Ashland College.

21. Joseph Buchtel (1830–1916), pioneer photographer, sports enthusiast and inventor.

22. Charles N. Scott (1846–1921), railroad administrator. Miss Giffen has proved unidentifiable.

23. Zenas F. Moody (1832–1917), merchant and surveyor; governor, 1882–87. John

FOOTNOTES 1882

Crawford (1815–99), Albany miller and financier.

24. John Adair (1839–1915); his wife, Dr. Bethenia Owens-Adair, said of him, "Colonel Adair is an optimist of a happy and cheerful disposition . . . he is usually among the clouds, and rarely gets down to *terra firma*."

25. Jonathan Bourne (1855–1940), lawyer and silver mine owner; he was then associated with W. H. Effinger's law office; U. S. senator, 1906–12.

26. J. W. Varney, one of the lessees of the Turn Halle.

27. Christina MacConnell (1841–1922), school teacher; McConnell in original.

28. John Leary (1837–1905), Seattle lawyer and town developer. Henry Yesler (1810–92), Seattle lumberman and civic leader. John C. Haines (1849–92), prominent Seattle attorney. Thomas Burke (1848–1925), Seattle lawyer and jurist.

29. Julie Rive-King (1857–1937), notable pianist.

30. Clara S. Foltz was admitted to practice in California in 1878.

31. Samuel T. Cushing (died 1901), subsistence officer. Nathaniel Bloomfield, Vancouver attorney.

32. Frederick R. Marvin (1848–1918), Congregationalist clergyman. Gordon Blanding, San Francisco attorney.

33. Annie Abernethy Hodges (1836–1911), wife of Colonel Henry Clay Hodges.

34. "Hazel Kirke," an enormously popular melodrama by Steele MacKaye.

35. J. C. Powers had been convicted of murdering Ben Cornelius in a drunken shoot-out at Portland on July 4. His sentence was commuted to life imprisonment. Preston W. Gillette (1825–1905), lawyer, legislator, real estate broker.

36. M. B. Rankin (1844–1909), real estate and timber man.

37. D. Solis Cohen, (1852–1928), attorney and leader of Portland's Jewish community.

38. Alfred Holman (1857–1930), journalist; *Oregonian* reporter and editor until 1903 when he removed to San Francisco to edit the *Argonaut*. Balsh in original. Mitchell labored mightily to deprive the youngest Balch children of their inheritance.

39. Charles J. Reed (1855–1912), businessman. C. A. McGuire (1829–1901), Seaside stagecoach operator and hotelman.

40. Lisa Dekum (1861–1931), afterwards Mrs. John Gill. Haley has not been positively identified.

41. J. Vender was pastor of the Swedish Lutheran Church. Charles E. Wantland, clerk of the O.R. & N. Co.; he lived at The Hill.

42. Arthur P. Stanley (1819–91), Anglican churchman.

43. Nathan (Doc) Sitton (1825–1902), Yamhill County farmer. Charles E. Fendall (1821–94), Yamhill County stockman. John H. Mitchell would be returned to the United States Senate in 1885, 1891 and 1901.

44. John Mott Smith, physician; minister of finance during the reign of Kamehameha V, 1863–72.

45. Owen D. Greene, MA, 1849; an A.A.G. officer, he retired in 1897.

46. Leslie Stephen (1832–1901), English writer and philosopher.

Among the "sights" of the eastern visit, the Deadys took in the Smithsonian Institution. The judge wasn't impressed with the "anthropological curiosities."

Col. Benjamin Mackall, old Barnesville friend. (Deady album.)

Edward Hamilton, attorney, good friend and Oregon Territory official.

Frederick V. Holman, then young attorney and later president of the Oregon Historical Society. Deady heard his first case.

In Juston's (above), Henders became alarmed at the silverware.

# 1883

*January 1 (Mon)* Did not make any calls. Alices baby buried today. Ella buried Xmas and James Holman Saturday before. In my chambers all day, but in the evening slipped in to see Mrs Stott in her new house and was glad to see her so happy and comfortable, then I came back by the way of the Hall w[h]ere I spent a pleasant half hour with last years lilies. . . .

*11 (Thu)* . . . Heard some Chinese cases on Habeas Corpus partly today—a girl and an actor. Are either of them laborers and may they show they are not by some other proof than an official certificate? Missed the Shakesp[ear]ean reading at Crans on Tuesday night. Was holding court until 9 and until 10 at night the day before. Mrs Deady went to Yamhill on Monday and I go to the Oak Grove Church tomorrow near Nesmiths in Polk county to deliver my lecture on "Trial by Jury." She will meet me at Amity and go up to Nesmiths with me where we expect to stay all night and return on Saturday. Got my draft this evening for Dec salary dated Dec 6. They have turned over a new leaf—$294.80. . . .

*13 (Sat)* Friday . . . went up on the West side train to Mrs [Beulah] Riggs about 3 miles this side of Derry and the same distance from Oak Grove Church, where I lectured in the evening on Trial by Jury to a good sensible rural audience of about 150 persons. Mrs Deady met me at Amity and went up with me and on to Nesmiths. I spent a very pleasant afternoon with Mrs Riggs. Got acquainted with her daughter Emma and her 2 sons Scott & Seth—a good family of people. The old lady told me all about Alvey Shaw who it seems was a bastard child of a Miss Riggs[1] a cousin of the late Mr Riggs, born in N J and begotten by a man named Alvey Compton. His mother then married a shoemaker named Shaw and hence his name A C R Shaw. He started to this country from Illinois in company with Mrs Riggs father, Mr Drinkwater, an Englishman, with sheep. Dr[inkwater] died in Mo and S managed to appropriate the sheep to his own use and drove them to Oregon in 1844–45 whence he got the name of Sheep Shaw. They were the first sheep driven to the country. From the lecture I drove home with Nesmith 5 miles, which occupied an hour and a half. Had some supper and sat up and talked until after 3 in the morning—Mrs D staying with us until ½ past 12. Came home today after a tedious ride on a slow train. Tonight, have heard of the death of Judge Stotts youngest child—sudden death.

*20 (Sat)* Sunday . . . Called at Stotts in the afternoon. Her baby of 18 months of age died the afternoon before suddenly while she was out calling and she is much stricken with grief. Poor woman she has plenty of children left. . . .

Monday heard In re Ho King on habeas corpus, an actor who came to this port on the British steamer *Hook* and discharged him, as a person entitled to come and reside in the U S. . . .

Friday sent letter to Villard directing him to have N P Bonds donated to the University registered in the name of Mr Henry Failing as agent, and to [M C] George concerning the judiciary bill. Got a letter from Sawyer, [dated] Jan 12, containing a copy of a very handsome letter written by him to Senators [J F] Miller & [J P] Jones[2] concerning the propriety of my being appointed one of the Circuit Judges. . . .

*27 (Sat)* . . . Thursday and Friday engaged in hearing Wells Fargo & Co v The O R & N Co. Same v The O & C Ry Co and same v The N P Ry Co, upon motions for preliminary injunctions. . . . Lewis, Fechheimer and Clarence A Seward were for the motion and Dolph and [James] McNaught contra. They all did well. Seward is a very accomplished man and the court room was packed to hear him. He brought me a letter of introduction from Hoffman. Had no time and but little means to give him any attention. But we had him to dinner last evening en famille, in boarding house and then took him to the Orchestral Union Concert at the N M Theatre . . . He is very pleasant and entertaining socially. He told a good story of [Martin] Travis of N Y to the effect that some friend of his who was bitten with a stock mania mortgaged his house to raise money to engage in this speculation, asked T what stock he had better invest in, to which he replied—"Buy the mortgage."[3]

. . . The weather has been moist the most of the week. K[earney] made me a present today of $100 to buy me some clothes with. Deposited it. . . .

*February 3 (Sat)* . . . During the week finished 1 vol of Bancrofts *His of the Pacific States*. The story of Alvarados conquest of Guatemala is a wonderful one. Ped[r]arias Davila is dead at last.[4] B calls him the Timur of Central America. . . .

Had a pleasant time at the Guild Friday evening. Mrs Holt Wilson was lovely in a tableaux as Marguerite, admiring the fatal gift of pearls. I bought a pair of silk stockings knit by Mrs Flanders for $5. Went to Muirs[5] last night to the Shakespeare club after working until 9. This evening attended the annual meeting of the library association and read my annual report, which I prepared during the week. After reading the report I called Henry Failing to the chair and I went to the Broom Drill given at Turne Halle by Trinity Guild. Rather a picturesque but monotonous affair, though very well done. The 12 brooms sold at auction to the admiring young men for $60. Kinross was the auctioneer and he distinguished himself. Dancing followed and I left.

*10 (Sat)* . . . Tuesday evening—Shrove Tuesday—called with Mrs D at the Bishopcroft the first time since the family moved into it. A pleasant roomy house, very. Ash Wednesday went to morning prayer at 11 oclock.

Sat in the C C & D C during the week. Nothing of interest done. . . . I have one more of the old Lownsdale cases, and then I am done after 15 years. The week has been cool and clear, the thermometer ranging from 30 to 6 degrees above zero. Skating on Guilds lake has been all the rage among the young people. I am going to take Mrs D down this afternoon to see the crowd. . . .

The supreme court of the state reversed my finding as referee in the Chadwick cases, holding that the sureties of a public officer were not bound for the exercise of any more skill or competency than he happened to have—so there is no risk in going surety for a fool. The *Oregonian* published the opinion under the headline "An opinion showing the uselessness of official bonds." . . .

*17 (Sat)* Sunday . . . at Trinity as usual. Got tired of the ill manners and indifference of Will Morris and David Lewis in my S S class and told them if they couldn't do better that I preferred they would not attend. Called at Dolphs (Jo N) in the evening and had an hour or twos conversation with him and bade him good bye. He left for Washington on Tuesday night to take his seat in the Senate on March 4th. . . .

Attended the S[hakespeare] club at Northrups on Monday evening, but no one there.

Attended the first bar dinner of the Portland Bar Association at the Maison Doree at ½ past 8. Judge Strong presided at one table, I at his right and Judge Stott at his left. The dinner was poor, but the feast of reason and the flow of soul thereafter was very fair. I responded to the first toast The Bench, and was complimented by Judge Strong. Whalley talked longer than anyone else and sang a good song.

James Gleason, under the combined influence of wine and mother wit was amusing in reply to the toast "The Ladies."[6] John Catlin presided at the second table and made quite a pleasant little speech. . . . Edward came into the court room yesterday and S [*name obliterated*] with him. He said he was going to recommence the study of law and get admitted. He looks very well. . . .

*23 (Fri)* Took John Hendersons note for $1843 payable to Mrs Deady in one year with interest at 10 percent. Amount made up as follows—note of Henderson and Hurst, March 23, 1881 for $800 with $160.66 interest; note of Hendersons, October 23, 1882 for $815 with $27.16 interest, & 100.18 cash for H B D, and deducting $60 paid by John to Mrs D on said notes; a portion of this amount belongs to H B D which I must figure up when I get time.

*24 (Sat)* . . . Wednesday evening delivered my lecture on "Towns and Cities" in the Unitarian chapel to a good audience. Had kind notices from all the papers except the *Standard.* Sat in the C C & D C during the week. Read Morses *Life of John Q Adams,* a judicious and friendly defense of an able, patriotic and industrious man without tact or sympathy.[7] Saturday attended the matinee of "Esmeralda" with Henderson at the New Market. Not much. Called at the Hall in the evening.

*28 (Wed)* . . . Tuesday evening attended Rev Mr [E T] Lees lecture at the Con church on the moral power of science. Took Miss Lydia. The performance sophomorical somewhat.

*March 4 (Sun)* . . . [*Friday*] evening went up to Salem and delivered my lecture "Trial by Jury" at the Pres church. Not a large audience, but they said much larger than usual for a lecture in Salem. . . .

*10 (Sat)* . . . Wednesday evening attended Library meeting and proposed the purchase of north ½ of Brookes block for the Library. But I am afraid our rich men are too poor to do anything. . . . The weather has been warm and clear all the week. Went to the chapel to evening prayer this evening and called in at the Hall where I met a number of people and was pulled in conversation with Mrs [Solis] Cohen which taxed my resources as well as my endurance. Mrs D has been confined with neuralgia for 3 days but is better now. In my opinion in the Proebstel case I attempted to pay Ch J Waite a compliment for one he paid me in Barney v Dolph in 97 U S.[8]

*17 (Sat)*. . . Friday morning went to Silverton by the East side and narrow gauge. Never passed over the country between Woodburn and the latter place before. A good country—the plows were going in every direction. Was met at the depot by Mr [E H] Ramsby. Saw Davis Shannon there. He was glad to see me and I him. One of the noble Romans. Ramsby took me to [Ai] Coolidges[9] where I was billeted. Had dinner at 12 and then took me all over the place where I met some good people. Delivered my lecture in the evening at the new Methodist church, on Trial by Jury to a house full of about 150 persons. Tim Davenport introduced me. Got up in the morning at 15 minutes after 4 and left in a carriage with Mr Ramsby for Gervais at 15 minutes to 5 which we reached a few minutes after 7, when I got on the express train and came to Portland in time to sit in the D C. . . .

The weather is still warm and clear, with a tendency to cold this evening. The N Y *Herald* has a respectful notice of my decision in the Chinese actors case, Ho King—the issue of Feb 27. Judge Hoffman sent it to me with a letter complimenting my lecture on Towns and Cities, a compendium of which I sent him in the *Oregonian*. Field writes me to know if I would like to hold the Circuit Court this summer in San Francisco and try the Debris case. I think I would, but I must know how it suits Sawyer first. . . .

*31 (Sat)*. . . Tuesday evening attended Shakespearean club at Arnolds. Read first act of "Coriolanus" in class and Agammemnons speech in "T[r]oilus and Cressida" myself. Pleasant evening. *Miss* Muir present for the first time. Good Friday, the 23 inst. Attended M prayer at Trinity at 11 oclock. Quite a congregation present . . . In the evening attended a banquet given by the members of the Bar to Mr Whalley on the eve of his departure to Europe. I presided and proposed the health of our Guest, in a speech of some 5 minutes in which I said among other things that "already the newspapers—the fountains of honor and dishonor in this country—forcasting his future had dubbed him Judge." There were about 40 persons present, the dinner was only tolerable but the wine was good and the company excellent. Everyone was called out and the responses were hearty and good. Got home at half past 2.

Easter Day, March 25. Rose early and attended . . . Trinity. Music in the morning noisy, meaningless and without melody, in the evening it was beautiful and grand. A collection taken up during the day for the church debt of $5000, amounting to about $3000 but $1350 was conditioned on the whole amount being subscribed . . .

*April 7 (Sat)* . . . Attended a Shakespeare at Muirs on Tuesday evening where we read the last 2 acts of "Coriolanus." Took Miss Muir to supper and had a pleasant tete a tete with her. She gave us a single reading. It was finely acted and if she had more voice would be a good reader. . . .

APRIL 1883

*14 (Sat)* . . . Had a Shakespeare in my chambers on Tuesday evening, with ice cream, cake and muscatel for refreshment. Bad night and not many present. Mrs D & Mrs Marvin came over and did the honors. We read the two first acts of "Troilus & Cressida" and some special selections. I read Volumnias speech to Coriolanus outside the walls of Rome. . . . Finished Trollopes *Pio Nino,* and was much pleased with it. The adoption of the dogma of Papal Infallibility is graphically told. The proceedings in method and purpose were a good deal like a New York caucus—and of no more authority. Wednesday attended the funeral of E J Northrup from his house. He was killed on Monday by falling through a hatchway at his store. He was a good man and his death was generally mourned. In the evening of the same day had a meeting of E & H Failing, Fechheimer & H W Corbett at my rooms to consider of rules and regulations for the R V Cemetery. . . . Read last night R Grant Whites article in the Ap[ril] *Atlantic* on Mrs Potts Bacon-Shakespeare craze as he calls it. It is perfectly inimitable and it pulverizes Potts badly. Called at the Hall in the evening with Mrs Deady and saw the girls and teachers en masse. Miss Rodney sang "Robin Grey" for me and young [Harry] von Holt[10] gave us the Sandwich Islands spear dance and chant with good effect.

*21 (Sat)* . . . Tuesday evening attended the Shakespeare at Arnolds. Finished "Troilus & Cressida." I read "Queen Mab." Took Miss Muir home. Thursday evening Paul and I went to Mrs Lewis' to see some parlor theatricals. . . . After this came dancing and refreshments, to the latter of which I escorted Mrs Kelly. Danced once with Katy Story. Mrs Deady was taken ill in the morning with a bilious attack and was not able to go. She is better now but still in bed. I had an attack of something of the same nature yesterday and do not feel well now. Yesterday Mrs & Miss Muir called and I showed them the town and surroundings from the cupola. Gave the latter my photograph. She returns to Canada on Monday. She is a bright pleasant woman and will be missed at the Shakespeare and elsewhere.

. . . Saw Koehler at Lewis' and asked him to extend the order giving the University students half fare on the west side. Got a note from him this morning saying he had done so.

*28 (Sat)* . . . Judge Sawyer arrived on Monday evening and sat in the C C on Tuesday, Wednesday & Thursday. . . . Wednesday evening Sawyer and I dined at Corbetts. The dinner was given to Villard. There were about 15 persons present and it was the most stylish affair I was ever at in Oregon. Mr Corbett sat at the west end of the table and Ladd at the east. Villard sat at Corbetts right and Sawyer on his left. I sat at Ladds right and [C H] Prescott at his left. Mr [Wm] Mead, the architect of McKim & Mead of N Y sat at my right and I found him an intelligent agreeable fellow.[11] After dinner we went to the Orchestral Union Concert. In the morning of Wednesday I took Sawyer to the meeting at the New Market Theatre to meet and hear Villard, called under the auspices of the Board of Trade. We with some 15 or 20 others were seated on the stage. The building was packed from pit to dome. Villard talked 1½ hours about his corporations, their progress and purpose so far as Oregon is concerned in general and Portland in particular. He talked slowly, sometimes hesitated for the right word, but generally waited until it came. It was very plain and simple on the surface but shrewd and well arranged for the purpose in hand and reads in the next mornings *Oregonian* like a book. He is evidently a strong, deep man and I think an upright one—at least compared with other Railway Kings and speculators of the U S. He called to see me on Sunday and we talked over the endowment of the University and alluded jocosely (he did) to my decision against the Ry Co in the express case. Thursday evening I dined at Schulzes where I met Mr Vs private Secretary, Mr Spofford and the Engineer of the Transcontinental company, a Mr [R E] O'Brien, whom I rather like. At 9 oclock went [with] Mrs D & Judge Sawyer to a grand reception at Senator Dolphs to Villard. There were probably 400 persons present, and altogether it was a decided success. Danced twice—once with Mrs Koehler and once with Mrs Deady. . . .

*May 5 (Sat)*. . . Sat in the C C & D C during the week. Nothing special. Prepared a portion of my lecture on "Trial by Jury" for the *Am Law Review*. Have almost finished it. The *A L R* for March–April contains a letter of mine of date Feb 24 to the editors protesting against the use of Oreg as an abbreviation for Oregon. It was republished in the *Oregonian* of Friday. I think I will send a copy of it with a note to the P M Genl, Judge [Walter] Gresham, as the P O Dept is where this abomination originated, I believe. . . . Had a very mean letter from J[esse] A[pplegate] this week, about his case, of date April 24. I don't think I shall ever recognize him again. He scolds like a drab and lies like a Cretan.[12] The week has been moist and cloudy and yesterday there was quite a windstorm. Today is bright and warm—perfectly charming. On Thursday evening attended the N M Theatre with Mrs D and saw the "Colleen Bawn." The audience small and unknown, but the playing was excellent. Have not seen the play for 20 years, not since [James] Stark used to play it here in the old Holmes Theatre. Irish plays are not much in vogue now. The Invincibles have given the very name an unpleasant sound.

. . . Wrote a letter today to Judge Gresham congratulating the country on his appointment as P M Genl suggesting that he was within reach of the Presidential lightning. I enclosed him a copy of my letter to the *Am L R* on Oreg cut from the *Oregonian* of Friday and suggested that his dept might be reformed upon this point.

*12 (Sat)* [*Last Sunday*] . . . went to a French Restaurant on Morrison St for dinner, which I had heard well spoken of. When we got there we found it rather a common place, but we were in for it and staid. Got rather a good dinner. But Henderson took fright at the furniture of the table and would not eat and had to let him go. . . .

Wrote to [W T] Meek on Thursday and sent him by express on yesterday a silver cup for his grandson and my namesake—Paul Deady Meek, born June 7, 1882, which cost me $18.75—marked $20. This is my first namesake and I can't afford many at this price. This is my 59 birthday, and I feel somewhat as if I was nearing the farther shore. Mrs D made me a present of a silver napkin hook and some napkins of a larger growth to keep the old man from soiling his clothes at meals. Last March I had been on the Bench 30 years.

*19 (Sat)* . . . [*Tuesday*] I went to Netta Brookes party where I found Mrs D & Paul, and enjoyed myself ever so much until nearly 2 oclock. Had one dance, but it was a jolly one, the lancers. Had Miss Pettys for a partner and Brooke and Miss Piper for vis a vis. Am nearly done with Farrars *Christianity.* He is multiplying words over the Epistle of St John and for that matter thats his foible generally. . . . Got a letter the other evening from Gilfrey enclosing a letter from Edmond Mallet giving [Gabriel] Franchères orthography of Wallamet in the original edition of his narrative, a copy of which he possesses.[13] It is Wollamat and proves my theory that the word is Indian and that the first syllable has the broad sound of *a.*

*26 (Sun)* . . . Thursday evening attended the dinner of the B B Society, at Eppingers Restaurant in a large room up stairs on the corner of First & A Street. About 100 persons present. I sat on the left of the President, Donald Macleay and Mr Corbett on my left. Senator Dolph was on the Presidents right and Judge Williams on his left. The dinner was very fair and the [wine] excellent and abundant. Williams made a good and entertaining serio-comic speech in which he saw a parallel between John Bull & Brother Jonathan in proposing the toast, The armies and navies of G B & U S. In the course of it he said that John Bull like most other men was ruled by a woman at which there were some smiles among those who are aware of the current impression that in the speakers case such was the fact. I responded late in the evening to the toast proposed by Arnold—The Bench and The Bar, in which I read from manuscript some thoughts that I had prepared during the day on the subject. Came home with Mr Corbett in his carriage, duly sober at 20 min past 2, but left quite a collection of the younger members there who pursued the matter beyond the menu.

The proceedings were published in the daily *Or* next morning in which my remarks appeared in full. They read well, and I have sent several copies of the paper away. . . . Took Ella DeHart to the Orchestral Union Concert at the New Market last night and enjoyed most of it.[14] A Mr Jackson sang, "Come Into the Garden Maud" in a manner not well calculated to attain his object. . . .

*June 2 (Sat)* . . . Gave Bancrofts agent Mr Lea[d]better a letter commending his *Histories of the Pacific States* to people of Portland on account of the space and labor devoted to Oregon in them. Read his first chapters on Oregon from 1834 to 1848 in proof sheets yesterday. The work is well done and the notes are very interesting. Wrote him a letter on the use of Wallamet, just before I received this proof. Got a very interesting letter today from Meek acknowledging the receipt of the silver cup I sent to my namesake his grandson, and giving me an account of the presentation ceremonies. Also a letter from Mr Lucien Eaton, informing me that my article on trial by jury will appear in No 3 of the *American* [*Law Review*]—the May–June one. The weather has been lovely this week, but at times a trifle cool. The thermometer stood at 72 and 66 in my rooms, between 9 A M & 5 P M, but not on the same day. Paid a dentist bill for Edward yesterday of $15, when I told him of it yesterday he took it as a matter of course. Miss Clementina Rodney went to San Francisco, last evening to attend the Wagner Festival or rather the [Theodor] Thomas concerts.[15] . . .

*9 (Sat)* . . . Tuesday morning Mrs Deady and I went to the Gram school in the morning and heard Hendersons Latin class examined. I suppose he did pretty well, but there were some things about his examination that I did not like. . . . Wednesday gave Edward $10 to help pay his board this month and he took it without a word. Gave him an order this evening on [A] Roberts for a summer Serge coat costing $5 such as I bought for myself this morning for office use, and he took that the same way. I wish he would recognize what we are trying to do for him, but I will endeavor to do what I can and in time it may come round all right. Had a long and serious talk with Paul last night about his duties and future. Visited the art dept of the Hall this evening and saw some attractive and good work. Tuesday evening went to Forest Grove and was present at the meeting of the Alumni. Took meals at Mrs Sloans[16] and lodged at Jo Watts. Went [with] Mrs Watt to the meeting. Came back on the early train next morning and had a most delightful ride. . . .

*16 (Sat)* . . . Monday afternoon attended the graduating exercises at St Helens —one graduate, Miss [Charlotte] Crawford. Bishop [Daniel] Tuttle addressed the class in the chapel from the motto, nil longa deo. It was both beautiful and practical. The chapel exercises including the processional and recessional were very interesting. Little Elsie Failing marched in the front of the procession. Tuesday evening attended the closing exercises at the B S Gram School. Dr Hill read his annual report. Rev Mr [W E] Potwine made an elegant address to the boys on "Manliness" which he said consisted of a fourfold strand of conviction, courage, purity and courtesy. Bishop Tuttle finished with a good offhand sermon, and then we adjourned to Bishopcroft where a reception was given to Bishop T and the clergy who had been in attendance upon the convocation. . . . Wednesday H B and I went to Eugene to attend the Commencement. Got there in time for the planting of the class tree—an elm from Mt Vernon, and the Alumni exercises. . . . In the evening heard Miss [Frances] Willard in the Presbyterian Church.[17] A sweet spoken, smart little woman. Thursday was called up at 6 to see Mr Geary who had lost his speech in a great measure. Made his will from written memorandum made by him. Dr Sharpless [came] and said that he did not think it serious. . . . Attended a meeting of the Regents in the evening and of the Alumni at Professor Ba[i]leys. There were 17 graduates and the essays and orations were the best in manner and matter I ever heard. Friday, had a final meeting of the Regents at 8 A M. Called to see Dr Geary & found him much better. . . . Came to Salem at 1 oclock and stopped off for the Pioneer meeting then in progress on the Fair ground. H B got off at the Salem station and staid over to visit Estelle Bush and will not be home until Monday morning. Heard [John] Caples make an impromptu speech at the Pioneer meeting in which he made a buffoon of himself and raised a laugh. Saw a good many old acquaintances . . . walked down to Marion Square in the evening where the Pioneer camp fire was lit, but we did not stay long. Got up this morning at 6 oclock and came home in time to sit in the D C . . .

*30 (Sat)* . . . Sat during the week in the C C & D C, Field with me in the former on Monday, Tuesday & Thursday. We heard the Express Co cases, which he has taken to S F with him to write a little opinion . . . It gives him an opportunity to say something not on the side of the Railways which I think he is rather pleased with than otherwise. We dined at Schulzes on Tuesday evening and at Kellys on Wednesday evening. Williams was at the latter place and F was in fine feather and did scatter his compliments most profusely. . . .

On Saturday evening last [*June 23*] called on Senator [Geo] Edmunds and party at Corbetts. On Sunday he and Mrs Edmunds and Corbett sat with me at Trinity. He reads the service or responds in a devout and manly tone. On Monday he called at the courtroom . . . He left that evening on the *North Pacific*, and made a very good impression. Field who admires his ability says he would sink a ship with a thousand persons on it against whom he had no ill will for the sake of drowning an enemy; but that is a flight of fancy. . . .

*July 7 (Sat)* . . . Nesmith called on the 3 & 5th and told some of his old stories with new lights and shades and one or two new ones. Spent the evening of the Fourth at Dolphs with Mrs D & Edward, pleasantly. This week has been warm and smoky. Finished reading the life of Monroe in Morses series, and found out that he had cut more of a figure in public affairs than I gave him credit for. Still it is quite evident that Jefferson used him and traded on his integrity and singlemindedness. Went to E prayer at Trinity last evening and read the service—the minister being absent and his supply failing to put in an appearance. Miss Rodney played the organ and sang, and altogether we did very well. Gave Edward $10 today to help pay his board and I hope it is money well invested. Read today a copy of a letter written by Jesse Applegate to B F Dowell in 1864 denouncing his daughter Gertrude for marrying (being debauched he called it) to the traitor Jim Fay[18] and asking Dowell not to recognize her or speak to her, saying, that he would never enter a friends house where she was allowed to visit or speak to one who recognized her. In a few years poor Gertrude was dead and A & F were cheek by jowl. The letter shows a bad heart.

*14 (Sat)* . . . Tuesday Mr Edwards Pierrepont[19] and son Edward called at my chambers with a letter from Judge Field. Staid an hour or so and talked pleasantly. Told me an interesting story of how he made Ben Butler pay a client of his $60,000 that he took from him at New Orleans and pretended he had turned over to the U S. Paul and I called on them at Schulzes the same evening where we staid until near 12. I played 3 games of billiards with the son and got beaten. Talked with the father near two hours on current topics and found him an elegant, pleasant and intelligent man. He is something of a dandy but that is better than being a boor. His son is a very handsome, sweet engaging fellow and looks as if he might carry more brains than his father. He was 8 years at school in England, graduating at Oxford.

Saturday evening last went with H B D to the Jaunashek[20] matinee and heard the "Hebrew Mother" and took Mrs D in the evening to hear "Marie Antoinette," and was much pleased with the former and less with the latter. . . .

*21 (Sat)* . . . Sat in the C C & D C during the week . . . and decided orally a couple of patent cases which I must confess I somewhat guessed at. I don't know but I am too old to begin the study of patent law and inventions. Sixteen years ago on the passage of the act of 1867 I took up the study of the subject of Bankruptcy with zeal and pleasure and think I did as much as most district judges towards a correct administration of the law. But then the subject was largely ethical and suited to my taste.

Monday Mrs Deady went to Yamhill and came back on Friday evening. H B returned from Hardings on the morning of the same day. Thursday evening a dinner was given by the business men of Portland to John Muir on the occasion of his transfer from Portland to St Paul. I was invited coupled with a request to respond to a toast to Mr Villard. Thinking on the whole that the response ought not to be made by me under the circumstances I declined on the ground of a previous engagement and said something nice about Muir whom I like. The dinner was a very pleasant one and the speeches and toasts were all in the *Oregonian* next morning including my letter of regrets. Purchased section 5 in pullman yesterday for Missoula on Monday for self, Mrs D and H B. . . . Sent letter and check for $25 yesterday to Mrs Fannie Roberts, nee Fannie Martin, at Canyonville.[21] She asked me to loan her $100 which I could [not]. I told her I gave her the $25 in remembrance of some days in 1849 when I was kindly entertained by her father on North Yamhill. Dear me how long ago! and what changes have taken place since. . . .

*22 (Sun)* Attended S S and M & E prayer at Trinity as usual. The Rector being absent Mr Dodd read the service and a sermon upon the text "Who putteth his hand to the plow" &c. Those who don't like him complained that in so doing he was calling attention to the plough he had for sale.

*28 (Sat)* Monday Mrs D & H B and I started for Missoula on the O R & N Co and N P Ry Co roads. Had a section in the regular sleeper but at the station Mr Muir who was going to St Paul in a private car insisted on our riding with him which we did. . . . We reached Missoula on Tuesday evening after an interesting ride, sometimes made disagreeable by the heat and dust. Here we parted with Muir . . . and left the dining car for Gen [H G] Wright[22] and party who are expected from the east. Met Bush & his 2 daughters and Mrs Charles Ladd returning from the east. Charles was there waiting for them. . . . Got back Thursday evening. The Pen d'Oreille lake is a large and beautiful body of water and must some day be a famous place of resort; and Clarkes Fork is a grand river and adds greatly to the pleasure of the road which runs along its banks for hundreds of miles. We had a dining car up and back to Land Point on the Lake. From there it went back to Missoula to meet the commissioners, who are coming out to inspect the 25 miles of the road last constructed, so as to enable them to act upon full stomachs. We paid $20 for sleepers and $7 for meals and servants besides our lunch basket at Eppingers [the cost of] which I have not yet ascertained, besides 4 bottles of wine we took with us. The road is well built and for its age in excellent condition. When I came home found a letter from [S O L] Potter enclosing some of Mitchel[l]s letters to his wifes sister Carrie Price, which are about the most love sick things I ever read.[A] . . .

*August 4 (Sat)* . . . Mrs Deady and H B D went on board the *R R Thompson* on Thursday evening en route to Victoria to join the *Idaho* on the trip to Alaska. Got their tickets for $50 and $25 = $75—they paying their rooms and meals to Victoria. Lotty Stout and May Montgomery went with her. I got Lottys ticket for her at half price $65. . . .

*11 (Sat)* . . . Monday, Major [Lucien] Eaton of St Louis and Managing Ed of the *Am Law Review* called. In search of Fishing & Hunting. Got him into a party—Fechheimer & Bybee—going to Trask river, Til[l]amook on Wednesday. Had him at lunch at Eppingers on Tuesday. Quite an attractive manly fellow. . . . Got 2 letters from Mrs D and one from H B D on Tuesday evening. They would sail on Sunday afternoon from [Port] Townsend. Were on board and comfortably fixed. The Marvins came back from Victoria the same evening having given up the trip at the last moment. The Dr is too dainty or finic[k]y for this world. Got an invitation last evening to attend the spike driving on the N P Ry on September. Don't believe I will [have] time to go. Would like to very much.

This afternoon walked down to the site of the proposed railway bridge, some ½ mile below Weidler saw mill, visited the office of the engineer and saw the plans. The draw is 170 [feet] in the clear on either side of the pivot pier, and the distance between the shore piers about the wharf line is 1186 feet. This portion is to be iron. The deepest water is fifty feet at high and 22 at low. Rode back on the car up 15th and down Washington. . . .

*18 (Sat)* Sunday . . . at Trinity as usual; and also a special service at ½ past 2 for the consecration of the banner of the Oregon Knight Templars [*sic*], at which Bishop Morris made a good address. The house was crowded and a liberal collection taken up for the Good Samaritan Hospital. There are some things about these pseudo Knights, their titles, pretensions and dress that make one smile, but on the whole I imagine the parties are improved by the process; and certainly it is better to have their banner consecrated in church and high purpose set before them, than to do so with a carouse in a beer hall. Called to see Gen Hamilton in the afternoon and dined with the Brookes. The old man is breaking up I think at last. We talked about a great many things—particularly the people we knew in Wheeling 45 years ago, he as a man and I as a boy. . . .

. . . This day 3 years ago I reached Victoria on my return from Alaska. I wonder where Mrs D is. On her way back, I suppose, but if she went to Mt St Elias or Glacier bay she won't be at Victoria probably before the 24 . . . am reading Mrs Carlyles letters. She certainly had the faculty of writing and I expect talking. Had a little south wind during the first of the week which blew away the smoke, but it is coming back. Major Eaton called on Wednesday. Had a glorious time on Trask & Wilson river fishing. Went to the Sound. Attended a German last night at Turn Hall, given by the young men. Danced the Lancers with Netta Brooke and Mrs Holt Wilson. The latter and I exchanged a good deal of pleasant chaff. Netta is a fine looking woman. Got home at ½ past 12. Think Reed and Maggie Green are in a fair way to become attached. Good thing for both of them I think. . . .

*25 (Sat)* . . . Friday Glen O Burnett called to see me.[23] I was very glad to see him and he me. He is near 76 but looks very well. He has been spending some weeks with his children in Yamhill & Polk and is now returning to Cal. Probably

I will never see him again. . . .

Friday evening Paul & I went out with many others on the *Lurline* to Vancouver to attend the reception given to Gen Sherman and Justice Gray by Gen Miles. About 150 persons present. Dancing, conversation and refreshments— Plenty of champagne. I danced with Miss Pet[t]is, Netta Brooke and Mrs Gen Morrow, and had some pleasant chats with Justice Gray. He is very genial. I am invited to meet him at dinner at Dolphs on Sunday evening. We all got home about 3 oclock and I was up this morning about 15 min after 7 not feeling much the worse. Have not heard anything of the return of the *Idaho* yet. The weather is still smoky and our visitors are losing the sight of our grand snow peaks. . . .

. . . [*Yesterday*] evening went to Dolphs by special invitation and accompanied them and Mr Justice Gray to the Pavillion, to attend the Sherman reception. Gray & I sat on the platform and after Sherman had spoken I introduced him [*Gray*] in a very short speech, to which he responded briefly but [in] so low a tone he could not be heard. Then the Sherman hand shake commenced and Gray and I left. There were probably 2000 persons present, and they were very enthusiastic over Sherman who made them a rather telling speech with nothing in it.

*September 1 (Sat)* . . . Dined at Dolphs [*on Sunday last*] at 7 P M, 16 persons at the table . . . Dolph at the head of the table and I at the other [end]. Dolph had Sherman on his right and Gray on his left with Williams and Grover immediately below the two latter. I had [Gen] Miles on my right and Kelly on my left with Corbett and Tidball immediately below the two latter. The rest were Gibbs, [Amos] Kimball, Prescott, [G M] Dodge,[24] Scott & Cy Dolph. The dinner was excellent and the wines abundant. We sat until ½ past 10 and left at 11, when Sherman & Gray with their party went aboard the steamer for San Fran. I enjoyed Mr Justice Gray very much. Altogether the visit and reception was a success except the fact that our mountains were veiled in the smoke.

. . . Prepared my report as President of the Regents and gave it to the *Oregonian* yesterday. This is the 7th report I have made in so many years. I must turn it over to someone else soon.

Mrs Deady & Henderson, with Lottie Stout & May Montgomery returned from Alaska via the Sound on Tuesday (28th) evening in good health and spirits. Brought me a handsome Chilcatt blanket from Carl Spuhn. Came to Victoria on Saturday and left there on Monday. The same evening we called to see her companions du voyage, at the St Charles, Mr & Mrs [James] Ruthven, married in May last—he a New York lawyer and widower of 66 years and she a belle of 38 or 9. She is a charming little brunette, and he a shrewd, genteel intelligent old gentleman. Both have seen the world but are willing to remain and see more.

. . . Got a letter from Sawyer this evening advising against the bill of review in the Bridge case, and saying that the Bridge people ought to take the case to the supreme court. And so they should—and shall—either the original case or the case in review as they may think best; and if that august tribunal can reconcile the Wheeling & the Chicago Bridge cases, as I think they can, they ought to have the opportunity. Wrote . . . yesterday accepting the Villard invitation to the "spike driving" on the N P on the 8th inst, the train to leave here on the 5th inst.

The names of the invited guests were published this morning in the *Oregonian*. The Oregon list is notable both for its *omissions* and *commissions*. The Judges of the supreme court among the former and the collector of this port among the latter. But he may have Transcontinental [?connections]. In my University report I was called upon to notice Villards donation of $50,000 of N P bonds to the Regents. I think I have done it in a way that will be acceptable to him, without indulging in any personal adulation or gush, and at the same time point a moral in the right use of riches for the benefit of our local closefisted narrow visioned millionaires. Thursday, H B went to Yamhill. Edward came home on Tuesday looking well, but has since gone astray. Got some money from his uncles I suppose for harvesting. [Henry Ward] Beecher[25] lectured at the Mechanics pavillion on Thursday evening on the reign of the Common People under the auspices of the Womens Suffragists. Mrs D & I had an invitation to sit on the platform, but did not go. Had a large audience I understand. I heard the lecture in San Francisco in 1878, but there is a good deal of change in the material according to the report of the Portland version which I read in this mornings *Oregonian*. A great deal of taking superficiality in it, with some things good, wise and true.

*12 (Wed)*. . . On Tuesday the *Queen of the Pacific* grounded on Clatsop spit coming in the river in the smoke with the California party for the spike driving on board. Got [off] at high water on Wednesday. The affair cast a gloom over the contemplated excursion to the spike driving. Wednesday evening at 8 oclock went on the train. Waited for the passengers on the [*Queen of the*] *Pacific* and *Oregon* until one-half past 11. Got a berth in Wallula, No 6, lower one, with Judge Hoyt [*of Washington Ter*] above. Reached the junction of Deer Lodge & Independence creek[s] in a pretty, unoccupied and sequestered valley on Saturday morning about 8 oclock, where the spike was to be driven. Had lain by the night before at a Y some 8 or 10 miles this way where we had a gentle rain.

The eastern trains did not get in on time. The speeches commenced with Villard about 3 P M and ended with Grant just before sundown. Then the track laying commenced, the band marching backward in front of the proceeding. As the sun went down the spike was driven—Villards 3 months baby taking hold of the handle of the hammer, when the crowd hailed him as "Henry the Second"—a pretty and for the moment a not inappropriate conceit. Then we all hurried aboard and started west. At daylight we were at Sand Point. In passing Pend d'Oreille we were treated to a heavy shower with thunder and lightning. Crossed Snake river about 1 oclock Monday morning and were at Wallula junction by 7 A M. There got into a special train with the expectation of reaching Portland by 7 P M, but were kept along as pilot for the Villard section, and did not reach here until ½ past 12 oclock. Had dinner at the Dalles and Villard made a speech. Nesmith kept the Portland train in a roar all the way with his inimitable stories—many of which were entirely new. Monday morning we met the Sunday *Oregonian* with a full account of the Driving.

Tuesday the procession took place—It exceeded anything that I ever saw. The guests were placed on a platform in front of the Court House where they saw the procession march and countermarch. I acted as one of the committee of reception and assisted in entertaining Lady Hilda Broderick and her husband an M P from Surrey, Sir William Gurdon, one of Gladstones secretaries, and the three English Judges—Sir James Hannen, Sir Arthur Hobhouse and Sir Charles Bowen. Drove with the latter to the Pavillion where the school children sang the song of welcome and [Congressman] George delivered a long and much irrelevant address to the same effect. It was read from manuscript and contained a heroic defense of the mouth of the Columbia river with rambling references to bars and banks in Europe, Africa and Asia. A Mr Charles Russel[l] an Irish M P and Q C made a very telling, taking and hearty response on the part of the English guests. [John] Kasson of Iowa made an interesting speech. At about ¼ to 5 we left [O D] Conger of Mich, sawing the air and flapping his coat tails finely and missed Carl Shirtz [sic] whom we wished to hear.[26] Dined at Henry Failings with the English judges and his three daughters. A very good dinner and some interesting conversation in which I took a part. All about courts, codes, lawyers &c. At 8 the party except Sir James went to the Pavillion and sat upstairs and listened to the Orchestral Union until 11 oclock. A very brilliant assemblage of about 3000 persons. The lower room was then cleared for a promenade, but we came home. Met Mrs Deady at the Pavillion and introduced her to the Judges. Saw many people, some of whom I had met before. Got to bed at 12 pretty tired.

This morning met the Judges at Mr Failings by appointment and brought them here to my chambers and had them on the Bench a little while in the Circuit Court. Took them into the cupola and showed them the town. Introduced them to the members of the Bar present—and the marshal and clerk. Gave them or sent to Mr Failings for them a copy of the *Am Law Review* and a copy each of my opinion in the Express case, the proceedings of the Pioneers containing my address to them, and my address to the graduates at Eugene—"To be or to Have."

Wrote to Mr Justice Harlan acknowledging his of July 17, 1882 and asking for the photographs of himself and wife that he had promised us. Mailed 20 copies of Sunday *Oregonian* this morning and 10 or 12 copies of the program of yesterday to sundry persons. . . . Gave $2.50 on the train to a collection for the cooks and dining room waiters and the same to the porter of our car. Came over the river in a small boat, rather than wait on the ferry until Villard should arrive. This and servant on train from the Dalles was .75 more—making $5.75 for the trip. This evening dined at Corbetts, where I met Evarts, Shirtz and Gov [J M] Rusk of Wisconsin, a good plain dinner and a pleasant party. I sat on Corbetts left, with Evarts on his right, with Mrs Cs niece on my left. Found her a pleasant young woman who could appreciate a compliment. After dinner called on [Frederick] Billings and MacFeely at Ladds and Grant, [John] Newton & [G W] Cass at Dolphs and Mullan[27] at Brookes. Mrs D and the boys, aunts & cousins went down to see the illumination. From Brookes I went down, they going with me. It was grand and beautiful and the throng of happy wondering people filled up the picture. Upon the invitation [of] Quan Tie I visited the Chinese Theatre where there was an elaborate performance and great display of rich wardrobes, for the benefit of the Villard guests and others. Met Sir James Hannen & Sir Arthur

Hobhouse there and MacFeely and Villard also and saw the British Minister, Mr [Sackville] West.

*13 (Thu)* Mr [W L] Warren of the *Springfield Republican* called with a letter from Bowles and spent an hour or so with me. A pleasant, earnest, genteel fellow. We went into the cupola and saw Mt Hood for the first time in Portland for about 3 months. In the evening I called on Mr [H D] Lloyd at the journalistic headquarters, Cor of 3 & B, and made the acquaintance of some bright pleasant fellows—[H L] Bridgeman, [H V] Boynton, [C P] Dresser, and met [E V] Small[e]y & [Noah] Brooks whom I knew before. Went to the theatre to hear the Spanish Students with Lloyd & Smalley. Sat in the north lower box, and spent part of the evening in the dress circle with Lottie Stout chaffing her . . . On the way home fell in with Mrs Holt Wilson and her sister to whom I was presented. Saw her in the theatre with Holt & Miss Couch and took her for one of Mrs Wilsons daughters, but I could not say which. Friday Mr [A W] Campbell of the Wheeling *Intelligencer* called.[28] He is a plain man of sense and ability and just the one to sit down on Roscoe [*Conkling*] at the Chicago convention as he did. . . . Mrs D & I purchased a velvet dress pattern at Crans for herself which I am to have made in San Francisco—13 yds $10 per yd, catalogue price $12. This is a secret until it is made. Yesterday got a draft for my August salary $294.80. Sent dispatch to Sawyer, saying I would sail on the 19th on the *Oregon* for San Fran to sit in the Debris case with him.

. . . Called at the Hall and bid Miss Lydia Good bye. She goes east with the Bishop on the 20th inst to be gone probably a year.

*19 (Wed)* . . . [*Sunday*] at Trinity as usual. Sir Arthur Hobhouse sat in our pew, and he and Sir James Hannen called at our rooms in the evening and said good bye. Bright, simple, cheery old fellows. In the afternoon we took a carriage and called on Mrs Villard, Mr & Lady Broderick and Sir William Gurdon . . . and then on to Gov Körner[29] at Dekums who was at dinner. Mr West and Mr Villard also called at our rooms.

Monday we went to the State fair. Spent the night at Mrs Holmans and came back by the morning train in time for court. Had a right pleasant day of it. Rained quite copiously at night and made the temperature and the landscape delicious ever since. . . . Dr [Edward] Lasker[30] of the German Parliament called this morning with Fechheimer. A plain, quiet man.

This is a lovely day. I am to sail at 12 tonight on the *Oregon* for San Francisco where I expect to remain a couple of weeks in the C C on the hearing of the great debris case. . . .

*22 (Sat)* . . . Went on board the steamship *Oregon* at Portland [Wednesday] at 11 P M room 49 on deck, bound for San Francisco. . . . Reached here [*San Francisco*] on Saturday at 9 A M, after a delightful voyage in which I did not miss a meal. Sat at the Captains (Pottman) table on his right—the only American among the ½ dozen Germans of the spike driving party who were returning by San Francisco . . . Some of them spoke English, but generally I listened to the gabble in Deutcher without understanding a word of it. Mr [A] Rosenthal the German consul for San Francisco was along also and sat next to me. On Friday evening we had some champagne for dinner and the party waxed warm and pleasant. Mr [Paul] Lindau showed us the photographs of his Frauw and four kinter and brother.[31] I ventured to remark that the children owed their beauty to their mother.

Lord Justice Bowen and Lord [Charles] Carrington were also passengers on the ship and I had some pleasant chats with them. The former I met in Portland but missed the latter. He is a very sensible and agreeable fellow. Maintains a correspondence with the Prince of Wales. Mr Lloyd of the Chicago *Tribune* was also a passenger and I improved my limited acquaintance with him. I think he is the making of a man if not already one. On Wednesday evening before leaving we had him and Mr Warren of the *Republican* at our rooms. Am lodged at the Palace, Room 366 on the first floor. Got a bath and a change of linen and down to breakfast at 11 which I took with Lloyd and his friend [Edward] King.[32]. . . Went to Miss Taubles, 516 Sutter street to see about Mrs Deadys new dress. Boy came back with me and took the 13 yds of black velvet and the silk waist to Miss Taubles. She says there must be at least 2 yds more of the material. . . .

On my way down read the *North American* for September. Kassons article on municipal governments is similar in many respects to my lecture on towns and cities.

Met Justice Field in the evening and we dined together. Had just finished the draft of his opinion in the Hong Kong Chinese Habeas corpus case. I told him how he would decide it—that the statute included the Chinese as a race and was not confined to the subjects of the Chinese Emperor. Had a pleasant time with him at dinner. He still dreams of the Presidency and may yet attain it.

. . . answered letter to Justice Field from Charles C Soule concerning the proper pronunciation of my name to be used in his dictionary of the reports. I told him to pronounce it *Deedy*. Got an invitation from Mr James T Boyd to attend the Pacific club. Read a good portion of [Delphin] Delmas' argument in the Railway tax cases.[33] It is vigorous, imaginative, and sometimes convincing but more often fallacious. . . .

*23 (Sun)* Got off at 40 minutes past 10 for Menlo Park where I arrived about 12. Miss Flood met me at the station and drove me to her fathers [*James Flood*] house nearby which is by far larger and grander than any house I was ever in. Met there . . . a daughter of General Robt Lee who had just returned from a 7 years wander around the world by the way of Japan.[34] She is tall and straight—very dark and very bright. Had lunch, dinner and breakfast while there—all elegant—the dinner being full dress. . . . Mr Flood and I took a walk about the grounds in the evening and I found him a pleasant sensible man—but I suppose a man with as many millions as he could hardly be otherwise.

*24 (Mon)* Came home this morning in time to go into the C C at 11. Judge Field delivered the opinion in the Hong Kong Chinese case, holding that the restriction act applied to the Chinese as a race wherever from. This conclusion is undoubtedly correct, but the Judge took occasion to propitiate the Sand Lot a little by talking the hardship of a white laborer competing with a Chinese one who was the more economical of the two and could live on much less. . . . Examined Fields opinion in the Railway tax cases this evening and suggested some verbal corrections. Went with Miss Charlotte Chamberlain to . . . the Palace to a little company and musicale. . . . I always feel an interest in Miss C. She has a sweet sad face and would grace a fortune. Wrote to Mrs Deady and am writing this line at 20 minutes past 12.

*26 (Wed)* Tuesday sat in the C C in the Debris case.[B] Pomeroy consumed the day in argument for the plaintiff. Called on Mrs [Sarah] Hiller (formerly Mrs Wes Ladd) in the House. She looks well. Said nothing about her troubles with William. Called on [Judge] Hoffman at the [Pacific] club, and had a pleasant chat with him. The new club House is elegant. Today met Mrs Dr Vanderpool in the parlor at her request and found she had been arrested on a charge of producing an abortion in connection with a Dr Jocelyn.[35] She told a good story of her innocence and helplessness and I gave her a card to McGraw and asked him to help her. Judge Sawyer had a severe headache this morning and could not sit. I opened the court and as Pomeroy preferred not to go on without him I adjourned and spent the day in examining the maps and pleadings. Talked with Field about the N P Bridge case. He did [not] know what to make of it, and at first was inclined to think the act did not confer the power to construct a bridge unless it was a high one. But upon further turning it over I think he modified his opinion. It is a difficult question. Had a talk with Sawyer about it yesterday with pretty much the same result.

Dined at the club with Hoffman . . . A very relishable dinner with a most excellent glass of sherry and a delicate plate of spinage [*sic*]. The meals at the Palace are not as good as Mrs Hills. . . .

*27 (Thu)* Sat in the C C in the Debris case. William M Stewart commenced his argument for the defts. Sawyer adjourned court at 3 oclock so he could go down to the Ferry & say good by to Mrs Field. She has captured him this summer. She said laughingly to me that he has been very agreeable this summer and she attributed it to the fact that she regularly sat down on him and told him he could not have Judge Fields place. Went to the Cal Theatre and heard "Lucia" or the greater portion of it. Madame Cagli-Gilbert did Lucia very well as did Signor G Coda in Edgar.[36] . . .

*28 (Fri)* Today sat in the C C in the debris case. Stewart continued his argument and warmed up to his work. . . . Worked on the N P Bridge case this evening after court. Had Muir to dinner with me this evening and we are going to the Mechanics fair tonight. . . .

*29 (Sat)* Was driven to Bancrofts library on Valencia street in the morning where I met Mr [H L] Oak and Mrs Victor and saw a large collection of historical materials relating to this coast. Had the pleasure of correcting some provoking but not material errors in some of Mrs Vs notes to the History of Oregon concerning myself. Got to my chambers about 12 and went with Judge [Geo] Sabin to lunch at the Rooms of the Bar Association. Judge Hoffman followed. Judge [W W] Cope gave the invitation. Had a good lunch and a pleasant time. Met a good many people, among others Judge [Harry] Thornton[37] and his son Crittenden who is a splendid talker but he requires an equally good listener. . . .

*30 (Sun)* It rained most all night, but the day came in with the sun shining through large rifts in the clouds. Finished a long letter to Mrs Deady and gave it to Muir who sailed at 10 oclock for Portland. Called at the Mercantile library and read the late *Oregonian* and thence to church at Trinity where I sat in Hoffmans pew . . . They have built a gallery for the choir since I was here. Music not equal to ours. I suppose the sermon by Dr Beers[38] was good but I could not hear it. . . . Went to the club in the afternoon where I met Hoffman and we engaged in a pleasant rambling discussion on many topics including phallic worship &c. . . . *October 1 (Mon)* Got up this morning early and went down to my chambers by 9 and commenced work on the Bridge case. Sat in the C C during the day in Debris case. Stewart still speaking for the deft. Cut up [Geo] Cadwalader, counsel for the plaintiff, a good deal. I wish he had been there to hear it. . . . Got an *Oregonian* this evening of the 27 ult. It is the face of an old friend. I see that [J H] Chapman—[L] Besser treaty for the municipal offices is attracting much attention.[39] It is 12 oclock and I must to bed.

*2 (Tue)* Called with Judge Sawyer on Mr[s] [Mark] Hopkins.[40] Found her an elegant quiet woman and apparently intelligent. A beautiful home and furnishings, but I could not see it at night and therefore had her leave to call on Saturday morning at 9 oclock. . . .

*3 (Wed)* Dined at Judge Sawyers, Judge Sabin present and the family. Stopped at the Vienna gardens as we (Sabin & I) came home and saw the Spanish Students for a while. The building was the same formerly occupied by Dr Bowie, and I could but think of the difference between the present entertainment and company and the dinners and parties I had enjoyed there in the Drs time.

*4 (Thu)* Dined at Mr Lorenzo Sawyers this evening—a good dinner and a pleasant party with some very choice wines. Mrs Sawyer took me in as the guest of the evening but strangely enough seated me on her left and Judge Sawyer, her relative on her right. Besides these I have mentioned there were Judges Hoffman and Sabin . . . and Belle Wallace.[41] The latter sat on my left and after doing my duty to my hostess I had a charming time with her. She told me of her engagement with young [James] Donahue and I told her how sorry I was &c&c. She is very bright but natural and is full of Shakespeare, Moore, Byron and so on. . . . Took H[offman] to the club a little the worse for the brandy but very entertaining. Got home at 12 oclock and found a dispatch from Mrs D, giving me the length of her skirt at 41 inches. . . .

*5 (Fri)* Sat in the Debris case. W C Belcher[42] consumed the day in argument for the defendant. Got to my chambers 20 minutes after 8 and worked on the draft of an opinion in N P Bridge case until I went into court at 11. Finished the draft today on the important point—the power of the company to build a bridge across the Wallamet and read it to Sawyer and he agreed with it, though his impressions were very much the other way when I first stated the case to him. Saw Miss Lee in the dining room this evening and chatted with her for a while. She has just returned from Yosemite. Had a dispatch this morning from Edward dated today at 10 oclock saying—"I passed, so did all of us"—meaning that he had passed his examination for the bar. Oh! how glad I was to hear it. I hope he may do well yet. I must make him a present of something to mark the event. Judges Belcher and Thornton called this evening and spent an hour.

*6 (Sat)* Called at Mrs Hopkins this morning and was shown over her house. Had a beautiful view of the city from the tower. She was very kind and agreeable, and I saw many handsome and interesting things. Among others [Randolph] Rogers marble Nidia and [E] L[e]utzes Washington besides [John] Vanderlyns Marcus in the Ruins of Carthage. Worked on my opinion in the N P Bridge case and then went to lunch at the rooms of the Bar Association, where I met McGraw. It is a pity that a man of his ability and worth hadn't some manners. . . . Dined with Miss Lee and accompanied her to her room and exchanged cards with her. I invited her to go to church in the morning and she is going. I don't think she is a happy woman—mostly I think for want of an aim in her life. She is not handsome, but has an elegant figure and the prettiest arm I ever saw. Called on Miss Hiller and met her and her husband.[43] Got them to tell me the story of William's dealings with her about her interest in the O S N property. He paid her share of the money they got from Villard and kept the bonds and stock— about 50 per cent of the amount and wrote her in reply to her enquiry that that was all she was entitled to. Afterwards she reproached Ainsworth about it thinking he was a party to it, and Ainsworth would not believe that William had done what he did. When Ainsworth went home I suppose, indeed I have heard, that he gave W a talking to about it. However soon after he sent Mrs H the bonds and stock in a roll with her name on them and said he had been keeping them for her in the safe. And Tilton told Mrs H that W thought she was married again and might get through with her money and he had laid that by for her for a rainy day!! In addition he charged her $3000 commission for a sale that she says he never made and that is what took the Hs to Portland some time ago, and after some time he paid it over. Mrs H was lo[a]th to talk about it. . . .

*7 (Sun)* Had my hair cut this morning. Went to Trinity church with Miss Lee. Sat in Hoffmans pew. Went to the library and read the *Oregonian* containing Chapmans letters to the *Mercury* defending his agreement with Besser for a division of the spoils of the municipality and Rev Eliots sermon on the same subject. A nasty mess but the expose will do good. Went to Whitneys 1067 on 14 St to dinner and got back at 10 P M. . . . The journey is, they say, 10 miles there and the same distance back and the cost including cable car to the ferry was only 35 [cts]. A great crowd of common but decent but [*sic*] well behaved people going each way. Mrs W gave me a book—*Vice Versa* to read and I left it on the seat of the dummy when I got off at the Palace. . . .

*8 (Mon)* Got up early and down to my chambers at 15 minutes before 8 and worked on N P Bridge case until 3 oclock. Did not sit in the court. The debris case was postponed for the calendar. At 4 oclock started to San Rafael and reached Mrs Butterworths. Found Mrs B and Mrs [Geo] Hooper and her two little girls Ethel and B (Betty) waiting to welcome me which they did very kindly. John the China servant was there also and as respectable and respectful as ever. Mrs B looks very well, and except for her gray hair looks but little older than she did in 1874. Mrs H looks well, but is stouter and in that respect shows the flight of time. Had an excellent and pleasant dinner, when Maimy (Mrs H) and I went down to see Mr Stoy who is the rector of the Parish. We did not find him at home but soon after our return he came up with his daughter, who is a very nice looking girl. Mr Stoy looked very well. He is comfortably fixed here and always will be when he is [?in] Mrs Bs neighborhood. Got up in the morning at 6 and walked about the grounds until 7 when we had breakfast. On the table there was excellent homemade milk and butter and delicious quail on toast. Mrs H drove me to the station in her aunts Phaeton by 8 and I reached the Palace by 15 minutes after 9 after a delightful ride on a delightful morning by boat, rail, and cable car. The visit was a very pleasant one. We talked of Julia Ames and her uncle Mr Butterworth who had both fell asleep since I saw the family. On the whole it has done me more good than anything that I have experienced lately. . . .

*9 (Tue)* Returned in the morning from San Rafael and sat in the Debris case. Heard [Dion] Boucicault in "Shaughraun" at the Cal Theatre.[44] The first look he gave the audience and the first word he spoke told of a man of genius. . . .

*10 (Wed)* Attended a dinner given to me at his residence 1900 Franklin street by Mr Gordon Blanding [and] I took Sawyer in my carriage, an elegant affair. . . .

*11 (Thu)* Went to a musicale at Mrs Hopkins, the mil[l]ionair[e] widow with the Sawyers. A grand affair. About 100 persons present. . . . The music was fair to middling. Given by professionals for hire. The supper was elegant and included terrapin, fried oysters and champagne. The hostess appeared very well. Mrs [Charles] Crocker and she wore the diamonds of the occasion. . . . Met Lord Rosebery—a handsome fellow. Mr[s] [Ben Ali] Hag[g]in had his arm and clung to him as if she had never seen a Lord before.[45]

*12 (Fri)* Finished hearing the argument in the debris case at 10 minutes past 1 today making in all 14 days consumed in it. At ½ past 3 started with Judge Sawyer and L L Robinson representing the miners and Judge Belcher the farmers to view the site of the mines and deposit of debris. Went to Colfax on the C[entral] P[acific] Ry and thence by the narrow gauge through Grass Valley to Nevada [City] where we arrived at ½ past 1. Started from there the next morning at 7 in a spring waggon for North Bloomfield, a distance of 15 miles up and down the mountain ridges over a good road. Got there at half past 11 and went down to Humbug Canyon to the mouth of the long tunnel and below to the "under currents" or riffles where the gold is saved and about a half a mile from the South Yuba. Rode and walked. The latter was fatiguing and warm. Went down into the bed of the Bloomfield mine and saw two giants playing streams of water 7 inches in diameter under a pressure of 450 feet (lbs) on the bank. A wonderful power. Got a small nugget that the foreman picked up from the bedrock that day. Saw a bucket of amalgam just taken from the sluices containing $28,000 of gold. Visited the Derbeck mine, a drift one, about a mile and a half north of the Bloomfield and just beyond the town of that name. Started in the afternoon for North San Juan, a distance of 13 miles. A short distance out met a Mr McMurray, the superintendent of the Eureka lake Co mines, lying between Bloomfield and San Juan on the same auriferous channel. I got in his waggon drawn by a very smart pair of little horses. We went along at a break neck speed, using neither [*illegible*] nor brakes. Stopped to see the mines along the way. Immense washing everywhere, and tailings deposited everywhere.

Got to San Juan at dusk and was well cared for.

*14 (Sun)* Left San Juan at 7. I in McMurrays team, to Sweetland, where we were met by a Mr Miller, the Superintendent of the mine who took me in his waggon. We went down into the bed of the mine and saw the giant play before we got to Sweetland. Crossed the South Yuba again. At Feeneys, near Smartsville on Deer Creek we were met by Mr James O'Brien[46] of the latter place with two waggons who drove us over the hill to a place called the Narrows on the Yuba, the site of the proposed dam to detain the debris in the mountains. Had a considerable walk to get to the site. At Smartsville we had lunch at O'Briens. He has a lovely home and a clever, good looking, bright daughter and son. He went there in 1853 and is now very rich. Has no education but is shrewd and bright. He has educated his children. Mary gave me a bunch of oranges which I am taking home to Mrs Deady. After lunch drove to Marysville going into the river in many places to see the effects of the debris. Drove to the Eliza tract below M[arysville] and then to town at dark. I rode with Judge Belcher in O'Briens waggon. It was a Kemble and jerked me fearfully. Had a good dinner and got to bed in season.

*15 (Mon)* Was up at 6 and took a walk. Met a character in an old colored man who blacked my shoes. His name is Gabriel Sims. Said he had been there since 1853. That he was the owner of property in the place once worth $8000 and now it was not worth one. He added pathetically "This debris has brought me to this"—accenting the last syllable of "debris," or rather pronouncing it like "this." Here the party were put in two carriages and with some of the citizens drove about 4 miles up and down the river inspecting the levees and the deposits of tailings. The Mayor, a Mr [A C] Brigham and Robinson were in my carriage. Got lunch and at half past 2 left on a special train for Sacramento, a distance of 50 miles which we made in an hour and a half including two considerable stoppages for orders. Got in an hour and a half ahead of the Overland. Visited the Williams flour mill. Saw the rolling and purifying process. Got dinner, and came down to the Overland. Got to the Palace at 10 oclock . . .

*16 (Tue)* Worked all day in my chambers formulating my thoughts on the Debris case which I propose to leave with Judge Sawyer. The Marshal paid me $310 for my expenses here in going and returning at the rate of $10 per day for 31 days from Sept 20 to Oct 21 inclusive. Called with Sawyer at Mrs Hopkins, the Lakes and Mr Clerk [Lorenzo] Sawyer. Saw Minnie and Anna Lake. They looked sad and poor and were very glad to see me. Called at the club and saw Hoffman and the rest.

. . . Sail tomorrow for home on the *Oregon*, room (Bridal Chamber) D. The trip to the mountains and the mines was a very pleasant and interesting one indeed.

*17 (Wed)* Finished the draft of my impressions of the debris case, and had them copied for Judge Sawyer. . . . Called on Mrs Ashburner . . . Had a squad of ladies at lunch. Just saw her. Looks as charming as ever. From there to Wallaces. Had written a note to Belle that I would call and see her and her mother about

2 P M and asked her to get her grandfather [*Gov Peter H Burnett*] there if she could. Got a charming note from her in reply. Found Mrs Wallace, Ada and Belle at home. Had a glass of wine and a cake. Belle and I drank to the present and the future Mrs D, the latter being herself to be married soon to young Donahue. After a while the Governor came in and we had a pleasant chat. Was there an hour . . . Came back to the Hotel and went to Miss Taubles for Mrs Ds dress. Not done, but came home since. Making and trimming $57. Dined this evening at the club . . . thence to S W Holladays[47] where we met Louise and Ruth, his daughters, and had some excellent music from them, vocal music. Thence home by 11 and commenced packing . . .

*22 (Mon)* Thursday (Oct 18) Got off on the *Oregon* in Room D at ½ past 10. Cost more to get away from the Palace than it does to stay in it. While sitting in the office waiting for the carriage met Miss Lee, walked in to breakfast with her and bade her good by. She looked right pretty this morning. A young Englishman of her acquaintance has just come over from Yokohama to meet his fiancee just from Scotland and is to be married this morning. Miss Lee is to put the veil on the bride &c.

Reached Portland Saturday at 9 P M after a pleasant voyage most of which was spent on my back. Got to breakfast on Saturday morning just outside the bar. The first time at the table . . .

Found Edward at the dock with a carriage for me. Found all well at home and glad to see me. Mrs D tried on her velvet dress. Fit her beautifully and looked very elegant. . . .

*27 (Sat)* Sat this week in the C C & D C. Have been busily and constantly at work when not in the courtroom on my opinion in the N P Bridge case. I drafted it in San Francisco, but have rewritten it throughout, and have just completed it except the syllabus which I will write tomorrow. Am pretty well satisfied with it. On Tuesday heard the application of Lee Tong for a habeas corpus on the ground that he was imprisoned by the city under an ordinance for the suppression of gaming which was void, and therefore without due process of law. . . .

*November 3 (Sat)* . . . Sat in the C C & D C during the week. Monday delivered opinion in the N P Bridge case to the effect that the company had a right to build a drawbridge over the Wallamet and dismissed the pltfs bill. . . . Worked during the week on opinion in Lee Tongs case and delivered it this morning to the effect that the petitioner was unlawfully restrained of his liberty because the ordinance of the council for the punishment of gambling was void—the power to punish not being included in the power to suppress. Called at the Rectory on Wednesday evening by invitation of the Womens Guild. Rather pleasant affair but not as numerous or enthusiastic as it ought to have been. The well to do are inclined to leave these pleasures to the poorer brethren. . . .

*10 (Sat)* . . . Attended the opening concert of the Orchestral Union at Masonic Hall with Mrs D last night. A handsome audience and a good entertainment. Mrs Hornick sang for the first time.[48] Does good plain work but the curlycues are too much for her, or at least she is not so attractive in them. . . .

. . . Called at the Hall this evening and met a new teacher, Miss Child, and saw all the Doves in the parlor taking a Saturday night. How they fluttered.

*17 (Sat)* Sunday (Nov 11) Attended . . . Trinity as usual. In the evening went to the Congregational "meeting" with the Marvins to hear the Dr on Luther. He did very well indeed; and the effort raised him in my estimation both as a thinker and speaker. . . .

Friday evening went with Mrs Deady to Vancouver on *City of Salem* to attend a reception given by the Ladies and Officers of the 21st Infantry to General and Mrs Miles on their return from the east. About 50 persons went over, and we had a very enjoyable time dancing, talking, eating and drinking at Sullys Hall until 15 min past 3 when we started home where we arrived pretty tired at 4 oclock in the morning. I danced all the square dances and enjoyed myself very much. . . .

*24 (Sat)* . . . Mrs Deady has spent the most of this week, both night and day in attending Ollie Failing who has been quite sick. Monday presented Edward with a copy of *Bouviers Dictionary,* in 2 vols late edition $15 in consideration of his admission to the Bar on October 5th.[49]

*December 1 (Sat)* . . . Sat in the C C & D C during the week. Tried U S v Hoginson and Boyle v Case et al in the former with a jury. The latter was an action against the vigilance committee of Astoria who gave the pltf 25 lashes on July 9 or 10 last because he did not leave town when they told him to on the 6th. Verdict for the plaintiff for a $1000. Williams made a speech in the case in justification of mob law, that he ought to have been ashamed of. . . .

Received from Bishop Morris yesterday the Rev Fultons *Laws of Marriage* with a request to present the same to the Library after looking at it. Ran half way through it yesterday and found it interesting. How the church did multiply senseless impediments to marriage during the middle ages; and often I suppose made much gain in dispensing with them. . . .

On the 10th ult Messrs Corbett, Failing, and Ladd wrote me a note asking me to select and accept a family lot in River View Cemetery in consideration of the service I had rendered them in the organization of the Association. The letter was written by Mr Corbett and was doubtless well meant but the language is not well chosen, and if it was not for Edward Failing through whom the request was made and who has a just appreciation of the value of my service, I don't think I would accept the offer. They sent me a verbal request to the same effect before through E F which I declined and hence this note. Among other things I prepared a long and complicated deed of trust by which the Cemetery property was vested in trustees to secure & pay the partys bonds to the amount of $75,000 representing the money which they had advanced to purchase and improve the property. Five hundred dollars would have been a good fair charge for the service and $250 a very small one. Besides this I drafted a set of by-laws for them and helped to do the same with a set of rules, which was worth as much more. The lots range in value from two to $800 and I expect to select one valued at $375 and I suppose they will think they have *given* me a lot. . . .

*8 (Sat)* . . . On Wednesday the 5th I purchased of Henrichsen & Greenburg a diamond earrings and pin for Mrs Deady for $800 payable in 6 months. They are solitaire, oblate, of first water and free of any & all possible faults or defects.

The rings weigh each 2⁵/₃₂ carats and pin 2¹/₃₂ carats. I was allowed 15 percentum discount of them and $10 off besides on the rings. The price of them was $600 and I got them for $500—15 per cent off and $10 and the pin $300 being 15 per cent off of about $350. Bought a pair of Munich bronze candlesticks at Gills today for $5.75 cash 75 cts off for Mrs D Xmas . . . Prof [B J] Hawthorne of the Agricultural school called today. He would like [C E] Lamberts chair (English literature) in the University. Gave him a note to Henry Failing. I rather like him. Received a pamphlet from Miss Lee containing the proceedings and address of Major Daniel on the unveiling of the monument to her father Gen Robert E Lee, at Lexington. The address is very fine indeed, but now and then a bit stilted. . . .
*15 (Sat)* . . . On Wednesday night about 10 oclock Ham Brooke came to the house and said Gen Hamilton was dying & that his [Hams] parents wanted us to come down and we went. He died at 20 minutes to 12. I sat by his side and held his hand for a half hour before he died and helped to close his eyes. This was just 33 years and 9 days from the first time I ever saw him, when he administered the oath of office to me at Oregon City on the evening of Dec 3, 1850 as a member of the H of Rep from Yamhill county. On Thursday I wrote a notice of the Gen, which appeared in Friday mornings *Oregonian,* that pleased me at least, and I learn is well thought of by some others, but of the Brookes I cannot say. I also had invitations prepared and sent to the 8 pall-bearers whom we selected the night of the decease. Friday I adjourned court on account of the funeral which I attended as pall bearer, but did not cross the river, as I was to sit in court at one oclock. The funeral was from Trinity church and was largely attended.

Had a formal call today from the Chinese consul at San Francisco, Huang-See Chen and his interpreter Chin Aid. Mrs Deady and Mrs Marvin were present by invitation and also Henderson. Louis Park and Quong Tai accompanied them. The consul is rather a good looking young man of a darkish hue and small stature. The interpreter, is a larger, lighter commoner looking man, and speaks rather poor English.
*22 (Sat)* . . . Sat in the C C & D C during the week until Friday when I went to Eugene to a meeting of the Regents. . . . Staid at Wesley Shannons all night at Eugene. Called at Murchs and dined at Prof Baileys. Henry Failing & McArthur went up with me. We declined Prof Lamberts resignation, except at the end of the school year, and employed Mr [A E] Gantenbein[50] as tutor in the place of Burke deceased by a vote of 4 to 3, Mr Geary voting with F, McA and myself. Same vote on Lambert. Travelled in the Pul[l]man from Albany down and found it very pleasant indeed. Had a full plain talk with Prof Johnson about his objection to the 2 by-laws on prohibiting the faculty from engaging in politics and the other to keep them out of the meeting of the Regents. He is a perverse little feist and not altogether ingenuous. . . .
*29 (Sat)* . . . Tuesday Xmas, went with Henderson to 7 oclock service at St Stephens and staid to breakfast at the Hall where we had the usual sausage and buckwheat cakes. Saw the tree also and had a present on it of a "Fingerer and Stamp Dampener" from Miss Rodney. . . . Xmas dinner at Mrs Hills was fair, but I lacked appetite. My stomach is giving out I am afraid. . . .

# NOTES

1. Beulah Drinkwater Riggs (1819–1904), widow of T. J. Riggs (1808–72). A. C. R. (Sheep) Shaw (1816-80), sheep raiser and town founder of Cincinnati—now Eola—Polk County; he was for a time warden of the state penitentiary.

2. John F. Miller (1831–86), California lawyer; Republican senator, 1881–86. John P. Jones (1829–1912), miner; Republican senator from Nevada, 1873–1903.

3. Clarence A. Seward (1828–97), New York attorney; expert in patent and public carriers' law. James McNaught (1854–1927), Washington farmer and banker. Martin V. B. Travis, New York attorney.

4. Pedro de Alvarado (c.1485–1541), conquistador; conqueror of Salvador and Guatemala. Pedro Arias de Avila (c.1440–1531), Spanish colonial administrator; enemy of Balboa, whom he executed.

5. John Muir (1847–1935), Canadian-born railway executive; traffic manager, N.P.R.R. Co., 1883–86; *post* 1898, real estate and investment broker.

6. James Gleason (1856–1912), Portland attorney.

7. John T. Morse (1840–1937), lawyer, editor and biographer.

8. This bit of mutual judicial backscratching was possible because both cases involved interpretations of the Donation Land Act.

9. E. H. Ramsby (1848–1909), Silverton stage coach operator. Ramsey in original. Davis Shannon (1811–89), Polk County farmer. Ai Coolidge (1823–1908), Marion County businessman. T. W. Davenport (1826–1911), farmer and politician.

10. The work criticized was *The Promus of Formularies and Elegancies by Francis Bacon,* edited by Mrs. Henry Pott. R. Grant White (1821–85), critic and man of letters; an acknowledged authority on Shakespeare. Harry M. von Holt (1863–1927), son of Hermann J. F. and Alice Brown von Holt Macintosh, and stepson of the Reverend Alex Macintosh. He had a long career as a successful Honolulu businessman. He was attending Bishop Scott while his sisters, Bertha and Maria, were attending The Hall.

11. Charles H. Prescott (c.1839–1905), manager, O.R. & N.Co. William Mead (1846–1928), architect; associated with Charles F. McKim and Stanford White.

12. Applegate's letter is long, accusatory, and full of bad law. It closed a correspondence that had continued without interruption for more than 30 years.

13. Miss Pettys cannot be identified. Frederick W. Farrar (1831–1903), Anglican divine. Edmond Mallet was a minor functionary in the Treasury Department. Gabriel Franchère (1786–1863), French-Canadian fur trapper; a member of the Astor party, he arrived at Astoria on the *Tonquin,* 1811, and returned overland to Montreal, 1814. His book, *Relation d'un Voyage à la Côte du Nord Oueste de l'Amérique Septentrionale,* published in 1820, was one of the sources for Washington Irving's *Astoria.* It has been translated a number of times.

14. For Ella DeHart, see DP.

15. Lucien Eaton, St. Louis lawyer and legal editor. Theodor Thomas (1835–1905), eminent conductor; his concert tours were highly successful.

16. Sarah A. Sloan (1828–1902), hotel keeper.

17. W. E. Potwine, Episcopal clergyman; served many years at Pendleton. Frances

E. C. Willard (1839–98), teacher and reformer; president of the W.C.T.U. from 1879 and an organizer of the Prohibition Party.

18. James Fay was a Breckinridge supporter and Southern sympathizer, Applegate was an old-line Whig turned Republican. After the Civil War they reached a political accommodation.

19. Edwards Pierrepont (1817–92), New York lawyer, U. S. attorney-general, 1875–76; ambassador to Great Britain, 1876–77.

20. Fannie Janauschek (1830–1904), German-American actress; famous for dramatic roles.

21. Fannie Martin Roberts (1841–1904), married A. H. Roberts, Yamhill County farmer in 1856.

22. Horatio G. Wright (1820–99), soldier and engineer; army chief of engineers, 1879–84.

23. Glenn O. Burnett, brother of Peter Burnett; merchant and Christian Church minister; removed to California, 1873.

24. John C. Tidball (1825–1906), soldier; MA, class of 1848. Grenville M. Dodge (1831–1916), Union soldier, civil engineer and railway lobbyist.

25. James A. Ruthven (1821–89), lawyer and traveler. Henry Ward Beecher (1813–87), Congregationalist preacher holding liberal positions.

26. Sir William Gurdon (1840–1901), farmer and MP; then an official of HM Treasury. Sir James Hannen (1821–94), English jurist; president of the probate and admiralty divisions of the High Court, 1875–91. Sir Arthur Hobhouse (1819–1904), barrister, jurist and member of the privy council. Sir Charles Bowen (1835–94), lawyer and jurist; later Baron Bowen of Colwood. Charles Russell (1832–1900), English lawyer and jurist; Irish MP, attorney-general, 1886–92; leading counsel for Parnell before the Parnell Commission, 1888–90; lord chief justice, 1894–1900; became Baron Russell of Killowen. John A. Kasson (1822–1910), lawyer and diplomat; Republican congressman for Iowa, 1863–66; 1873–77; 1881–84. Omar D. Conger (1818–98), Michigan politician; Republican senator, 1881–87. Carl Schurz (1829–1906), German revolutionary, Union soldier, Missouri politician and journalist; served as Republican senator and secretary of the interior.

27. William M. Evarts (1818–1901), New York lawyer; Hayes' secretary of state, 1877–81, Republican senator, 1885–89. Jeremiah M. Rust (1830–93), then governor of Wisconsin. Frederick Billings (1823–90), lawyer and railroad executive. John Newton (1823–95), soldier and engineer; army chief of engineers, 1884–86. George W. Cass (1810–88), engineer; president of Adams Express Co. and, 1872–75, of the N.P.R.R. Co. John Mullan (1830–1909), explorer and army officer; MA, class of 1852; associated with I. I. Stevens in exploring railroad route from St. Paul to the Pacific, 1853–54; discovered Mullan Pass; was chief of construction of a military road from Fort Benton to Walla Walla after which he resigned from the army, 1863; subsequently practiced law at San Francisco and in Washington, D.C.

28. Herbert L. Bridgman (1844–1924), journalist; then representing *Frank Leslie's Illustrated Weekly.* H. V. Boynton (1835–1905), representing the Cincinnati *Commercial Advertiser.* C. P. Dresser; Chicago journalist. E. V. Smalley (1841–99), journalist and then public relations expert for the N.P.R.R. Co. Noah Brooks (1830–1903), journalist; then editor, New York *Times.* The Spanish Students were a singing and dancing act. A. W. Campbell, as the leader of the uncommitted portion of the West Virginia delegation at the Republican convention of 1880, he did much to block Conkling's attempt to control the nomination.

29. Gustav P. Körner (1809–96), German-American jurist and historian; lieutenant-governor of Illinois, 1852–56. Kroener in original.

30. Edward Lasker (1829–84), great German liberal leader.

31. Paul Lindau, German journalist, represented *National Zeitung.*

32. Lord Charles Carrington (1843–1928), Earl, and later Marquis, of Lincolnshire; early friend and confidant of Edward VII; sometime royal governor of New South Wales. Edward King (1848–96), journalist and war correspondent.

33. Delphin M. Delmas (1844–1928), accomplished trial lawyer. James T. Boyd, San Francisco lawyer.

34. James C. Flood (1826–89), silver magnate; with John Mackay and James G. Fair exploited the Comstock Lode. Mary or Mildred Lee; probably Mary.

35. Neither Mrs. Vanderpool nor Dr. Jocelyn can be positively identified.

36. William M. Stewart (1827–1909), California and Nevada lawyer and politician; Republican senator from Nevada, 1864–75, 1887–1905; in 1893 and 1899 he ran successfully as a member of the Silver Party. Madame Cagli-Gilbert and Signor G. Coda were not well received by San Franciscans and closed after a brief engagement. History does not remember them.

37. Henry L. Oak, *post* 1868 Hubert Howe Bancroft's librarian and associate editor. George M. Sabin, attorney and jurist; died 1890. W. W. Cope, San Francisco lawyer and California state supreme court justice. Harry Thornton, San Francisco attorney and jurist.

38. Hiram W. Beers; Episcopal clergyman.

39. J. A. Chapman, former mayor, Luzerne Besser, sometime chief of police, and Thomas Connell, a contractor, agreed that Besser and Connell would finance Chapman's mayoralty race and that Chapman, when elected, would appoint Connell chief of police and Besser street superintendant. Connell became dissatisfied with the arrangement and leaked the agreement to the newspapers.

40. Mary Frances Sherwood Hopkins, widow of Mark Hopkins.

41. Lorenzo S. B. Sawyer, nephew of Judge Sawyer and clerk of the U. S. Circuit Court. Belle Wallace was the daughter of Judge William T. Wallace and the granddaughter of Peter Burnett.

42. William C. Belcher (1836–1902), lawyer and jurist.

43. Randolph Rogers (1825–92), American sculptor. Emanuel Leutze (1816–68), German-American historical and portrait painter. John Vanderlyn (1775–1852), American painter. Sarah Ladd had married Dr. David A. Hiller of San Francisco.

44. Dion Boucicault (1820–90), Irish-American actor and dramatist.

45. Archibald P. P. Rosebery, 5th Earl of Rosebery (1847–1929), prominent English politician; prime minister, 1894–95. Mrs. Ben Ali Haggin, wife of James Ben Ali Haggin, leading San Francisco lawyer.

46. James O'Brien, California miner.

47. Samuel W. Holladay (1823–1915), San Francisco attorney.

48. Mrs. C. W. Hornick (Harnock in original), wife of the chief clerk, traffic department, N.P.R.R. Co. She afterward toured the Pacific Coast and received favorable reviews.

49. *Bouvier's Law Dictionary,* a standard reference work.

50. Wesley Shannon (c.1820–1903), Marion County farmer. Ambrose E. Gantenbein, afterwards a Portland businessman and publisher; died 1925 at age 65.

# APPENDIX A

### ALIAS JOHN H. MITCHELL—II

There seems to have been no satisfying John H. Mitchell's appetite for amour, nor his taste for variety. At age 27 he had already crowded seduction, fornication, adultery, lewd cohabitation and bigamy into a busy schedule, a record which would have taken a lesser man a lifetime to achieve. In his later years he was notorious as a regular and admired patron of the better brothels of whatever city in which he happened to be sojourning. But the most extraordinary of his romantic adventures was the seduction of his wife's younger sister, Carrie Price, a seduction accomplished with knowledge of—and perhaps abetted by—his own mother-in-law.

This liaison apparently began in 1866, when Carrie was 21 and Mitchell past 30, and continued about five years. Carrie was then living with her family in Oregon City. Mitchell was living with his wife in Portland, and commuted. Unquestionably he promised to wed his sister-in-law, and it is not improbable he whispered to her, under a bond of strict secrecy, that his marriage to Mattie was bigamous and of doubtful validity.

These assurances contented her until 1871, when a growing suspicion that Mitchell's intentions were not altogether honorable gave way to total disillusionment, and she became engaged to Samuel Otway Lewis Potter, a government draftsman and engineer. Rumour of this shocking inconstancy reached Mitchell at San Francisco, where he had gone on business, and on December 16 he wrote her a letter of protestation:

My Dearly Loved Carrie
. . . Oh! *My own dear Carrie,* will you believe me when I say that since I last saw you I have been the most miserable, I expect, of all living men. I have felt as I have never felt before. My thoughts have been of you, and you alone, and although you promised me *faithfully,* my own girl, that you would not leave me *now*—and you have never told me a lie in your life to my knowledge—yet, notwithstanding all this, I have continually felt doubts creeping into my mind . . . you have given me, my dear good girl, too many proofs of that love.
. . . I will love you and be your friend, and also that of your mother. I know that your mother knows we love each other dearly, and that it would be a sin to separate us . . .

He had already written her a number of other notes and letters, some unsigned, some signed by a *nom de guerre,* and all bearing the instruction that she read and burn immediately. A fatuous instruction, for a sensible young woman will put a love letter anywhere but in the fire.

She married Potter. He discovered the letters and the truth, and promptly divorced her, premarital chastity being, in that day, the most essential of wifely virtues.

These were the letters Potter turned over to Deady, with the stipulation, however, that they were never to be released for publication so that what remained of his former wife's tattered reputation might be preserved. This stipulation the judge chose not to accept.

# APPENDIX B

## THE DEBRIS CASES

Hydraulic gold mining, as practiced in the last century, was often enormously profitable, never particularly efficient, and always shamefully destructive of any watershed where such an operation was conducted.

Hydraulicking was placer mining done on a grand scale. Entire hills of gold-bearing gravel were washed down by streams of water delivered by high-pressure nozzles, called giants, capable of delivering 90 pounds per square inch and above. The rubble was delivered to sluices and carried by stream-flow, sometimes augmented, over a series of wood or iron riffles designed to trap the coarser gold and to break the larger stones into manageable size. A series of strategically placed screens led to side sluices which recovered finer gold. The residuum, sand, gravel, and very fine gold, which could not be captured by the process, was allowed to escape into the stream itself where it was washed along until the current became too sluggish to propel it and it settled and began to accumulate.

For some years property owners along the banks of the Yuba and Feather Rivers in north-central California, dismayed by the encroachment of the inexorably mounting debris, sought relief from the state legislature and in the state courts. The legislature, paralyzed, persuaded and occasionally purchased by the mining companies' wealth and political clout, and by the reiterated threat that closure of the operations would throw hundreds into unemployment and mean an end to the payrolls upon which, it was said, the prosperity of the area depended, refused to act. The state courts were no more sympathetic. At length the case of Woodruff v The North Bloomfield Gravel Mining Co., et al, was brought in the California federal district court, which accepted jurisdiction because the mining was being conducted under federal law and license and because outfall from the Feather was beginning to pollute the Sacramento River, a navigable stream. Deady and Sawyer, sitting as U. S. circuit judges, heard the appeal from the lower court's decision.

The nature and extent of the environmental destruction is described in the record:

> The Debris thus discharged has produced the following effects: It has filled up the natural channel of the Yuba to the level of its banks and of the surrounding country, and also the Feather below the mouth of the Yuba, to the level of fifteen feet or more. It has buried with sand and gravel and destroyed all of the farms of the riparian owners on either side of the Yuba, over a span two miles wide and twelve miles long . . .

It has polluted the natural clear water of these streams so as to render them wholly unfit to be used for any domestic or agricultural purposes . . .

The plaintiff argued the circumstances. Attorneys for the defendant miners argued the law: That an act authorized by law, i.e. hydraulic mining, cannot be a public nuisance. That the state and federal legislatures together had the power to authorize hydraulic mining, with its consequent damage to navigable streams. That the use of streams under a claim of right confers a right, by prescription, to continue such use as against the owners of private lands. And finally, with bare-faced impudence, that the piling up of sand and gravel on privately held lands over a period of years had effectively excluded the original owners from the use and enjoyment of those lands, and that therefore title to such lands passed to the mining company by right of adverse possession.

Sawyer found for the plaintiff in an opinion that is long, exhaustive and conclusive. Deady's concurring opinion is shorter and pithier, but no less conclusive, and contains a concise statement of an enduring truth:

> . . . it is a fundamental idea of civilized society, and particularly such as is based upon common law, that no one shall use his property to injure the right of another . . . From this salutary rule no one is exempt—not even the public—and the defendants must submit to it. Without it the weak would be at the mercy of the strong and might would make right.

(For details, see *Sawyer's Reports,* Vol. IX, pp. 441–551.)

Mrs. Deady: the black velvet gown.

*The Northern Pacific Railroad Company requests the pleasure of your presence at the opening of its Main Line from Lake Superior to Portland, Oregon, and Puget Sound.*

*The Company expects to be honored by your taking part in the act of joining the two ends of track at a point in Montana near the western approach to the tunnel piercing the main range of the Rocky Mountains.*

*The arrangements for the entertainment of the Company's guests are fully set forth in the enclosures.*

*Henry Villard,*
*President.*

Deady's invitation to the Northern Pacific Gold Spike event. (Deady Collection.)

"The people under the electric light were a pleasant sight." Mechanics' Fair Pavilion, S.W. 3rd between Clay and Market, site of present Civic Auditorium.

Aurora S.P. station, in the Wallamet Valley.

Northern Pacific Gold Spike celebratory page from September, 1883 *West Shore,* with sketch of Henry Villard (center), surrounded by (clockwise from noon) R. E. O'Brien, H. Thielsen, C. H. Prescott, R. Koehler, Paul Schulze, J. M. Buckley, T. F. Oakes, and Gen. Adney Anderson. At the corners are John Muir (top left), A. L. Stokes, Theodore Wygant (lower right) and C. J. Smith.

Decorating 1st Street for the Northern Pacific celebration, September, 1883.

The first train from St. Paul to Portland never arrived, since no bridge was built over the Wallamet until five years later. (There was a ferry.)

# 1884

*January 5 (Sat)* . . . Wrote and mailed yesterday a letter to Mr Villard condoling with him in his misfortune[1] and another to Mr Billings asking him to retain Schulze in his present position. Tuesday New Years Day was dry and cold. I started out to call at ½ past 12 afoot on some persons near our rooms and at 1 oclock took a carriage and got home at 7. . . . The most palatable refreshment I got was at the Hall. Miss Clem called it "Tipsy Parson" but the young lady that waited on me called it "Trifle." Mrs Deady received in her room with Lucy Murch and Mrs Molson. She wore for the first time her black velvet and diamonds and looked lovely. She had more than the usual number of calls. Paid off my bills and squared accounts for the year, and had $90 left after giving $10 to the Hospital. But I have found about $10 of odds and ends since then to pay so that I really only had $80 left. . . .

. . . Edward has been on a drunk since Wednesday. His mother is very sad and for that matter so am I. I don't know what will be the outcome of it. The steamer *Oregon* came up last night. She was off the bar three days on account of rough weather. . . .

*12 (Sat)* . . . Edward came to see me on Monday [last] and asked me to speak to [Horace] Nicholas[2] to let him come back to the office again. Made many good promises, which I hope he will be able to keep, and I saw Nicholas and Catlin, who said yes. The latter left on the Steamer the same evening for California on account of his health. . . . Went to the Masonic Hall last night and witnessed the exhibition of Mr Knights deaf-mute School and was much pleased and instructed.

*19 (Sat)* . . . Monday delivered opinion in Gilmores case denying motion for new trial. Put a good deal of work on it and am pleased with it. It occupies advanced ground on the subject of a masters liability for injury to a servant caused by the fault of another servant. On Monday and Tuesday heard arguments in the C C on application for injunction in the Dundee Mortgage Cos case to prevent collection of taxes upon their loans under the mortgage tax act of the last legislature.[3] Effinger for the motion and Gilbert, [Andrew] Hurley and Thayer contra. . . . On Thursday sent telegram to Mrs Wallace congratulating her on the marriage of her daughter Belle signed the Deadys. . . . The weather has been beautiful this week, frosty at night and clear and warm during the day. On Thursday I paid to Mr Catlins order $500, the balance of the purchase money for the undivided ½ [interest] of lots 1 & 2 in Block 1 in McMillens addition to East Portland for Mrs Deady. Ordered a ring for Mrs D for her birthday in February to be made by Henrichsen—a ruby surrounded with diamonds cost $100. Nesmith called during the week and told some stories mostly old ones and some very dirty but funny ones. . . .

Called at the Hall in the evening. Met a Major & Mrs Wilson there. She is a bright handsome, somewhat affected woman. He was in the British Army in India, I believe. Both Scotch, now poor and in trade. . . .

26 (Sat) . . . Got a gushing letter from Judge Pratt of the 18th inst over my obituary notice of Gen Hamilton and the decision in the "Debris case." The papers in California generally approve of it I see and the Sac[ramento] *Bee* goes wild over it, and exhausts the commendatory adjectives in praise of Sawyer, but I come in for a small share. Well, he earned his in the work he put in on the case. Snow fell on Thursday night some 3 or 4 inches deep and is still mostly on the ground. In the meantime, it has thawed, rained and snowed with clear intervals and is snowing now. Thursday evening, I attended a concert at the Masonic Hall, given by the Caledonia Club, on Burns birthday. Heard one or two Scotch songs well and naturally sung by a little Miss Mair[e], and saw two Scotch dances "weel bobbed" in costume by a Mr Robertson.[4] Friday night attended the organ concert at the Congregational church with Mrs Deady & Lucy Murch. Full house and good entertainment. From there we went to the dance at the Turn[er] Hall[e], where we staid until after 12. I danced with Mrs Good and we had an explanation of Mr Goods not calling after his marriage and declining to call on her on that account on New Years Day. He and she called since. Brought him to his manners. . . . Got a letter from Mr Villard this morning of the 18th inst containing a grateful acknowledgement of my letter of sympathy to him of the 4th inst.

This morning found George Kane guilty of obstructing the mails in the late attempt at Pendleton to detain the train to Portland, unless the rioters (discharged hands) were brought to Portland free of charge and fined him $25. Will write an opinion in the case I think.[5]

February 2 (Sat). . . Thursday heard the case of the *Ulloch,* a libel against a British bark for pilot fees on account of an alleged offer of pilot service in and over the bar of the Columbia. Involves the usual mendacious contradiction between the crew of the bark and the pilot boat as to what was done by the latter towards tendering a pilot to the former and the question of whether the territory of Washington is a state within the meaning of the act of Congress allowing a vessel to take a pilot from either of two States adjoining a pilot water. Friday paid monthly bills to the amount of $201 including a contribution of $20 to Mother [Abigail Scott] Duniway for female suffrage campaign. . . .

16 (Sat). . . On Wednesday evening, the 13th, we celebrated Mr & Mrs Hendersons Golden Wedding at Edward Failings. There were about 40 persons present including 7 children with their wives or husbands and 18 grandchildren and 1 great-grandchild. Paul made a nice address to the old people, presenting Mr H with a goldheaded cane from his children and Mrs H with a thimble, chain and shawl pins from her children and grandchildren. I wrote an account of the affair which was published with Pauls address in the *Oregonian* of the 15th, and made a very good showing. The young folk (including egomet) danced the Virginia

Reel and Lucinda (Johns wife) took fright and left in high dudgeon. I pity her, but she don't know any better and must be excused.

Last evening I attended a little party at the Rev Mr Eliots, given to Mrs [Sarah] Cooper & daughter, the Kindergarten women of San Francisco,[6] where I met a lot of good plain people of the schoolmarm order and had an excellent bait of eastern oysters and an excellent dish of tea.

. . . Yesterday I heard a motion to strike out parts of a complaint in Goldsmith v Balch—Kelly & Williams for the pltf and Willis & Watson for the defendant. The suit is an attempt I suppose to get the decision of the Supreme Court in the Balch case indirectly set aside or reversed.[7] Judge Williams made one of his characteristic arguments in which he displays his ignorance of or indifference to the law. . . .

*March 1 (Sat)* . . . Monday & Tuesday evening attended with Mrs Deady the Mother Goose entertainment given by the ladies of Trinity Guild at N M Theatre. It was a pleasant affair, particularly the vocal lancers. The house was full both times and in a very good humor. Paul and Henderson were both in the cast. H B as the maid in the garden hanging out her clothes and Paul as the batchelor who went to London to get himself a wife and spilled her (Miss Morris) out of the wheelbarrow as he brought her home.

Tuesday was Mrs Ds 49th birthday. I gave her a ring that I had made for the occasion—a . . . ruby . . . worth $32 set with 10 . . . diamonds . . . worth $56—costing in all $100.

. . . Paid my bills today including City taxes which were $69.30. The weather is warm and clear today. Went downtown without my wrap—the first time this winter. A train came through on the North Pacific today—the first one for a week or more.

*15 (Sat)* . . . [Tuesday the 4th] was Hendersons 15th birthday and I bought him a knife and his mother got him a book. He will soon be a man. Worked on mortgage tax law case when not in court, which I delivered on Thursday, holding the act void for want of uniformity. . . . During the week tried in the Circuit Court with a jury . . . U S v Keefe (Friday & Saturday) . . . for murder committed in Alaska, the defense was insanity caused by drinking.[8] The jury under the suggestion of the court found a verdict of manslaughter. I forgot in the hurry or rather interest in the Keefe trial to make this entry last Saturday as I should. Missed my lecture before the medical class on Friday on account of the jury. . . . sentenced William A Stillwell to 2 years imprisonment in the penitentiary for stealing $85 from the mail sack in his charge as carrier between Camas Valley, Douglas County and Angora in Coos County on December 19, 1883, by means of a false key with which he opened the sack. In Dec 1849 I ate dinner at his grandfathers house on the North Yamhill. He is a boy I think of feeble intellect aged 17 years and I am quite sure was advised and aided in the matter by his brother in law Daniel Hill, who made and furnished him the key to open the sack. Have attended the Friday evening service at Trinity during this lent. Mr Plummer is delivering a course of lectures on the evidenciary value of the "Holy Eucharist" as he styles "The Lords Supper." The[y] have the merit of brevity . . .

*22 (Sat)* . . . Wrote a great many letters this week. Cleaned up my correspondence. Paid Hendersons school bill today for the Easter term $205.70, state and county taxes $101.10, and Mrs Ds ring $100 = $407.10. . . .

*29 (Sat)* . . . Monday signed the diplomas of the 10 Graduates of the medical college as Prof of Med Juris. In the evening attended the graduating exercises at the M E Church. Good and interesting except that the Rev Isers address was entirely too long. . . . The bill to increase the salaries of the district Judges passed the Senate early this week. But I am afraid of the inertia of the House.

*April 6 (Sat)* . . . Sat in the C C & D C during the week. Mrs D and Edward went to the farm. Read some plays of Wycherly, Congreve, Farquar and Vanbrugh. Had read about these dramatists of the Restoration before, but never had any adequate conception of their lewdness. Worked some on Kelly v Herral, involving the validity of a tax title. Troublesome question, that the supreme court of the state ought to have decided for me. . . . Thursday got a telegram from Harvey that Edward was dangerously ill, and went up that evening on the 5 oclock train to McMinnville where I took a conveyance and reached Harveys at ½ past 9. There I found Edward better. Had been having severe convulsions from 10 oclock Wednesday evening until 1 oclock P M of that day. Remained there until Saturday morning when Harvey drove me to Amity from whence I came home on the train. Paul went up on the evening train and expects to be home on Monday morning. Drs Goucher—father and son—were attending Edward.[9] The former lives at Amity and the latter at McM[inn]ville. It is difficult to say what will be the issue of his sickness. The ultimate cause of it intemperance; and unless he could and would reform he had better die and so he told his mother. Mrs Brooke & Netta called last evening to ask for Ed and they wanted me to come there and spend the afternoon and dine, but I hadn't time or heart to go.

Attended . . . at Trinity. Mrs Molson asked me to dinner but I declined. Henderson went to the Hall last night and has gone out walking this afternoon with Wistar. Paid Harvey $5 that he paid for E when he was at Amity last fall, on account of a horse hiring when he was intoxicated. . . .

*12 (Sat)* . . . Mrs Deady came home on Thursday evening. Brought Edward with her. He had a bad turn on Sunday night after Paul left. But is quite well again. I don't know what is to become of him. Judge Sawyer came up on Thursday evening. Has not been in court yet. Good Friday I adjourned court and went to church at 11 oclock and in the evening. G F is getting to be the vogue. I never saw as large congregations in Trinity and the Congregationalists and even the Unitarians had services in the evening.

. . . Heard argument for 4 hours today on a motion for an injunction in Kahn v Salmon et Burman—Fechheimer on the one side and Simon on the other. A *Jew*dicial affair truly.

*19 (Sat)* . . . Sat in the C C & D C during the week, Sawyer on the bench Monday & Tuesday. Had Sawyer, Mrs Deady and Paul to dinner at Eppingers on Tuesday evening. A very fair meal at $1 a plate. A bottle of claret $1 and of champagne $5—in all $10. Wednesday morning S left by the N P, the Utah Northern and the C P for home. Had a pleasant visit with him and counseled with him as to three or four important cases I have on the consideration block. . . .

Mrs D and I dined at Stotts on Sunday and had a good dinner and a pleasant time. Lotta looked very charming and was bright and sensible. I contributed $50 to the church debt on Sunday—quite as much as I was able to and more in proportion than some of my richer friends. But everyone must give for himself. . . .

Edward came home last night very sick and out of his head with drink. We sat up with him all night or rather his mother did. This evening she and Dr Strong took him in a carriage to the G[ood] S[amaritan] Hospital where he will stay until he is well. In the meantime I hope to get him on board a ship bound for Europe and if that don't save him from the demon of drink nothing will but the grace of God which I cannot command and may not deserve. . . .

*26 (Sat)*. . . Thursday & Monday went to the hospital to see Edward. Have made an arrangement with Capt T B Howes of the ship *Helicon,* now at Tacoma, to take him to sea. The voyage will be to Melbourne with lumber, thence to Sydney for coal, thence to Hong Kong and beyond that it is uncertain. I am to pay $20 a month for him, and furnish the $5 for wages allowed him on the articles which he signs to do such work as he can and berth with the carpenter &c. Got a telegram today from the captain, saying he would sail on the 6th of May. Wrote last night on this account to Ashland postponing my lecture there until Tuesday the 13th. Went with Ella DeHart last night to see "Patience." For an amateur performance it was excellent. Called at the Hall in the evening. The first time for a good while.

*May 3 (Sat)* Sunday . . . Trinity as usual. Went to the Hospital in the afternoon to see Edward. Have been out twice since this week. He is getting along very well, but still remains in bed most of the time and seems weak. . . . The *Am Law Review* for March-April is occupied a good deal with my name complimentarily and critically.

Sunday dined at McCrackens where I met Gov [Geo] Perkins, Mr [Milton] Andros[10] and Judge Williams. Had a good plain dinner, a good glass of wine and pleasant company. . . . Found Gov Perkins a very good man. Not surprised that he is popular. . . .

Col Benj Stark and his son Ben dropped in on us last evening. Just came over on the N P Ry and looked very well. Staid an hour and a half and we enjoyed him. . . .

*10 (Sat)*. . . Wednesday at noon started from the House with Mrs D in a carriage for the Hospital where we got Edward and started for the ship *Helicon* at Tacoma. Met Capt Howes at the Dock (Ash St) with his bride of an hour, Miss Comstock, who was born in the Fifties—between '53 & '58 on the North Umpqua, not far from our place on the Camas Swale. We reached Tacoma about 10 in the evening and remained in our berths in the sleeper until morning. Then got breakfast and went on board the *Oakes* at the invitation of the master Capt Cliff and saw the first iron vessel built at the Gorringe shipyard in Philadelphia and drank a glass of wine with the Capt, who seems a very pleasant man. In the forenoon drove over to Old Tacoma, taking Capt Cliff with us, where the *Helicon* was lying. At noon we all took dinner on the *William A Campbell,* a Maine vessel loading with lumber with the Capt & his wife—Harthorne—very pleasant people. We had three New England skippers at the table and two of their wives, one of the latter—Mrs Howes—being an Oregonian, and they were a very creditable lot. In the evening we got on the *Helicon* and were towed to Port Townsend where we arrived at 4 in the morning. We got breakfast at ½ past 7 and had Capt Howes sign a paper stating the actual terms of Edwards shipment on the vessel and gave him $175, to be applied to the payment of his wages $5 per month and his board and lodging $20 per month for the period of six months, when it is supposed the vessel will be at Hong Kong and $25 to be used to meet an unforeseen casualty or circumstance. Marshal Kearney gave me $50 for Edward on Wednesday to be applied as his mother might advise. At her suggestion I paid a bill of clothing which he owed at Waldon & Becks as from himself and adding $4 to the remainder gave the sum to Capt Howes as above stated. I gave Capt Howes a certified copy of the writing. About 8 oclock we got ashore in a little tug and parted from Edward. As we left the vessel I gave way and had a hearty cry. I don't know what will be the issue of the experiment, but it is the best thing I could devise and I pray God it may turn out well.[11]

At 9 we left P[ort] T[ownsend] on the *Olympia*—a grand and beautiful steamer and reached home this morning at ½ past 8, sleeping last night on the cars on the road and at Kalama. Mrs D has stood the fatigue and anxiety of the trip very well, but I am afraid her heart is very sore. The expense of the trip was $19.20. . . .

Gave Edward some of my old books that I have had on my shelves many years. Three vols of Websters works that I bought of O C Pratt in 1853, and read and reread during the long winter evenings and rainy days in the Umpqua between then and 1860; 7 vols of [George] Bancrofts History, covering the colonial period, Whipples *Literature of Elizabeth,* and the *Orators of France.*

*17 (Sat).* . . Monday started for Ashland with Mrs Deady, Mrs Marvin and Butler on the sleeper. . . . Reached Ashland at 5 oclock on Tuesday after a very pleasant ride. Drove to the Ashland house, where we had a good breakfast. In the afternoon drove out the road south with Mr & Mrs [Jacob] Thompson. Rained in the evening. Delivered my lecture on Law and Lawyers in the Ashland College in the evening to about 150 people—apparently attentive and intelligent ones. Met Elisha Applegate, Capt Tom Smith, Col [John M] McCall[12] and others I had known in times gone by. The place and its surroundings are very beautiful. The tavern is good and Mrs [Johanna] Houck, the landlady is a kind dignified woman with a pleasant eye and the sweetest of German accents.

Wednesday morning we drove to Jacksonville in Mr Thompsons thoroughbrace, reach[ed] there about 12 oclock. The distance is 18 miles and the drive was a charming one. Found the rooms in the hotel unendurable and while I was looking round for some rooms came across [C C] Beekman who took us to his house nolens volens, where we were lodged and fed in the best of style. Thursday morning started with Mr Frank Ennis up in a two horse thoroughbrace for Capt Ankenys Sterling mine. Mr Ennis is the superintendent and came over for us by direction of Ankeny. It rained pretty hard on the night before and laid the dust well and threatened to continue but did not. I sat in a chair in the hind part of the waggon and as my head was too near the ceiling to wear a hat had it covered with a piece of lace. We went by the Crescent City road to Applegate creek and then up little Applegate to Sterling Creek and thence up that to the mine, travelling about 15 miles and making almost ¾ of a circle. We arrived at the mine at half past 1 and walked down into the pit which is about 2000 feet long and an average of 240 feet wide and 60 deep. Two pipes were playing under pressure of about 500 feet through 5½ and 6 inch nozzles. Mrs Deady picked some specimens of gold from the bed rock and Mr Ennis gave me 3 specimens worth about $3½. He also gave Mrs D & [Mrs] M some amalgam each from which they think of having rings made to commemorate their adventure. After this we returned to the mess house where the Chinese Cook gave us an excellent dinner of stewed chicken, gravy potatoes with delicious bread and butter. Mrs D[eady & M[arvin] gave him $1 apiece after which he felt as well as we did. At 20 minutes to 4 we got under [way] to Jacksonville behind the same black ponies by the direct route up Sterling and Poor Mans creeks in length about 10 miles and reached there at 6. Here we parted with Mr Ennis whom we found to be a first rate fellow. Friday came in clear and warm and I visited the cemetery in company with the Sexton, my old friend Sergeant [R S] Dunlap, where I found many of my old Jackson county friends and acquaintances.[13] It is a beautiful place on the slope of the hill to the west of town. When I first knew it in 1853 it was bare but it is now covered with young oaks, laurels and mancenito bushes. I saw there the grave of a child marked "Little Mary." Dunlap told me it was the antenuptual child of Ben Holladay and Esther Campbell that died at the Sisters and was called by them Mary Van Cam[p], Child of sin and sorrow. It was born in Sam Smiths House in Portland, in August 1869, and after being kept [t]here for a short time by an Irish woman named Bryan was taken by the Priest here and Holladay to the Sisters at St Pauls in Marion county and thence to the Sisters at Jacksonville, where it died at 4 years of age.

In the afternoon we all went up to Peter Britts gardens where we drank some pleasant claret made from his own grapes and he sat me twice for a photograph. He sat me once before, either in 1860 or 1869, I don't remember which. I have not been in Jackson county since I held the last court there in the fall of 1848 [1858] or the spring of 1859 except in those years. From there we went to the courthouse where I found the old records that I wrote with my own hand of the courts I held then commencing on Sept 5th, 1853. Called to see Mrs Kinney nee Lizzie T'Vault, found her somewhat aged and hardened but very kind and natural. Saw the old lady her mother on the street. She is 74 but appeared strong and well, though the face is beginning to have a vacant expression. Got an early dinner and started on the stage for Medford at 5 P M where we took the train at 7:20 for Portland and reached home at ½ past 4 today. Had Mrs W H Odell with us on the train from Salem. She looks old, yet the Mrs Thurston of 33 years ago is quite apparent in her appearance.[14] Our expenses to Ashland and back were $23.55 and if we had paid for the Hack to Medford as we ought and must in some way they would have been $25.55. Beekman paid it without my knowing it.

*24 (Sat)* . . . Yesterday I received a postal order from the *Am Law Rev* of $50 for my article on Trial by Jury. Came just in time and after I had forgotten all about it. The secretary said it had been overlooked. . . . Wednesday evening had Ben Stark Sen & jr, Mr & Mrs Brooke and Mrs D & Paul to dinner at Eppingers—cost $15.75. Pleasant evening, but the dinner was not as good as it might have been. After the dinner the young gentlemen went to the Tivoli [Gardens] while the rest of us got in the street car and went out to Mother Jones to make our party calls. Saw her new house and admired it much. She invited us and the Starks to dinner on Tuesday. Nesmith was here during the week. Rather green and grouty and I may add dirty. I am invited as usual to the dinner of the B B Society tonight in honor of the Queens birthday, and booked to respond to the toast—the U S, a large and hackneyed subject. Got Stark an invitation and will ask him to respond to the Early days of Portland. . . .

*31 (Sat)* . . . Got a letter from Justice Field on Sunday [*last*] enclosing one to Sidney Dell, which he asked me to read and seal and drop in the post office unless I thought it best not to do so. I sent it. He also enclosed me Dells letter to which it was a reply, in which I found a passage referring to myself that I did not like. I will get rid of him as easy as I can. He is a pestilent fellow. . . .

*June 7 (Sat)* Sunday (June 1) . . . at Trinity as usual. Pretty severe lightning and thunder in the afternoon. In the evening went with Miss Lottie Stout to see the new Roman Catholic church, St Lawrence. Heard vespers sung and saw incense burned. A pretty little church, but a small Congregation. The plate when it came to me had been down one aisle and halfway up the next and it did not contain more than 8 or 10 pieces of money, and they were either nickels or dimes at the most. I dropped a ½ dollar in and the man looked at me with surprise. . . .

*14 (Sat)* . . . Monday heard H B examined in German. Think he did very well. Tuesday evening attended the closing exercises at the Gram School with Mrs D. Dr Nevius made the address—a mystical misty affair of round full and sometimes endless sentences on "Trails." Wednesday afternoon attended the graduating exercises at the Hall. Miss [Alice] Chance was the only graduate. She read an essay in German and one in English. The latter was rather long and Cyclopedic. But they were both well written and read. The exercises in the Chapel including the processional and recessional of the clergy and scholars were very beautiful. The Bishop delivered a characteristic address on "Simplicity."

Estelle Bush was married on last Wednesday at her Grandmother Zeibers to Claude Thayer, by the Rev T L Eliot. What a *lame* and impotent conclusion![15] The weather has been beautiful this week, but today it rains and is gloomy. Mrs Victor called this morning and I spent an hour answering her questions about Oregons early days. . . .

*21 (Sat)* . . . Tuesday went to Salem to the Pioneer meeting. Walked in the procession under the banner of 1849—only 4 of us. H Y Thompson delivered the regular address in the morning and F O McCown in the afternoon. Both were excellent in their way, though I think the way of the latter is the superior way. The first was noticeable for its rhetoric and delivery, the latter for its vivid personal narration and Original Thought. I wrote a note to the *Oregonian* concerning the affair which appeared in the paper on Thursday. Stopped at Mrs [Joseph] Holmans. Lunched on the fair ground with Judge Waldo and wife, together with the Dekums, Nesmith and John F Miller. Saw Harding and Bush in the afternoon. The latter invited me to dinner with Judge Pratt, but I was engaged to stay at Holmans. Besides, I thought if he wanted me at his house he ought to have invited me before I left home. For many reasons, I have made up my mind never to visit his house except upon a direct and pressing invitation and then it will depend on circumstances.

Wednesday went to Eugene to attend Commencement and the meeting of the Regents. Stopped at the St Charles. Attended the meeting of the alumni in the afternoon. Called at Murchs in the evening. Thursday, attended the graduating exercises in the forenoon and afternoon. Had a meeting of the Regents in the morning, at noon and in the evening, and the next morning. Wrote a note to the *Oregonian* of Wednesdays proceedings which was published in Fridays paper and of Thursdays proceedings which was published in todays paper. We elected a new professor (Hawthorne) and tutor [B B] (Beekman). I voted for both of them and urged Hawthornes election. Established a School of Law at Portland and elected Mr Richard H Thornton Professor. He went up with me. This was done at my instigation and I drafted the Resolution establishing it. Dined with President Johnson on Thursday evening—Prof [E B] McElroy,[16] Thornton & Hawthorne present. A very primitive, but wholesome and welcome dinner. McArthur and I went to the Alumni party at Mrs Underwoods about ½ past 10 where we had a pleasant time until after 11. Came home Friday and sat in the C C and took Mrs D to the opera—"Don Pasquale"—in the evening. . . .

. . . This evening had vestry meeting and accepted Mr Plummers resignation unanimously. I advised it, and there was an affectation of holding back by some. Called at the Hall later.

*28 (Sat)* . . . Sat in the C C & D C during the week. Read and corrected my opinions for 9th Sawyer and sent them to Judge Sawyer by W[ells] F[argo] & Co on Wednesday the 25th inst. There were 42 cases ranging from May 10th, 1883 to June 14, 1884—a pretty good years work. Indeed I think my best and that does not include my opinion in the Debris case. . . . Wednesday & Friday had special meeting of the vestry in connection with Mr Plummers resignation. Passed a resolution on the subject which I prepared and ordered a subscription for a purse to be given him. Paul took the subscription this morning to see what he could do with it. . . .

Bishop Morris and Mr [E P] Anderson called this morning and spoke very favorably of Mr Foote of San Jose as Rector of Trinity Parish.

*July 5 (Sat)* . . . Tuesday settled the quarters bills. Paid out $596.69 and had $150.43 left in bank and $71.35 in my purse, out of which I have since paid $8.25 belonging to that quarter. This pays everything I owe in the world, up to date except $800 for Mrs Deadys diamonds, which if nothing happens I will settle this year. I believe I have paid all of Edwards bills about town also. My payments on his account during the past 3½ months have been $368.80. Monday evening went to Coles Circus. Took Mrs D, Ella DeHart, Paul and Henderson. Said to be 10,000 persons present. No riding of any consequence, but a very large elephant, wonderful trapeze performance and a woman walking on a ceiling head downward like a fly by means of magnets or artificial suckers on her feet. Thursday evening took Mrs D and Henderson to the Bijou opera to see "Orpheus & Eurydice." A pretty good comic show. The ladies wore "stockings"—very long ones. I saw Aimée in the same play once in San Francisco.[17] It was even more loosely done there than here. July 4. The day was not celebrated in Portland and the people scattered in every direction. About noon I walked over to East Portland and out to the Park where there was to be the usual celebration, with Gov Grover as orator. I was invited on to the stand and heard his address. It was well composed and well calculated to please the average good American with himself and the future of his country. The delivery occupied 48 minutes and was only tolerable. In the evening had a party of ladies and gentlemen from the house up in the cupola of the post office to witness the fireworks, of which we did not see much, but saw what was prettier by far—the town by a lovely bright moonlight. Henderson had fireworks at the house also. . . .

*6 (Sun)*. . . at Trinity. Twas Mr Plummers last Sunday. He chose for his text the reply of St Paul to the people of [Ephesus] who had followed him to the sea shore and fell upon his neck and wept—"I have not [shunned] to declare to you the whole counsel of God." It was an excellent selection. But he wasted the opportunity by dwelling too long and obscurely upon his "The whole counsel of God." However he finally made a tolerable application of the saying in its surroundings to the circumstances of his own case.

*12 (Sat)* Monday evening (June 30) had a vestry meeting and authorized me to take up a subscription for Mr Plummer. Turned the matter over to Paul who got $240 by Saturday, on which afternoon I took the book and by 9 oclock that evening I added $120 of which $70 was in 14 five dollar subscriptions. Monday evening July 7 had a vestry meeting and I had raised $15 more for the Plummer fund making $375 in all whereupon Mr Lewis put up the other $25 making it $400. Voted to call Mr Foote of San Jose. Adjourned and proceeded to the Hall to attend the reception given to Mr Plummer. Here I presented Mrs P with a purse of $150 from the Womens Guild of Trinity and Mr P with a purse of $400 from the Congregation with a little speech. . . .

. . . Had a letter from Judge Gilbert of Brooklyn asking me to look after his son who sailed from N Y on March 3 for this port on the *Belle of Oregon* as a treatment for "dypsomania." Poor fellow. What a singular coincidence between his case and Edwards. . . .

*19 (Sat)*. . . Henderson commenced work in [C W] Townsends[18] office—drafting—Thursday and is quite pleased with it. Townsend says he has talent for the work. His work was copying a draft of a sternwheel on a scale reduced by [*to*] one inch. Have been reading Drydens *Aeneid.* Am now in the 10th book, where Aeneas has returned to the Trojan camp with the Tuscan allies. Wonderful ease of versification. I find that my early reading of Popes *Iliad* and *Odyss[e]y* prejudiced me against the Trojans, but Virgil presents their case well in the after piece.

*20 (Sun)* . . . Trinity as usual. Mr Ferguson officiated. Finished the *Aeneid* in the afternoon. Virgil makes a good pedigree for the Romans. What an easy thing fighting and killing is in a poem like this. Life is held as cheap as dirt. . . . Went with Mrs D to a Calico party at Mrs Lewis' on Thursday evening, and wore a fancy necktie which was highly complimented. Life is made up of trifles and this is one of them. . . .

Got a letter from Dr [J C] Mackenzie of Lawrence school advising me that Henderson could be admitted as a scholar there, which I answered last night.[19] Got a letter yesterday from the Rev Mr George W Foote, accepting the call to the rectorship of Trinity church on some minor conditions that I think the vestry will allow of course. . . .

Talked with Jo Teal this afternoon at the Holton House, and he told me about the arrangement that was made last year between B G[oldsmith] and Sol Abrams by which the latter for $20,000 was to procure Judge Watson to change his judgment in the Balch case and vote for a rehearing and that as B G informed him it was arranged. Sol operated through Lowery W[atson]. He retained him on a contingent fee of $5000 and had arranged to give him $5000 more for Judge Ws daughter, by his first wife; and that Sol assured him personally in July, August and September that the matter was all arranged and he would gain his suit, but for some reason when the pinch came Watson went back on them and they had to pay Sol several hundred dollars for his expenses.[20]

*August 2 (Sat)* . . . [Last Sunday] evening went to the "Meeting House" to hear Dr Marvin answer Pilates question to Jesus—quid est veritas. An excellent and interesting sermon, but I did not like his criticism of the Apostles Creed—to the effect that it did Pilate injustice, when it says—suffered under P P, when he no more suffered under P P than Tiberius Caesar. Said P P was a coward not bad; which is admitted. But nevertheless, Jesus "suffered under" him, because having authority to prevent it he consented to his death.

. . . Wrote and mailed letter to Sawyer yesterday containing a statement of my expenses while holding court in San Francisco last fall, amounting to $180.30 and asked for Mr M M Drew, the Marshal, for $129.70 that being the difference between the account and the allowance of $10 per day or $310 in all. The department refused to pass the item unless expense stated in detail. Heretofore I have always received $10 per day and no question has been made about it.

Friday morning the new Marshal, Mr Penumbra Kelly, qualified and entered upon the duties of his office.[21] He appears like a very clever fellow. Poor Kearney went out quietly but I think reluctantly. Rotation in office may keep the "Outs" on the alert, but it does little to keep the "Ins" industrious or upright but the contrary.

Have been dipping into Cookes [*George*] *Eliot* during the week.[22] In the chapter on her philosophy now. Rather deep or foggy, but I make out that her idea was that our notions of God and morality are our notions of ourselves subjectively considered or what we would be and hope to be. . . .

*10 (Sun)* . . . Friday afternoon went to Tacoma to attend a ball in honor of Mr [Charles] Wright on the occasion of the opening of the New Hotel. Reached

Tacoma about 10 and got room 19 at the Hotel where I managed to make my toilette by candlelight—the first time for a good many years, say 25. There is no gas in the town and the Hotel was generally well lit up with Kerosene lamps. I remained in the ballroom until about 4 in the morning, having danced the last dance on the program, with Miss Wright. There were about 250 persons present, most of them from elsewhere than Tacoma of course. Very few from Portland, myself and Ella DeHart, who by the way was one of the belles of the evening, Mr & Mrs John R Foster, Schulze, Mrs Koehler and Mrs [Henry] Muller—the latter two being boarders. Danced all the square dances—one of which was with Miss Lilly Blye—a very charming girl from Chestnut Hill near Phil. She is with Mr Wright and his daughter. Saturday morning I was up and down to breakfast by ½ past 9. In the forenoon drove up to Bishop Paddocks and thence to his Seminary taking him along. Went over the new building which I think is being very well and conveniently constructed. Met Mrs [Lem] Wells there. They (she & her husband) are going to take charge and are just moving in. Saw Miss Fanny Paddock at her fathers. What a pronounced manner she has and what a talker she is and very pleasant withal. She was at the hop and bared her pretty plump arms without reserve. Lunched at ½ past 2 with Mr Wright in his private dining room with Miss Wright & Blye, Mr Wright jr, Mr Scott[23] of Phil and Mr Hosmer. A good meal, sat between the young ladies and enjoyed them both. Got on the train at 6 oclock and got to Portland at 6 this morning. Got on the boat at Kalama and to bed about 12. The first thing I heard when I got home was [that] Butler (James H) [had died] in Colorado on Friday. Poor fellow! He has been with me now as bailiff of this court and janitor of my chambers for about 22 years. I shall miss him very much. He was a very capable and true man, and I am afraid I will never get another to fill his place. Nesmith came in this afternoon and told me some remarkable stories, and he appeared to be duly sober.

*16 (Sat)* Monday . . . Nesmith called in the morning and talked about falling in the street near Molsons and Fred Holman coming to him with water and saving his life, soon after he left me on Sunday afternoon. He looked badly and cried like a child at times. He is not drinking much now, but I think he has been before he came to town. Poor old fellow, what a pity it is to see such a man a wreck. . . .

Paid $400 on Mrs Deadys diamonds on Tuesday. Thursday (the 14 inst) was the 18th birthday of the "Brooke Boys" Mac & Scott—and I gave them a Scarf pin apiece—gold with a "Tiger Eye" stone for a head. Cost $3 apiece. . . . Mrs Eddy & Mary called at the house on Wednesday. Just arrived over the N P. I called on them on Thursday at the Esmond. Mary is bright and pleasant, but somehow she looks faded and jaded. The mother has a hard selfish look, which is growing on her. Living a life of mere pleasure and for self alone must tell on anyone. What a pity with their means and abilities they are not led to try to do some good in this world—to make someone the better for their having lived in it. . . . Mrs Deady has made up her mind to go east with Henderson the last of this month, and I must look around for the money and make the arrangements.

*23 (Sat)* . . . Mr Justice Miller called Thursday on his return from Alaska. Well pleased with the trip but not with Capt Carrol[l]s want of politeness. Mrs Deady and [I] called on him and the ladies at the Esmond in the evening. Had a pleasant chat and in the course of the conversation we stumbled onto Aunt Kate (Mrs George H Williams). She [*Mrs Miller*] says her true name is Ann—that her first husband—Ivens—was a Mormon and that she followed him from Keokuk to Kirtland, Ohio, to marry him when she was 16 and that Ivens did not want to marry her then but his mother made him and that after she had lived with him and had a child—which I understood was begotten out of wedlock—she left him and went home to her father and got a divorce on the ground of his infidelity before Judge Williams. She left the child with the father and never claimed it. That afterwards she fell in love with [Mr] George and he left her and went to Pikes Peak when she went into fits and they sent for him and brought him back and he married her.[24] Her father Hughes carried on the cooper business in Hooppole, a suburb of Keokuk. She had a sister Ruth who went to the bad and kept a bawdy house &c&c. . . .

Mrs Deady started to Salem this morning but missed the ferry. However she went this afternoon. Goes to visit the Bushs. Eugenia wrote for her to come. A dispatch from San Francisco informed us that R R Thompsons house in Alameda was burned and everything in it—a loss of about $300,000 including all the paintings, books and bijouterie that he has been collecting for some years. Considering that he got this out of the *"Oregonian* steal" the old proverb applies—"What comes under the devils belly goes over his back."[25]

Mr C E S Wood (too many initials) has delivered a couple of briefs this week that show a good deal of original thought and much care, research and taste.[26] He ought to succeed at the bar. If he can get anything to do he will attend to it.

*30 (Sat)*. . . Had a spell of diarrhea during the week. Justice Miller called at my chambers on Thursday and at our rooms with Mrs M on Friday. He is a pleasant sensible old gentleman and a most excellent judge. Today Mrs Deady and Henderson got off on the Northern Pacific for New York. Eugenia Bush went with her. Mr Bush and Paul and I went to Albina with them and came back as far as the Ry ferry with them. Gave Mrs Deady passes, tickets and money to buy sleeping car tickets to New York and meals twice a day ($21) east and $28 over for incidentals—$150 in all, and Ladds drafts on N Y for $650. Gave her a pearl shell opera glass at $16 cost $12 and she had a sealskin sack and muff made at $240. . . .

*September 6 (Sat)* Sunday . . . Dined at Cyrus Dolphs in the afternoon with Justice Miller et ux. Paul was along. Had a good dinner and a pleasant time. Miller sketched Williams to me as he was on the bench in Iowa, halting between two opinions, timid and uncertain. Monday morning Justice Miller had a reception in my chambers where about 25 lawyers called on him before going into court. He talked to them very entertainingly and then sat in court with me until 11, when he joined his wife and daughters and started for the Northern Pacific. I have enjoyed his visit very much. Had a meeting of the vestry in the evening in which we resolved to ask Bishop Morris to "institute" or induct Mr Foote into the Rectorship of the Parish at M prayer on the 1st Sunday in October. Tuesday morning got a telegram from Justice Field that he was coming and he came that day. Had the Circuit Judges chambers fitted up for him and he is lodging and working there and living at the Esmond when he is not dining out. . . .

. . . Went with Mr Justice Field to dinner at Williams at 7 in the evening today. Sat down at ½ past 7 and rose at 11. A very good dinner and well served and champagne (pint bottles) gilore [sic]. . . . The house was elegant and the madam had just returned from the Sulphur Springs looking as well as she did twenty years ago. Judge Field plied her with flattery which [she] took in the best part.

*13 (Sat)* Sunday . . . Dined at Col Kellys in the evening with Justice Field. Mrs Grover there. Growing large and exceedingly dignified. She is bright however and says things, just as she did when she was a child. Had a good dinner and a very pleasant time. Mrs Kelly grows better looking and more agreeable with age—and I may add good fortune. . . .

Thursday morning Cyrus Field called with his two sons and in the evening Paul and I called on them at the Esmond, where we met Mr Field and Mr [J H] Hall[27] of N Y, Justice Field, Mr Corbett and Mr Williams. Cyrus F is a character and a brusque but agreeable and entertaining man. Mr Hall is a very fine looking man and so far as I saw a man of ability and character. I was sorry to hear him characterize some of Mr Villards financial operations as criminal.

. . . Paid H & G $250 on Mrs Ds diamonds which leaves only $150 more. Field and I dined together at the Esmond Monday and Tuesday and will again this evening after which we will call at the Hall and Brookes, when he will go on board the steamer for San Fran. He has been here this time 11 days and I have enjoyed his company very much. True he don't allow anyone to do much talking where he is, but I can afford to listen to him once in a while. . . .

*October 4 (Sat)* . . . Thursday evening [*Sept 16*] went to Mrs Williams to a grand party given the young people generally and a few "deservable" people no longer in that category as Mrs Lewis phrased it. Had a good time. It was a splendid affair. I danced with Katy Story, Netta Brooke and Etta Failing. Left between 1 & 2 drove home, changed my clothes and went down to the O R & N Companys dock and went aboard the steamboat for Astoria where I slept and lounged until 9 the next morning. . . . Saturday, went to Skipanon on the *Sam* and drove thence to Grimes with Monroe. Got there a little after 1 in a slight rain, and I was in the surf in less than no time. . . .

I had a quiet pleasant time at Grimes. Bathed every day but 2, Monday & Tuesday (Sept 29 & 30th) when the surf was too strong. Got knocked down with it on Sunday. Walked and read and wrote the rest of the time. . . . Got a pair of Elk Horns from a young Indian for $2.50. They are a beautiful pair with 5 prongs or spikes indicating that the animal was 5 years old. He was shot on the Tillamook Trail on the 1st day of October about 2 miles south of the Seaside House. I intend to have them mounted and sent to Justice Field. Mrs Monroe Grimes gave birth to her second son on the morning of Tuesday the 30th of September. She sat at the fire chatting with the rest of us the evening before as cheerful as a bride. The affair created quite a ripple in our otherwise monotonous life. . . .

*11 (Sat)* . . . Wednesday evening, went to the dock to meet Mr Foote and wife on the steamer *Columbia*. Met Dodd & Glisan my co-committeemen there, and about ½ past 9 the steamer came to the dock with Mr Foote. Went on board and got him off and in a carriage bound for the Bishopcroft, with Dodd & Glisan. I did not go myself because I do not feel at liberty to enter the Bishops house since his conduct towards Henderson.[28] . . .

Tuesday evening attended a tin wedding at Alices. About 40 of the Kin and connexion there, and altogether it was a hearty, pleasant affair. I contributed a toaster for Mrs D and muffin rings for myself and Paul and I furnished the candy. I got away pretty early and wrote to Mrs D an account of the affair. . . .

Friday evening, opened the law school and introduced the subject and prof Thornton in a few remarks which are published in this mornings *Oregonian*. About 20 or 25 persons present. Bishop Morris there. He gave me an invitation from Mrs Morris to dinner tomorrow to meet Mr Foote, which I declined, I am afraid rather awkwardly, on account of the conventional previous engagement. . . . I thought I had closed my accounts last week with a balance of $150 in the bank, but I find I was mistaken and I only had $77.75 with an account of $15 still out which I have since paid. . . .

*12 (Sun)* Attended . . . Trinity. At the morning service Mr George W Foote was "instituted" by the Bishop as Rector of the parish. Bishop Paddock was also present in the chancel. Dr Glisan and I as the Wardens of the parish and representatives of the Congregation received Mr Foote into the church and I as the vestry or Senior warden presented him with the Keys of the church. The House was very full. Bishop Morris preached a heavy long sermon. In the evening Bishop Paddock preached another. He makes a good deal of noise on the drum ecclesiastic. Bishop M indulged in a good deal of denunciation of which he was pleased to call "sensational preaching," and doubtless there is a tendency in this direction that deserves to be curbed and merits rebuke. But after all, what is the pulpit for unless it is to call the peoples attention to their everyday duties and obligations in this world and urge the due performance and acknowledgement of them.

. . . Dined with John Catlin at Mary Strongs and had a good dinner and a glass [of] claret. Mary & Tom are very comfortably fixed for young people and evidently live well. Went to the New Market in the evening where I heard [Geo] Miln as Hamlet.[29] He is an actor of superior parts and with experience will be distinguished. Read proof of my report after the play and got to bed at 12. A busy day. Thursday evening Paul and I went to a party at Mrs Cyrus Dolphs. Got home at 1 A M. . . . Had a chat and promenade with "Aunt Kate." She was elegantly arrayed in light blue silk which did not make her look any the less. Friday . . . took Agnes Catlin to the Fair in the evening. Henrietta Failing was to go with us, but the news that Ham Corbett was probably dying deterred [?] her. At the Fair Mrs Ladd told me that they had a dispatch at 6 in the evening that Hamilton was dead. Died at Santa Barbara, Cal whither he had gone a few days before of Hemorrhage of the lungs.

. . . On Tuesday sent Mrs D a draft on N Y for $125 to the care of Mr Knott, 216 St Paul street, Baltimore, and paid B Goldsmith $125 here for that sum advanced her in New York.

She had had, besides the last named draft $839 in cash and her disbursements according to the bills and accounts she sends me are $713.69 including $210 paid to the school at Lawrence for Henderson, which would leave her with $125.21 while she writes me that she has $168. Probably some bills that she has reported are also in her Hotel bill. I suppose I have found one in her Brevoort bill of $47.65. According to her account when she received my draft, and she will on Tuesday, she will have $293. Thayer of the Supreme Court called this morning and consulted me about a case against the Indian Agent at Klamath for seizing liquor in transit through the reservation. The defense does not state that the trespasser was a "white person or an Indian" and the statute authorizing a seizure seems to be limited by its language to that class of cases. This is a blunder of the lawyer which makes the law appear lame. . . .

25 (Sat) Sunday . . . at Trinity as usual. Rev Mr Foote officiated. His sermon upon the saying of Paul—"we are ambassadors for Christ"—was a fit and wise exposition of his relation to the Congregation and what he was there for. His manner and presence are very good and everybody was pleased. . . .

. . . Monday evening called at Mrs Stotts and Mrs Dolphs. Played billiards at the latter place. In the course of the evening Mitchel[l] and the Price family became the subject of the conversation between Mr & Mrs D and myself and I finally told Mrs D the fact about Ms guilty relations with his wifes sister from beginning to end. She was indignant. Cyrus knew all about it before, that was evident, but had never told her.

Attended the funeral of Ham Corbett on Friday at the house of his father. Many people present and a great wealth of flowers—this overdone. Rev Lindsley read the Episcopal burial service and added a prayer of his own which did not improve it. I understand that Ham told his mother in his lifetime how much he liked this service and she agreeing with him, they then and there agreed that whichever went first the other would see that the service was read at the funeral. A quartette sang "Jesus lover of my soul" and "Abide with me" and murdered them both. Paul was one of the pall bearers. I went to the grave—in the Riverview Cemetery—in a carriage with Donald Macleay, Mr Molson, and Capt [Frederick] Bolles.[30] The scene at the grave was very affecting and the view from the height looking north and east was beautiful. We got home at 5 oclock. The funeral ought to have been in the church where people could see and participate in the service in an orderly and comfortable way.

Old Mrs Harvey died Friday evening after a somewhat lengthy illness—softening of the brain. I wrote a notice of her last night at the request of John McCracken which appears in this mornings *Oregonian* signed "DD"—the symbol for Deady; and I have promised to act as pall bearer at her funeral tomorrow from Trinity church. . . . This mornings *Oregonian* contains a very nice notice of Hendersons drawings in the Mechanics fair, but attributes his education to the Public School instead of the Grammar School and calls him Henderson "P" instead of "B." And this is fame. Had a letter from Henderson dated the 15th and got another from his mother written to her on the 10th. He had been to Phil to visit the electric light exhibition and was much pleased. . . .

*November 1 (Sat)* . . . [*Sunday last attended the*] Montefiore celebration[31] at the New Market in the evening where I sat on the stage on the immediate right of the president, Mr Laidlaw, the British Vice Consul. The House was packed from pit to dome. The address of the evening was made by Solis Cohen and it was admirable in both matter and manner. The Revs Lindsley & Eliot spoke also, but I thought they fell below themselves. . . .

. . . Took Henrietta Failing to the New Market last night to hear Mrs L H Smiths elocutionary entertainment.[32] A slim and rather a good performance. Sleep scene from "Macbeth" was well done as a pantomine—particularly the placing of the taper on the stand . . . forgot to say that I attended Mrs Harveys funeral on Sunday as pall bearer. She was buried at 2 P M from Trinity church.

. . . Have been reading [S H] Gays *Life of Madison* during the week. An interesting book in some respects but very lopsided on the slavery question. Fifty years will have to roll by before the popular mind recovers its equilibrium on this question. The war and the result of it have made a man who owned Negroes or obeyed and respected the injunctions and limitations of the Constitution on this subject, look like a criminal by [*sic*] this generation. . . .

*16 (Sun)* . . . On Tuesday the 4th inst dined at Lewis' where I met the new Rector & his wife, Mr & Mrs Foote, and Mr & Mrs [*omitted*] lately of New York. About ½ past 10 oclock went down to the *Oregonian* office and met the news from New York that indicated the election of Cleaveland [*sic*] which was this morning after many fluctuating reports has been finally confirmed. I hope Cleaveland will prove true to his civil service record and general disposition to administrative reform, and if he does, his elevation to the Presidency will be a great benefit to the country. But the greater portion of the party behind him have no sympathy with him in this respect and there lies the danger. Blaine had no sympathy with adminstrative reform and was unworthy of the Republican nomination, but the core of the party have, and may have controlled him in the right direction. . . . On Thursday the 6th inst Agnes Knott was married at Chicago in St Vincents church to Mr M T Flemming. Paul and I sent her a handsome silver spoon which cost $10 without a box and had a picture of Mt Hood engraved on it. . . .

*22 (Sat)* . . . Have heard from Mrs Deady and Henderson regularly during the week and written them also. This writing to them takes up a good deal of my time I find. A letter of 4 pages every other day takes an hour at least. And although there is nothing particular in them, yet I never know when to quit chatting and gossipping. I am not certain about the two pp's in this last word, but better one too many than one too few.

. . . Mr Justice Gray sent me a copy of his opinion in Elk v Wilkins in which he decides that an Indian is not born within the allegiance or jurisdiction of the U S and is not therefore a citizen thereof and cannot become one without the consent of the U S. In it he quotes from my opinions in McKay v Campbell and U S v Osborne in a manner complimentary to myself. I wrote him acknowledging the receipt of the opinion and thanking him for the compliment and complimenting him on his opinion in the legal tender cases. Sent a letter to O P Shiras with L & Ts exchange on Chicago for $25 as my contribution to keep Mr Hageman at Washington to look after the passage of the district judge salary bill. I hope it will prove bread cast on the waters. Fechheimer took me to the Casino last night to see Je[a]nnie Winston and troupe in "Juanita." Poor trash. She makes a good Tom Boy and screeches rather melodiously. Went to the matinee this afternoon to see "Felicia" and was well pleased. Pat Malones son [*John*] played Capt John and did it well.[33] I went behind the scenes and talked to him after the curtain fell. Called at the Hall this evening. The "doves" were in the parlor reading, singing &c. . . .

*29 (Sat)* . . . Thursday was thanksgiving. Went to M prayer at Trinity where I heard an admirable sermon appropriate to the occasion. The offering which I think was quite large went to the G S Hospital. In the afternoon took Ella DeHart to the matinee at New Market where we saw Rose Etynge in "Led Astray." Malone did the husband very well. Took dinner at Alices where we had an excellent turkey and other things to correspond except wine. . . .

*December 6 (Sat)* . . . Got a letter from Edward last evening dated Newcastle, N[ew] S[outh] W[ales] Sept 19 and Oct 10th. The ship was about starting to China at the last date with a Cargo of coals. E seems dissatisfied and wants to come home, and I don't know what to do with him or say to him. We are both to be pitied. God help us. Got a letter from Mrs Deady yesterday also dated Nov 28 at Baltimore. She was homesick for the first time since she has been gone and wrote me a scolding letter which I suppose I deserve or at least can bear. . . .

*13 (Sat)* . . . Sat in the C C & D C during the week. Trial jury came in the former. Tuesday & Wednesday tried Broderick v Sturges, a breach of promise case in which there was a verdict for the plaintiff for the sum of $1500. A number of well written and interesting letters of the parties were read in evidence. . . . [*Today*] Adjourned at 11 until Monday and went over to the Unitarian church to attend the funeral of my old friend Mr Orville Risley. At the request of the clergyman, Mr Eliot, I made a few remarks at the close of the service, in the course of which I referred to the fact that this day 35 years ago I walked into the town of Lafayette where I finished the final end of my long and weary journey across the plains where I first met the deceased. . . .

*20 (Sat)* . . . Commenced blowing and snowing on Monday night. Snow fell the next day near a foot in Portland and Wednesday at 8 oclock the thermometer stood at 14—the lowest point it had reached this year. The train from the east has not come through since Tuesday, being snowbound between here and the Dalles. Have not heard from Mrs Deady since this day week. . . .

*27 (Sat)* . . . Tried Balfour et al v City of Salem Co on Monday with a verdict for the pltf. Scotch Reid being a witness for the deft and his brotherinlaw, [William] Dunbar, a conflicting one for the pltf, the pltf impeached his character for truth and veracity by the oaths of Burns, Rogers, Macleay and Townsend. This suggests, when Scotchman swears at Scotchman then comes the tug of war.[34] . . .

Went to the Chapel to M prayer at 7 oclock Xmas morning and staid for the usual breakfast of buckwheat cakes and sausage. Gave Miss Lydia an illustrated hymn—"My faith looks up to The[e]," and she gave me a copy of Bishop Doanes poems—*Songs by the Way*. Went to M prayer at Trinity where Mr Foote preached an excellent sermon on the teaching of the life of Christ. The thermometer stood at 42 when the service commenced and 46 when it closed. Sat in my chambers all the afternoon and bathed my head in cold water for an ache. In the evening went to Catlins to the Henderson Xmas tree. There were 47 persons there including four generations, that is Grandpa and Ma Henderson and their three great grandchildren—Mary Strongs babies. The tree was beautiful and well laden with presents. Rachel Holman and family, Henry Failing and family and Judge Strong and family were there. There were more pretty girls in the company than I ever saw before under one roof. Mrs D got a handsome crazy quilt from her mother—her own handiwork.

On Xmas eve I sent Netta Brooke[35] a pretty portable French clock as a wedding present from Mrs Deady and myself with a note of congratulations which she answered very handsomely the next day. The clock was imported by Henrichsen from Paris and the price was $54 and he said it would cost $60 in a retail store in San Francisco. He let me have it for $40. I did not make many presents this year. Sent an illustrated book to each of Harveys, Johns & Wills children. Gave one to Elsie Failing & $2.50 worth of cake and candy to the Catlin tree. Gave Paul, a pocketbook, gloves, comb & nail brush, costing $5 and Mrs Hill a brass set hand glass worth $7½ which Ayer let me have Xmas eve for $5. I enclosed a slip of paper with the words "From your oldest boarder—when you look in the glass and see there a sweet honest face, remember the giver." She was much pleased with the glass and the words—particularly the latter and I was glad that she was. She deserved something. . . . During last night the weather moderated and the water was dripping from [the] roof this morning as if it were raining. The mercury at one oclock today stood at 44. I have been requested by the board of trade to act on a committee for the revision of the city charter. The committee met last night, but I could not meet with them; but will this afternoon at 2 oclock. I prepared the original charter in 1864 and the present one is substantially the same. . . .

*31 (Wed)*. . . Tuesday evening attended the dinner given by the Medical Society of Portland. A very pleasant affair and a good dinner. I had the place of honor on the right of Dr [S E] Josephi, the President, who presided admirably. Judge Williams, the only other non-medical man present except the press, sat on the right of Holt Wilson, the vice President. I responded to the first toast, The Bench, and spoke of the relations between the administration of justice and the medical profession, considered as experts, and the urgent need there was of a reformation in that particular. I don't think I was particularly happy in my remarks but Joe Levisson made a very pretty paragraph out of it in his report of the affair published in Wednesdays *Oregonian*. Got home with Dr Marvin, who represented "the cloth" at 2 in the morning . . . [This] evening attended a brilliant party at Lewis' in honor of the debut of Miss Eva. I danced with the debutante and Mrs Koehler. The refreshments were very good as usual. I had Mrs McKee to supper. Had quite a tete a tete with Mrs Effinger. Willy and I bowed to one another and nothing more.[36] . . .

# NOTES

1. A huge deficit put the N.P.R.R. Co. into receivership and Villard had been forced out as president.

2. Horace E. Nicholas (1850–1922), Portland attorney; for a time associated with John Catlin.

3. The Dundee Mortgage Trust and Investment Co. vs School District No. 1, arose out of application of an act of 1882 "whereby land or real property, situate in no more than one county of this state, is made security for the payment of a debt, together with such debt, shall, for the purposes of assessment and taxation, be deemed and treated as land and real property." The Dundee Mortgage Trust and Investment Co. was a foreign corporation with headquarters at Dundee, Scotland. It therefore qualified to bring action in the federal court. Deady granted the injunction prayed for on the grounds that the act was unconstitutional.

4. Jeannie Maire and Andrew Robertson. Mr. Robertson operated a "hot Scotch shop."

5. The N.P.R.R. Co., in order to effect economies, had discharged a number of men, some of them train crews, at Pendleton, then a tiny community. The discharged men demanded they be allowed to ride the freightcars free to Portland, where they might find some opportunity for employment. When the railroad company refused, the men attempted to take over the cars by force. They were accused of obstructing the mails.

6. Sarah B. Ingersoll Cooper (1836–96), philanthropist; founded a number of free kindergartens in the San Francisco area. Her daughter, Harriet, worked with her.

7. B. Goldsmith had purchased a portion of the Balch claim. Litigation arose over the ownership of certain lots and portions thereof along the common line.

8. Patrick Keefe, a Sitka saloonkeeper, had shot and killed a personal friend, one William Morton. Keefe was apparently deranged.

9. G. W. Goucher (1829–93), Amity physician, and E. E. Goucher (1858–1936), McMinnville physician.

10. George C. Perkins (1839–1923), banker, shipowner and politician; governor of California, 1880–83. Milton Andros, San Francisco attorney.

11. The extended sea voyage as a treatment for alcoholism was not uncommon at this time. Around the turn of the present century one semi-prominent Portlander, rather more economical than Deady, arranged to have his son "shanghaied" and placed aboard a ship bound for the Orient. In that case the cure was complete. The young man contracted tuberculosis and died shortly after returning home.

12. Jacob Thompson (1827–1911), Ashland liveryman. Tom Smith (1809–c.1910), miner and farmer. John M. McCall (1825–95), flour and woolen mill owner.

13. Cornelius C. Beekman (1828–1915), Jacksonville banker and express agent. R. S. Dunlap was sexton of the Jacksonville Cemetery until his retirement in 1904, having then served for more than 30 years. He moved to the Oregon Soldiers' Home at Roseburg and presumably died there.

14. Peter Britt (1819–1905), pioneer Jacksonville photographer. Elizabeth T'Vault Kinney (1834–1911), widow of Daniel M. Kinney (died 1860), Jacksonville attorney. Rhoda

Boone Burns T'Vault (1810–86), widow of Wm. G. T'Vault. Elizabeth Thurston Odell (c. 1816–90); her first husband, Samuel Thurston, (1816–51), was Oregon's first territorial delegate. She subsequently married Wm. H. Odell (1830–1922), surveyor and newspaperman.

15. Estelle Bush (c. 1856–1942), married Claude Thayer (1858-1923), the son of former Governor W. W. Thayer. They lived in Tillamook, where they operated a small bank. The young man was slightly lame, which explains Deady's punning reference.

16. B. B. Beekman (1863–1945), son of Cornelius Beekman; he later practiced law at Portland. Richard H. Thornton (1845–1925), attorney, law professor and dean of the U. of O. law school. Ebenezer B. MacElroy (1842–1901), educator; superintendent of public instruction, 1882–90.

17. Offenbach's comic "Orphée aux Enfers" was commonly played as "Orpheus and Eurydice," the title of Gluck's great work. Marie Aimée made her New York debut at the Grand Opera House in 1870; she was particularly successful in opera bouffe.

18. C. W. Townsend, draftsman for the River Department, O.R. & N. Co.

19. James C. Mackenzie (1852–1931), Prebyterian clergyman and educator; founder of Lawrenceville School (in New Jersey) and its headmaster, 1882–99.

20. Edward B. Watson (1844–1915), lawyer and jurist; justice of the state supreme court, 1880–84. Sol Abrams (1828–1901), Roseburg merchant. David Lowery Watson (1842–1917), county judge, Coos County, 1866–94. Those inclined to believe this kind of story may believe this one, though it is delivered to Deady third hand.

21. Penumbra Kelly (1845–1908), logger, rancher and public official.

22. George Willis Cooke; he was a Unitarian clergyman.

23. Charles B. Wright, president of the N.P.R.R. Co., 1874–79. Barbara Muller, wife of Henry, partner in the furniture firm of Muller & Hannemann. She died, 1890, aged 44. Mr. Scott of Philadelphia cannot be positively identified.

24. George Ivens, Mr. George, and George H. Williams; hence Williams was George the Third.

25. Deady's own conscience was clear. The cases brought by the other stockholders against Ladd, Reed, Ainsworth and Thompson were settled, largely because of misgivings on the part of Ladd, who had been acting as trustee and agent for some of the plaintiffs. (See 1871, Appendix D.)

26. For Charles Erskine Scott Wood, see DP.

27. John H. Hall (1828–91), paper manufacturer and financier; a director of both the O. R. & N. Co. and the N.P.R.R. Co.

28. On June 11, 1884, Bishop Morris wrote Judge Deady as follows: "I think I ought to show you the enclosed letter which was returned to the Grammar School a few days since. No one has seen it but Mrs. Morris & Myself—& no others will know of it—except Henderson & Willie.

"Very improper letters, though not of *this* character—from Henderson to one of the girls at the Hall, have been intercepted & I have forbidden his visits to them. I saw Henderson at the wharf, as Mr. Plummer's party was leaving, & told him that I should send the letter to you. He told me there was nothing in Willie's letter to him to call out a reply of this character, and that Willie had never written Such a Style to him. Of course I know that you will be deeply grieved at this discovery . . ." The Judge apparently felt less grief than grievance.

29. George C. Miln was a Congregationalist minister out of New York state who had dramatic aspirations.

30. Capt. Frederick Bolles for many years captained ships on the Portland—San Francisco run.

31. Honoring Sir Moses Haim Montefiore (1784–1884), the great Jewish philanthropist.

32. Louise Humphrey Smith was a local teacher of elocution.

33. Oliver P. Shiras (1833–1916), Iowa attorney and jurist. Jeannie Winston; singer,

dancer and comedienne. John Malone, actor; made New York debut in 1880; supported Warde, Booth and Otis Skinner. His father, Pat Malone, had been a journalist in Oregon before moving to California.

34. William Dunbar, as an official of the defendant, City of Salem Co., ordered 50,000 sacks at 8.275 cents per sack from the plaintiff, Balfour Guthrie. When the sacks were delivered, William Reid as president of the defendant company refused to accept them. Balfour Guthrie was forced to sell the sacks at a lower figure and sued for the difference. Reid insisted Dunbar was not authorized to make the purchase. Dunbar insisted that Reid had so authorized him. Dunbar's future career is instructive. Shortly after Judge Deady's death, he, with a number of others including James Lotan, sometime collector of customs at Portland, and Seid Back, Portland's leading Chinese merchant, were convicted of smuggling opium and Chinese subjects into the Northwest. Dunbar escaped to China where he remained for 20 years, or until 1914, when it was arranged that he should return and make payment of a $1,000 fine.

35. Netta Brooke was marrying Lieut. J. S. Parke, U. S. Army. He retired in 1916 after 38 years of service.

36. Simeon E. Josephi (1849–1935), physician; member of faculty, Willamette Medical School; dean of the U. of O. Medical School; a sometimes controversial figure. Newman J. (Joe) Levinson, then city editor, the *Oregonian;* he was later associate editor, the *Telegram.* Deady's relations with Col. Effinger were increasingly chilly.

C. E. S. Wood, rising attorney.

Estelle Bush (Deady album).

Mrs. Deady took Henderson to the Lawrenceville (N. J.) School in 1884. Photographed in Baltimore where she visited, she wears the sealskin sack and muff. The diamonds are not visible.

1884 election scene in Jacksonville. (Britt Collection.)

In Jacksonville, Oregon, the Deadys in 1884 visited photographer Peter Britt's home (still standing). (Britt Collection.)

Jacksonville, an 1885 Britt photo, with courthouse (with cupola) right center (now a museum).

Rev. Thomas Lamb Eliot. (Buchtel & Stolte.)

William "Dundee" Reid. (Buchtel & Stolte.)

Portland waterfront, early 1880s. Stark Street ferry right.

# 1885

*January 3 (Sat)* New Year . . . remained in my chambers all day doing chores, writing and adding my accounts and writing to Mrs Deady & Henderson. Sent off the letters by steamer which sailed at midnight. . . .

Friday, prepared 4 subdivisions of sec 37 of the charter, in place of the present 3, 4 and 5, concerning the licensing, taxing, regulating and restraining certain professions, trades and employments; and providing for the punishment of gamesters, whores and whoremongers and opium smokers. Met with the Committee on revision of charter in the evening at the Council Chamber, where my amendments were adopted with one or two additions—ins agents & livery stables.[1]

Had a telegram from Mrs Deady this morning dated Jan 2 at Washington. Just returned from Baltimore. Henderson at school. I have just telegraphed her $100 through L & T. Footmen brought the letter mail down from the delayed train last evening. . . .

Found that I have received during the year from all sources $6796.06, and after paying all my current bills including the $100 sent Mrs Deady this morning and my annual contribution of $10 to the G S Hospital, I have $217.33 in bank. During the year I paid $900 for diamonds for Mrs D.

I still owe $272 for furs and $115 for books and $40 for a present to Netta Brooke, in all $422.

*10 (Sat)* . . . Engaged much of the time [*this week*] in drafting and redrafting provisions of the new charter. Sunday afternoon drafted a scheme for a board of commissioners to have the patronage of the city government, make all appointments and removals from office and employ all persons in the fire and police departments and supervise the discharge of their duties, and on Monday redrafted Chap 9 of the charter on the subject of opening and widening streets. This was mostly a mass of obscure verbiage, originally contained in an independent act passed for that purpose and subsequently transferred to the charter in some revision. I put a days work on it and made something intelligible of it at least. Moreland was on the committee with me and gave me some valuable suggestions, which I put in. At the meeting on Monday the report was adopted as a whole. My scheme for a city commission was then thoroughly discussed and adopted with only three votes in the negative—Pennoyer, [B] O'Hara & [D P] Thompson—out of 13. Afterwards I drafted and put into shape Mr Failings ideas about Commissioner of Streets and public works which title I furnished him in debate. I put this in good working order also. I also drafted a chapter for the fire department, taking the act of 1882 largely as my guide, after weeding out the most of it. At the meeting on Thursday night both these drafts were adopted and also two sections which I drafted, one for repeal and the other as to the act taking effect and the disposition of the present incumbents of the city offices.[2] On Wednesday morning at 1:30 the delayed train came through from the east with about 500 passengers and the mails. . . .

Friday evening heard "Fra Diavolo" at the Casino and was much pleased with it. Kinross was magnificent in the wolf song. I never heard it all before. The music of the song—"On yonder rock reclining" was tune number 2 in the band which I once belonged to in Barnesville, and is among the first airs whose melody I mastered. The sound of it brought back many associations. The house was packed. During the evening I visited Mrs Goldsmith in her box and sat with her during the second act.

. . . On Monday evening attended a meeting of the Shakespeare club at Arnolds and had a pleasant time. Walked home with Mrs Montgomery. The snow is about gone except a few secluded places. The weather has been charming the latter portion of the week. Got my invitation yesterday to Netta Brookes wedding on the 14th inst. . . . Finished "Antony and Cleopatra." The Egyptian doesn't appear to advantage and probably ought not.

*17 (Sat)*. . . Wednesday evening attended Brooke-Parke wedding at Trinity and the reception at Mr Brookes. The church was packed full. The bride was elegantly dressed and the six maids looked pretty and picturesque—the ushers were all of the Army except young Morrow and Paul Deady. The Bishop and Mr Foote jointly officiated.

The reception at the house was very pleasant. The refreshments were delicious, the champagne abundant and excellent. After supper there was dancing. I took part in one Lancers with Miss Pettis. Got home at 2 oclock in good condition. Kissed the bride and presented her with a bo[u]quet. . . .

*24 (Sat)*. . . Went to see "Boccacio" at the Casino on Monday evening. Came away at the end of the second act tired. Took Mrs Catlin and Paul and Mrs McKee to the Casino this evening to see the "Prince Methusalem," which we rather enjoyed. My throat is quite sore, commenced yesterday morning. Got a telegram from Mrs Deady this evening.

*31 (Sat)*. . . My throat very sore during the week—the vocal chords much affected and about Thursday developed into a cold in the head with coughing. Am better now but cough painful and severe at times. Drank some Ponds extract [*witch hazel*] this morning. Missed the parlor theatricals at Lewis' on Wednesday evening on account of my cold. Got two letters from Mrs D—one the 20th the other the 22–3 and also two from H B. Mrs D is well again and enjoying Washington festivities much and don't know when she will come home. I look for her the middle to the last of February. Had a letter from Justice Field yesterday in which he informed me that the second photograph of himself that I received on Xmas was intended for Mrs George H Williams (Aunt Kate). I sent it to her this morning with a note. Had a rule served on me this morning to show cause why a mandamus should not issue to compel me to direct the payment to [Ellis] Hughes of the balance of the attorney fee in the MacAllister case. Hipple attorney of course. It shows an ugly and contentious spirit on the part of Hughes which I may remember hereafter.[3] Have not done much this week, not been able to. Did a little miscellaneous reading in the magazines. Read "Much Ado about Nothing" . . . last evening. How improbable the final action of Leonato and Claudio is in the matter. But the piece sparkles with the verbal wit and double entendre of Benedick and Beatrice. But after all, I imagine the official stupidity and drollery of Dogberry has done more to give the play its circulation and celebrity than anything else. This is a lovely day. The sun shining bright and warm with a soft light mist or haze in the distance . . .

*February 7 (Sat)* . . . Had a note from Bishop Morris asking me to call and see Bishops Sillitoe and Paddock at his house on Wednesday. Could not go on account of library meeting. Saw Bishop S and wife at Mrs Williams. They remembered me from meeting me at New Westminster in 1880 and spoke with me. I suppose I must call this afternoon on them, though I don't feel like going into Bishop Ms house. I am invited to Mr Goods today to dinner at 6 and at Molsons tomorrow at the same hour. Got a telegram and letter from Mrs D yesterday. Says she will leave for home on the 11th at the farthest.

Called at the Bishops a little after 4 on Bishop & Mrs Sillitoe & Bishop Paddock. Met a good many people there. . . . I rather liked the Sillitoes—apron and leggins notwithstanding. She was much dressed in comparison with her good sister, Mrs Morris, and exposed somewhat a very pretty neck indeed. Brooke, who was there says he saw more of her in that short time than he had of Mrs Morris in many years of acquaintance.

*14 (Sat)* . . . Went to Salem on Wednesday evening and attended Gov & Mrs Moodys reception. Quite an affair. Some 4 or 500 people present. They were better dressed and mannered than any crowd I ever saw at Salem before. Staid with Mrs Holman. Returned home Thursday morning. Dr Marvin went up and came back with me. . . .

*21 (Sat)* Sunday . . . Henry Failing called at my chambers at ½ past 1 and consulted me about the propriety of allowing Tim Davenport to publish a letter of his to Tim on the subject of corporations, National Banks, civil service reform &c. The letter was written in reply [to] one from Davenport asking his views on these subjects in view of the fact that he was a possible candidate for the Senate. The letter was a shrewd and sensible [one] and as long as it had been written I advised him to consent to its publication. At his suggestion I examined it and suggested some verbal alterations. But I have not seen it in print.

. . . Monday had a telegram from Mrs D that she would leave Washington that day, and yesterday had a telegram from Springdale, Mon[tana] that she would be at the Dalles tonight. I am going up on the train this afternoon to meet her. Edward Failing is going east on the same train. Mrs D and I will get here tomorrow afternoon. It is now near six months since she went away, and I am quite elated at the thought of meeting her. Her old Father & Mother have been waiting here patiently to see her for weeks. . . . [*Wednesday*] afternoon left on the eastbound train to meet Mrs Deady. Edward Failing was with me—he being bound to New York where he has not been since 1852. Staid about 6 hours at the Dalles and reached Alkali, between one and two Sunday morning where I met the westbound train and found Mrs Deady in a private car with Mrs Muir. Got home 15 min after one, the day was beautiful and the ride lovely. The family soon commenced pouring in to see Mrs D and the house, or rather her rooms were filled up with an eager happy crowd ranging from 5 to 75 years of age. In the evening the Brookes and Stotts came in—the former staying until late. Mrs Deady left home on Aug 30th and was gone six months, lacking six days. . . .

*28 (Sat)* . . . Tom Strong called on me on Monday and wanted me to postpone his Seeley cases until Sawyer was on the Bench and suggested that his client was alarmed on account of rumors &c.[A] When pressed to state what they were he said that the defendants—Ladd & Reed, I suppose—had furnished $2000 for Mrs Deady to go east on and the same amount for Henderson to go to school on. I felt like kicking him out. He is as big a fool as his father. I told him I would not comply with his wishes and that he ought to be ashamed to make a request based on such reasons. Mrs Deady and Henderson went east before the suits were commenced. Mrs D spent $1000, which was her own money, that her brother John has had loaned [out] for her some years in Yamhill. As for Henderson, I am paying for him by the term, and it doesn't cost me as much as it did when he was here. . . .

*March 21 (Sat)* . . . Friday [*March 13*] went to Eugene to attend meeting of Regents. Took Mrs D and Lucy Failing with me. Brought the latter back and the former remained with her sister Mrs Murch. Henry Failing went up also and his daughters Etta & Millie as far as Albany. The Regents met and considered the subject of the new building for which the last legislature appropriated $30,000, and adjourned to meet at my chambers on the evening of the 8th proximo. Came home on Saturday. The weather was lovely and the country looked beautiful. Some persons told me that Prof Condon was the source of the opposition to my reappointment as Regent, whatever there was of it. But it is just as well for me to know nothing and think nothing about it.

. . . Tuesday the 17th San Pat had possession of Portland. Having concluded the draft of the opinion [*in the Or Ry Co case*] by evening I went to the New Market to hear a play produced by Irish R C society in which the Irish tenant is arrayed against his landlord or rather his agent as usual. A young man by the name of O'Reily delivered a eulogism on Ireland, which was well composed and declaimed, but was in the main a stranger to truth. He asserted in almost so many words that Ireland was the seat of Christianity and that the Faith was carried from there all over Europe including even Italy itself. From there about 10 oclock I went to the Ball of the H[ibernian] B[enevolent] S[ociety] to which I had a complimentary invitation. There I staid an hour and was made welcome, and came home. This is not a church society and holds its annual ball on San Pats Day in despite of the protest of the clergy. The assembly was composed of decent common people who enjoyed themselves immensely, and when they balanced to partners instead of dancing to one another they clasped their arms around one another and spun around on their heels like a top. Wednesday I got a letter from Lawrenceville that Henderson had 18 marks and would be suspended at 20. I telegraphed him the same day,—"You have 18 marks. Save yourself by all means," and wrote him and Dr Mackenzie on the subject. On the 10th of February he only had 6⅔ marks. Something serious must have happened. Mrs Deady returned from Eugene on Thursday. It is good to get her home again. Wrote a letter to Judge Strong yesterday commending him to the President for the office of Minister Resident at the Hawaiian Islands or Gov of Washington Territory. He asked me for it, and I couldn't refuse him, but I am afraid his mind is affected—indeed I am not certain that he was ever altogether sane or well balanced. . . .

*28 (Sat)* . . . Friday decided three cases in C C and admitted Mary A Leonard to the bar.⁴ . . .

*April 4 (Sat)* . . . Wednesday April 1 settled and paid off quarter bills, spring taxes included. The latter are very high this year. $114.20 for State & Co $57.70 for City and School $20.30 in all $192.20. Paid out in all $509.18, leaving only $79.75 to my credit, to which I added on the same day a deposit of $75 = $154.75. Good Friday I held no court and attended morning prayer at Trinity. Quite a congregation present—the women as usual being largely in the majority. If some men are saved it will be by their wives. . . .

*11 (Sat)* . . . Sawyer arrived this afternoon. Met him at the Gilman. . . .

*18 (Sat)* . . . Tuesday evening dined with Judge Sawyer and Mr Andros at Aliskys restaurant. A good dinner and a pleasant time. Wednesday heard the Seeley cases on demurrer to the bills for multifariousness. Dems sustained and plaintiff had leave to file amended bills against Reed & the company, Smith Bros & Watson & the company and a new bill against Ladd if he desired. Sawyer delivered the opinion and I hope Tom Strong is satisfied.

Sawyer left on the steamer Wednesday night. Had a pleasant time with him and got a good many items. He is urgent that I shall come down in the fall and try the Sharon case if it goes to trial on the merit.

We changed Rule one of the circuit court so as to provide for the appointment by the court of a committee of 6 on admission to the bar, and that an applicant for admission shall have the certificate of some two of these as to his moral character and professional standing. We also appointed George H Durham standing master in chancery and examiner of the court.

Thursday, attended Henry Greens funeral as pall bearer. Took place from the house. Rather a private affair. Coffin loaded with flowers. I won't say ad nauseum for they were beautiful, but to such excess that they lost their significance. The face looked very natural. It showered a good deal of the time at the house and on the way to the cemetery but fortunately was dry during the interment. Mr Foote officiated and looked seraphic.

In the evening went to the concert of the St Andrews Society with Mrs D. It was a sort of slovenly affair. [Jeannie] Winston came late but sang two songs and two encores. One was "Come Under My Plaidee." A Mrs Irvin sang two or three Scotch songs in an excellent voice, naturally and with good effect. One was

"Robin Adair." Winston was dressed beautifully, but was painted and acted like a wanton. Took the DeHarts with us to Aliskys and had some oysters.

*25 (Sat)* . . . Dined last evening at the Arlington Club with Mr Macleay and Robertson. Sat at the table until 12 and sipped champagne and chatted about the Old Country and the new Burns, Walter Scott, &c&c. A very pleasant evening. . . . Today I was called as a witness upon the application of the Strongs to have a guardian appointed for their father and testified that I thought his mind was impaired and that he was liable to waste his property.[5] He was there and cross-examined me. . . .

*May 2 (Sat)* . . . From the morning paper saw that the ship *Helicon* had arrived at Victoria from Hong Kong on the 25th ult. Edward is on her. Had a note from him since dated the 27th saying he wanted to come home and wanted money. Telegraphed Capt Howes on the 30th to bring him over with him today as I understood that he was coming here. Got a dispatch from him this morning to the effect that he was not coming and would write. Wonder what the result will be.

. . . Attended a party with Mrs Deady at McKees on Thursday evening. A lovely affair and an elegant supper. Staid until three oclock in the morning to witness the German. Mrs Deady and Mrs Ladd presided at the table w[h]ere the favors were distributed. They both looked well and I may be excused if I say very well. Paul was there looking as handsome as anyone. . . .

*9 (Sat)* . . . Wednesday evening attended a library meeting and passed a preamble and resolution settling the terms of the purchase of the north ½ of block 214 for the library. I feel like congratulating myself now that this is accomplished. Henry Failing raised $8000 for the purchase and the remaining $12,000 will be paid out of the fund on hand or borrowed at 7 per centum while ours is bearing ten per centum. . . .

*16 (Sat)* . . . Thursday went to Corvallis taking Mrs Deady and her two sisters, Mrs Catlin and Mrs Strong with me. Stopped at Mrs [S A] Hemphills. Mr [Wallis] Nash met us at the depot in a carriage. In the evening we went to his house to supper—the ladies going out in the carriage and he and I walking. The place is about a mile back of town on a pretty elevation on the Agricultural College farm. The Nashs have been and are somebody but they are evidently poorer than they have been sometime in their lives. She is a fine looking, heavy, serious, genteel appearing Englishwoman. Friday we drove in the afternoon to Philomath about 7 miles west of Corvallis. The ride was a pleasant one and the country exceedingly picturesque. Called at Mrs Averys when we came back. Met Mrs Holgate there, nee Ann Watt, who came to meet us and was very glad to see us. She went to school to me in the winter of 1849–50 and I was at her wedding 25 years ago. She looked and appeared very well. Mrs Avery looks old but very well and is very comfortably fixed. In the evening took a walk up the river and had Prof [B L] Arnold and [E] Grim[m] call on us later and also Mr & Mrs [James] Cauthorn —nee Martha Mulkey. On Friday morning called on John Burnett and he accompanied me to the Agricultural College, where I met Prof Arnold and [W W] Bristow. Had a pleasant visit with the former. Came home today, John Burnett and daughter on the train.[6] Got acquainted with her and found out her mother is a daughter of Roland Hinton whom I used to know in early days about 14 miles south of Corvallis whose wife was a Richardson, sister of "Old Doc" [*Aaron*] Richardson, which accounts for her looking so much like the McBrides, who are closely related to the Richardsons. On the whole she is a bright interesting woman, though not highly cultivated. The weather has been variable from bright sunshine to cool and cloudy with a few light showers. Corvallis has grown much in the last ten years and the shade trees in which it abounds have grown still more. Found an invitation to Queens birthday dinner when I got home, for tonight. Don't think I can attend. It is good to decline sometimes. I see I am expected to respond to the toast—the Army and Navy of Great Britain & the U S—which is not in my line anyway . . .

*23 (Sun)*. . . Friday evening took Mrs Deady and Blanche Catlin to New Market to hear "Virginius" by [Frederick] Warde. It was well played throughout. Some common places in the composition that do not harmonize with the surroundings. It has rained most of the week, but looks now as if it might clear off. Have been reading . . . Fitzjames Stephens *History of the Criminal Law*. D'Anestys case, which he cites as showing the inconvenience of following the King in the Curia Regis round the country to get justice, which led to the localization and separation of the common pleas, is a very extraordinary one. The suit was to recover his uncles land and because there was a question of the validity of a marriage involved he had to send twice to Rome for a writ from the Pope to try the case. No wonder they reformed the papacy out of England. Friday purchased a ticket for Edward to come from Victoria here and wrote him to the care of Welch Rithet[7] at Victoria enclosing $5. Got a telegram on the morning of the same day from Capt Howes advising me that he would send Edward from Nanaimo to Victoria on Tuesday next.

In the evening attended the Queens Birthday dinner at the Esmond. Sat on the right of the president Mr [James] Cameron[8] and responded to the toast "The Armies and Navies of Great Britain and the United States." My remarks are public. . . .

*30 (Sat)*. . . Weather moist and cool the first of the week, but warm and dry since until today which is a little overhanging. Thursday had a letter from Capt Howes of the *Helicon* from Nanaimo dated 25th saying that Edward would leave for Victoria on the 26th, that the balance due him including something for watching ship there was $4.17 and that he had sold his bed and blanket for $5. He has not come home yet but Paul learned from a passenger who left Victoria on Thursday that he was there on Wednesday and sober, and expected to come over with him.

Wednesday got a nativity from W H Chaney of myself which both amused and interested me.[9] There are certainly some singular coincidences in it. This is Decoration day and the soldiers and firemen have been drilling and parading in front of my chambers, and great crowds of people have collected here to look on to see the supposed stay of the country in the day and hour of danger. . . .

*June 6 (Sat)* Sunday (May 31) . . . About ½ past 1 Edward came home, after a voyage to Melbourne, Sidney, Hong Kong and return to Victoria, B C of over a year on the ship *Helicon,* having left the Sound on her on May 9, 1884. He was looking well and duly sober. He has been living with us at Mrs Hills and I hope is going to do well.

Sat in the C C & D C during the week. Worked on the application of Dis Atty to enter satisfaction of judgment in U S v Griswold—a disgraceful transaction in which Hipple is managing the treasury dept for the benefit of as great a rogue as himself.[10]. . .

Thursday evening dined at Gen Miles, with Senator Sherman and Mr John [*sic*] Francis Adams. Went over in the afternoon on the *Wide West* with Prescott, Mr Adams, who had just arrived overland on the Oregon Short Line, Judge Williams, Henry Failing and Donald Macleay, who constituted the dinner party with the additon of Col [L C] Hunt of the 14th Inf and young Mr [Frank] Sherman of Iowa. The dinner was very good and the party pleasant. I sat at my hosts left and Mr Adams at his right. The Senator occupied the other end of the table with Judge W on his right and Mr Failing on his left. I had Mr Prescott on my left and found him a very pleasant companion on such an occasion. The host did well and looked the same. Mr Adams gave us an epitaph on Ebenezer Rockwood Hoar:[11] "Here lies E R H who when judge of the Supreme Court of Mass always regretted that he could not decide against both parties and that while Atty Genl of the U S had the pleasure of snubb[ing] 70 Senators." No wonder the Senate refused to confirm his nomination as Justice of the Supreme Court. We returned to Portland on the *W W* by 10 oclock.

Friday afternoon I attended the reception given by the Board of Trade to Sherman and Adams at the Masonic Hall, and sat on the platform. S & A made good speeches for the occasion which are fairly reported in this mornings *Oregonian.* Adams talked well on railway management. . . .

Today (this morning) Senator Sherman & nephew called at my chambers while I was in court. Had him on the bench a little while and then a pleasant call from him in my chambers for a ½ an hour. Adams went up the valley yesterday evening and the party goes to the Sound today. Weather cloudy and cool. Called at the Hall in the evening [on] Miss Lydia, still unwell. . . .

*13 (Sat)* . . . Tuesday attended the graduating exercises at St Helens Hall. Millie Failing the only graduate. She looked both lovely and womanly for so young a person and read an excellent essay on early Christian art and a French composition that I will [not] attempt to criticize except that it was easily and naturally spoken. Mr Thornton delivered the address, which he entitled "Needlework" for the reason I suppose that there was very little if anything about that kind of work in it. There was something about Christian art and puritan iconoclasm and ugliness that was well said but out of place.

At the Convocation today, a report was read giving forms of establishing a mission which was the work of the same hand, in which the Bishop was addressed as the Right Reverend Father in God and made to describe himself as "We Benjamin, by the Divine Grace &c." I moved to refer the matter to the Bishop and the standing committee saying that the language and conception of this

# JUNE 1885

scheme was archaic and unAmerican, which was done. There is a disease which affects certain scholarly good people that ought to be called d____d foolism and this is an instance of the same.

*20 (Sat)* . . . [*Monday*] Intended to go to Oregon City to the Pioneer reunion, but at the time of starting (10 oclock) it began to rain and I gave it up and worked . . . I read Williams speech since, and it reads well. He does that kind of thing about as well as anyone. Wednesday had a telegram from McArthur announcing Nesmiths death at 15 min to 12 that day. Went to Eugene on Thursday. Fell in with Henry Failing on the Ferry (Stark St) bound for the same place, the annual meeting of the Regents of the U of O. At the station we boarded what we supposed to be the train when we found ourselves among the Iowa Journalists. I soon stumbled on Gov Moody who introduced me to Dr [Geo F] Magoun, Pres of the Iowa college, Mr [C F] Clarkson the oldest editor in the state and the agricultural editor of the *State Register* and Mr John Makin of the *Journal,* Muscatine. The party verified my idea of Iowa people, that like the state, they are a very good average lot, with neither great nor small. At Salem we took the regular train, the excursionists going into town for a few hours. Failing and I were carried down into town on the train and had to run for the station to catch the regular train. I fell behind and F just made it and stopped the train until I came up. At Eugene had a meeting of the Regents, and adjourned to see the excursionists about 4 oclock, who spent half an hour at the station talking and being talked at in return. Had an evening session until 10 when Failing, Bush and I went to the reunion at Mrs Underwoods. Had another session in the morning of Friday. A good deal of talk and not much doing. Awarded the contract to build the new U building at $18,000 and some odd dollars. Friday took the train for the north. Lucy Murch, Miss Etta and Emily Failing on board and Gov Moody, Mr Bush and Dr Anderson also. At Salem Mr F, B and myself got into Gov Moodys carriage and he drove us to Nesmiths where I met Mrs Deady and Edward. The burial service of the Episcopal church was read by the Rev Mr [J T] Chambers of Salem and then we followed the body to the grave, myself and 11 others, including ex Senators Kelly, Corbett, Gov Moody, Mr Bush & Failing walking beside the hearse as pall bearers and 100 neighbors and pioneers walking in front. We walked up the creek a half mile to the bridge crossed over and down about half as far on the south side to a high point on the Ric[k]reall in a clump of fir timber where we buried him. About 9 oclock the McMinnville express train backed up to Nesmiths and we who were northward bound ran down on it to McMinn. Mrs Deady remained and Mrs Wilson came on. At 15 min before 6 we started for Portland and got here at ½ past 8. Barnhart and his son Henry came down with us. On the way down H F gave me an account of the inside of the late O[regon] R[ailway] & N[avigation] election which resulted in placing Mr Ives[12] in the board by the votes of the Oregon stockholders.

Today, wrote an account of Nesmiths funeral for the *Oregonian,* at the request of the family made by McArthur. Got a good selection from Shakespeare to begin and end with. Will be published in Sundays paper. In the evening attended a banquet given by the Board of trade to the Iowa Journalists at the Masonic hall.

*469*

Donald Macleay presided. At his right sat Mr [A W] Swalm the President of the editorial Association.[13] I sat next to him and Mrs Swalm on my right whom I found a well educated, sensible pleasant lady. There were covers for about 300 persons. The dinner was fair and the company good, and we did not get through until near one oclock. I proposed the toast—The State of Iowa, upon very short notice and did tolerably well.

*27 (Sat)* Sunday (June 21) . . . The proceedings of the banquet are published in this mornings *Oregonian*. The address of Macleay and the speeches of Williams, Woods and Holman are given at length, while mine is well condensed into a few lines. But theirs were written out and furnished to the paper beforehand, while mine was in a great measure impromptu and made without a note.

. . . Friday wrote an article for the *Oregonian* on the early laws of Oregon, showing the derivation from Iowa, the same being an amplification of some thoughts thrown out in my remarks at the banquet. Called at the Hall in the evening and saw the Misses Rodney. Shocked them by speaking jocularly of ritualism as "frippery," which was really more than I meant, but Miss C is so thoroughly dozed on the subject, that nothing less than strong terms will affect her.

*28 (Sun)* Attended . . . Trinity as usual. Attended the Baptist church in the evening and saw Henrietta Failing baptized—immersed. The preacher, Mr [J Q A] Henry, treated us to a long, loud, and common discourse on some fancied analogy between the Hebrew cities of refuge, and our relations to God as a refuge from our sins. I felt sad when I thought of these nice, cultivated girls of Edward Failings being stupified and commoned by this material, noisy nonsense not a whit above the level of peasants and proletaires. . . .

*July 4 (Sat)* . . . [*During the week*] Prepared my Oration for today. Made it out of my Roseburg Oration of 1877. Wrote a Portland prologue for it and some reflections on the origin of the Thirteen Colonies, the germ of which was in a speech I made at the Queens birthday dinner some years ago.

Today rode in the procession with the chaplain, Rev Mr [G W] Chandler of the Methodist church, Mr [Henry] Northrup, the Reader, and Mr Dodd, the President of the day, and delivered the Oration from a stand in front of the court house. I held my manuscript in my hand and indulged in some gesticulation and demonstration. I spoke about ¾ of an hour and did quite well, better than I ever did before, and was much congratulated. As to the matter of the speech, I know that it is good from my standpoint and pretty well put together from any standpoint. Northrup read the declaration better than I ever heard it read and Mrs [Louise] Smith declaimed Drakes address to the American Flag superbly. The day was very warm.

*11 (Sat)* . . . Thursday, Mr Goode, the Solicitor General called. A pleasant, respectable looking gentleman. Mr Elijah Smith, Pres of the O R & N Co and Mr [Robt] Harris, Pres of the N P Ry Co called during the week.[14] Smith looks like a rugged jolly fellow. The thermometer touched 100 in the shade this week—I think on Monday. The committee of arrangements have noted to publish 500 copies of my "able and patriotic" oration in pamphlet form and I have prepared the copy for them.

Examined the Marshals and Pauls accounts today in the C C—the latter $300.[15]. . .

*25 (Sat)*. . . Grant died Thursday morning at 8 oclock and we had the news the same morning in the *Oregonian* for breakfast. Three hours difference in time made [this possible]. Died from a cancer produced by excessive smoking—"Better is he that ruleth his spirit than he that taketh a city." Everybody is trying to out-mourn his neighbor—or appear to. If he had died a year ago, the result would have been very different. He was great I suppose in war but certainly little in peace. He meant well enough probably, but his taste for low company kept him in a bad atmosphere. His second term as President was the most corrupt and low we ever had or have had since. . . .

Got a letter this evening from Sawyer with a check for $123.90, being one half of the royalty at 60 cts per volume on the sale of *Sawyers Reports* for the half year ending June 30th. Heretofore I have only had one third, but furnished fully one half of the matter. This report of sales includes the first sale of *9 Sawyer.* Sawyer has set the Sharon-Hill case[B] for the 8th of September for me to try. . . .

*August 1 (Sat)*. . . Thursday attended a meeting of the Board of Trade by invitation of the President to hear an address from the latter to Senator Dolph and his reply. Both did very well and kept within the bounds of good taste. . . . Mr Charles E Whitehead, a lawyer of New York, called and presented a letter from Hall McAllister. Told me the story of Barnes (W H L) "kissing and telling of it" when he was a young man at Yale and for which he was thrown into Coventry and denied graduation by his class. The ladys name was Lillie Devereux, and is now married the second time and [is] Mrs Blake, a distinguished womans rights woman.[16] Had a letter from Miss Lee this morning anent my oration . . . Bright and pleasant. . . .

*8 (Sat)*. . . Mailed and distributed some 200 copies of the pamphlet containing my Fourth of July Oration. A beautiful pamphlet printed by Walling at the expense of the Com on arrangements. Wednesday evening Dr Curtis C Strong drove me out to his mountain summer home where I had dinner with Alice and the children. Got back by 15 minutes to 8 in time for the library meeting. Just 40 minutes coming in—4½ miles. . . .

Friday evening Agnes Catlin and I went with the Brookes to the New Market to see "The Private Secretary." It is a silly lot of common place horse play. I was bored to death.

*15 (Sat)* Sunday August 9th. Attended S S and read morning prayer at Trinity and a sermon of the Rev Phil[l]ips Brooks on the text from the Corinthians— "Brethren the time is short." Quite a good congregation and I got along very well I believe. . . . Went to Calvary church in the evening. A Mr Reed of Manchester, somewhat of a modern evangelist, preached. An odd place, but doubtless a good one.

. . . Tuesday afternoon, drove out to the site of the pumping works of the water company with John Green. Thursday evening called on Mr Levi Anderson by invitation where I met Archbishop Gross and Daddy Fier[e]ns.[17] The Bishop appeared a pleasant talky man, but his talk was not about anything of any moment. Friday evening dined at the club with Mr [William] MacKenzie and 12 others. I acted as croupier and responded to his toast the Queen and the President, the rulers of the Anglo-Saxon race, and proposed several others one of which was Virginia, the mother of states and statesmen, premising that a Virginia President, Mr Jefferson had sent two other Virginians Lewis & Clarke to explore the Columbia river at the opening of this century to which fact the subsequent settlement and occupation of Oregon by immigrants from the western states is largely due, and called on Effinger to respond, which he did quite well. Had an excellent dinner and did not get home until 2 oclock. Today attended the dedication of the Roman Catholic cathedral—Church of the Immaculate conception—at 10 oclock, by special invitation. Service lasted 3 hours. Archbishop Gross preached an hour and sung high mass. The music by the choir was very elaborate and quite good. But the toggery, the robing and disrobing and genuflections were simply silly and disgusting. The sermon was animated and in a sense eloquent but intellectually it was pitched very low. . . .

22 (Sat) Sunday (Aug 16) . . . at Trinity church. Dodd not being present I conducted the S S and Mr Foote being absent read the morning prayer and a sermon from Rev Boyds "Thoughts of a Country Parson," on Christian denial from the text "If any man will come after me &c" St Luke 9:23. . . .

. . . Wrote a letter yesterday of 5 pages to Bush about Grants early days in Oregon and particularly his potatoe raising speculation, which he asked me for on account of a wild statement in the Springfield *Republican* that he wanted to write Bowles about. I consulted Brooke about my statement. . . .

29 (Sat) . . . Sat in the C C & D C during the week except Tuesday, Wednesday and Thursday when I was at the Sulphur Springs [*St Martins*] at the Cascades. Found George H & Mrs Williams there. Brooke came up on Wednesday and returned with me on Thursday. Aunt Kate talked all the time, and dilated especially on her study of German and French while she was in Europe a few years ago. One day we were sitting on the porch all there reading, Williams having a volume of Macauleys Essays, came across the phrase Parc aux Cerfs, and asked Mrs Williams what it meant. I was sitting at some distance from them and ought not to have heard what passed but I did. She stumbled at the question a while and then she said Let me see the book [saying] "Them French words have so many different meanings all depending on the context you can't tell without looking at the book." After looking at it for a while she said she thought it meant some kind of park or square, but was evidently at fault as to the literal meaning of the phrase—"a deer park"—but was totally ignorant of the historic significance of the phrase, from its being the popular appellation of the private and famous place of assignation of Louis 15th at Versailles. I think her knowledge of these languages is limited. . . .

Attended the Regatta . . . [*this*] afternoon. Sat on the Coloma Dock. The races were well contested and the collection of people in small boats on the river was very picturesque. At the close I presented the prizes to the winners with a few remarks. The prizes were very handsome and for the most part silver goblets. In the evening I attended the dinner given to the winners at Aliskys. The "cups" were filled with claret punch brewed by the Captain, Mr White[18] and drunk to the winners—I proposing the toast and calling on Mr Joe Teal to reply. About 10 oclock I slipped away.

During the week and principally during the two days I was at the springs I read Blackmores *Lorna Doone* an English story of the time of Charles & James the Second, supposed to be written by the principal character, John Redd, in the time of Anne. It is a remarkable production. Full of rich, racy and quaint Old English and redolent of the country life of England, than which there is nothing finer and better in the world. The botany—plant and tree life—of the scenes are sometimes overdone, but earnest honest love was never more naturally and powerfully portrayed.

*September 2 (Wed)* Sunday (Aug 30) . . . at Trinity. Mr Foote returned and officiated . . . I expected to read the service and to read a sermon of Phil[l]ips Brooks from St Paul—"I have kept the faith" that I was sorry the congregation missed. . . .

Will sail tonight on steamer *Columbia,* room 32 for San Francisco to sit in the C C in Sharon v Hill.

Called at the Hall last evening and met the Misses Rodney just returned from Astoria and the seaside looking very well. We all indulged in a little shouting over *Lorna Doone,* which they had read some time since. Paid off my bills yesterday including $176.50 in repairs to the House and $200 sent to Lawrence School and $50 each to Mrs Deady and self for contemplated expenses, which gives me $90 in my purse for my journey to San Francisco. I leave $427 in bank to which my July salary will be added in a few days. Got a new suit of clothes made at Curriers for $65 which I put on Sunday—the coat a single breasted frock. Will never have a coat made again other than a frock of some kind.

*6 (Sun)* Went on board the *Columbia* at Portland on Wednesday evening (the 2 inst) at 10 oclock bound for San Francisco. Had room 32 to myself. Owing to the fog we did not get off until 9 oclock Thursday morning. Stopped at Astoria an hour and a half and crossed the bar at 7 P M. I was on the Bridge. The water was very smooth and the weather calm all the way down. We reached here at half past 2 yesterday, having been detained some hours in the last 50 miles by fog. We found the entrance in the fog, but never could have done so but for the fog horn at the head. . . . [Met] Col & Mrs [Geo] Trusdell and son and a good agreeable maiden lady with them, Miss Sophy Little who is not very little either. They are from Washington City and have been in Portland some days looking around. Stopped at the Occidental, room 224 third floor, Parlor, bedroom and bathroom for $3½ per day. Found a note here from Justice Field written on the supposition that I would have reached here in the morning as I would if it had not been for the fog, and saying that he had delayed his departure since Tuesday so as to meet and asking me to call on him at once on my arrival, as he had much to say to me and was going east on the afternoon train. But I was too late. Sorry for it. Sawyer called in the afternoon and we discussed the situation of the Sharon case, which I expect to sit in on Tuesday. Went with him to the Mechanics Fair last night. Called on the P[acific] club on my way home where I saw Hoffman, [James] Boyd, [Richard] Mayne and others at the post prandial game of cards as usual. Saw Tom Madden at dinner.[19] Looks well and was pleasant and friendly. When I asked him where all the rest of the old timers were he answered that he had buried the most of them. . . .

Went to church at Trinity in the morning and staid for Communion. Sat in Judge Hoffmans pew. Met William Alvord as I came out of church and Miss Little with the latter of whom I walked down to her hotel—the Lick House. Dr [Hiram] Beers the Rector of Trinity has a very unpleasant voice. There must have been 150 persons staid to Communion, but the offering I think was light. There were 3 clergymen in the chancel. The people went to and came from the Communion rail as opportunity occurred and they were served, the chancel being full of those standing and waiting their turn. . . .

*12 (Sat)* Monday (Sept 7) Called at Bancrofts. Saw A L[20] and the young man his nephew, who has succeeded Stone in the law dept. In the afternoon rode out to the Park on the cable car, Miss Little and her Washington friends chanced to be on the same car on the same errand. Went through the Park with them. Sat near the Garfield Statue with Miss L and Mrs Truesdell, when the conversation naturally turned on Garfield when they both said quite plainly that he was in fact anything but a good man and that his wife was about to separate from him when he got the nomination for the Presidency. I think this represents the average unpolitical opinion of Washington. I went on in the dummy engine through the Sand hills to the Cliff house. This place and its surroundings is now given up to coarse and vulgar Sunday amusements. In the evening took Capt [John] Mullan with me to the Cal Theatre where we saw (couldn't hear) "A Prisoner for Life," a melodramatic play copied from the French, which had some affecting situations in it.

Tuesday sat in the C C and commenced the hearing of Sharon v Hill. The day was consumed by [W H L] Barnes in reading testimony for the plaintiff. In the evening Sawyer and I went with Mr & Mrs [Chas G] Howard to the Baldwin and saw and heard "In His Power," which notwithstanding the adverse criticisms of the Press I like better than "A Prisoner for Life." Sat in a box which I afterwards learned was Lucky Baldwins, which Mr Howard had the run of as his attorney in some one of his woman cases.[21] Mrs Howard appears to be a very cultivated and elegant woman, while he is a merry, bright offhand fellow. They are Catholics. He is a perfunctory one, I suppose. He remarked in her presence that he said his prayers regularly every day but he did not think it did him much good.

Wednesday being the anniversary of the admission of California into the Union the court did not sit. I was occupied the greater part of the day in reading the testimony and examining the exhibits in the S-H case. Called on Hoffman at the club in the afternoon, or rather dropped into the club where I met H. We had a pleasant chat and discussed the feasibility of getting the law so changed that we might retire after 25 years of service on full pay without reference to our ages. Visited the panorama of the battle of Waterloo which is the most marvelous illusion I ever saw or heard of.

Thursday sat in the C C. Testimony of the plaintiff—finished reading, and ex-Senator [William] Stewart commenced the argument for the plaintiff. Friday, sat in the C C, at ½ past 9 and Stewart finished his argument by 12 oclock, when the case was adjourned until Tuesday. In the afternoon I went to Sacramento to visit the State fair. Stopped with Bernard Steinman at the depot house where I had a good bed and an excellent dinner and breakfast. Paid $4.40 for a ticket for the round trip, and 50 cents for a seat in the Pul[l]man each way. Distance about 90 miles. Made the acquaintance of Mr Creed Haymond on the up train. Went to the Pavilion in the evening with Mr Shearer of Oakland.[22] We travelled from New York to San Francisco together in January, 1860. He was just married and was a bright clean young fellow. But I am afraid he is now in danger of dying a drunkard. Had some excellent Burgundy at dinner at Steinmans from Gov Stanfords winery, which S said he sold at 75 cents a gallon. The Pavilion is a mighty handsome building and the exhibition was very fair. But the people had a village and country air as compared with the crowd at the mechanics fair in San Francisco.

Saturday morning rode out to the fair ground in the edge of the town. Met Haymond there who introduced me to "Ned" Marshal[l], atty Genl of the state. I met him here in 1878 and in May 1849 I saw him back of Leavenworth on the back of a bucking mule. He was attached to the Collier party,[23] then about to start across the plains to take possession of the custom houses at San Francisco and elsewhere in Cal. Met Mrs Marshal[l] & daughter and Mrs Haymond in the stand in the afternoon. Mrs M is a pleasant, genteel woman and her daughter is very plain but well bred. Mrs Haymond is showy. I made a bet with her of a pair of gloves on the afternoon trotting race which I left in the course of being run. But I see by this mornings paper that her horse Dawn, won.

The show of horses and cattle was very fine. As it paraded around the track it was more than a mile long. We left in the parlor car at 50 minutes after 2 and got here by 7. Made the acquaintance of Mr [Marcus] Boruck the publisher and editor of the *Spirit of [the] Times*.[24] A good general average man I think. Sacramento is a lovely country place. The eucalyptus tree is redeeming California from the reproach of barrenness.

*18 (Fri)* . . . Monday, being law day I did not sit in the C C but spent the day until 2 oclock reading the testimony in H v S. In the afternoon visited the Panorama of Waterloo and the Japanese exhibition with Cap Mullan. The former I have spoken of. The latter is a very interesting place. Saw all kinds of Japanese work going on including cloisone [*sic*], pottery, embroidery, bronze, painting and silk. Went into a tea [room] where a good looking Japanese woman gave us a tiny cup of delicious tea.

Tuesday sat in the C C in S v H. [O P] Evans[25] spoke for the pltf and made a masterly argument, but it would have been improved by more force in the delivery. . . .

Wednesday, [Geo] Tyler[26] commenced for the defendant, reading evidence all day with some sparring with the court and counsel. . . .

Thursday, Tyler still reading evidence. Got along about as usual. At the adjournment for the day Miss Hill asked through Mr [Sherman] Houghton to speak. I said yes, but you stand by. She came up to the platform and I stepped down. She said I might have her papers if I would return them to her but she wouldn't trust Sawyer with them, for fear he would let Piper have them.[27]. . .

Friday, Tyler closed his reading of the testimony and commenced the argument. . . .

20 *(Sun)* Saturday, got up at 6 and got off on the Narrow guage [*sic*] ferry for Monterey via Santa Cruz at ½ past 8. Judge Sawyer was with me but his boy Howie got astray and he had to go back. Reached S C a little after 12. Had lunch at the Ocean House and was driven about for a couple of hours by a stableman named Miller who had lived there 19 years. An interesting place. But the ride through the tunnels, one 1¼ and the other 1⅛ miles in length—and over the coast mountains was the most interesting . . . At 4:20 went on by the broad guage and at Pajaro[28] was transferred to the train to San Francisco on which I found Judge Sawyer and Howie. We got to Delmonte between 6 & 7 and had dinner. Went to bed in room 214 with a bath between that and 213 in which the Sawyers slept. Before retiring we wandered through the public rooms in the Hotel. The billiard room and the parlor are immense affairs in which hundreds of people can be comfortably disposed.

In the morning we rose early and had breakfast and by 15 minutes to 9 we commenced the 17 mile drive around [the] Point. We got back just before 12, had lunch and started back on the 1 oclock train and reached this Hotel at ½ past 6. At Gilroy the thermometer marked 94. Delmonte is the most beautiful place I ever saw. The building is grand and the grounds are lovely. The great old oak and pine trees scattered all over the grounds add much to the place. The dining room is a marvel of lightness and beauty as well as vastness, and the table is excellent. . . .

24 *(Thu)* Monday . . . being law day I did not sit in the court. At 11 oclock I called at Gov Stanfords by invitation of Miss [Anne]Lathrop and was shown through the art gallery, the Pompeiian & Indian rooms and the dining room. The gallery is very interesting & Miss L was very kind and obliging. . . .

Wednesday sat in the C C and heard Tyler in S v H. He closed in the afternoon and Terry[29] commenced on the same side. Tyler is a man of some ability and energy with much power of presenting facts, and if he was not so habitually disingenuous he would have great effect. . . .

Today sat in the C C and heard Terry in S v H. He closed just before 4. [W H L] Barnes will commence for the pltf in reply tomorrow. We have been sitting from 10 to 1 and from 2 to 4. I suppose it will take Barnes two days to get through. . . .

This evening I was so annoyed by the frequent discharge of urine that I sent for Dr [David] Wooster.[30] He came and examined my water and said there was sugar in it, that I had diabetes, and must quit the use of all food that contains starch or sugar.

25 *(Fri)* Dr Wooster came in the morning and took a quantity of water that I voided during the night for the purpose of making a quantitative analysis of it. Came back in the evening and spoke rather cheerfully of the case saying that there was only about 2 per cent of sugar in the urine and that with proper diet I would

get well. Sat in the C C during the day. Barnes spoke for the pltf in S v H all day and did it elegantly as well as forcibly. His sentences are sometimes too long drawn out and his comparisons overdone and strained. But altogether I think it was the most accomplished effort I have heard at the bar. His costume was admirable and in keeping with himself and the occasion.

In the evening called . . . on the Haymonds in the hotel. He is a good deal of a man with very pleasant manners. She is really a beautiful woman, a little overdone about the head. She talks well also, as far as she goes, and the prejudice I conceived against her when I first met her at Sacramento begins to wear off. She knows Mrs Dr Hawthorne and sent love to her.

*26 (Sat)*. . . Read [Francis] Newlands argument in Sharon v Sharon on a question of alimony. His treatment of Sharon his father in law, was just and judicious and his excuse or justification of the part he was then taking in the case is simply sublime. . . . Presented Mrs Haymond with a pair of gloves (2.75) that I lost to her on the bet at Sacramento, she betting on a horse named Dawn against the field.

Went to the Pacific club in the evening. Called on Mr [Evans S] Pillsbury there but he was not in. Left my card. Met a Mr Platt the attorney for "Hen Owens" the Oregon Swampland Angel and his assignee Mr [C N] Felton of this place.[31] Hoffman, Stewart, Delmas and Barnes made a ring and talked. In the course of the conversation Stewart unburdened himself about Sumner, who he said was an equal compound of "egotism, cowardice and mendacity." He also told the story how Sumner came to be removed from the chairmanship of the committee of foreign relations. Sumner was at a dinner given to the members of the Alabama Commission, and some[one] said that Grant seemed to be very popular and that he supposed he would be elected the second time. The remark was not addressed to Sumner nor was he near the speaker. But he heard it and immediately replied in his loud voice, "No, he will not be reelected. He will be impeached and convicted of high crimes and misdemeanors first." Of course there was an aw[kw]ard pause until someone diverted the conversation into another channel. The next day the matter was reported to the senators and at the request of the Republicans Mr [H B] Ant[h]ony called a caucus and sent for Mr [Hamilton] Fish [who] was present at the dinner and asked him about the matter when he stated it as above. Thereupon Sumner was sent for and denied the statement in toto and retired. Everyone believed that he lied and Fish told the [truth] and out of indignation at this mendacity rather than what he said, a motion was then and there made to depose [him] from the leadership of the committee which passed unanimously without a word.

Came home at 11 and made this memorandum. . . .

*30 (Wed)* Sunday (Sept 27) Went to morning prayer at Trinity church and then across the bay to Col [Southard] Hoffmans in Ross Valley with Judge Hoffman and Mr Charles Mayne. Met and enjoyed a very pleasant family at Col Hs. Mrs H is from Alabama, and was wooed and won by her young husband when he was fighting for the Union in the war of the Rebellion. She is [a] charming woman and an excellent mother if I may speak on an hours acquaintance. She has 5 children—2 fine looking manly boys at the adolescent stage, 2 girls and a little boy. The oldest girl May is about 12 or 14 and very sweet and winning with a sound basis I take of good sense and feminine tact. Told her I would swap Paul for her and give some[thing] to boot. . . . From there we drove up to Gen [Lucius H] Allens also nearby. He had just lain down and excused himself very politely. Saw Mrs Allen, whom I never fancied much, and their two sons. These are all lovely places, occupied by nice people and the region might well be called Happy Valley, for a better reason than that described in *Rasselas.*[32]. . .

Monday sat in the C C and heard the continuation of Barnes argument in the Sharon-Hill case. It was very good. Dined in the evening at Mr William T Colemans at 1299 Taylor street. The dinner was given to me. The table was double ended. Mr Coleman & I sat at the head, I on his right and Mr [Thomas] Brown of the Bank of Cal and Mr Freeborn at the other end. Judge [John] Hager sat at my right and Gen [Henry] Heth at Colemans left. Besides these there were present Mr Good[e], Mr [Geo] He[a]rst, Mr [I M] Scott[33] and Mr [Evans] Pillsbury. The dinner was elegant and the company pleasant. Hager rather surprised me with some smutty stories, but they were good ones. I got away at 11 oclock and left the party in the billiard room.

Tuesday sat in the C C and heard the conclusion of Barnes argument in the S & H case. She [*Sarah Althea*] was present and I think he was deterred from saying much that he intended to and what he did say, while it was well said, was under the circumstances drawn very mild. She interrupted early in the morning with a taunt, but we told her she must shut up or she would be made to. Presented my account for expenses to the marshal for 31 days at $8 per day from Sept 3 to Oct 3, both days inclusive and was paid $248. . . .

Called at the Sutros this morning where I was taken to see Adolphs wonderful collection of books on Battery St. At 1 oclock Mr Gustave Sutro called for me at the Occidental and drove me through the park and to Sutro Heights where we spent an hour looking at the wonders that are and to be of the place.[34]

This evening I took a farewell dinner at the club . . . Got home at 10 P M, settled my bill, 26 days $91, wine, carriage and washing $18.45 more, in all $103.45 which leaves me with $24 cash and a draft on Portland for $200. Made this final entry and commenced packing up for the homeward journey in the morning. Bot [*sic*] a straw hat this evening for the trip $2. Send my trunk home on the steamer by Wells Fargo & Co and my silk hat by Meusendorfer of whom I bought the straw one. *Finis.*

### *Portland*

*October 8 (Thu)* Left San Francisco on the morning of Thursday, October 1 in company with Judge Sawyer and reached Delta about 8 oclock.[35] Thence in the stage or rather on the outside of it at a breakneck pace to Sissons at the foot of Mt Shasta by daylight of Friday the 2d. The mountain looked cold and austere in the gray of the morning but hardly majestic to one accustomed to Mt Hood. Took breakfast and changed horses and driver at Buteville a few miles this side of Shasta. Sorry to lose the driver (Frank Hovey) who is a very sensible, safe fellow.

Friday, Oct 2, made Ashland at half past 8 where we found Mrs Deady & Brooke on the train to meet us. Had a pleasant ride in the forenoon through Shasta valley but from Yreka on to Coles [Station] it was warm and sometimes tedious. The ride over Siski[y]ou was grand. We raced down 6 miles on this side in the twilight in 30 minutes. In getting off the stage at supper station 7 miles beyond Ashland I hurt my knee pretty badly from the effect of which I am still a little lame. Came down to Portland in the Pullman and got home by 5 oclock Saturday evening and went to the new house which Mrs Deady and Mrs Hill had furnished very neatly. The ceilings of our room were [*elegantly*] frescoed with paper.[36] Koehler sent us the Presidents car to come down in from Ashland but I preferred the ordinary sleeper and did not take it. . . .

. . . Am going to fort Stevens tonight on the Steamer *Columbia*. Have secured room 44.

*17 (Sat)* Friday (Oct 9) Reached Astoria at 10 in the morning on the steamship *Columbia*. Met Senator [J P] Jones and his wife on board returning from Alaska. He had been quite ill in Portland. Got over to Fort Stevens in the *Sam* by 2 oclock. The Captain was going to Skipanon and went by Ft Stevens with me for which I gave him double fare—$1. Went by invitation to the house in the quarters occupied by Mr & Mrs C E S Wood where I met Mrs W[ood] and Miss Emma Lewis. Staid there until Wednesday and had a very pleasant time. Went in bathing every day on the beach below the jetty. Miss Lewis went in with me on Saturday which was one of the loveliest days I ever saw. Mr Wood came down from Portland Sunday evening . . .

On Monday Capt [Geo] Flavel came over and drove me to his farm about 2½ miles down the beach where we staid with his tenants, Mr & Mrs Pitkins all night. Pitkins was in the army of the Potomoc from Minnesota some three years and told us some very interesting stories of his battles and adventures. I found Mrs Wood a very bright interesting woman without a particle of affectation or pretense. Miss L is devoted to her and enjoys her hugely, as I think. . . .

*24 (Sat)* Took Mrs D to New Market on Monday evening to hear Mrs Custer Calhoun read, Paul and [Stewart] Linthicum were ushers.[37]. . . The reading was good, but there was a deal of it, and one voice grew monotonous. There was an interlude on the cello by a Mr Ottendorf which I enjoyed. Forgot to say that Mrs C lectured under the auspices of the G A R and was introduced by Mr F K Arnold in a very neat and appropriate speech.

The weather has been clear and warm all week until last night when a shower of rain fell which was very welcome. The ground is so dry that the farmers cannot plough.

*25 (Sun)* . . . Called on Ollie and Frank. The former is getting ready to have a son as we all hope while we fear it may be the eighth daughter.

*November 1 (Sun)* Sat in the C C and D C during the week. Occupied the Circuit Judges chambers while the court room was being calcamined—chromeoed I might call it as there are 6 colors used. The collector left the manner of it to my judgment. . . .

*7 (Sat)*. . . Thursday evening we had Mr Foote to dinner. After dinner the 'bus called for me by arrangement and took me to John Muirs to a Shakespeare reading with others. Brought home in the same way between 12 & 1. The 'bus was crowded and the going and coming was quite jolly. We read from "Lear," omitting the Edmond parts as being rather gross for ladies. Yesterday a committee of Tax payers made arrangements with me to draft an amendment to the charter for the construction or purchase of water works. I had hardly time to do it, but consented in view of the public interest in the matter. . . .

*14 (Sat)* Friday commenced work on the Sharon case and today the dispatches announced that he died the same day. Got the *Northwest* magazine for November published at St Paul and devoted to Portland and its celebrities. My face is in it among others with a rather kindly but not discriminate biography from the pen of Tom Merry.

The weather has been lovely today and most of the week. This mornings *Oregonian* contains the Mitchel[l] love letters to Carrie Price his wifes sister. They must fix him with the decent part of the community, but with his particular henchmen I imagine it will make no difference unless his pretensions to piety disgust them. He is alone in making fornication a means of salvation. This evening attended a meeting of the Water Committee at Ladds bank and helped to consider the bill I drafted for the committee in company with . . . the Multnomah delegation. Reduced the amount of the bonds from $1,000,000 to $750,000, struck out the water rate on unoccupied lots, and reduced the qualification of a tax payer from $100 to $25 city tax.[38]

*21 (Sat)* . . . Mitchel[l] was elected to the Senate on the third ballot on [Wednesday] by 55 votes, 17 of whom were Democrats. It is a disgrace to the state and a reproach to humanity. Thursday evening we had Gov [W C] Squires to dinner with us. A very pleasant, plausible man, and I think a genuine good one. Friday evening heard Miss Clara Foltz lecture on the life of Col Baker. A pretty good lecture from the popular stand and quite well delivered. Spoke with her at the close of the lecture. Have been at work on Sharons case whenever I could get a moment of time, and am making some progress. I discussed the case as if he were still alive, as the decree will be entered as of some day before his death and after the hearing.

*28 (Sat)* . . . Yesterday the Collector by orders from Washington had this building draped out of respect to the memory of the vice President, Thomas Hendricks the last of the Copperheads, and a pretty good man according to his lights, which were not of the first order by any means, particularly on the subject of patronage. In that respect, his death is no loss to the country. . . .

*December 12 (Sat)* . . . Acted as pall bearer at Mrs Effingers funeral on [Wednesday] last.[39] I did not expect to be invited. Saw Col E[ffinger] the same evening at Brookes and had some pleasant chat about Mr Foote and funerals—how appropriate and effective he was or is on such occasions. It may be the beginning of pleasant relations again, but I don't know that I can ignore the past without some excuse or apology. Maybe he thinks the same. We will see.

*20 (Sun)* . . . [*Last Sunday*] afternoon and evening worked on opinion in S v H. Commenced to rewrite and revise, and Roswell [B] Lamson commenced to copy with the type writer.[40] Closed it up and put it up for the express today at half past 2 oclock. Have been at work on it night and day all this week when not in court and since half past 9 this morning. It covers with syllabus 70 pages of legal cap type written and contains over 24,000 words. I think the work is well done and that there are passages in [it] which will attract attention and probably criticism . . .

. . . Went to the Tabernacle to hear Mrs [Margaret] Hampson in the evening at ½ past 7.[41] The house was well crowded when I got there listening to Mr [Wm] Wadhams and his cochanters singing a rather nursery style of hymns. At 8 oclock Mrs H made her appearance on the platform and consumed probably a half hour in a hymn, prayer and reading of the Gos*pil* as she called it according to St Luke including the parable of the unjust Steward.

After that she spoke with much unction and earnestness until 20 minutes after 9 from the words, "And I say unto you, make to yourself friends of the mammon of unrighteousness."

She has a good voice a little worn at that time, a vivid imagination and a good command of suitable language to the occasion. She is probably an intelligent woman, without early education for she used *h*evil for evil and 'air for hair. But she kept that audience of 3000 persons mostly plain men, absorbed in what she said, and I believe she did them good. For my tastes, she dealt a little too much in the old fashioned campmeeting death bed scenes and stories, of which she was generally a part.

Mr Ladd sat in his crib in the aisle in front of me and in speaking in praise of men who sought and obtained the mammon of this world by industry economy and judgment she exclaimed "A self made millionaire (meaning an honest one of course) is the noblest work of God" or words to that effect. I told L that the compliment was evidently suggested by him if not intended for him.

*26 (Sat)* . . . On Thursday afternoon went out and got 5 perpetual memberships taken in the Library—which was well. In the evening got a telegram from Sawyer saying that the opinion in S v H received and that passage out at the end of page 65. On examination I found that page 66 had gotten into the retained copy, and yesterday morning I telegraphed it to him at government rates—355 words in all at 1 cent a word. How could we get along without the telegraph. . . .

On Wednesday Mrs D and I went with the Dolphs to hear Col [R B] Sprague[42] of Mills College, Oakland lecture on John Milton as a teacher. There were but few present, but they were well paid for their attendance. His manner was the most elegant without a particle of affectation, I ever saw. But about his matter, there is of course a difference of opinion as there probably always will be. I met him at Cyrus Dolphs yesterday evening and was much pleased with him. . . .

Our Xmas was a quiet and pleasant affair. But just as we sat down to dinner Mrs D learned that Mrs Brooke was sinking and she had to leave the table and go down there where she staid all night. I called this morning and found Mrs B had rallied a little, but it is not thought she will last long. Poor thing! how we will miss her.

On Tuesday Mr Corbett for the committee paid me $300 for preparing the water Commission act. It ought to have been $500, but as I said to him I ought to contribute something to the general good as well as the committee.

*27 (Sun)* I sat up last night with Mrs Brooke and helped close her eyes at 10 minutes past 3 this morning. She was dying from 6 oclock the evening before and knew no one. . . .

*29 (Tue)*. . . attended Mrs Brookes funeral. Acted as a pall bearer with Col Kelly, Mr Lewis and Judge Williams. We went from the house to Trinity church at 1 P M where the services were held and from there to the R V cemetery where the interment took place. And this is the last of this world for my dear friend, but I hope to meet her in the life beyond. . . .

# NOTES

1. Whether Deady's additions were to be licensed, restrained or punished is not clear.

2. A commission form of government was not adopted until 1913. According to Joseph Gaston, Bernard O'Hara (1836–1908), came to Portland in 1857 and took up any honest labor which offered. Later he became a policeman, a street contractor and a real estate operator. Joseph Gaston, *Portland—Its History and Builders,* vol. II, p. 750.

3. Attorney Ellis Hughes had brought suit against the Dundee Mortgage Trust Investment Co. for legal fees allegedly due him for lawsuits brought and other legal business. Because the company was a foreign corporation the case was brought in Deady's court. Deady rendered a verdict for Hughes, but materially reduced the amounts asked in the complaint. This was early in 1883. Hughes then divided up the items on his original account and sued on each one separately, again in Deady's court. Deady found against him in each instance, on the ground that having sued and been given a judgment for all the business, he could not now come in and sue on the individual items. The mandamus in the MacAllister case was an attempt to embarrass Deady. Hughes took his cases to the supreme court and Deady was upheld in each instance.

4. For an account of the life of Mary A. Leonard, the first woman to be admitted to the practice of law in Oregon, see: Malcolm Clark, jr., "The Lady and the Law," *OHQ,* Vol. LXVI (June, 1955), pp. 126–39.

5. John Robertson; Portland contractor. The Strong family was denied its guardianship.

6. Mrs. S. A. Hemphill was proprietor of the Hemphill House. Wallis Nash (1837–1926), writer and railroad promoter; member, board of regents, Oregon Agricultural College. Ann Watt Holgate was the wife of Erastus H. Holgate, Corvallis lawyer. B. L. Arnold was the first president of the Oregon Agricultural College, 1872–92. E. E. Grimm, professor of agriculture. James A. (1838–1901) and Martha Cauthorn; he was a grain merchant. W. W. Bristow was principal of the preparatory department and professor of bookkeeping. Burnett had married Martha, daughter of Roland Hinton, a Benton County farmer.

7. Frederick Warde (1851–1935), actor; played with Booth, Janauschek, Charlotte Cushing and others. James F. Stephens (1829–94), English lawyer and jurist; Richard de Anesty spent five years, 1158–63, trying to secure the inheritance of his deceased uncle's property; because part of the litigation involved the validity of a marriage, recourse was had to the ecclesiastical as well as civil courts; both were dilatory. Welch Rithet was a combination of Welch & Co. of San Francisco and R. P. Rithet of Victoria. R. P. Rithet was a prominent shipping broker and was also president of the California & Hawaiian Sugar Co.

8. James R. Cameron, partner with Clement Caesar and Henry Hewett in the firm, C. Caesar & Co.

9. W. H. Chaney (1821-c. 1900), astrologer, minor politician and probably Jack London's father.

10. Deady had ruled, however, that though the treasury department might release

Griswold from paying that portion of the judgment owed the government for the frauds he had perpetrated, it could not release him from that portion due to B. F. Dowell.

11. John Sherman (1823–1900), Ohio legislator; U. S. senator, 1861–77 and 1881–97; secretary of the treasury, 1877–81. Charles Francis Adams (1807–86), politician and diplomat; minister to England, 1861–68. Col. Lewis C. Hunt, MA, class of 1843; died 1886. Frank Sherman was a nephew of Senator John Sherman. Ebenezer R. Hoar (1816–95), lawyer and jurist; attorney-general, 1869–70, he demanded that federal judgeships be removed from patronage; the Senate refused to confirm his appointment to the United States Supreme Court.

12. George F. Magoun (1821–96), Congregational minister and educator; president of Iowa College, 1862–84. Coker F. Clarkson (1811–90), Iowa journalist. Brayton Ives (1840–1914), New York banker.

13. Albert W. Swalm (1845–1922), Iowa journalist and diplomat.

14. John Goode (1829–1909), Virginia lawyer; his appointment as solicitor-general was not confirmed by the U. S. Senate. Elijah Smith; president of the O.R. & N. Co. Robert Harris; director and later president of the N.P.R.R. Co.

15. Paul was U. S. Commissioner.

16. Donald Macleay was the out-going president of the board of trade. Charles E. Whitehead, a New York lawyer and philanthropist. Lillie Devereux Blake (1835–1913), author, reformer, feminist.

17. Levi Anderson (1810–89), investment broker. William H. Gross (1837–98), Roman Catholic prelate; archbishop of Oregon City *post* 1885. John F. Fierens (1828–93), Roman Catholic prelate; Vicar-general of the archdiocese of Oregon City and pastor of the pro-Cathedral at Portland; one of the founders of St. Vincent's Hospital.

18. Coloma Dock was between Oak and Pine. T. Brook White (c.1854–1914), attorney and civil engineer.

19. George Trusdell served with the California militia during the Civil War. Truesdale in original. Thomas P. Madden; San Francisco real estate man.

20. Albert L. Bancroft (1841–1914), brother of H. H. Bancroft; publisher of legal and school books.

21. E. S. (Lucky) Baldwin (1829–1909), promoter and womanizer. Charles G. Howard, Los Angeles attorney.

22. Creed Haymond (1836–93), lawyer and frontiersman; a Stanford associate, he was attorney for the Central Pacific. Shearer cannot be definitely identified.

23. James Collier was sent to California in 1849 to take over the customs houses.

24. Marcus D. Boruck (died 1895); California journalist.

25. Oliver P. Evans (1842–1911); California lawyer and jurist.

26. George W. Tyler; California lawyer.

27. Sherman O. Houghton (1828–1914), California lawyer and Republican politician; member of Congress, 1871–75. Dr. R. M. Piper was the handwriting expert.

28. Pajar in original.

29. Davis S. Terry (1823–89), California lawyer, jurist, politician; following service in the Mexican War moved to California, practiced law, became a justice, and subsequently chief justice, of the California Supreme Court; changed politics from Know-Nothing to slavery Democrat; killed David C. Broderick in a political duel; served in Confederate army; returned to California after a brief stay in Mexico and took up practice of law. He was chief attorney for Sarah Althea, whom he subsequently married. His death is described later in the diary.

30. Deady had consulted Dr. Wooster in previous visits to San Francisco; the doctor was a graduate of Western Reserve, class of 1849.

31. Evans S. Pillsbury (1843–1937), attorney; represented Wells Fargo for many years. H. G. Platt, San Francisco attorney. C. N. Felton (1828–1914), speculator; Republican congressman, 1885–89; senator, 1891–93.

32. Southard Hoffman served as an A.A.G. officer of volunteers during the Civil War.

Happy Valley was the home of the hero of *History of Rasselas, Prince of Abyssinia,* Samuel Johnson's now widely unread philosophical romance.

33. Thomas Brown; cashier, Bank of California. Freeborn is either James Freeborn, San Francisco capitalist, or William Freeborn, a stockbroker; probably the former. John S. Hager (1818–90), lawyer and jurist. Henry Heth (1825–99), soldier; MA, class of 1847; served in Mexican War and in the West; resigned to enter Confederate service and rose to rank of major-general. George Hearst (1820–91), California miner and publisher; Democratic senator, 1886–95; father of William Randolph Hearst. Irving M. Scott (1837–1903), foundryman and shipbuilder; constructed, among others, the battleship *Oregon.*

34. Adolph H. J. Sutro (1830–98), mining engineer; conceived and built the famous Sutro tunnel. Gustav was his cousin and partner in banking, street railway promotion and merchandising.

35. Delta, Shasta County, was then the northern terminus of the California & Oregon Railroad.

36. Mrs. Hill had removed her boardinghouse to 163 Tenth at the southwest corner of 10th and Morrison.

37. Margaret Custer Calhoun, sister of George Custer. Through his efforts she lost two brothers, a husband and a nephew at Little Big Horn. She supported herself by elocutionary readings. Stewart Linthicum (1861–1911), Portland attorney.

38. These are the letters S. O. L. Potter gave Deady with the injunction that they should never be published. It was not intended under the water bill that the water be metered. Anyone paying $25 or more in city taxes would be eligible for water; anyone paying less than that amount would not.

39. Amanda Effinger; W. H. Effinger's mother-in-law.

40. Roswell B. Lamson (1868–1911), later a Portland attorney.

41. Mrs. Margaret Hampson was an English evangelist.

42. Robert B. Sprague (1829–1918), educator; president of Mills Seminary, 1885–87; later president, the University of North Dakota.

# APPENDIX A

## SEELEY VS REED

The Oregon Iron & Steel Co. was formed to buy out the assets of the Oswego Iron Company. L. B. Seeley and Simeon Reed were stockholders in both concerns. The new company showed no better profitability than its predecessor and Seeley, who was an experienced iron master, agreed to manage the property for two years under a complicated arrangement which required, among other things, that Reed buy up $150,000 in company bonds. This did not work out to the satisfaction of the parties and Seeley sued in an attempt to make Reed and W. S. and W. M. Ladd, who were also shareholders, buy out his interest. Among other things he alleged that Reed and the Ladd & Tilton Bank had improperly loaned the company $270,000 in an attempt to force it into bankruptcy. After a long contest, this suit was overturned in the federal courts.

Seeley then enlisted the support of the New York financier, Elijah Smith, who represented certain Eastern stockholders and a voting trust was formed, aimed at Reed. The Ladds switched sides and joined the trust. A new suit was instituted in the state courts with Reed as the sole defendant. Reed fought back furiously but was brought to terms by a stiff letter from Smith, who pointed out that Reed had disposed of the Oswego Iron Company at an inflated price, and was holding a large block of stock for which he had subscribed, and on which he had paid nothing. A settlement, not advantageous to Reed, was reached in 1887.

In his private correspondence Reed characterized the litigation as blackmail, and he was bitter at what he considered the Ladds' duplicity.

# APPENDIX B

## SHARON VS HILL

William Sharon was born in Ohio, studied law with Edwin Stanton, removed to California in 1849, accumulated a modest fortune dealing in San Francisco real estate, and lost it. In 1864 he persuaded William Ralston to appoint him manager of the Virginia City branch of the Bank of California. In a dozen years a combination of canny investment, judicious stock-jobbing and Machiavellian chicanery had made him a multi-millionaire and U. S. senator from Nevada.

In 1880 Sharon was an aging and by no means handsome widower whose most attractive feature was the size of his bank account, and he had come to feel that amorous dalliance with a young woman of suitable youth and beauty might stir his sluggish blood. He was in this frame of mind when he happened upon Sarah Althea Hill.

Sarah Althea was young enough, about half Sharon's age, and she was undeniably beautiful, but she was not, according to the story as she afterward told it, notably complaisant. She was willing to entertain the advances the infatuated Sharon was tearfully pressing upon her only if he would first legitimatize their relationship. Sharon was unwilling to go through a formal civil or religious ceremony but he did prepare and sign a contract:

> In the City and County of San Francisco, State of California, on the 25th day of August, 1880 A. D., age 60 years, in the presence of Almighty God, take Sarah Althea Hill, of the City of San Francisco, Cal., to be my lawful and wedded wife, and do here acknowledge myself to be the husband of Sarah Althea Hill.

To which Sarah duly responded:

> I, Sarah Althea Hill of the City and County of San Francisco, California, aged twenty-seven years, do here, in the presence of Almighty God, take Senator William Sharon of the State of Nevada as my lawful and wedded husband, and do hereby declare myself to be the wife of Senator William Sharon of Nevada.

To which she added, presumably at Sharon's request:

> I agree not to make known the contents of this paper for two years, unless Mr. Sharon himself sees fit to make it known.

The affair having been legitimatized to her satisfaction, Sarah Althea allowed herself to be moved into a suite in San Francisco's Grand Hotel and for more than a year thereafter they lived openly as man and wife, he even squiring her to his daughter's wedding reception. Toward the end of 1881, however, Sharon demanded the return of his contract and when she refused throttled her with such application that she fell senseless and he stuffed her body into a hotel closet, believing her dead. This on the word of Sarah Althea. Persuasion having failed, Sharon had the rooms of the suite searched with such thoroughness that her belongings were ripped to ribbons, but without the contract being discovered. This second failure hardened Sharon's heart, and he ordered Sarah Althea evicted. She did not propose to leave the matter there. Repeated efforts to bring the senator to acknowledge her having failed, she took advantage of a moment of weakness on his part. In September, 1883, he was hauled in for having committed adultery with Gertie Deitz, he being then the lawful and wedded husband of Sarah Althea Sharon.

The criminal case was dismissed, but Sarah Althea promptly brought him into court on a civil action, flourishing her wedding contract. Sharon, using the argument that he was a citizen of Nevada and thus outside the jurisdiction of California courts, counter-sued in the federal district court. In the state courts Sarah Althea won a smashing victory in December, 1884, a confirmation of the validity of the marriage—she had meanwhile bolstered her contract with letters addressed "Dear Wife" and purportedly written by Sharon—and a decree of divorce. Deady's decision found otherwise, almost exactly a year later, finding the contract fraudulent and the letter forged.

Sharon died November 13, 1885. On January 7, 1886, Sarah Althea married her principal attorney and ardent admirer, that redoubtable fire-eater, David Terry. Terry did not propose that his little bride be lightly treated by the law, and he hurried back to court as soon as he decently could after the celebration of the nuptials—to the state courts, they being the more agreeable—and brought suit against the executor of Sharon's estate under the divorce decree. The case wended its way slowly to the California Supreme Court, where a decision was handed down, which, when finally modified, allowed the new Mrs. Terry $7,500 in lump settlement and $1,500 a month for the remainder of her life. Whereupon Sharon's executor returned to the federal courts and the case eventually came before Judge Field. The sequel is described in the diary.

William Sharon (from "Men of Mark," Bradley & Rulofson, S.F.)

Henderson, age 16, at Lawrenceville.

Ladd & Bush Bank, Salem.

The Reed Opera House, Salem. (Cronise photo.)

During Deady's stay at the Oregon coast in 1885, he visited the C. E. S. Woods at Fort Stevens, and "bathed below the jetty," then just begun. The view of officers' quarters and barracks, looking across the Columbia's mouth to the northwest, must have been taken just preceding that time.

In Benton County in May, 1885 (Corvallis, the Agricultural College, Philomath) the Deadys passed through this kind of country. (S.P. Collection, OHS.)

The Grand Court of the Palace Hotel. In 1886, The judge preferred the Occidental.

G.A.R. Arch, Market Street, San Francisco, Cal.
Aug. 3rd. 1886.

The Cliff House of that period, with ships approaching the Golden Gate in the distance. (Hazeltine Collection, OHS.)

Fort Point and the Golden Gate. (Hazeltine Collection.)

Drill Grounds in Golden Gate Park, 1890s. (Battleship Oregon Collection.)

Telegraph Hill and the Bay, 1880. (Hazeltine Collection.)

"U. S. District Petty Jury," 1886–87. 1, Matthew P. Deady, Judge U. S. District Court; 2, R. B. Lamson, Dep. Clerk U. S. Courts; 3, R. H. Lamson, Clerk; 4, L. L. McArthur, U. S. Attorney; 5, W. H. Williams, The Dalles; 6, J. S. Medley, Cottage Grove; 7, M. S. Williams, Hillsboro; 8, J. F. Anderson, Salem; 9, G. M. Allen, Amity; 10, Chas. S. Emerson, St. Helens; 11, J. P. Milhorn, Junction City; 12, W. Dunagan, Silverton; 13, G. W. Snell, Portland; 14, J. T. Callison, Pleasant Station; 17, John W. Pugh, Shedd; 18, Al. W. Herren, Salem; 19, Hiram Adams; 20, G. P. Lark, Oregon City; 21, H. Allen, Silverton, 22, W. F. Kirk, Oregon City; 23, W. W. Collins; 24, R. A. Woodruff, Cleveland; 25, Penumbra Kelly, Marshal; 26, D. J. Cooper, The Dalles; 27, F. P. Close, Eugene City; 28, F. P. Devney, Jefferson; 29, John Buoy, Creswell; 30, J. T. Apperson, Oregon City; 31, J. N. Fullilove, Bailiff; 32, N. B. Sinnott, The Dalles; 33, Levi Henkle, (Reside photo.)

# 1886

*January 9 (Sat)* . . . Paid off my bills on Saturday the 2 amounting to near $1000, and had something over $380 left which has since increased to $790. My receipts during the year appear to have been $6148. On Wednesday Dec 30th Mr Corbett gave me $50 more on account of the water bill which makes $350 in all. Read Barcourt, something of a squirt after all, though his comments on American manners 45 years ago are very entertaining at times.[1] An upper class Mrs Trollope.

*15 (Sat)* . . . Last evening I received the proof of my opinion in S v H from Bancroft and will read it carefully tomorrow and return it on same steamer. Sawyer is very thin skinned and is scared because some county newspaper in Cal is howling because I said that Sharon was more responsible than Hill and so far more likely to tell the truth. . . .

*23 (Sat)* . . . Tuesday evening sent proof of my opinion in S v H to Bancroft & Co by express on Steamer. Put a good deal of work on it. Worked much of Sunday afternoon and until 11 oclock at night on it, and think it pretty near perfect now. Refused to leave out what I said about Sarah Althea being an unimportant person without position or property as Sawyer suggested because criticized by the Colusa *Sun*, but put in an explanatory paragraph.

On Wednesday and Thursday snow fell nearly 8 inches deep. Last night it rained and the snow is going off. Last night took Edward to the Casino to hear the "Beggar Student." It was well rendered and has some pretty music and striking situations. Am going again this evening and will take Mrs D. Heard Norelius v Warren et al, a libel by a seaman against the master and mate for assault and battery. I have got so much business on hands that I don't know when I will catch up. No mail from the east yesterday or today. Snow slide at Bonneville, prevents the passage of trains.

*30 (Sat)* . . . Thursday delivered decision in Norelius v Warren et al—a seaman agt his master and mates for personal wrongs. Gave him $250 agt the master and $50 agt the first mate and would have given him $1000 agt the third mate if he had been found.

Took Mrs Deady, Edward and Jess[i]e Murch to hear "Pinafore" last night. The performance was excellent. Agreed with Mr [John] Wentworth of San Francisco to pay him $75 for a picture and sketch of myself to appear in the March number of the *Resources of California,* with the rest of the trustees of Stanford University.[2] Sent him a photo and letter last night by steamer. Alfred Holman will write the sketch. Sent L S B Sawyer a pair of elk horns on last nights steamer— the pair I got from Ed Faye on the Coquille some time ago. Mr Grimes sent the largest and handsomest pair this week from Clatsop I ever saw. Expected to send them to Sawyer, but concluded to keep them and send the others. . . . Called in the evening at the Hall, where I spent a pleasant hour with Miss L & C without a word about brasses and surplices.

*February 6 (Sat)* . . . Sat in the C C & D C during the week. Finished opinion in Ah Lits case and delivered [it] . . . on Thursday to a large audience. Discharged the Chinaman on the ground that the city had not the power to punish persons for smoking opium elsewhere than in a joint or public place. . . .

Thursday evening on my way home I stopped in to the Casino about 10 and was taken by the manager, Mr Thompson, to the right hand box, where I met and was introduced to Gen Gibbon.[3] Not a very prepossessing man in appearance, but had a hearty self reliant look. Got my January salary today—this beats Republican time. Evidently a working administration.

Attended the annual meeting of the members of the Library Association held at their rooms in the evening and read my annual report. Mr Corbett and I were reelected as directors for the ensuing ten years. It is not likely that I will serve the time out, but he may. From there I went at ½ past 8 to the Grammar School to witness an exhibition of Mrs Jarleys wax works in which Mr Oliver Cole personated Jarley with great success—in fact Mr Cole is very droll.[4] The entertainment was given under the auspices of the Womans Guild of Trinity and many of the Congregation were present.

Mrs Deady and the Catlin boys went out early in the evening and when we came home we found that Alice Strong had another boy, and she was another Aunt.

*7 (Sun)* . . . Trinity as usual. Bishop Morris preached one of his old full ½ hour sermons. Life is getting too short for that kind of thing. . . .

*13 (Sat)* . . . Much excitement in town this week over the Anti-Chinese Congress (mob) that meets here today, and I understand the citizens are well prepared to put down any act of lawlessness, like driving out the Chinese and to punish the actors. I hope so. Rev Mr Eliot and Mr Thielsen had timely articles in the *Oregonian* this morning on the subject.[A]

. . . Got letter from Henderson yesterday and his accounts in which he speaks of his incidental expenses as his *acci*dental instead of his *in*cidental expenses. Called at the Hall this evening.

*20 (Sat)* . . . Called to see Fechheimer on Thursday evening [*the 11th*]. He is quite ill with enlargement of the liver and some impediment or affection of the stomach or intestines. Called again at noon on Friday and bade him good bye. He went on the evening train to N Y for medical or surgical aid and advice. Poor fellow! He is just fixed to live and it seems hard to die. I would miss him very much and so would many others. Thursday evening took Mrs Deady to the Casino to see "Billie Tailor," a rough sort of "Pinafore" in which Miss [Beba] Vining appears to advantage as usual. Got Hendersons report of his standing for the half year in which the average of 7 studies is 3.9 on a scale of 5 or .9 above average, while his marks are 57. Sent a draft for $225 to the Treasurer through Dr MacKenzie, $25 of which is to be placed to H Bs credit for incidentals. Got another report today with the same result, but changing Latin from 4 to 3.5 and English composition from 4 to 3.5 and reducing his marks to 56. . . .

. . . Sunday afternoon and evening [*the 14th*] I looked over the draft of the tax law which Mr Failings commission was getting up. They need a draftsman very badly. I made a good many suggestions for Failing and drew him a provision to be added to one of the sections embodying the purpose of the Block law allowing debtors to agree to pay taxes on the security where the interest does not exceed 8 per cent. . . .

. . . Called at the Hall . . . [*this*] evening where I met a Mr Hickman from Stockton who was disposed to champion the cause of Hill as against Sharon because he did not think the U S court had jurisdiction for that S was a *resident* and therefore a citizen of California. This I doubt not is a common impression among those who do not know the difference between mere residence and citizenship, and to put the case before the country in its true light on this point I discussed the question of citizenship in general and Sharons citizenship on the facts proven, even against Sawyers earnest advice. But I think he is now pleased with what I did.

*21 (Sun)* Attended . . . Trinity as usual. The coal gas escaped from the new furnace into the church in the evening so badly that the sermon was omitted. . . .

*27 (Sat)* . . . Heard the case of the *Saraca*, Dennison libellant. Decided it this morning. A ship chandler furnished $140 in money to a drunken master in hopes of getting his trade for sea stores, and when he lost the trade by reason of the master being displaced, he pretended that the money was furnished to the master to pay seamens wages and sued the ship for the amount. Sentenced Richard Breckenridge to 6 months imprisonment for breaking into the P O at Roseburg and taking some trifling matter out of a private box. He was only 12 years old and plead guilty, and I directed the sentence to be executed in the jail at Roseburg where his mother lives.[5] . . . Yesterday was Mrs Deadys [*omitted*] birthday. I presented her with a necklace of gold beads that I had made for her out of some old jewelry and some fine gold from the Sterling mine belonging to Capt Ankeny. The cost of manufacture was $40 and the value of the material about $30. They are large and handsome. . . . Gov Moody called on me this morning and talked over the situation with reference to the anti Chinese demonstration. I advised him to issue a proclamation by the 10th or 15th of next month based on the action of the so called Congress here and the expulsion of the Chinese from Oregon City since, stating the right of the Chinese here and warning all persons against undertaking to carry out the direction of the Congress and the penalty they would incur if they did. I think he will. Said he had been thinking of it. Sent Henderson a box on the 24th for his 17th birthday, March 4. It contained a razor, strop brush & cake of soap . . .

*March 13 (Sat)* . . . Monday evening went with Mrs Deady to the Casino to hear "Falka" and then by previous invitation to Mrs Laidlaws to a petit soupe where we met a number of people—mostly young or youngish and had an elegant spread including a glass of delicious [*omitted*]. Judge Williams and I sat at the table with Mrs L—I on her right. Met the young artist there, Mr [Edward] Espy—a rather striking prepossessing fellow with the odds in his favor of an occasional stammer.[6]

   . . . Called [*at Fechheimers*] Thursday afternoon by special invitation and had an hours talk with him or rather he with me. He is arranging for his end which he thinks quite nigh with as much method and deliberation as if he were about to go on a journey to a far country. He thanked me very cordially for all I had done for him in the last 18 or 19 years of our acquaintance, and told me some particulars of the disposition he had made of his property—particularly for charity and the Library. Saw him a moment yesterday afternoon and took him by the hand. He is going fast. Has a hard cancer of the stomach and bowels. . . .

   . . . Went to Eugene on Friday and returned on Saturday to a meeting of the Regents. Took Jessie Murch with me to her folk. Got a resolution passed designating the new College building as Villard Hall, in acknowledgement of his benefactions to the University, of which I have had a copy handsomely engraved to send him.

*14 (Sun)* . . . Notice this morning of Fechheimers death in the *Oregonian*. Died Saturday night near 9 oclock. Poor fellow. I am sorry that he is gone. Mrs D and I stopped at Brookes as we came home and Mrs D put a gold necklace (beads) on her Goddaughters neck—Genevieve Park[e]. We sent to New York for them. Cost $25 and are very pretty indeed. Worked in the afternoon a while and then called at Ollies and thence to Fechheimers, where I found Arnold and [Henry] Ach disagreeing over the question of whether Rev Mr Rosenberg should make some remarks at Fechheimers grave—the latter being for it and the former against it. I told them that Mr Arnold was Mrs Fs brother and the matter was in his hands. They both wanted me to make some remarks at his grave but I declined, saying I could not do so without being misunderstood and that I could properly say what I ought or wanted to say from the Bench when the resolutions of the Bar were presented.

*20 (Sat)* Monday court adjourned out of respect to Fs memory and his funeral took place from his house at 2 P M. The Bar attended in a body. There were no services. I had a carriage placed at my disposal in which I took Judges [Seneca] Smith & [Loyal] Stearns[7] and Paul. At the Cemetery (R V), Hughes and Bellinger made some agnostic remarks, the latter closing up with a characteristically politic remark to the effect, that whatever might be wanting in hope for the future "at least they had nothing" to fear. Hughes had no policy and was brutally materialistic. It was sad to see so good a fellow buried like a dog. Tuesday sat in the C C & D C. MacArthur as District Attorney, at my suggestion, presented the Bar resolution on the opening of the court in a few eloquent and well chosen remarks. He was seconded by Mr Ach, who did admirably well. Then came Thomas N Strong in a rather pretentious disquisition but well delivered. [H Y] Thompson made some personal observations of the deceased. Wood (C E S) closed the requiem in a speech of near half an hour delivered in excellent style and containing some very appropriate and beautiful things, but he got on to Fs peculiar notions, which were evidently his also and grew tedious and inappropriate. I followed with a 5 minute speech which I jotted down the night before closing with a stanza from Whittiers "My Psalm," of anti-Agnostic flavor. The proceedings were published in Wednesdays *Oregonian* and Thursdays *Telegram* with my remarks in full.

Worked . . . getting some thoughts together for my charge to the Grand Jury on the 23 on the subject of Anti-Chinese agitation and outrages.

The week has been cool and moist. On Wednesday sent a certified copy of the resolution of the Regents naming the new College building Villard Hall, to Mr Henry Villard, at Berlin. Dropped into the Turne Verein, where the Hibernians were celebrating San Pat with a ball. I always get a complimentary and go and look on a while. They were a decent well-behaved crowd of common people. Got a letter from Dr Mackenzie today dated the 12th saying Henderson had been suspended for his marks and that he had taken him to his house where he would be kept for a week when he would be returned to school. The letter was kind and considerate and gave hopes that Henderson was penitent and determined to do better hereafter.

*27 (Sat)* . . . Tuesday empaneled Grand Jury and delivered charge to them—the part relating to the anti-Chinese rioters was in writing and was published in the *Oregonian* the next day—the 24th. It reads well and I have had many compliments for it—both as to matter and manner. But I suppose I will get scorched for it in the *Alarm* and *Pulse* that are issued today. . . . Wednesday Mr Edward Espey sent me a pastel of his, representing the surf at the mouth of the Columbia river near Fort Stevens. It is a very attractive picture, and is worth with the frame as I learn not less than $150. I wrote him a letter Thursday acknowledging the receipt of it, and saying that the picture had a special interest for me as I spent some days in October last in that very surf about the time he was making the sketch—and that in days to come which I hoped and predicted would not be many, when Edward Espeys name stood high on the list of artists I would take pride in exhibiting my picture, as an early proof of his genius and promise of his future distinction. I have taken some interest in the subscription of $1000 for his large picture "Repose" to be presented to the Library association. Mr Laidlaw has the matter in charge and yesterday he called and told me that the amount was raised. Espey returns to Paris in a few days to finish a large picture of a sunset at sea for the Salon of 1887.[8] . . .

*April 3 (Sat)* . . . The Grand Jury were discharged on Tuesday. They found 13 Indictments against the Anti Chinese under § 5336 of the R[evised] S[tatutes]. On Thursday April 1 got a telegram from Sawyer suggesting that the counts be inserted on § 5519 and 5508 of the R S. Too late, the jury gone . . .

*17 (Sat)* . . . Got a letter yesterday from Dr Mackenzie to the effect that Henderson had gone for Easter holidays without his consent and that he had opened a letter to him from me that came the day after he left about which he was in much distress. Telegraphed him at once, that opening letter all right and wrote him today at length that H had our permission to go to N Y or Phil and was sorry that he had failed to get his and hoped it would turn out there was some mistake about it.[9]. . . Edward went along splendidly this week but last evening went over the dam again. Poor fellow.

*24 (Sat)* . . . [Monday] Made order, which I prepared, for the building of the Santiam bridges on the Narrow Gauge Ry and otherwise putting the road in repair and working condition and authorizing the receiver to borrow $100,000 on the security of the road for that purpose. Wednesday evening delivered my first lecture at the law school. Subject the land law of Oregon. Will deliver 8 or 10 more on constitutional law before the close of the year.

. . . Good Friday, adjourned court and attended M prayer at Trinity. Mr Foote preached an earnest sermon—a little long and slightly what old [W G] T'Vault used to call "repetitious" and somewhat monotonous. But these two are characteristic of all his sermons. During the week having been looking over the *Harleian Miscellanies* came across Henry the 8ths letters to Anne Bullen. Most of them are written in French, the originals are given with translations. They are rather decent and well turned love letters. He does say in one of them that he would like "to kiss her duckies"—whatever they are . . . Had a long letter from Mr William Mackenzie of Dundee today, which is not as interesting as the writer is. My opinion in the Sharon case is the subject of quite a long editorial in the Dundee *Advertiser* of the [*date omitted*]. It is quite complimentary to me. Mackenzie says it was either written or inspired by Dr [John] Leng.[10]

*May 1 (Sat)* Sunday (Ap 25th) Easterday . . . [attended] Trinity and afternoon service at the chapel, where I saw a large class confirmed—the women and girls being prettily and becomingly arrayed in white, and the men, among whom was a negro, and boys "as you please" . . . Monday evening took Mrs Deady, Edward, Jessie Murch and Agnes & Blanche Catlin to the Casino to hear "The Bohemian Girl." It was very well done and it was a real pleasure to see how these young girls enjoyed it. It was all knew [*sic*] to them but it will never be to me again.

Wednesday lectured to the senior class in the law school. Finished the subject of the land law of Oregon . . . Thursday evening went late to the Mikado Tea at Mrs Lewis' given by the Womans guild. A pretty sight, but more a success as a spectacle than socially.

*8 (Sat)* . . . Got a letter yesterday from San Gabriel—very complimentary of me and my charge to the Grand Jury in the Anti-Chinese matter, the signature of which I cannot make out. The writer speaks of Justice Field as a familiar friend. I think I will enclose the letter to him and ask him who the writer is. I think the name is Shorb, but there is a De something in front of it. It can hardly be Dr [James De B] Shorb who used to cut such a figure in Democratic politics in San Francisco.[11]. . .

The weather has been cool and moist during the week. On Wednesday evening I lectured before the class in the law school on constitutional law—commencing with the decalogue and ending with Magna Charta [*sic*]. Got my salary for April today which brings my bank account within $9 of even. . . .

*15 (Sat)* Sunday . . . at Trinity as usual. Water gave out and motor wouldn't work, and no music until after the "Te Deum," when they got the boy on the bellows . . .

*22 (Sat)* . . . Sat in the C C & D C during the week. Monday decided motion for provisional injunction in Seeley v Reed, denying the same. Tom Strong had [Wilson] Hume[12] report my remarks without letting me know it. A scurvy trick. But Hume showed me the extension before he gave it to him and allowed me to correct it. Allowed application of Receiver Scott to permit other warehouses along line of the Narrow Gauge road. In the evening lectured at law school. Wednesday called . . . at Kellys where I spent an hour very pleasantly, and had some fun over some of Aunt Kates peculiar speeches, in which she constantly fortifies her statements by saying, "Yes, I told the Judge."

. . . Friday evening lectured in law school, and called with Mrs D on the Corbetts. Mrs C looks very well after her winter in New York, but I notice when she smiles that her mouth is beginning to be drawn out of shape . . . This evening went to the minstrel performance for the benefit of Company G, given by the members of the company. I bought tickets and attended because the young gentlemen who composed the company stood up bravely and promptly for law and order during the anti Chinese troubles last spring.

*29 (Sat)* . . . Monday evening attended the celebration of the Queens birth day at the Esmond. Sat on the right of the Vice Consul Laidlaw, who sat on the right of the Chairman Macleay. Williams and Gibbon sat on his left. Major [W A] Jones[13] sat on my left and Whalley on his left. I replied to the toast—The State of Oregon. The speech was published in the *Oregonian* of the 27th and reads well. The dinner was good and the wine also and the company pleasant and well behaved. Williams in proposing the British Empire, made an entertaining speech of some length which he marred by speaking at the close of Canada as a place of refuge for our defaulting cashiers and "licentious Sunday School teachers."

. . . Lectured at the law School on Tuesday and Friday evening at the former on the formation of the State Constitutions, and the latter on the law of the land "per legam tenae." Rather like it, but wish we had a larger class . . .

*June 5 (Sat)* . . . Lectured before the law school on Tuesday evening and Friday evening on the power to regulate commerce. This makes 10 lectures and completes my allotment. On the whole I rather like it, and am moderately well pleased with myself. . . . Wednesday attended the French exhibit at the Hall, and discussed the Lords Supper with Miss Lydia afterwards. I am afraid she thinks I am a heretic . . .

*19 (Sat)* . . . Tuesday [*June 8*] went to Eugene to attend Commencement. Took Jessie Murch with me. Henry Failing and Mr McArthur went up also. Delivered my address in the new Villard Hall at 3:50 in the afternoon. The Hall was about half full of what appeared to be an attentive and appreciative audience. Came home on Friday. While at Eugene attended all the exercises, and made a little impromptu speech at the dinner of the Alumni Association. The addresses at the graduating exercises were excellent in manner and matter, and I think showed the good effects of Prof Hawthornes careful training in composition. . . .

*26 (Sat)* Sunday . . . Met Judge Sawyer at Trinity in the evening with some ladies who had just returned from Alaska with him—Miss West, Miss Jackson, Miss Geis and two Misses Watson. After service on[e] of the Misses Watson wanted to see

Miss Rodney with whom she was at school at St Marys, Burlington. So we all walked up to the Hall where we met the Misses Rodney and where after a few moments I left the party to come here and write some letters.

Monday Judge Sawyer sat in the C C with me . . . His lady friends came up with him and sat in the courtroom. In the evening I took the Judge and Miss West and Miss Jackson to the Lawn party at McCrackens. I also invited the Misses Catlin and Failing but got Paul to take them on my account. The affair was very pretty and picturesque—the Gipsy camp especially, where Miss [Kate] Trevett told my fortune and gave me 95 years of life for which I paid her 25 cents or double price.[14] Danced with Miss J and Mrs C E S Wood and ate a philopena with the former for which I exacted payment when I bade her good night . . .

Thursday (the 24th) was the 34 anniversary of our marriage, and also of Cyrus & Mrs Dolphs. We dined with them and went to the Green-Burr wedding at Trinity which was a beautiful affair.[15] . . .

*July 3 (Sat)* . . . [During the week] Decided U S v Kelly in which I found some very singular slovenly work in a hearing transcript containing a statement of differences as to the defts property accounts and returns as clerk of the Indian School at Forest Grove, and some suspicious tinkering with the defendants retained papers.[16]

Friday evening dined at Whalleys with Mrs Deady . . . Miss Whalley looked lovely and was charming. I was stupid enough to beat her at a game of billiards. Tuesday I tried U S v Bewley & Son without a jury for obstructing the mails, and found them guilty and fined them $10 apiece.[17] . . .

Mr Harris, Pres of the North Pacific called this morning with a Mr Thorn of New York. Mr Horace White of the *Evening Post* called yesterday.[18] A quiet pleasant man, whom I am glad to know. He tells me Villard will be in New York this fall at the head of a large banking establishment based on German capital. . . . Monday, July 5, went in the procession. Gov Moody and Secretary [Rockey] Earhart in my carriage. The day cloudy but pleasant until we got to the stand when it began to sprinkle and continued to drizzle throughout the exercises. Tom Fitch delivered the oration which taken altogether was the finest thing of the kind I ever heard.[19] On Friday evening I heard him lecture at Masonic Hall on the life hereafter, ludicrously and belit[tl]ingly named "The Invisible police." It was a gem of rhetoric, and word painting and most original and appropriate thought and suggestions as well. And yet poor fellow, after 20 years of experience and opportunity on this coast, his life is generally understood to have been a failure, and even a fault. While I sat on the stand and listened to him I felt that if anyone were to offer my choice of a million of money or his gift of eloquence I would take the latter without hesitation. And yet it has done him no good. . . .

. . . Was taken Tuesday evening [*the 20th*] with an attack of billious diarhea, which pulled me down for a day or two, but I came to my chambers and worked in my chair. Heard application to settle amount of supersedeas bond in Hickox v Elliott, on behalf of Joseph Holladay. Wrote opinion after reading up on the subject very thoroughly which I delivered on Friday holding that the decree was not otherwise secured within the meaning of rule 29 and the amount of the bond must be $75,000.[20]

Friday Mr Justice Waite arrived with his daughter from the east. Sent James [Fullilove][21] down with my card, and in the afternoon the old man came to my chambers and we had two hours of pleasant chat. Took him into the cupola where we had a splendid view of Mt Hood & Helen. At half past 5 Mrs Deady and I drove to the Esmond and took the Chief Justice and his daughter, Miss Waite and drove them to R V Cemetery and then back through town and returned them to the Hotel at 15 minutes after 8 when we drove to Koehlers to say good by to Mrs K who starts for Germany today. Got home about 9 when I went down town and in returning while getting off the car was thrown down and hurt my right knee . . .

*26 (Mon)* . . . Friday went to Tacoma. Took Mrs D with me. Staid all night at Tacoma House. Met Ladd and some of his party returning from Alaska. Saturday we went to the Chautauqua grounds 8 miles this side of Seattle, where I was booked to deliver a lecture on "Constitution Making." Spent the afternoon lounging about, looking at the bathers &c. At 9 oclock 200 or so people came down from Seattle and between that and ten I began my lecture which lasted 40 minutes. We got on the boat by 11 and to Seattle by 12. Sunday morning we got off at 6:40 A M for Tacoma. Passed over a beautiful rich country full of hop yards and many comfortable houses and places. Got to Tacoma for breakfast at 9, and went to church at St Lukes where we heard Mr Wells preach. . . . Came home today and sat awhile in the Circuit Court. Made the acquaintance of Judge Tripp of Yankton, Dakotah (Bartlett Tripp, formerly of Maine, but went to D in 1868).[22] Had his daugher and a female friend with him. Mrs Deady was not well since yesterday morning and I have been troubled with lumbago in my back ever since I have been gone and am yet. . . . The Chautauqua was a humdrum sort of affair. I had a pretty good lecture, a good share of which I extemporized, but I doubt if the people took much interest in it and yet they sat it out well. My expenses were $27 one half of which I will charge to Chautauqua at least.

*August 7 (Sat)* . . . Have been much troubled with lumbago in my back, but it is better this evening. Dr Strong has been attending me, giving me an alkali and a linament for external application. Got a letter today from J H Blair of Marshal, Iowa [enclosing] a brief in a railway case and a letter in which he quotes largely and lauds loudly my opinion in the Narrow Gauge v the O R & N Co. Well I can stand it. . . .

. . . Saturday [*14*] went on the *Olympian* to Ilwaco, leaving at one P M. Pleasant ride. Reached the wharf at 8 P M. Slept on board. In the morning walked up to Mrs Holmans where I found a warm welcome and an excellent breakfast. Between 10 & 11 I rode over to the beach in company with Fred Holman and called at Whalleys cottage and thence to the seaside where I found the Misses Whalley, headed by Susie . . . After strolling about and lounging in the sand, Fred H and I went into the surf awhile. Had a very enjoyable time indeed. The weather was lovely and the water delicious. Then we dined at Whalley's, Capt [J N] Allison being present also, and I think he means business as to Miss Susie. After dinner he "took" us all as a group with a sort of pocket camera which he carries with him. Then I drove back to Ilwaco and got aboard the *Olympia,* where I soon got in bed and woke up in the morning at Portland in thick fog, and got home to breakfast. Monday evening (Aug 17) Mrs Deady went out to drive with Chief Justice Waite and daughter and Mr Cyrus Dolph. Tuesday evening called with Paul on the Chief Justice and Mrs Waite who returned from Alaska on Monday, laying by some days at Victoria and the Sound. In the parlor of the Hotel we met Gov Hoadly, wife and daughter and pension Commissioner [J C] Black & wife.[23] Wednesday evening dined at Williams. Dinner given to the Chief Justice. In Mrs Williams absence Mrs Wood was hostess. The Chief Justice sat at her right and I at her left. Hoadly sat at Williams left and Miss Waite at his right. No other ladies present . . . The dinner was very good, but the champagne was limited.

Thursday Mrs Deady, Paul and I went up the Columbia on the *Wide West* to the Cascades on an excursion given by Mr Cyrus Dolph to the Chief Justice. The Hoadlys went along on their way home. The boat was filled with Grand Army people returning home by the North Pacific from the encampment at San Francisco. Among others was Gov [Lucius] Fairchild[24] and Comr Black . . . We had a pleasant day and a good dinner—champagne galore. Got pretty well acquainted with Mr & Mrs Hoadly and liked them both very much. On leaving the boat we bade the Waites good by. They started overland yesterday morning for California. He is a very pleasant sensible man, who bears his honors well and Miss Waite is his own daughter.

Wednesday (Aug 18) was a field day in the C C. By invitation the Chief Justice and Gov Hoadly sat with me in the court. There was a large attendance of the bar. I decided three cases orally and delivered one written opinion. Then I announced we were honored with the presence of the Chief Justice and that we would take a recess for a few moments to give the members of the bar an opportunity to pay their respects to him. Thereupon we stepped down onto the floor and I presented the company to him and Gov Hoadly.

The *Central Law Journal* [of St Louis] published an editorial on my address on "Towns & Cities," commending my presentations of the evil of our present municipal system, but condemning the proposed remedy as impracticable as interfering with male suffrage which the writer seems to think is fixed for all time and circumstances. Well we will see. If the municipal suffrage is not weeded and purified it will soon become so diseased that it will have to be bodily cut out and destroyed in the interests of order and property. By means of this article I suppose I have had several applications from persons in the east and west for copies of the address.[25]

*28 (Sat)* . . . Sat in the C C & D C Monday and Tuesday. In the former announced Judge Sawyers opinion affirming my decree in the case of the *Abercorn* the contested point in which was that Washington Territory is a "state" within the meaning of that phrase as used in the Congressional Pilot Act of 1837 . . . I first held that it is in the *Panama,* in 1862, and have been affirming it occasionally ever since and I am glad that it has been taken to the Circuit Court. Wednesday, we started for Yaquina with a party made up by Mrs Deady mostly, consisting of 31 persons consisting of myself, Mrs Deady, Edward & Henderson, Mr Brooke & Scott & Mac Brooke, Judge & Mrs Stott, Alice Strong and Fred, Mrs Catlin and

Seth & Blanche, Mr Henry Failing and May, Mr & Mrs Wood and "Nan," David & Sallie Lewis, Couch Flanders, Gre[t]chen & Mabel Breck, Rodney & Florence Glisan, Will Ott & Mal Effinger, Mr Linthicum, Mr Koehler and the colored boy James Fullilove—in all 31. Paul was to have gone with us but could not get away. However he came on the next day with Mr Valentine which made 33.[26]

We reached Newport at ½ past 7 after a very enjoyable ride through the mountains, and a splendid lunch on the cars, and stopped at the Ocean House—the young men being put in tents.

Thursday morning we bathed on the north beach, just inside the heads. In the afternoon we drove up the coast 5 miles to the lighthouse on Cape Foulweather so called, the real cape of that name being some miles farther north. We all went up in the lighthouse. Looking at the shore and surf through the lens showed a magnificent panorama in which all the colors of the prism were mingled in the most brilliant confusion. Friday we drove to the seal rocks 10 miles south—a delightful drive on a hard smooth beach.

After clambering up the rocks we dined at Mrs [James] Brasfields—a good dinner with the best of bread, honey and butter.[27] The honey is made from the flower of the Sallal bush and is very clear and perfect in taste. Saturday we came home, stopping for dinner at Hemphills in Corvallis. Here the party was grouped for a picture by the local photographer. The day being the tenth anniversary of Mr & Mrs Stotts marriage, Mr Linthicum got a tin cup at Corvallis and Mr & Mrs Wood a nutmeg grater, and on the way down, near Derry, I presented them to Mrs Stott in a little speech. Then Mr Failing filled the cup with wine and Mrs Stott having tasted it was passed around to the health of the company. Stott was called for a speech but he did not respond. At Amity we dropped Henderson. His uncle John was there to meet him and take [him] to the farm, to see his grandfather and mother before going east. Farther down Stott made a little speech giving thanks to the party to which I replied to the effect that each one had done something to make the party a success for which I was obliged to them, but that much was due to Mrs Deady for a happy selection of the guests. The grade on the last 5 miles of the ascent coming east from Yaquina was 116 feet to the mile and there are two long tunnels and two more than horseshoe curves in that distance. We had a car free all the way and back and everyone paid his or her expenses beyond this. It cost me for Mrs Deady, Edward, Henderson and self $39—$12 of which was for hack hire to Foulweather & Sealrock. I believe there was not an unpleasant incident that occurred on the whole trip.

*September 4 (Sat)* . . . Henderson left yesterday for Lawrenceville to return to school. I hope for the best, but I have fears that he will not exert himself and will fall behind, and be dropped out. Paul has been behaving badly this week and altogether I am not in a happy state of mind. There is one consolation. Edward is doing well. . . .

*11 (Sat)* Sunday (Sept 5th) Attended S S and M and E prayer at Trinity as usual. The choir was back and sang well. Mr Foote is getting a little monotonous. Called at Ollies in the afternoon and found her and her seven daughters and Agnes Catlin at dinner—also the father of the interesting group. Owing to the number of girls therein and the fact that the front door of the house is always securely locked, I have given the place the name of the "Nunnery."

. . . Thursday the Rev Mr [J C] Eccleston[28] called to see me in company with Capt Barnett. He will lecture here on Tuesday and Wednesday on Westminster Abbey and St Pauls with the aid of the Stereopticon. Came over the Canadian Pacific and spoke with rapture of the game he saw on the [way] and which he expects to take a shot at on the way home—from which I infer he is not altogether a fisher of men. He is a fine looking man and they say he is a fine speaker.

. . . On Wednesday evening Mrs D and I made a very pleasant call at Sim Reeds. So far as this world goes, they appear to be well fixed and happy. The break with Ladd annoys him though, and I don't wonder at it.[29] The weather has been beautiful this week, but yesterday and today are rather warm. The thermometer in my chamber is now—2:25 P M—at 84.

*18 (Sat)* . . . Sat in the C C & D C during the week except Friday when I went to the State Fair, where I saw some old friends, and good livestock and some pretty horse racing and trotting used primarily as a gambling device . . . Have been dipping into the first volume of Ruskins *Fors Clavigera* during the week. Read Ouida on woman or female suffrage—a trenchant reckless article and very readable indeed.

*October 12 (Tue)* . . . [*Tuesday, September 21*] went to the New Market to hear Minnie Hauk,[30] on the invitation of the Reeds. Mrs Deady went also. Was disappointed in her. After the performance I went on board the *Thompson* en route for Clatsop where I arrived on Thursday and staid until Thursday the 7th of October when I started home reaching here Friday evening on the *Reed* in the rain.

On the Thursday, Sept 30th, Mrs C E S Wood came down with her 4 children and a nurse and I left them there. They got home this evening. I bathed every day I was there except the last rain or shine and enjoyed it very much. Had Mrs Wood in some times. Tommy Strowbridge was stopping at the Clucher house and came over and spent much of his time with us.[31] I enjoyed Mrs Woods company very much, but she is such a slave to her children that she has little time to spare for anyone else. . . .

Found Mrs Deady very sick when I got home with neuralgia in the shoulder. She is out of bed today for the first time. Found Paul had been gambling and drawing checks in the name of the firm again to pay gambling debts. Upon consideration with Whalley I agreed that he ought not to be expected to keep Paul in the firm any longer. Saturday Oct 10th Paul signed articles of dissolution and left the office. Including his interest in the library he had $2200 coming to him. Of that he gave me a check of $1540 to pay a note of $1500 at Ladds which I gave on July 5th to raise money to pay his debts. $420 more was taken to pay checks drawn in the firm name to pay gambling debts. What he will do I don't know. He has used about $8000 in eighteen months and has nothing to show for it—not even a decent suit of clothes.

Sawyer came up and held the Circuit Court from the 4th inst. Went home this morning. Dined with him last night and had a pleasant chat. Heard the *Noddleburn,* Curtis libellant today. Suit for damages for injury sustained by the breaking of the crane line. Edward appeared for the libellant and examined his witnesses very well. His voyage to Australia was of service to him on the occasion. Capt Lamson said it was the first intelligent examination of witnesses on a nautical subject he had ever heard in the court. Of the 14 days I was in Clatsop it rained more or less on three of them. We had some very delightful weather—just perfect. The thermometer stood in the surf at 54. September is the month to spend at the seaside. My expenses for the 17 day[s] were $33.

Sunday, Oct 11, attended . . . Trinity. Young Mr [Frederick] Post[32] officiated in the absence of Mr Foote who is attending the general convention. He has a very good voice and is an elegant reader. He preaches an effective well written 20 minute sermon and is generally very acceptable. . . .

16 (Sat) Sat in the C C & D C since Tuesday last. Wednesday heard the argument in the *Noddleburn* case, Daniel Curtis libellant, having heard the evidence the day before. Edward appeared for the libellant, and considering that it was his first case he did very well. The libellant fell from the rigging by the parting of the crane line between the after foremast shroud and the back stay and fractured the outer malleolus or projection of the fibia, which has united so as to stand out and therefore leaves the ankle liable to turn out whenever the man steps on an incline or uneven surface. Thursday and Friday heard the evidence and arguments in the *Don*—Daniel Rankin, libellant, a suit by the seamen for wages and dissolution of contract on the ground of danger to life if they returned in the vessel to England by reason of the drunkenness [*sic*] of the master and mates. . . . Thursday night went to the Casino and heard Michael Davitt.[33] A plain sharp man who stated the case against the Irish Landlords and Dublin Castle with considerable ingenuity and effect, and the audience, chiefly Irish, cheered him lustily and often. As a substitute for Irish landlords he proposed the Parliament of the Irish Nation that is to be, who are [*sic*] to own the land in trust for the tillers thereof. A landlord is a blessing or a curse owing to the character of the person occupying the position. An absent landlord is necessarily a bad landlord, even if he would be a good one; and an Irish Nation as a landlord, would be neither good nor bad. . . .

23 (Sat) . . . Worked on opinion in *The Noddleburn*, Daniel Curtis libellant and delivered opinion in it this morning for the libellant for $1500 and $70 wages. This was Edwards first case in my court and he did very well in it. I wrote an opinion in it as much as anything else because I did not like to decide a case in his favor without giving my reasons for it and putting them on record and I think I would have given the libellant $500 more if he had not been his attorney. I also decided this morning the case of *The Noddleburn*, Gustave Rolleofs et al libellants, *The Don*, Daniel Rankin et al, libellants, and *The Alliance*, James Hanna libellant, all for the libellants . . . Attended a drive whist party at Mrs Stotts last night and had Mrs Montgomery for a partner. Made 27 points and lost 28. My first experience. A very pleasant party. Mrs Deady is better but still continues weak and uncomfortable. Got Hendersons account of the $75 I gave him when he started east on September 3. It is very cunning indeed. One item of "Tip," 15 cts . . . Visited "the fat cattle show" on Tuesday afternoon and saw much that was

interesting. Saw some Hereford cows that I think are the handsomest horned cattle I ever saw. Sent Wentworth a draft for $75 for my place in his *Resources of California* for September . . .

*30 (Sat)*. . . [Sunday] afternoon Mrs Montgomery drove Mrs Deady and me over the river to the garden of John Bro[e]tje and then into Ladds Dairy.[34] It was a lovely afternoon and a beautiful drive. We saw 80 odd cows being milked in the stalls and the process of separating the cream from the milk by centrifugal force.

Monday went up on the N[arrow] G[auge] to examine the bridges on the Santiam with Mr Robertson and Mr [E P] Roger. Took with me Miss Daisy Buckingham and Mrs Capt [Uriel] Sebree.[35] Went up and back the same day. Had a special train on the N G from Woodburn under the charge of the Receiver Scott and a good luncheon on board. The day was beautiful and the country interesting and the ladies were charmed and charming. . . . Gov Stanford sent me 100 copies of the Sept number of the *Resources of California* for distribution. Received from Bancroft the first volume of the *History of Oregon*. It is a worthy monument to the pioneers of Oregon and contains a notice of Mrs Deadys family which I furnished.

*November 6 (Sat)* Sunday (October 31) . . . at Trinity as usual—Mr Post officiating. Mr Footes long dull sermons will seem doubly tedious after listening to the bright short ones of Mr Post. . . .

Mrs Deady went to Salem to visit the Bushs on Tuesday and on Thursday week on to Eugene to visit the Murchs. For the week ending on Monday she visited a Mrs [J A] Root, a mind cure[r] once a day for the neuralgia and was apparently cured. I am afraid though it will come back again but as she says it was worth the cost ($14) to have so many days existence free from pain.[36]. . .

Have been at work during the week in spare hours on Dumbleton v Talkington, in which I read near 1000 pages of legal cap of testimony. The transaction out of which the suit arises was the exchange of a Salem Saloon and gambling house for a half interest in a 1000 acres of land on the line of the railway on N Umpqua, in which the owner of the land gave $500 [to] boot and in less than three months resold the Saloon to its former owner for $50. It is evident that in this case a knave and a fool met and the Saloon Keeper was not the fool. The weather has been delightful during the whole week. A light white frost at night and warm and hazy during the day. Called in the evening at the Hall where I met the Rodneys and read them a passage out of Ruskins *Fors* illustrating the difference between the Justice of Despotism and Republicanism, the one being an execution on the ship of Sir Francis Drake of a comrade who had misbehaved and the other the hanging of a lot of innocent Chinamen at Los Angeles by a Hibernian mob. . . .

*20 (Sat)* . . . Wednesday evening attended the [Charles] Reed—[Margaret] Green wedding at Trinity church.[37] It was an elegant affair of course with good music.

Got letters from Barnes & Newland saying the Sharon estate would advance the funds necessary to publish 11 Sawyer containing the case of Sharon v Hill. There was some very nice compliments to me in Ns letter. I sent Reed as a wedding present a pass for himself and bride over the O & C Ry to Ashland and back. Called at the Hall this evening where I met the Misses Rodney and had the usual salmagundi chat.

*27 (Sat).* . . Friday evening dined at Schulzes where I met Senator Dolph, Cyrus Dolph, Donald Macleay, Mr [Alex] Mackintosh & Col McCracken, and helped eat an excellent dinner. Played pool awhile after dinner for the second time in my life and succeeded in pocketing a ball besides the cue one . . . Thursday, Scott had a terrible review of Mitchel[l]s methods in the Balch case and the Caruthers case in the D *Oregonian* including his letter to Price[38] arranging for a trade with Ladd & Knott whereby he was to throw off on the state in the supreme court in their favor for 10 acres of the land.

This afternoon took Mrs Deady, Jessie Murch and Blanche Catlin to the New Market to *see* and *hear* the McGibeny family. The phenomenon of their existence was worth seeing but their performance was only so so.[39] . . .

*December 4 (Sat)* Sat in the C C during the week and tried 6 cases with a jury. One against [Tom] Jordan for hiring Tom Mountain to disobey a subpoena in an election bribery case.[40] The deft was found not guilty on proof of an alibi the only material part of which rested on the evidence of one "Doc" (Milton) Howe . . . Monday evening gave a dinner to Senator Dolph at the Esmond to which I invited Judge Williams, Col Kelly, Cyrus Dolph and John Catlin. Sat down at ½ past 6 and rose at near 10. The dinner was very good and the company quite agreeable. Dishes & wine, sherry, claret, appolonaris and champagne. Cost me $35. Took Mrs Deady last evening to the Unitarian Baza[a]r, where I spent $2.10—$1 of the amount for a selection from Mrs Eliots poems. From there we went to Catlins and joined in a taffy pulling. . . .

*11 (Sat).* . . Monday evening attended the young ladies hop at Masonic Hall with Mrs Deady on invitation of Miss Lizzie Story. Had a delightful time. Worked this week all spare hours on Hickox v Elliott et al on application for order of sale of property in possession of Joseph Holladay. The facts are so numerous and complicated that the statement of the case is growing under my hand.

. . . On Wednesday [H] Wise & [J] Centner withdrew their plea of N[ot] G[uilty] and plead Guilty to indictment charging them with bribing [J D] Piercy to vote and I fined them $100 apiece and required them to pay the costs of the prosecution. . . . Spoke to C E S Wood today about taking the professorship of equity in the law School. It struck him favorably and I hope he will take it.

*18 (Sat)* . . . Monday evening took Mrs Deady, Alice and Velina Molson to the New Market at Je[a]nnie Winstons opening in "The Lace Handkerchief." Full of rubbish, but a crowded house and one or two good songs. Wednesday night dropped into the Casino and saw the first act of "Macaire," the opening night. Called on Mrs Ach in a box with the Wassermans. Called on Miss [Kate] Hanover, who was there with Edward.[41] Not pretty but decidedly genteel and somewhat distingue. . . .

*26 (Sat)* . . . On Xmas eve I took a stroll among the shops and bought Mrs D a mahogany card table for $16, and sent 1 pound of candy to each of Mrs Deadys sisters children and ½ a pound to her nieces children—Mary Strong. Gave Mrs Hill a bottle of cologne. In the morning I went to early service (7 oclock) at the

Hall, and staid to breakfast as usual of sausage and buckwheat cakes. There were presents on the tree for Mrs D and Me, and we put some on for the ladies. I gave Miss R my photograph and Miss L Ruskins *Athena or Queen of the Air* and L gave me [George] Herberts poems. . . .

*31 (Thu)* . . . Settled my quarters accounts on Monday and a few yearly ones, gross amount $714.19, which left me $152.08 in bank, that I have since increased to $232.08. Got a handsome notice from my old friend Peter [*Richard*] H Taney-hill of Barnesville in the Holiday number of the *Enterprise.*[42] Speaks of me as a "tall awkward looking boy with a large head, curly sandy hair and prominent blue eyes." What a change since then, February 17, 1841. . . .

# NOTES

1. A search of the catalogues of the Library of Congress, British Museum, Bancroft's Library, Yale Library and the Newberry Library of Chicago has failed to discover any book on 19th Century America ascribed to an author named Barcourt.

2. John P. H. Wentworth, California editor and publisher.

3. Apparently William A. Thomson, proprietor of the Casino Drug Store, which was in the same building as the theatre. John Gibbon (1827–96), soldier; brigade, division and corps commander during Civil War, after which he served largely in the West.

4. Oliver H. Cole, Portland insurance man.

5. Deady was being less lenient than he wanted to appear. The sentence was handed down despite the fact that the U. S. District Attorney had recommended clemency.

6. Edward Espey (1860–89), son of W. W. and Mary Jane Espey.

7. Loyal B. Stearns (1853–1936), Portland lawyer and jurist.

8. The Oregon *Alarm* and the *People's Pulse* were local anti-Chinese sheets published respectively by Nat Baker and John W. Gibson. The present location of Espey's picture has not been determined.

9. On April 26, 1886, Dr. Mackenzie wrote Deady, "I am fully satisfied that Henderson left us on Wednesday of vacation week . . . with the full and proper permission of his mother, tho he acknowledges now that I had not a drop of evidence to this effect at the hour of his departure.

"I accidentally learned that he spent Wednesday evening at the house of Mr. Charles E. Green, so that he accompanied Miss H only to Trenton.

"Of his friendship with Miss H I see no reason to take any other view than that advanced by yourself. She is a woman of 33 or 34 years of age who is lacking in certain senses that fine delicacy & kind of propriety which differentiates the perfect lady from one who constantly attracts your attention to what she is doing or saying. Henderson's friendship has gone as far as I think it ought to go . . ." The Judge rightly considered Henderson the most precocious of his three sons.

10. John Leng (1828–1906), editor and proprietor of the *Dundee Advertiser;* Liberal MP, 1889–1905.

11. James de Barth Shorb; California politician and vintner.

12. Wilson T. Hume (1859–1931), at that time a law clerk but later a Portland attorney.

13. Maj. W. A. Jones, MA, class of 1860; in charge of river and harbor division, corps of engineers at Portland.

14. Kate Trevett, daughter of T. B. Trevett.

15. Katherine (Tissel) Green married 2nd Lieut. Edward Burr, who graduated from the Military Academy at the head of the class of 1878.

16. David C. Kelly had formerly had charge of the Indian school at Forest Grove. The U. S. sued for items unaccounted for at the time of his departure. The suit was brought for the sum of $121. Judgment was rendered for $21.38 including interest.

17. James F. Bewley and his son had been driving hogs along a country road when the stage driver tried to force his way through. The Bewleys held the bridles of the team

and prevented the driver from proceeding until the hogs were clear. The incident led to feelings between the driver and Bewley and eventually it was charged that Bewley shot at the driver at some subsequent time, though Bewley insisted that it was the driver who shot at him. The Bewleys were arrested both for impeding the mails which were aboard the coach, and for shooting at the driver when he was carrying the U. S. mails. The jury found them guilty of the first charge, and acquitted them of the second.

18. Thorn cannot be positively identified. Horace White (1834–1916), journalist and economist.

19. Rockey P. Earhart (1837–92), public official; served as Indian agent, state legislator, secretary of state, 1878–87, and collector of customs at Portland, 1890–92. Thomas Fitch (1838–1923), Nevada and California lawyer and journalist; Nevada congressman, 1869–71; famous for his oratory.

20. Ben Holladay had transferred title of much of his property to his brother, Joseph, in order to protect it from his creditors. Joseph refused to return what he had been given and a long series of law suits was required before the various judgments were satisfied.

21. James Fullilove was a young Negro. He remained Deady's bailiff until the Judge's death, and after continued on for a time in government service before opening up a barbershop. He died about 1916.

22. Bartlett Tripp (1842–1911), Dakota Territory lawyer and jurist; chief justice, territorial supreme court, 1885–89; minister to Austria-Hungary, 1893–97.

23. James N. Allison, officer in the 2nd Cavalry; MA, class of 1867. Despite the fact that Deady insisted on elevating him to the rank of Captain, he was carried on the rosters as a 1st Lieut. George Hoadly (1826–1902), Ohio lawyer; Democratic governor, 1884–86. Hoadley in original. John C. Black (1839–1915), Illinois lawyer and Democratic politician; commissioner of pensions, 1885–89; commander of the G.A.R., 1903; chairman of the federal civil service commission, 1904–15.

24. Lucius Fairchild (1831–96), Wisconsin soldier and diplomat; Republican governor, 1866–72; commander of the G.A.R., 1886.

25. Considerable interest was generated by Deady's suggestion that the municipal franchise be limited to those who paid property taxes, either directly or indirectly. At the present day this would enfranchise very nearly everyone, since Deady would have included as qualified those who rented. But in that day there was a large floating population which was voted by the political bosses, and in most cities these made up the bribe-takers and repeaters.

26. William S. Ott was then living with and studying law under W. H. Effinger. J. Townsend Valentine, Portland businessman; he lived at The Hill.

27. James Brasfield and his wife had purchased Seal Rocks in 1883.

28. J. C. Eccleston was a New York clergyman.

29. Reed and the Ladds had fallen out over the Seeley case.

30. Minnie Hau(c)k (1852–1929), notable soprano; debuted, 1866, in New York as "Norma."

31. Thomas H. Strowbridge (1859–1902), Portland insurance man.

32. Frederick H. Post; Episcopal clergyman, Salem and Roseburg.

33. Michael Davitt (1846–1906), Irish revolutionary and labor agitator.

34. John Broetje; florist and nurseryman. Ladd's farm was near the present Reed College campus.

35. Uriel Sebree was the area lighthouse inspector.

36. Mrs. J. A. Root advertised herself as a metaphysician. It is clear many of Mrs. Deady's ills were of a psychosomatic origin.

37. Charles J. Reed's marriage to Margaret Green produced the famous writer and radical, John Reed, author of *Ten Days That Shook the World.*

38. John B. Price was Mitchell's father-in-law.

39. There were, all told, 13 McGibenys.

40. Tom Jordan was sheriff and Tom J. Mountain a circuit court bailiff. Jordan had

allegedly been drinking with Dr. Howe, a local dentist.

41. "Macaire," a melodramatic farce by W. E. Henley and Robert Louis Stevenson. This is Deady's first mention of, and probably was his first meeting with his daughter-in-law-to-be, Katherine Hanover (1857–92).

42. Richard H. Taneyhill (1822–98), Ohio lawyer, journalist and historian; author of a history of Belmont County and of a little book, *The Leatherwood God,* which served as the basis for Wm. Dean Howell's novel of the same name. Tanneyhill in original.

# APPENDIX A

## The Anti-Chinese Riots

At the beginning of 1886 the country was at last working its way out of three years of depression, but recovery came slowly in the Pacific Northwest. The failure of the Northern Pacific in 1884 had brought a temporary halt to railroad building, throwing thousands of men out of work and cutting off the flow of payroll money upon which hundreds of small businesses had come to depend. 1886 was also the year of the Haymarket incident and the founding of the A. F. of L., each of which events was, in its way, a response to the grinding conditions imposed by the massive corporations which controlled not only the private economy, but a majority of the elected officials. The anti-Chinese riots cannot be considered separate from this atmosphere any more than the equally shameful "relocation" of the Japanese in 1942 can be separated from the wild hysteria which followed the attack on Pearl Harbor.

The Anti-Coolie Club was formed at a meeting held at the New Market Theatre on January 27. A local insurance man, M. G. Griffin, was in the chair. The principal speakers were attorney John Caples, hotel owner L. P. Q. Quimby, and Nat L. Baker, a radical journalist whose *Oregon Alarm* borrowed its name, significantly, from a leading Socialist weekly. A steering committee of ten was elected and it was decided that a grand organizational meeting be held on February 15.

On February 7 and 8 rioters at Seattle routed some 400 Chinese from their homes, drove them to the waterfront and loaded them aboard ships whose captains were ordered to take their unwilling passengers elsewhere. This act of mass savagery created much excitement in Portland. The organizational meeting of the Anti-Coolie Club was held two days earlier than planned. John Myers was elected permanent president. It was decreed that all Chinese must vacate the area within 40 days or face the consequences. Boycotts were voted against the *Oregonian* and the *Telegram,* and against all merchants who advertised in their columns. The *News* and the *Standard,* which so far had expressed sympathy for the movement, were given rousing votes of commendation.

Inflammatory speeches and the bombastic editorials published by Baker and by John W. Gilson, whose *Popular Pulse* also took its name from a leading Socialist weekly, were causing the authorities much uneasiness, and this was heightened when the Emmett Guard flatly refused to take an oath of loyalty. In the event of trouble the burden of maintaining order would fall upon the city's remaining militia company, the Washington Guard, and an understaffed and poorly trained police force.

Trouble arrived on the evening of February 22, coming by way of Oregon City. As a thousand men and boys marched through the streets of Portland in a torchlight parade, armed men drove 160 Chinese, all of them employees of the Oregon City Woolen Mills, from their homes and barracks, and shipped them to Portland on the river steamer *Latona*. It was the first of several forced evacuations conducted in the next three weeks at Albina, East Portland and Mt. Tabor. Armed raids were directed against Chinese truck gardeners at Guild's Lake, and Chinese laundries in the center of Portland were blown up by dynamite.

The heat generated by these acts of vandalism and armed coercion did not hurry the city fathers into precipitous action. Not until the second week of March did Mayor John Gates call for a meeting of the law and order forces, to be held on March 13. It was a ludicrous fiasco. Led by L. N. Hamilton, editor of the *News,* and Sylvester Pennoyer, the anti-Chinese packed the assembly hall, elected Pennoyer chairman, and passed resolutions calling for Chinese expulsion and exclusion.

It was the climax of the campaign. The Anti-Coolie club was already fragmenting under the pressure of internal rivalries. The citizens demanding law and order met elsewhere, but they met, and organized, and clearly meant business. Pennoyer was anxious to be elected governor and he was acutely aware that a continuation of the troubles would disadvantage him. He urged his followers to seek relief at the ballot boxes. Which was as well. An increasing number of people were recalling, uneasily, the great fire of 1873.

Judge Lewis Linn McArthur. As U. S. District Attorney, "a few eloquent and well chosen remarks."

Simeon G. Reed broke with the Ladds over the Seeley case.

Morris Fechheimer. Court adjourned out of respect to his memory.

Sylvester Pennoyer. Deady thought him a Jacobin.

In August, 1886, the Deadys and friends had a vacation at Yaquina. Returning, the party celebrated the Stotts' anniversary at Corvallis with a party and a photo. Standing: 4th from left, Henry Failing; Mrs. Deady; a Brooke twin (straw hat); Lloyd Brooke; young lady in ruffles, possibly Blanche Catlin; Edward Deady in straw hat and mustache; Mrs. Stott; Mrs. C. E. S. Wood and C. E. S. (wool hat and beard); next man to right, Judge Stott (skullcap); Richard Koehler, in bowler and beard; next to end, Judge Deady. Sitting, from left: James Fullilove; Paul Deady; young man in bowler may be Seth Catlin; 5th from left one of Brooke twins in straw hat; girl sitting at right end with staff may be Alice Strong. Small children in center, David and Sallie Lewis, with Nan Wood (in white); behind her to right Henderson Deady.

# 1887

*January 8 (Sat)*. . . Today got a perpetual membership for the Library from Col Kelly and a check for $1000 from S G Reed for the Home fund. I had both these transactions put into last years accounts so that the year should not go by without an increase of these funds. . . .

*15 (Sat)*. . . On Wednesday Sylvester Pennoyer was inaugurated Governor of Oregon and delivered a message to the Legislature in which he gathered together all the grievances, crotchets and whimsies of his life. He criticized my judicial action in several cases as usurpation and said that if the offense was repeated it would be the duty of the legislature to memorialize Congress for my impeachment. He has made a laughing stock of himself as I knew he would if elected.

On Friday morning McArthur presented resolutions of the bar on the recent death of Gov Gibbs in London and moved their adoption which was seconded by Gov Grover and Mallory, and responded to by myself.[1] The proceedings were published in the *Evening Democrat* of yesterday and I understand will be also in the Sunday *Oregonian* tomorrow. The proceedings were instituted through my suggestion to Grover . . .

*22 (Sat)* Sunday (Jan 16) Attended S S and M prayer at Trinity. Called in the afternoon at Fechheimers, Whalleys, Kearneys & Dr Strongs. Met Susie Whalley and spoke of her engagement in the Hall, and told her I would take my last kiss which she gracefully allowed. We then walked into the room where I found her betrothed Capt Allison, sitting on the sofa, where he overheard all we said and did. The affair ended in a hearty laugh all round. . . .

. . . Lunched Wednesday & Thursday with Mrs Deady at the luncheon set by the Trinity Mission Guild. Plenty of pretty girls acting as waiters with their napkins on their arms or over their shoulders as if they were waiters born; and all for sweet charity. A very clever caricature in this mornings *Oregonian* copied from the Benton *Leader* on Pennoyers message. It professes to be the original draft of the instrument and sounds very much like it.[2] Nell Corbett has a "tea" this afternoon to which I am invited but will not go, because she did not invite me to her wedding.

*29 (Sat)*. . . Wednesday evening I lecture[d] in the lecture room of the Unitarian Society on "Constitution making"; and after that went with Mrs D to the Benedicts ball at Masonic Hall. A large assemblage of married people and none others. Danced with Mrs D, Bellinger, Stout and Corbett (H W) and walked a waltz with Mrs Jones (Savier) and others. The affair was a success and ought to be repeated once a year at least. Dr Joseph W Hill, of the Grammar School, seemed to be the principal manager and led the Grand March, and did it well.

Today wrote an article for the *Oregonian* in reply to an interview of Pennoyers with the Salem reporter of the *News* concerning my lecture. It gave me a good opportunity to correct an impression that some people have made on the public mind to the effect that before the war I was a States Rights Democrat and all that, when the fact is that I never was and since 1884–5 [*?64–5*] at least, when I read Jeffersons works, Websters speeches and Marshalls *Life of Washington,* the trial of Burr and much other contemporary matter, I have been substantially a Federalist. Got hold of Theophile Gautiers *Sappho* today and read some pages in it. I had heard so much about its indecency that it really seems tame. So far it does not compare with passages in Rousseaus "confessions." But it is very Frenchy. The literary & art life of France is thoroughly Heathen and animal. It has rained incessantly nearly all the week. Prepared this week and [*sic*] amendment to the water act, giving power to appropriate land and water for the purpose of the act. Put the amendment into the first section of the act. Called at the Hall in the evening . . .

*February 5 (Sat)* Worked on and finished my annual report as President of the Library Association which I will read tonight. Wednesday night heard [Emma] Abbot[t] & Company in "Il Trovatore" at New Market. Quite well done. Friday night took Mrs D, Jessie Murch & Blanche Catlin to hear "Lucrezia Borgia," by Abbott & Co. Well done also. But I think A is naturally a better actor than singer. Indeed her dramatic power is something unusual. Got two tickets for Mrs D for the matinee today—"Carnival of Venice"—and two tickets for her and myself tonight—"Linda of Chamouni" [*Linda di Chamounix*]. The largest investment I ever made in opera at once in my life—principally for the reason that I never had the opportunity. Snow fell Sunday night and on Monday & Tuesday and is still on the ground, a few inches thick. The thermometer has been down to 12 above zero. The weather is clear and bright since Tuesday. This evening went to hear Abbott in "Linda" at the New Market, and was much pleased.[3]

*12 (Sat)* . . . Wednesday evening listened to a pleasant lecture from Mrs Eliot at the Unitarian chapel on "the rights" of man or rather their duties. Snow is still on the ground and bobsledding is all the rage, but the weather has moderated. The thermometer has not been lower than 20° this week. Finished *A Generation of Judges* by the Reporter.[4] The book contains interesting sketches of the English Judges of the past 30 years or thereabout.

Called at the Hall this evening, and Miss Lydia called my attention to a sonnet by Mrs Preston[5] in the February *Century* on Keats "Grecian Urn." This led to looking up Keats for the Urn which we found and read. To know the sonnet and the Ode are well worth an evening spent in their search and perusal.

*19 (Sat)* . . . Went to the opera four nights this week. Monday took Mrs Deady and Henrietta Failing and Agnes Catlin to hear "Lucia." Tuesday went with McArthur to hear "The Bohemian Girl." Wednesday Mrs Deady and I were invited to the Reeds to dinner and thence to the opera where we occupied the lower right hand box. The piece was "Mignon" and was well done. After the opera Reeds drove us to their house where we had a Welsh rabbit (rarebit) and then sent us home. Thursday evening I took Jessie Murch to see "Somnambula," which was I believe the best performance of the Abbot[t] troupe. Friday went with Mrs Deady to Mrs Williams party, where I danced the Centennial lancers three times, once with Katy Story, Mrs Burns and Virginia Wilson each. After supper the German commenced. We left about ½ past 1. It was a beautiful party and the young girls looked very well.

This day has been bright and clear, but the snow still hangs on in patches in the shady places. The legislature adjourned last night in a merry mood, and everybody breathes freer. The bill to prevent foreign corporations from suing in or removing suits to the National Courts in this district failed. Died in the judiciary committee of the House. When the Legislature met it was a popular measure before the country and passed the Senate by an almost unanimous vote. It was inspired by the attorneys, clerks & sheriffs of the Cow Counties for the fees there is in the business for them if done in their counties. Well there is a good deal of human nature in that.

Mr. Corbett paid me $150 Thursday on my work of drafting the statutes for the Water Commission, making it $500 in all. It ought to have been $1000, but I suppose I ought to contribute something to the public good as well as the committee. Got a letter from Henderson today in which he said the examinations were closed, that he had failed in French and passed in everything else. Called at the Hall in the evening and had a word fight with Miss Clem over music and the basso of the Abbott troupe as well as some features of Abbotts vocal gymnastics. She always assumes that I don't know anything about music and that she knows everything, a proposition which I am not supposed to admit by any means.[6] Miss L bless her good soul was distressed about it.

*26 (Sat)* . . . Monday evening Mrs D and I attended a masked ball at Masonic Hall. I wore a domino and mask, but my beard and hair gave me away. Danced with Mrs Brockenbrough, Mrs Jones, and Miss Ott.[7] We came home immediately after the supper. The costumes were very pretty and striking and altogether the affair was very enjoyable. Tuesday morning at ½ past 9 Edward was married to Miss Kate Hanover, by Archbishop Gross at John Catlins. All the family were present from Grandpa Henderson to Rhoda Failing and a few others. After the ceremony there was a breakfast and the young couple started for Victoria. The affair passed off very pleasantly. There [were] a number of presents. Mrs Deady gave them $100 worth of silver and gave Kate a pin which cost $25. I gave her a purse with $25 in it. Tuesday evening Mrs D and I went to a musicale at Mrs Ladds, and got home before 12 tired and glad that the season was over and the next day was Ash Wednesday. Thursday sent $300 to Lawrenceville School on H Bs account and yesterday I got the report of his semi-annual examination in which his average is only 2⅞ in a maximum of 5 and he has 26 marks in a limit of 60 for the year. He failed his French or else he would be over average—3. I am very sorry and disgusted with him and so wrote him yesterday. . . .

*March 5 (Sat)* . . . Moved back in our rooms or rather commenced to sleep in them again on Thursday. Dead rat in the wall kept us out nearly a month. Heard

[Lucius] Bigelow lecture on Wednesday evening on the war. A vigorous and eloquent composition read after the manner of an earnest rustic. Heard Mr [John] Doughty on the same evening during the last half hour of his lecture on the atonement in which he made it pretty plain that the apostles taught that God was in Christ reconciling man to him, and not that the latter was Gods sacrifice as an atonement for the sins of men and thereby reconciling God to man and appeasing his justice.[8]

Went to Franks last night and witnessed the young peoples dancing class that met there. It was a very pretty spectacle. Congress adjourned yesterday morning and I am afraid the bill to increase the district judges salaries was lost between the two houses. I feel like say[ing] d—n the House, but what of it. Finished "Endymion" last night. What a wealth of adjectives and sensuous description. I find the word "lush" used quite frequently and it might be applied to the poem. Some of the erotic scenes are portrayed very vividly and without reserve. But as the female is some sort of a supernatural the case is outside of the ordinary rules.

Called on Edward & Kate on Sunday evening on their return home. They were comfortably fixed and looked happy. I haven't made her out yet, but I think she is all right. . . .

*12 (Sat)* Sunday . . . at Trinity as usual. Finished opinion in the afternoon and evening in the Ordway timber cases which I delivered on Monday, holding the N P Ry Co had no such interest in the land ceded to it for the purpose of building its road before the construction of a section thereof to waste the co terminus lands, by disposing of the timber thereon and that if the defts cut the timber in question believing in good faith that it belonged to the N P Ry Co from whom they had a license they were only liable for the value of the timber in the tree. . . . Dipping into Keats . . . last evening after going home between 10 & 12 oclock and into Bancrofts *British Columbia* in the morning at my chambers. Read "Lamia" and "St Agnes Eve" in the former. Both are full of beautiful and sensuous imagery and end abruptly and unsatisfactorily. The latter is evidently unfinished. K is more at home I think in the Grecian myths than in the Gothic ones.

I think Bancroft is repeating himself in this volume more than usual—making mountains out of mole hills, but that may [be] partly excused on the ground that there is not much else to make them out of. He also appears to criticize [Sir James] Douglas unnecessarily and waspishly. Besides there is a tone of mocking levity running through the book that don't belong to the subject. This is a beautiful day clear and bright but a little cool. . . .

*19 (Sat)* Sat in the C C & D C during the week. Not much done. Did some miscellaneous reading including the Cyclopedia articles on Heat and the correlation of forces. The old materialistic doctrine that heat or calorie was the substantive thing or agent is exploded and heat is merely matter in motion. Well what will be the next theory I wonder.

Got a letter from Henderson this week (the 17) dated March 7. It was detained three days on the way by washouts and overflows on the Yellowstone. Am still dipping into *British Columbia.* It is a desultory common place sort of book I think. This may be owing to the subject. The weather has been variable this week between wet and dry with a breath of spring in it all. This is a lovely day. I saw the lawn mower at work at Mrs Hills yesterday, on the green grass. Took up *Fors Clavigera* again last evening and will stick to it to the end. There isn't much more of it, and as old T'Vault used to say of his adversarys pleading it is "repetitious."

*26 (Sat)* Sunday . . . afternoon [13] attended the laying of the cornerstone of St Josephs church (German R C) by invitation of a committee of the Congregation. Mr Levi Anderson, Mayor [John] Gates of Portland and Mayor [J H] Steffen[9] of Albina and I rode in the same carriage in the procession. The ceremony was long and except to the initiate, senseless, being in the Latin tongue. Bishop Junger of Nisqually delivered a very spirited and apparently eloquent address at the close of the ceremony in German.

Sat in the C C and D C during the week. On Tuesday empaneled and charged the Grand Jury in the District Court. There were 18 persons sworn . . . The jury has been called at the request of the government and are engaged in the investigation of alleged crimes in the selection of swamp lands by claimants under the state.[10] . . .

Have not done much this week except miscellaneous reading connected with some cases I intend to decide on Monday and a lecture I intend to deliver before the senior class in the law school on Wednesday. Called at the Hall in the evening and had a tilt with Miss Clem on whether it was proper to say the litany at an afternoon service and whether the Nunc Dimittis ought to be said before or after the benediction.

*April 2 (Sat)* Sunday (Mar 27) . . . afternoon called at Capt [Charles] Beebes where I found Mrs [S R] Bowne, his mother in law, a charming middle aged woman. They were at 2 oclock dinner and insisted on my sitting down at the table which I did. Mrs Beebe is a very pleasant one also and altogether I had a very enjoyable call. I told Mrs Bowne the story of the French Count who said he would prefer Mattie Mitchel[l][11] as the wife of his friend rather than his own, and she appreciated it. . . .

*9 (Sat)* . . . Sat in the C C & D C during the week. Grand Jury returned on Tuesday and on Friday were excused until Monday again, when it is expected they will close their labors. . . .

. . . Signed a testimonial for Dudley Evans directed to the President endorsing his fitness for official position. It was very generally signed by the leading and substantial people of the town.

The weather has been variable but mild. Sunshine and shower.

This afternoon at 4 oclock the medals for saving life were presented to Charles Richardson and five seamen in my courtroom by Lieut Sebree of the U S Navy. At his request I made a little address on the occasion. The court room was well filled with nice people. Altogether the affair passed off very well.[12]

I suppose my remarks will appear in the *Oregonian* in the morning, and I think they will read well.

*16 (Sat)*. . . My address on presenting the medals to the seamen printed in . . . [*Sunday*] mornings paper and murdered by Alfred Holmans neglect, first to give out the copies so that I could read the proof before 12 oclock and then neglecting to read the proof himself. Judge Strong died at 2 oclock this morning at the residence of his son Thomas N in his 69 year, and was buried from Calvary church on Tuesday in R V Cemetery. I was invited and went to the church and from there to the grave. Bush called in the afternoon and when I told him he was buried from the church, referring to the fact that he never went to church in his lifetime, he said it was taking an advantage of the old man to carry him in in his coffin. I had so little respect for him morally, intellectually or otherwise that I hesitated about attending his funeral. But Mrs Deady and Ed Failing thought I had best on Dr Strongs account at least and I thought so too and went.

Judge Sawyer arrived overland on Saturday evening and dined with us on Sunday. He sat in the C C on Monday, Tuesday, Wednesday and Thursday and went home on Friday. . . . Took Mrs Deady to the Casino last evening to hear the amateurs sing the Mikado for Wilder Peases benefit.[13] It was well done, Miss [Kate] Wallace was excellent as Yum Yum and Adams was elegant as the Mikado. Paul is in trouble again about his debts and the prospect is that I will have to put up $1200 for him.

*23 (Sat)*. . . Drafted a sketch of Dr Gearys Oregon career at the request of Prof Straub of Eugene for a memorial volume that is to be published concerning him. Will revise it and send it up tomorrow.

Borrowed $1375 of Ladd on the 20th inst payable on or before a year wherewith to pay Pauls debts which amount to $1372.95. He is going to make a new start in life and I hope he will succeed. He has been a dead failure so far—and what is more a reckless spendthrift. . . .

. . . Last night got a file of the Sacramento *Bee* from Sawyer containing the story of the Kissane family.[14] It is a remarkable revelation. It beats Mitchells "youthful indiscretions" in several particulars. However on the woman question M is a long ways ahead, and some of the back counties of Pennsylvania still to hear from. . . .

*30 (Sat)* Sunday [*18*] . . . Met Koehler at my chambers and talked over a trip to Ashland on my next birthday. Then rode out to the end of G street on the horse car and called at Cohens. They have a commodious comfortable cottage and Mrs C is as pleased and silly as a pullet with her first hatching.

Sat in the C C & D C during the week . . . Monday delivered my third lecture at the law school on the origin and formation of Constitutions, and Friday evening delivered my fourth on the origin and growth of the Constitution in Oregon. Each occupied an hour and was delivered from copious notes not much used. The principal benefit of them was in preparing them.

Finished Arnolds *Literature and Dogma* on Thursday evening. A singular book, but an effective one I imagine in time. . . . His definition of God as something not ourselves that makes for righteousness, is original and plausible. Picked up Ruskins *Fors* at January 1875 last night and will keep it on the table until I finish it. . . .

Friday sent a postal order to Dr West of St Clairsville Ohio for $20 for the aid of the sufferers from the cyclone on the 15th inst, with a suggestion that if

Mrs William Kennon Sr need[ed] it to give it to her.[15] The money I got very opportunely a few days before from Capt Flanders for some advice about his will. I did not want to take it but he insisted on it. It seemed providential. . . .

*May 7 (Sat).* . . Monday evening vestry meeting and organization of vestry. James Reed elected to fill vacancy and chosen Treasurer. I was again chosen secretary—a place which I have filled by annual elections since 1886 [1866] or 21 years. I think I have earned my discharge. . . .

*14 (Sat)* . . . Tuesday afternoon started to Ashland on the O & C with a party on the occasion of my 63 birthday which occurred on Thursday the 12th. Mr Koehler went with us and furnished us a sleeper. The party consisted of Edward Deady and wife, Paul Deady, Katie and Lizzie Story, Fred & Katie Holman, Ella DeHart, May Montgomery, Mary Stout, Mr & Mrs Molson, Mr & Sallie Bush, Elsie Failing, Herbert Murch, Mr Linthicum, self & Mrs Deady and the colored man James Fullilove. We left in a shower and sunshine and arrived at Ashland next morning about 10 oclock in a clear sunshine and cool crisp air—the recent snow still lying on the summits of the highest hills. Had breakfast at Medford as we went up and supper in the evening before on the train out of our lunch baskets to which Mr Koehler contributed the claret. Spent Wednesday wandering about Ashland and its romantic surroundings. Had lunch on the sleeper and took dinner at the Hotel which I took the pains to order, notwithstanding which it was as near nothing and that no account as you can imagine. Hitched onto the freight train on Thursday morning—a lovely day—and came to Roseburg in daylight—taking breakfast at Medford. The ride was delightful and the company agreeable. But I had an attack of diarehia [*sic*] in the morning and was compelled to keep quiet during the day. At Roseburg the party had dinner at the Hotel, and in the evening a deputation of lawyers and others visited me in the car. [Lafayette] Mosher & Mrs Mosher and the Rev Mr Post & wife called also, and the former staid until nearly 12. Mrs M looked remarkably well, the only drawback being that she wore a mop of false, young hair on her forehead. Mosher begins to shew age and abstinence from whiskey.[16] At 12 at night we hitched onto the express train from Ashland and reached Eugene at 5 oclock where we dropped Herbert Murch. Arrived at Albany for breakfast where it was raining, but soon cleared off and has not began again as yet. At Salem we dropped Mr Bush and Miss Sallie. I had a very pleasant time with B and Miss S won all our hearts—particularly mine and my friend Mr Lloyd Brooke, whom I forgot to mention was one of our party and a very entertaining one. Thence we soon came to Portland and by 20 minutes to 11 I was on the bench of the circuit court listening to the "jawmen" at the bar.

Yesterday and today I have been at work on my 6th lecture in the law school that I deliver on Monday. I went through the Supreme Court reports on the subject of the last three amendments to the Constitution. Got a letter from Dr. Mackenzie yesterday on the subject of Hendersons suspension and telegraphed him today to put him in charge of clergyman as he suggested instead of sending him to the village.

Today signed writing to Oliver & Clayton[17] giving them the refusal of ¼ of

Block 103 in Portland Heights (Grovers Ad to Portland) for [$]1200 until July 1—$500 down of which $100 was paid and the rest to draw interest until July 1 and the balance to be paid in a year with interest at eight per centum, secured by mortgage on the land, the mortgagor paying the taxes. And so ends my 63 year—I hope my 64 will end as pleasantly. Called at the Hall in the evening to read Dion Boucicault articl[e] on the Opera in the *North American* which provoked a fight with Miss Clem, over the merits of music—I asserting that "Music is a sensuous art" and she denying the proposition with scorn. I don't think she stopped to think or knew what I meant, but assumed that it was something derogatory to her vocation.

*21 (Sat)* . . . Attended the Charity Ball given by the Womens Guild of Trinity church at the Masonic Hall. A pleasant but small affair . . . It used to be said of the ladies that they bared their bosoms to the enemy on these occasions, but now they bare their backs also. Of the two I prefer the former. . . .

*28 (Sat)* Sunday . . . Called in the afternoon at Mrs Stotts, but she was up at Waldos. Had a pleasant call with her children. Called also at Alices and Franks and at McKees and Townsends. [If] it wasn't for Sunday afternoon I don't think I could keep up my calls. . . .

McArthur and Mallory had a splendid spat before the jury and a little one yesterday before the court. In the opening of the case, Mallory said that McArthur had written to a friend of the defts, stating that what they had done about cutting timber on [W R] Smiths alleged preemption was justifiable and now he was here prosecuting them for it. Mallory had no right to say this because he could make the proof if he had it, and did not undertake to. McArthur characterized it as a coarse and brutal assalt and abused M in fine style. Mallory came back with a good deal of fierce and rattling denunciation. To this McArthur replied in grand style and closed the encounter. Both behaved well, taking his punishment in silence. Mallory said that when the pot boiled the scum rose to the top. McArthur replied yes and when the political pot boiled in Oregon some years ago, the scum rose to the top, and the state disgraced itself by sending this man (M) to Congress.

*June 18 (Sat)* . . . Have overlooked my weekly entries here for three weeks. Have been very busy in that time and very much afflicted with a severe cold and catarrh in the head and throat. . . .

Tuesday evening the 14th we attended the closing exercises and annual party at the grammar school. On the 15th inst I attended the Pioneer celebration at this place and met many old friends and acquaintances. Rode in the procession with Gen Gibbon, S W Moss and [W G] Buffum.[18] At the Pavillion I made a little speech presenting the painting of Dr McLoughlin to the Pioneers and then I slipped out and went to the graduating exercises at the Hall where Henrietta Failing and Jessie Murch were graduated. In the evening I attended the Pioneer ball a short time and danced the Lancers with one of the native daughters—Velina Molson *nee* Nesmith.

On Thursday Mrs Deady and I went to Eugene to attend the commencement exercises and the annual meeting of the Regents. Got to Villard Hall in time for the afternoon exercises, which included Lura Murchs essay.[19] This was the best written and read essay I ever heard in the school. . . .

Have attended the two courses of the [John] Fiske lectures in the Tabernacle—the battles of the west and the making of New England commencing with the Orientals, Romans & Teutons. They are very interesting and instructive. [William] Cogswell finished my picture on Monday the 13th inst, and I think the coloring is very good.[20] I believed it was ordered by Mr Kearney and others for the Library.

Went to the Jubilee pic nic in the afternoon with Edward & Kate at the White House. Went up and back on the boat. Mrs Deady went to Yamhill.

*25 (Sat)* Sunday . . . Dined at Kearneys where I met the lecturer John Fiske—a solid, dull man in conversation. Heard him lecture in the evening on the problem of good & evil, taking his text from Genesis. Rather heavy but strong and clear. . . . Dined at the Arlington on Tuesday evening with the Britishers and had a very enjoyable time. I made a little impromptu speech in reply to the toast—The U S of America, in which I said that the U S was the latest and the highest form of the English idea and that the same was the brightest jewel in the Queens crown, considering her as she is the representative of the English speaking race. Some of my friends were kind enough to say I did well, at which I was not offended. Got home at 12. I was na fou but just had plenty. Justice Field arrived last evening and took up his lodgings in the C J chambers which I had furnished for him. . . .

*July 2 (Sat)* . . . Tuesday [*June 28*] drove Field to the White House and the Cemetery and over town and dined him at Baums. Wednesday Mrs D and I dined at Mrs Williams with Field. An elegant dinner and a pleasant company of 12. I took Mrs [H A] Dutard of San Fran to dinner and found her a pleasant companion. She brought me a pleasant message from Tom Madden whom she knows well . . . Friday dined with Field at B Goldsmiths en famille. A delicious dinner. From there I took F to the New Market to hear Miss Kate Field,[21] and thence we walked down to the steamer *State of Cal* where after a few friendly phrases I bade him good by and bon voyage. Altogether I have had a good time with Field and so he has with me and others. . . . On Thursday made a deed of my ¼ block on the Heights to Mr Clayton for $1200. Paid $700 for it in April 1886, though I purchased it in 1884. The first thing I ever sold for more than I gave for it in my life I believe. Paid my quarters accounts yesterday. Pretty stiff, but $158 was for grading.

*9 (Sat)* Sunday . . . Called on Mrs Dutard and Mrs [Samuel] Heitshu[22] in the evening and went to Grace Church (Methodist) in the evening with Mrs Deady to hear Carrol Stratton preach. He delivered a very good sermon on the Living God—it was well digested and as an intellectual and logical exercise it was very creditable to him. Like the rest of us he has aged some.

Sat in the C C & D C during the week. Delivered the opin on the Interstate Com act on Monday, and it was published in the *Oregonian* today and telegraphed to the 4 quarters of the globe. The returns [that] have come back are so far favorable but they are mainly from the cities on the Atlantic and Pacific that have the benefit of water traffic and competition. Spent the 4th pleasantly looking on at the pageant of which for once I was not a part.

Purchased 500 shares of the Sierra Nevada today from Bernard Goldsmith for $100. It is a Coeur de Alein [*sic*] mine. Expect it will be worth $300 in six months. Attended the funeral of Gov Gibbs this afternoon as a pall bearer. The services were held in the church, Mr Driver[23] making the prayer and Carrol Stratton the discourse. The latter was very good of the kind, but too cold and philosophical for the occasion. This duty ought to have been assigned to Driver, who knew Gibbs well in early days in the Umpqua, and who would have put some feeling and emotion into the affair. . . .

21 (Thu) Thursday [the 14 at] ½ past 10 started for Wilhoit Springs on the Narrow Gauge in company with Lucy Murch & Henrietta Failing. At Mt Angel I left the train and they went on to Coburg. Here Mr C Cleaver drove Mr Scott (C N) and myself over to the springs in a 2 horse spring waggon. The distance is near 14 miles—the first 7 being nearly level. Then we left Butte Creek at Mr Scotts place—a grand farm along the hills on either side of the creek and went across the ridges about 1500 feet high to Rock Creek where the springs are. The last part of the ride was a tedious and tiresome one. The springs is a beautiful place—a little valley between high wooded hills. The water is delicious and drinks like champagne—particularly in the matter of titillation. Found several Portland people there, Mr Brooke and Ham B, Miss [Abby] Atwood and her mother, and Mr & Mrs [Frank] Dayton. Plenty of people in the cottages and camps all around the spring. The tavern is very fair. Good clean beds, large airy setting rooms, big roomy porches and a good billiard table. I had a pleasant game or two of croquet with some girls from Champooic—my partner was named Miss Kennedy. Miss Atwood and I ascended the hill on the west side of the house and looked over into the Molal[l]a valley. The distance was about 1½ miles and the elevation 1500 or 2000 feet. Saturday afternoon a party came in from Salem including Mr Bush and Sallie, whom I enjoyed very much. Mr. Cleaver came in Saturday evening and drove Mr Brooke and myself out to Mount Angel on Sunday morning. There we met Mr [Harvey] Scott with an *Oregonian* excursion party bound for Coburg and they took us along nolens volens. The road to Coburg is through grain fields much of the way. At Coburg I got down to Murchs a few moments and saw the family including four sweet pretty girls—Lucy, Lura and Jessie Murch and Henrietta Failing. On the run back we had supper at Brownsville with nothing to eat. Got to Mt Angel at 20 minutes past 10 where we met Prior Adelhelm of the Mt Angel monastery with his wagon waiting to take myself and 4 friends up to the monastery, a distance of about a mile from the station. Mr Brooke was tired and did not go. Messrs Scott, Pittock, Coldwell[24] and William Reed went along. At the monastery we had a bite to eat including some good year old cider and a spoonful of apple jack to finish with which was strong with the boquet of apple blossoms and was an excellent substitute for a glass of Chartreuse.

The prior put me in the Episcopal chamber and I slept well. Got up at 5 and as I had to go out through the church where I found the Prior saying Mass and ten or a dozen lay brothers and a few German country boys from the neighborhood at their devotions, besides some three or four sisters who went to Communion. I set down my valise and remained during the service kneeling and rising with the congregation. Before breakfast the prior drove us up on the Mt and showed us the site of the proposed monastery. It is a lovely place and a grand view. After breakfast we drove down to the village and then went on the Narrow Gauge to Woodburn where we took the O & C to Portland where I arrived in time to go on the bench at 10:20.

The Prior is a Swiss German and the monks are of the Benedictine order. He is a great talker and something of a blatherskite without much dignity. He asked me if I did not get tired of listening to the lawyers so much. I replied about as much as you listening to long winded confessions. He laughed and said yes, particularly when the penitent wants to repeat his dull story. . . .

*30 (Sat)* . . . Saturday afternoon went [to] Ilwaco on the *Alaskan.* Called at Mrs Holmans in the evening. Slept on the boat and breakfasted there. Then drove over to Stouts. Linthicum was with me. We called at Woods and had the pleasure of finding Mrs W & Miss Lewis in bed at 10 oclock. Called on Mrs Corbett and Ward Stevens.[25] Then lunched at Woods and started afoot with the intention to call at Whalleys and have the hack overtake me there. Called and met Susi[e] (Mrs Allison) looking none the worse for the change of name and condition. Linthicum soon came along with Mrs Woods phaeton and venerable steed and drove me over to the landing. Got home at 11 oclock. It misted all day on the beach, but I enjoyed the jaunt notwithstanding. . . .

*August 6 (Sat)* . . . I went [*last night*] to the New Market to see the "Devils Auction." Saw a fine display of female legs and male gymnastics sandwiched into a lot of nonsense. The week has been warm and yesterday was quite sultry. Dined with Mrs Deady at Brookes yesterday—had an excellent dinner, but sat on Nettas left which I did not expect or I must say relish. . . . Bush called this afternoon and talked over the publication in todays *Oregonian* of his and Thayers letters on Bill Watkinds, which he don't like. I talked with S[cott] on the subject of W and the *Oregonians* apparent shelter of him and condemnation of his enemies. He avowed there was no such purpose and I don't think there is consciously, but as I told him it has taken such a shape that it has that effect and many good friends of his and the *Oregonian* were grieved at it. I told him he must take the first favorable occasion to drop him overboard in a way that the public would not mistake it, and he said emphatically he would.[26]

*13 (Sat)* Dr Robert Bruce Wilson died about midnight on Saturday the 6th inst or in the first hours of the 7th inst of typhoid pneumonia. I called in the evening. Saw Mrs Lewis and Mrs Holt W. They didn't think he would last long. Went over to Lewis' a while. Mr L didn't think he would live. Called at the house on Sunday evening. Attended the funeral on Monday as pall bearer. We met at the house. Saw no one but Mr Burns. When ready to move we went into the front parlor viewed the corpse when the coffin (a plain wooden one draped in black) was closed, and we carried it out to the hearse. Then we saw the family come out and get in the carriage. At the church the funeral service was read by the Bishop and Mr Foote and no music or singing. The church was full of people. At the grave, which was private, when the earth was all in, the Drs four daughters and Mrs Holt stepped forward and placed the floral decorations on the grave. The five of them in black were an interesting sight; and the only pathetic thing about the funeral, the rest of it being very staid and stupid.

Have been reading at odd hours Montesquieu and am getting quite interested. I have often said that it requires more virtue to *run* a republic or a democratic form of government than any other, but did not know that he had anticipated me in the opinion.

Thursday night it rained some—the first for weeks. My German friends Donnerberg and Keller got $5 out of me on the 8th inst for St Joseph church, which pays I suppose for being hauled around by them at the laying of the cornerstone last spring. . . .

*20 (Sat)*. . . Friday evening went to the tabernacle to hear Robert Collyer lecture, Subject, "True Grit." Took Mrs D, Miss Thresher[27] & Paul with me. We were all wonderfully pleased. Went home with Mrs Townsend and had a little supper of which Ginger Ale was something . . . Henderson went to Clatsop on Thursday to stay until the last of next week. Gave him $25 with strict instructions not to borrow or go in debt. . . .

*27 (Sat)* Sunday . . . Called on Robert Collyer at his sons in the evening. A genial old fellow—he is old indeed.[28]

Sat in the C C & D C during the week. Read Swinburnes Trilogy of "Mary Stewart" in the first part of the week. Had a sort of poetic debauch on it. What a wealth of words and I may say waste of them. But he has the true conception of Mary—a false hearted, adultrous woman with a dowry of beauty and brilliancy. . . .

. . . . I see that a fellow called Flournoy undertook to ridicule my opinion in the Sharon case before the Supreme Court of California the other day when Judge Thornton sat down on him heavily.[29] . . .

*September 3 (Sat)*. . . Wednesday night the 31 of August the rain commenced to fall. On Thursday September 1, 1853 I started from my place that I had just purchased in Umpqua (Camus Swale) for Jacksonville to hold the first term of court there. At the Canyon [*of Wolf Creek*] I overtook Lieut Grover (since Gov & Senator) with an advanced detachment of Nesmiths company on the way to the Indian war, which was then in a State of truce. I staid all night in camp sleeping under one edge of Grovers blankets. In the morning we woke to find the rain dropping on us—one day sooner than this year. . . .

*23 (Fri)* . . . Thursday [8] went to Clatsop on the *R R Thompson* and reached Grimes that same evening. Found Jessie Murch on board. Had a good room at Grimes on ground floor opening into the parlor where I had a writing table and a good fire. Friday, Sept 9th. Up at 7 and walked on the beach before breakfast where I met Mrs Person of Memphis, Tennessee and sauntered up the beach with her. A bright, chatty well mannered woman. Bathed at 3 P M with Mrs [M C] Crosby of Astoria . . . Saturday, Sept 10. Walked in the forenoon with Mrs P down the beach to the Seaside House and back to Grimes on the inside. . . . At ½ past 3 bathed with Mrs P and then walked with her and her son through the ant hill region. Mrs P is in raptures over the place and the surroundings. Played whist in the evening, Mrs P and I beat Crosby and Richard [Person] a rubber.

She thinks it great fun as she says she never won before. Sunday, Sept 11. A lovely day. Cool but bright sunshine. . . . Walked to the shell beds in the forenoon. Bathed in the evening alone and finished [Tolstoi's *Anna*] *Karenina* at 12 oclock P M. What a mob of characters the work contains and what a picture of Russian life. Poor Anna and Bronsky [*sic*]. They worked out their own punishment. And dear little Kitty and Mig Lavin I hope they lived happy, but I am not at all certain of it. Monday, Sept 12. Rather laid up with a sore foot . . . Bathed with Mrs P at ½ past 4. The surf is splendid. In the evening she and I beat C & R a rubber at whist. They got no game and Mrs P was delighted. . . . Tuesday, Sept 13. Beautiful day. Worked on report. Mrs P played the piano and we had some singing. She has a beautiful voice, not much in use. . . . Tom Strowbridge called in the evening. He had just returned from a weeks hunt in the mountains. On his way home Tuesday he caught 75 trout in the Lewis river and sent me a dozen of them for dinner. Played a rubber of whist in the evening and Mrs P and I were worsted at last. She returns to Astoria in the morning and we bade each other good night and good by, but I hope not forever. She is a charming woman, with good sense and taste as well as good manners. . . . Wednesday, Sept 14. Beautiful day. Bathed alone at ½ past 9. The water was glorious . . . Thursday Sept 15. Beautiful day with fits of sea fog . . . Friday Sept 16. Read *Nana*. Bathed at ½ past 11—probably I needed it after wallowing in that stye. Richard Person came down to go hunting. He wants a pair of elk horns of his own shooting so to speak. He brought me a nice bunch of grapes. A beautiful day. Finished *Nana*. A "brutal photograph" sure enough. . . . Called at the district school where I met Miss Amy Powell, the teacher. A bright, ambitious and energetic young woman. In the evening went to the beach to take a farewell of the lonely shore, where I met Miss Powell and had a pleasant ramble with her. In the morning went down to the mouth of the creek in a small boat with Allbright, a Baltic sailor and fisherman where we lay some time between the off and inshore breakers waiting for the tide to come in and help us up. On the way down he took 26 large crabs in the creek with a pitchfork. Thursday Sept 22. Pleasant day. Left the beach. Drove up to Skipanon and then over to Astoria in the *Electric*. Had 18 crabs that Allbright boiled and boxed for me. Got my crabs on the boat in the ice chest as soon as the *Queen* came down. Called at Col Taylors in the evening where I met the family including Mary and old Mrs Welch about whose hearth I passed an evening with General Hamilton in February 1851 listening to young [J K] Hackett,[30] afterwards for many years, Recorder of New York take off Negro preachers and the like and Judge Strong tell Yankee storys through his nose. Went on board at night. Friday Sept 23. Reached home at 4 oclock and sat in the D C a short time, and spent the evening looking over my piled up correspondence.

*October 4 (Tue)* Saturday (Sept 24) Went with Mrs D to McMinnville, where we stopped at Harvey Hendersons and attended the meeting of the Cumberland Presbytery, where I saw some marked specimens of reverend rusticity. In the evening John Henderson drove us up to the farm where we staid until Monday when we returned to McMinnville via Amity. . . . The old place looked lovely. On Sunday Mrs Deady and I went down the creek and found the place covered with wild rosebushes, where the cabin stood in which we were married on June 24, 1852. At McMinnville we stopped at Will Hendersons, and in the evening I lectured at the Opera House for the benefit of the Womens Guild of St James church (Episcopal) Subject (Law & Lawyers) audience small and select. Tuesday [27] morning came to Portland by 9 oclock and sat in the D C. . . . Thursday went to Eugene to attend a meeting of the Regents. Mrs D went with me, and from there she drove over to Murchs and came back Friday evening. Had a pleasant meeting of the Regents on Thursday afternoon and evening. Just a quorum present. No one from the north but myself. Increased the salaries of the professors up to the point where I proposed at the organization of the school—$2000 for each professor and $2500 for the President.

Saturday morning got on the through train at 4:45 and came to Portland at 10:30 where I sat in the D C and attended to my quarterly accounts and correspondence. In the evening called at the Hall and saw the ladies. A third person called—sat me out—and spoiled my visit. . . . Monday sat in the C C—the first day of the term—and called the docket. Rained last night but clouds and sunshine this morning. I am glad that Cleveland is having good weather for his visit at St Louis and that the Greedy Pensioners of the Republic had bad weather.[31]

*8 (Sat)* Wednesday . . . evening dined at Montgomerys, where I was invited to meet George Alfred Townsend and also to meet Mitchell, O'Meara and Tom Merry, besides Williams, Cameron and [Geo] Markle.[32] The dinner was excellent and the company tolerable. I don't think they were well selected and were rather in one anothers way. Mitchell and I spoke and took hold of hands when he came in. We had not spoken before since 1873. Townsend is rather a pleasant fellow, but I don't think he was much drawn out that night. He told a story of what Daniel Webster found on Justice Keelings tomb in England—a very clever and smutty quatrain—which I wish I could remember . . . Henderson commenced attending lectures at the Medical School this week and appears quite interested in it or them. Wrote up my correspondence this week which gets to be more and more of a burden and I must try and choke it off. . . . The subscription to the $250,000 subsidy to the new hotel drags its slow length along—it has not reached the first $100,000 yet after near a months time.

*15 (Sat)* Sunday . . . Attended the morning service at the R C Cathedral and witnessed the ceremony of conferring the pallium (blanket) on Archbishop Gross by Cardinal James Gibbons.[33] The old Greek and Roman blanket has been reduced to the size and shape of a neck yoke, such as we used to fitten the geese with to keep them out of the gardens and grain fields. The whole performance was a piece—a tedious piece of august frivolity. The sermon of the Cardinal was a smooth piece of sophistry and misrepresentation of facts.

. . . [*Monday*] evening attended the reception with Mrs Deady given to the Cardinal at the Casino, but did not occupy a seat on the platform to which I had been specially invited by the archbishop. [Henry] McGinn made an address of welcome to the Cardinal in which he complimented him on his defense of the Knights of labor, while the Cardinal in reply took occasion to say there ought to be no conflict between capital and labor, but the brain and the arm must be

united, for which I give him credit. Wednesday evening presided at the opening
of the fourth year of the school of law of the University of Oregon, when Prof
Thornton read an interesting paper on "Unusual Punishments" which was pub-
lished in the next mornings *Oregonian*. Thursday I was at a breakfast (½ past 11
A M) at Mr Richard Knapps where I met the Cardinal and the Bishops of the
W T, Montana, Idaho, Archbishop Gross, Dr [P L] Chappelle[34] of Washington
City, Father Fier[e]ns of Portland, Gov Pennoyer, John McCracken and Henry
Failing. The breakfast was delicious and the appointments elegant and lasted
until 2 oclock. I proposed the health of the Cardinal at the special request of Mr
Knapp to which he replied happily. Pennoyer proposed the health of the Archbishop to which he replied with his usual volubility and egotism—good natured
egotism however. In one way or another everybody at the table was got on his
legs and made to say something—even the taciturn old Fier[e]ns, whom I toasted
as the Nestor of the clergy. Dr Chappelle responded for Washington City in the
course of which he made the only bon mot of the occasion—the Republican party
had behaved very well during the three years it was out of power. Pennoyer had
the opposite end of the table, the Cardinal was at Mr Knapps right and I at his
left. Mrs Knapp met us in the Hall as we were leaving and bade us good morning
and good by. Mrs Deady was very much offended with me for accepting an
invitation to her house. Mitchell was also invited, but he fell ill of a chill just before
we went into the breakfast room, and went upstairs where he was when we left.
Of course some evil minded persons will be found to say that M preferred to
spend the time with his hostess upstairs. . . .

   Am reading Schurz *Life of Henry Clay.* An admirable book. What an irascible,
ignorant, prejudiced old savage history is making out of the political and military
hero of my boyish days—Andrew Jackson. More and more it grows on me that
his strength with the people, after the luck of New Orleans, arose from the fact
that he was socially on their plane—good and common—as compared with his
contemporaries. . . .

*22 (Sat)*. . . Finished *Henry Clay* last night. A pleasant and suggestive book, with
a strong anti slavery bias and a disposition to judge men on the Slavery question
by the circumstances of today rather than then. The weather during the week has
been delightful—brown autumn days. Took lunch with the Young Ladies of
Trinity Mission on Thursday. Miss Lou Trevett did the honors and I presented
her a boquet. A very attractive woman.

*29 (Sat)*. . . Mrs Deady purchased a handsome bible yesterday and sent it to
Harvey Henderson to be presented to the C P church on the occasion of the
dedication tomorrow. I wrote this inscription in it for her,

"This volume of the Holy Scriptures is presented to the Congregation of the
Cumberland Presbyterians at McMinnville on the occasion of the dedication of
their New Church on October 30, 1887

By
Mrs Lucy Henderson Deady
daughter of
Mr Robert Henderson"

*524*

She did it to please her old father who has taken great interest in the erection of the new church and whose long, laborious and blameless life is now drawing to a close. I trust he may be able to go down to the dedication tomorrow at least.

Got an invitation from Major & Mrs Moore of Barnesville, Ohio on Thursday evening to attend a reception at their House to be given to William Meek on the evening of the 20 inst and last evening I got a copy of the *Republican* of the 21 inst giving an account of the affair. Wrote the Moores last night acknowledging the invitation and regretting that I could not be there. Meek must have enjoyed it, and so did Tanne[y]hill. Called at the Hall in the evening . . . Met Rev Mr Post there. He doubted the right of a state to pass a prohibitory liquor law, "because the Constitution of the U S did not give it the power"! and of such is the kingdom of heaven.

*November 5 (Sat)* . . . [*Last Sunday*] Went to the funeral services of Father Wilbur at Taylor St Methodist church. Mr [H K] Hines read a biographical address which was very good. House was crowded to do honor to the memory of a man who deserved [it]. If he had been born in that station in life, so to speak, he would have made an admirable vicar general of the Order of Jesus. . . . Trial jury came on Tuesday. Tried three jury cases—U S v Adams one of them which closes up a matter growing out of his being robbed of public money in the steamer between here and San Francisco—$20,000 in February 1886 [*1866*]. He has an interview about it in the *Oregonian* this morning in which he speaks well of the bridge that carried him over—Judge Deady.[35] Worked on opinion in U S v [Henry C] Owen, dem to Indictment, and about finished [it]. This is the famous conspiracy case to gobble up lands of the U S on the pretext that they are swamp and belong to the state. The action is barred by the statute of limitations I find and will so decide. Another case of great cry and little wool—but the defts preferred not to go into the merits of the matter. . . .

Am reading Bancrofts volume on the Vigilance Com of San Fran of 1856. It is a fascinating story and told in a unique and sui generis way. Hits right and left, above and below the belt, and occasionally lauds someone or ones without stint.

*12 (Sat)* . . . Finished *Wuthering Heights* this week. The Bronte men as a rule are fine specimens of brutes, yet I was pleased with the result—the marriage of Catherine and Hareton—but the relation between Heathcliff and Cathy Earnshaw is the feature of the book and if I remember rightly after the forty years since reading *Jane Eyre*, it is another case of Jane & Rochester. Still dipping into or rather wading through Bancrofts Vigilance Committee of San Francisco. Hetherington and Brace have been swung off and Terry has been found guilty and let go.[36] . . .

*19 (Sat)* Mrs Deady went to Yamhill on Tuesday morning to see her mother who was not well. Had a letter from her last evening in which she says her mother is better. I am still nibbling at Bancrofts account of the San Fran Vigilance Com and am nearly through. Gave the *Oregonian* a bon mot last night—"Sparks *has* resigned and everybody *is* resigned."[37] It appears in the paper this morning with the "and" left out. . . .

*December 3 (Sat)* . . . Appointed G G Gammans Receiver in the case of the Creditors bill v Holladay to sell the property in the hands of Weidler trustee to pay outside creditors whose claims amount to over $300,000 . . . The telegraph announced yesterday morning that John Myers was appointed Marshal of this district—an appointment not fit to be made I think when his conduct touching the anti-Chinese agitation two years ago is considered.[38] Called at the Hall in the evening.

*10 (Sat)* . . . Monday evening there was a vestry meeting, when I resigned the secretaryship of the parish which I had held continuously since July 5, 1886 [1866], a period of over 21 years . . . preparing for old age which comes on apace . . .

*17 (Sat)* . . . The spike driving excursion left here on the train for Ashland this evening. I was invited but had to decline. Beside[s] I did not want to go. I was at the Spike driving on the Northern Pacific where the audience was gathered from the four corners of the world. Anything of the kind seems tame after that.

The weather has been mild and moist during the week.

John Myer[s] the new Marshal went into office on Monday morning. After his commission was read Kelly the incumbent vacated his seat and took Myer[s] by the hand and led him to the Marshals desk. . . .

*31 (Sat)* . . . Saturday Dec 24 Xmas eve there was a family tree at Catlins and we were all there. Mr & Mrs Henderson and 31 of their lineal descendants besides connexions, collaterals and a few friends making in all 65 persons. The gifts were pretty and plenty. I had a very handsome gold headed cane given me by my Chinese friend Seid Back.[39] I made a few presents but left the matter mostly in Mrs Deadys hands who spent some money and more [time] in that behalf. . . .

This morning delivered opinion in U S v Kee Ho & Lee Art on the demurrer to the Indictment charging the defts with importing, buying and receiving opium "contrary to law," sustaining the same on the ground that the illegality of the importation is not sufficiently indicated by the words "contrary to law.". . .

Gave Miss Lydia for Xmas, *Sesame and Lillies,* and Miss Rodney, the *Paris Sketch Book* and a hand painted card. Gave Mrs Deady a brass candlestick and pair of Bisque figures. Paid $17.50 for them at a sell out at Ackermans. The proprietor assured me that they cost $27 and that the regular retail price was $35—may be so. Since Thursday the 23 inst I have obtained 10 perpetual members for the Library Association, which constitutes an addition of $2500 to the Book fund, and $250 in cash for the purchase of Fechheimers picture for the Library. Attended a Library meeting this evening in which the Whidden plans for the new library building were examined and discussed, with a decided preference for the north front plan. The only thing now to be done is to persuade Dives to put his hand deep enough in his pocket to build it. $50,000 in addition to the $25,000 we have will do it, and I hope there are five men or at most ten who will put up the money.[40]. . .

# NOTES

1. Addison C. Gibbs, at the time of his death, was trying to sell Oregon real estate to British investors.

2. Deady undoubtedly best enjoyed that part of the take-off which went, "Some years ago I had a law suit with Mr. Neff. It was in the federal courts and finally in the Supreme Court of the United States, and was decided against me. I have carefully examined the federal constitution and I do not find there any authority delegated to the federal government to decide a case against me. That decision was, therefore, a clear usurpation. That decision soured me on the federal courts."

3. Emma Abbott (1850–91), the best-known American operatic soprano of her time, she toured extensively.

4. The name of the British court attache using the pseudonym "The Reporter" is not given in the catalogues of either the British Museum or the Library of Congress.

5. Margaret Junkin Preston (1827–97), novelist and poet.

6. Deady apparently wrote "supposed" for "disposed."

7. Mrs. J. B. Brockenbrough, wife of a special agent of the General Land Office. Miss Ott was apparently a sister of Will S. Ott.

8. Lucius Bigelow, journalist and Civil War veteran; then associate editor of the *Oregonian;* died 1917. The Rev. John Doughty was a Swedenborgian pastor from San Francisco.

9. John H. Steffen, proprietor of the Albina Hotel.

10. Since the nature and extent of the irregularities practiced by claimants under the Swamp Land Act had been known for a decade, the statute of limitations had long since run and the parties involved in the frauds were safe from danger.

11. Charles F. Beebe (1847–1922), merchant and soldier; married Emma, daughter of Mrs. S. R. Bowne. For Mattie Mitchell, see DP.

12. The life-saving medals were given to Charles Richardson, first officer of the vessel *Manzanita* and certain crew members for saving the life of a fisherman whose rowboat had been caught by the current of the Columbia and swept to the bar.

13. Wilder Pease, singer and entertainer; he specialized in Gilbert & Sullivan parts.

14. William Kissane was a prominent Sonoma County Democrat. In 1887 it was discovered that his name was not Kissane but Rogers, that he had allegedly taken part in riverboat piracy on the Mississippi and had been convicted of forgery in New York, served a sentence and thereafter joined William Walker's filibustering expedition in Nicaragua.

15. The cyclone was the most severe St. Clairsville had experienced to that time. Many buildings were destroyed.

16. Mosher was, it will be recalled, one of the two temperance candidates at the Democratic state convention in 1872, the other being Curry.

17. Augustus W. Oliver and Benjamin F. Clayton were real estate agents.

18. Sidney W. Moss (1810–1901), pioneer merchant and businessman; operated Oregon City's first hotel. William G. Buffum (1804–99), Yamhill County farmer.

19. For Philura Murch, see DP.

20. John Fiske (1842–1901), philosopher, historian and lecturer. William Cogswell (1819–1902), painter; painted portraits of Lincoln, Grant and his family, McKinley and at least two of Deady.

21. Mrs. H. A. Dutard, wife of a San Francisco merchant. Mary Katherine Keemle Field (1836–96), journalist, actress, author and lecturer.

22. Mrs. Samuel Heitshu (1849–1912), wife of a prominent Portland druggist. Charles Carroll Stratton (1833–1910), Methodist minister and educator; president, Univ. of the Pacific, 1877–87; chancellor, Willamette Univ., 1890–91.

23. Isaac D. Driver (1824–1907), Methodist clergyman; evangelical, unyielding, controversial, he was frequently at odds with his brother Methodists; a prohibitionist, he was married five times.

24. Columbus Cleaver, Marion County farmer. Frank Dayton was a Portland hardware man. Miss Kennedy was one of the two daughters of Barney and Arah Kennedy, Mary or Sarah. Adelhelm Odermatt (1844–1920), O.S.B. E. L. Coldwell (c.1840–1908), longtime *Oregonian* reporter; Caldwell in original.

25. Ward Stevens (died 1891), then deputy U. S. marshal.

26. Upon Thayer's election to the governorship in 1878, Watkinds resigned as superintendent of the state penitentiary and was replaced by Bush. Subsequently Thayer brought actions against Watkinds alleging massive irregularities in his accounts while Watkinds was serving as superintendent. Nothing ever came of these charges, but Watkinds was understandably irritated both with Thayer and with Bush. Watkinds published a letter in the *Oregonian* from Bush to Thayer, dated June 29, 1885, warning that Watkinds was on his way to Washington, D. C. in search of an Alaska appointment and must be prevented from getting one. Thayer wrote President Cleveland on July 23, 1885, enclosing Bush's letter and describing Watkinds as an utter incompetent. Watkinds charged that Bush had opposed him because he had refused to support Bush for the Senate and that Thayer and Bush had taken $2,000 to support Dr. E. J. Dawne, a lawyer and physician, for the position Watkinds desired. Dawne received the appointment, but he had no more than reached Alaska when he was forced to resign and return to Oregon to face criminal charges which had been brought against him. Dawne's appointment was an embarrassment to the Cleveland administration, and Watkinds was using these letters to embarrass Bush and Thayer in their turn.

27. Robert Collyer (1823–1912), Unitarian pastor at Chicago and, *post,* 1879, at Church of the Messiah in New York. Miss Thresher has not been identified.

28. Collyer was a year older than Deady.

29. Probably George Flournoy, Jr., San Francisco attorney. James Thornton was then on the California supreme bench. Shawn in the original.

30. Wife of Magnus C. Crosby, Astoria businessman and railroad promoter. John J. Hackett (1821–79), New York lawyer; resided in California, 1850–57.

31. The G.A.R. met in St. Louis on September 28–30, 1887. A torrential rain fell during its parade.

32. George Alfred Townsend (1841–1914), journalist, novelist and war correspondent. George B. Markle (c.1856–1914), banker; his career in Portland was brief, he failed and departed. Merkle in original.

33. James Gibbon (1834–1921), Roman Catholic prelate; highly influential in making the voice of American Catholicism heard; made cardinal, 1886.

34. Henry E. McGinn (1859–1923), Portland lawyer and jurist. Richard B. Knapp (1839–1907), Portland businessman; he was, interestingly, a Mason; he had married the daughter of his eldest brother's second wife, which may account for Lucy Deady's objections. Placide Louis Chapelle (1842–1905), Roman Catholic prelate; afterwards, 1898–1905, archbishop of New Orleans.

35. Harvey K. Hines (1828–1902), Methodist minister, journalist and historian; served in both Oregon and Washington, *post* 1853. In 1861 W. L. Adams was appointed collector of customs by President Lincoln. While carrying customs receipts to San Fran-

cisco in February of 1866, Adams was robbed of more than $20,000 in gold coin, apparently by three persons, one of whom was a member of the crew. Adams was eventually exonerated of any blame, but during the Cleveland administration the government brought an action against him to secure the money which had been lost. Deady decided in Adams' favor, which accounts for the doctor's generous praise of the judge.

36. Joseph Heatherington and one Brace were hanged by the Vigilantes on July 29, 1856, for assorted misdemeanors. Terry steadfastly opposed the Vigilante movement and his resignation from the state supreme court was demanded. He refused to be intimidated although there were some who urged he be hanged as well.

37. William A. J. Sparks (1828–1904), Illinois lawyer and Democratic congressman, 1875–83; commissioner of the General Land Office, 1885–87, his reforming zeal aroused much opposition in Congress.

38. G. G. Gammans (1857–1910), Portland lawyer. John Myers had been president of the Anti-Coolie Association.

39. Seid Back (1851–1916), merchant and importer.

40. The new library was to be built on Stark between 7th and Park.

Judge William Strong. Deady's views were pronounced.

Jessie Murch, in graduation dress, St. Helens Hall. De
attended the ceremonies in 1887. (Partridge photo.)

Also graduating that June was Henrietta Failing, photographed with sisters "Millie" (Emily) and May and Mrs.
Henry Corbett (in stripes) on the Failing house porch.

The 1870s exterior view of the Henry Failing home, between S.W. 5th and 6th, Yamhill and Taylor, was one of a series of stereo views from "Dudley A. Cozad's Imperial Gems of the Pacific Slope." The interior conveys Oregon opulence of the latter part of the 19th century.

Visible achievements in Portland during Deady's life included the Frank Dekum residence, S.W. 11th (above, left); the Cicero H. Lewis residence (above, right) on the block of N.W. 19th and 20th, Glisan and Hoyt, now the Couch School playground; the Capt. J. C. Ainsworth residence, at S.W. 3rd and Oak (ca. 1876), below.

Compared to the homes of Portland magnate W. S. Ladd (above, left) and U. S. Attorney General George H. Williams (right), built about 1881–82 at S.W. 18th and Couch, Judge Deady's house (below), on the southwest corner of 7th and Alder, was modest. He stands in the yard in this late 1880s view.

# 1888

*January 7 (Sat)* . . . [Tuesday] commenced the trial of Maconnaughy v Willey and 5 other cases between the same pltf and other defts for the possession of certain hay cut on 6 different pieces of land on the margin of Lake Warner which the pltf had purchased from the State as swamp and which the defts have since entered on with a view of entering the same under the preemption or homestead acts. Finished the same on Wednesday. The case is supposed to turn on the question of whether the land is swamp or not. Have been at work on opinion on reargument in U S v Barnhart. Thursday took Mrs Murch and Mrs Deady to the Cyclorama of Gettysburg. The country—the landscape—is beautiful and the old Dutch farm houses and stone fences look picturesque. The armies and the fight are very realistic and I suppose largely imaginative and much exaggerated. Snow fell 2 inches deep or more on Tuesday night which still remains on the ground. The weather has been growing colder and last night and this morning our thermometer marked 14 above zero. . . . Sunday I also called on Mrs Murch at Thomas Strongs—a place where I don't go except for some such reason. He was not at home. This noon went by invitation to the Esmond and witnessed some of the Mind Reader [W I] Bishop, wonderful performances.[1] I saw no ground for supposing that there was any imposture in the matter. I was on the general committee named by the persons present. . . .

*16 (Mon)* . . . Friday evening took Henderson to the Casino to see and *hear* [Thomas] Nast make caricatures.[2] The performance was simply wonderful. . . .

. . . [Sunday] evening went to dinner with [William] MacKenzie at the Esmond. Had a good dinner and a quiet time. Went up to his room and chatted a while and then to Bishops room where we staid the better part of an hour, drank a lemonade with whiskey in it and heard the mind reader talk and tell stories. He has dined with crowned heads and American legations are his amusement.

This morning my thermometer marked zero—the first time since I have kept one in Oregon. I do not remember that I had one in the winter of 1861–2 when there was a prolonged freeze in January. It is now 10 degrees above (4 P M) and the snow is falling fast. . . .

*23 (Mon)* . . . Thursday evening dined at Williams where I met Nast and Bishop. After dinner the Saviers and [T B] Trevetts came in and Bishop amused them with some extraordinary tricks with cards. He is a very good mimic and told some good stories at the table concerning encounters between English barristers and witnesses and Judges. But I don't fancy him as a man however much he may excite my astonishment as a psychological phenomenon. I rather like Nast, but it will take longer to find him out. . . .

Saturday evening attended a Library meeting. Talked with Henry Failing about the new Building, not much encouragement. The rich men of Portland will never do much for it until they die, and maybe not then. . . .

*28 (Sat)* . . . Friday took Henderson to the Pavilion to see and hear Nast again. He was very clever but the novelty was not equal to the first night. He took off Bishop in pretending to make a sketch of Ben Butler, while blindfolded, his son writing the name of the person [ *?to be*] sketched on a piece of paper and putting it in his pocket. The caricature of Bishop was delicious and brought down the house.

Have been reading in *Littell* this week . . . A paper on the Borgia family is very interesting. I did not know before that the elder was a Spaniard. The church that could hold them needed reformation if not extermination. Think of a Pope with 5 illegitimate children begotten on the body of another mans wife while he was a Cardinal priest!

. . . Called in the evening at the Hall and had a little of Ruskins *Fors*. In the meantime the ladies had read in the Sunday *Oregonian* the account of Ruskins marriage and divorce and his post nuptial relations with his wife and her second husband—Millais, and they have soured on him, particularly Miss Rodney.[3]

*February 5 (Sat)* . . . Read my annual report this evening at the annual meeting of the members of the Library Association. It will appear in tomorrows *Oregonian*. I had something to say about the "rich" men helping to build the library building which I hope will warm them up.

*11 (Sat)* . . . Friday went to The Dalles in the 10 oclock train, McArthur with me. In the evening lectured for the Y M C A in the Baptist church, to a good and attentive audience—subject "Law & Lawyers." McArthur introduced, and the President Mr McDonald, thanked me, and both were very complimentary. Came home this morning in the through train. Left The Dalles at 4 A M and got to the Ry ferry at 8 and home at 9. Altogether it was a pleasant trip and the change agreeable. Paul is still confined to his bed and is very weak and I am afraid far from well.[4] In the evening the Dr came in and said he thought there was no danger of Pauls having typhoid fever. His mother brought him down and made a bed for him in the parlor yesterday. . . .

*18 (Sat)* . . . Monday went to the Coursen concert and then home and went with Mrs Deady to the Academy armory party where I met Mr Lansing B Mizner and his wife returning from Olympia to Benecia.[5] Paul has been confined to his bed all week but is slowly improving. I have been quite under the weather all week with a sore throat and general aching all over. . . .

*25 (Sat)* . . . Went to church Wednesday and Thursday afternoons. Attend[ed] the "Ballad Concert" last evening at the Tabernacle. Very good, but few ballads according to my idea of what a ballad is. . . .

*March 3 (Sat)* . . . [Sunday the 26] was a lovely day and I concluded I was better off in the sunshine than within the stone walls, so instead of spending my afternoon in my chambers delving as usual I went down to Storys, and with Miss Katie went out to the hill and called on Mrs Burnside the first time I have seen her since the death of her husband. . . . Lectured before the class in the medical school on Thursday & Friday, in the building on the G S Hospital Grounds. Three women students present, all married. At work on the Gist case—the Eldorado ditch, on the plea of Grover that he is a bonafide purchaser for value. Case commenced in 1878 and has been lying fallow since 1879 until last fall when Mr Zera Snow got hold of it for the plaintiff and is putting life into it.[6] Paul is still unwell. Had a relapse or attack of malaria this week which kept him in his bed again three days. Went to prayer in the afternoon of Wednesday & Thursday. The male attendance is light—very. Mr F gave a talk about "knowing and loving God," and nothing about "living" God. . . .

*10 (Sat)* . . . Sat in the C C & D C during the week. Had jury in the former after Tuesday. Tried and disposed of seven cases. Lectured on Med Jurisprudence on Monday at the School and on Thursday evening in the Circuit judges chambers. The weather has been pleasant—a little cool one evening. Paul is still confined to the house. He gains strength very slowly indeed. . . .

*17 (Sat)* Sunday . . . at Trinity as usual. The Rev Mr Short from Astoria [*conducted services*] . . . and preached a model sermon from the parable of the laborers and the vineyard. What a relief and pleasure, compared with Mr Footes humdrum. Spent the afternoon in my chambers where I had a confidential talk with Bernard Goldsmith in relation to the debt he owes Lowenstein. He talked well and like a man who was more than willing to pay his debts if he could. I felt very sorry for him indeed.

. . . Had a talk with Mr Henry Failing yesterday about the money for the Library building when he told me he would give $10,000 of the $50,000 we want for that purpose. He goes East today to be gone 3 or 4 weeks he told me. I attended the commemorative services on the death of Kaiser William last evening at the Tabernacle.[7] The house was filled with a sympathetic audience and the exercises were interesting and appropriate. I occupied a seat on the platform. . . .

*24 (Sat)* Sunday . . . at Trinity as usual. Spent the afternoon in my chambers. Sol Hirsch called and spoke to me of a book which had found its way to the library from Dekums book store— *The Original Mr Jacobs* or some such name—a fierce, brutal and mendacious tirade against the Jews. He left it with me and I ran it through during the week, and found it all he said. Yet there are some things in it, that it would be good for the Jews to read upon the principle that a wise man prefers to know what his enemies say of him rather than his friends.

. . . Wednesday evening went with Mrs Kate D to the celebration of the silver jubilee of Bishop Gross at the Hall of the G R A. The place was crowded with rather decent looking middle class and somewhat below people, mostly women, many of whom were misses. The Bishop made a response to an address that was made him that had a good deal of stump speech humor and cleverness it it, and much brag and bosh. The audience were delighted and so was he. He reminds me of Caples a good deal. . . .

A meeting of the Regents was held in my chambers last evening. Voted to proceed with the construction of the observatory building on the University grounds, at a probable cost of $3000—the tower for the equatorial telescope to be added later. At the close of the meeting I took the Regents to Aliskys, where we had some oysters and beer.

Yesterday word came of the death of Chief Justice Waite just after I got out of the C C, but I had an entry made of the fact and the consequent adjournment not nunc pro tunc but qua tunc. I was interested in reading in this mornings dispatches the various opinions expressed of him—honesty and justice were the oft repeated epithets used in the remarks. Garland said he administered the business of the Supreme Court well—only that and nothing more. The decision in the Telephone case was not a week old.[8] He was a good man and a good judge, but he had a mischievous hobby and that was to limit the jurisdiction of the National Courts. He was largely instrumental as I am told in the passage of the Confederate Judiciary act of 1887. Requiscat in pace dear old man.

*31 (Sat).* . . . Attended E prayer at Trinity except on Good Friday when I attended M prayer. Mr Footes lenten talks are dutiful platitudes. Oh dear! But he is gruesome. . . .

Paul was out again yesterday for the first time since his second attack of gathering in the throat. I hope he is going to get well after 10 weeks of sickness.

On Wednesday the committee of the Bar presented Resolutions in the C C on the death of Ch J Waite. Effinger presented the Resolutions in behalf of the Committee without any remarks and McArthur seconded the same in a short speech, admirably delivered. I responded in a few words, devoted largely to the importance of the Supreme Court. The proceedings were published in the *Oregonian* of Thursday and read well.

Went to the Minstrel Show in the evening at the Casino. The house was packed with people I did not know—people from the lower middle walk of life mostly. The performance was plentifully seasoned with jokes and sneers at wedded life and sexual chastity which seemed to please mightily. A bad school I am afraid for the young men and women of whom there were plenty present.

*April 7 (Sat)* . . . Attended a library meeting on Wednesday evening where on behalf of the subscribers I presented the Association with a portrait in oil of the late Morris M Fechheimer, painted by William Cogswell and costing $400. I also presented a scheme of subscription for the $50,000 we want for the library building which was approved . . .

*14 (Sat)* . . . Judge Sawyer arrived Sunday morning and came to my chambers at 2 oclock and we spent the afternoon together and he went to dinner with me. . . . Wednesday I took him and a few others in a car up to Oswego to see the new Iron Works. He left for home on the afternoon train. . . .

*21 (Sat)* . . . [Friday] worked on the decree in Bogert v Holladay, which I have just finished. The decree provides for the sale of the Stock of the Or Real Estate Co owned by Ben Holladay, which represents Holladays addition to East Portland, to pay debts aggregating $330,000. It has been a long chase on the creditors part but I suppose the game is bagged at last. On Wednesday we attended the wedding of Miss Lizzie Story and Capt [S T] Hamilton U S A[9] at Trinity church and went to the house where we met about 75 pioneers and their descendants and had a pleasant time and refreshments. Our host opened the champagne without stint and we drank it as freely. The bride looked queenly. I have known her intimately since she was a child and a better woman don't live. Have not read anything this week. Have been too busy. Friday commenced my lectures in the law School, and will continue twice a week until the close of the school about the last of May. Today paid $1000 on note to L & T given one year ago yesterday for $1375 with interest at 6 per centum to pay Pauls debts. It strains me but I couldn't help it. . . .

*28 (Sat)* . . . Monday evening called with Mrs Deady at the Rectory to see Mr & Mrs Foote. They went to Cal Thursday on the steamer *Columbia* on account of his eyes. I doubt if he will ever come back again. There was a called meeting of the vestry on Sunday after morning prayer, at which Mr Foote was given 2 months leave of absence . . . Thursday evening saw Warde in "Rich 3." Rants too much in some parts. "In my kingdom for a horse" he roared and spread the word "horse" all over the stage. The scenes—the courtship of Anne and the interview with the Mayor and citizens when he reluctantly consents to accept the crown were well done. Last evening heard Mrs Julia Ward Howe at the Unitarian Church, subject, Greece revisited.[10] She is an elegant looking old lady, who looks as if she had eaten a many a good dinner. The lecture was a light, personal reminiscence, and pleasant affair. It was not pitched on the Key of the "Battle Hymn of the Republic" by any means. . . .

*May 5 (Sat)* . . . Sat in the C C & D C during the week. Spent the most of the time in my chambers working . . . [and reading] "Why Priests Should Wed"—an awful book, that is not all a lie by any means. Monday & Thursday evenings heard Mrs Howe lecture. Dined with her at Trevetts on Thursday, before going to the lecture. A grand, shrewd cheery old dame. I asked for the genesis of the line in the Battle Hymn—"In the beauty of the lilies Christ was born across the sea" —She said in art the Angel of the Annunciation holds a lily in his hand and Christ often spoke of them. These were the suggestions. Attend[ed] the party given by Company K at the Armory on Wednesday evening with Mrs Deady. Met Mrs Howe there and walked her around. Lectured twice . . . Attend[ed] the funeral of John Hanover, Kate Deadys brother at the R C church this morning with Mrs Deady.[11] Mass was sung and much time consumed to what seemed to me no purpose, unless it was to make business. . . .

*12 (Sat)* . . . On the 9th I received $5 the monthly and first dividend on Mrs Deadys 50 shares of the stock of the Sierra Nevada mine. Yesterday Mrs Deady received through the mail a card of natural flowers from Mr Lehman gathered at Bethany Jerusalem.[12]

*19 (Sat)* Sunday (May 13) . . . at Trinity as usual. Mr Costelle officiated, and preached an elegant sermon, of a reasonable length.[13] So different from the dreary and dolorous platitudes we have been accustomed to for some time. . . . On Wednesday morning coming down the street to my chambers as I struck my right heal pretty hard on the pavement I felt a sharp pain in it which immediately radiated towards my toes and passed off. On Thursday morning my heel was quite sore and reminded me of what we used to call a stone bruise when I was a boy. Yesterday it grew worse and I sent for Dr Strong who said I had bruised the nerve that ran over the heel and was distributed to the toes. He gave me a prescription for it—chlorate of am[m]onia—and it is better this morning. . . .

*26 (Sat)*. . . Got petition signed by W W Thayer, Charles Sitton, Raleigh Stott, Frank Dekum and Henry Failing asking the appointment of supervisors to guard the coming election for Representative in Congress in this city. Made an order apprising the chief supervisor of the fact and directing him to discharge his duty in the premises.

. . . Finished *As in a Looking Glass,* the smart and dramatic sketch of watering place life in England and on the Continent and the Chevaliers [d']Industrie male and female that haunt them. Notwithstanding poor Lenas impudence and rascality I felt sorry for her at the end and wanted to murder that selfish brute "Jack" . . .

*June 2 (Sat)*. . . appointed supervisors for the coming election in this city 22 in number for 11 polling places, half republicans and half democrats. Lectured in the school of law on Monday and Friday the last being on the subject of Code pleading making 12 in all. . . . On Wednesday I was in a procession of the G A R and at the tabernacle in the evening where I heard a pretentious, rambling and rather irrelevant address pretty well delivered by Col Anderson of the 14 Infantry.[14]

*9 (Sat)* Sunday . . . Attended Trinity in the evening where the boys from G S Academy attended en masse a sort of Commencement service in which Mr Costelle preached an excellent sermon so far as I could understand it. He don't speak United States exactly, and he lards his speech with Irish, Scotch, English and French Brogues. . . . [Newton] McCoy resigned the criership of the courts at the end of May and I have appointed Maurice McKim in his place and taken him as a student on the usual terms. He is a nephew of Miss Rodneys. Mrs Deady and I met his parents at St Marys Burlington in 1881. She was a lovely woman. The election went all one way on Monday. The Republicans were very much aroused by the much exaggerated stories of what the administration was doing to capture Oregon for the Democrats; and the discussion of the tariff question on the basis of the Mills[15] bill did the latter much harm for it made the fact prominent that the Democrats were for protection for sugar and rice in the south and no protection for wool and lumber in Oregon. Apart from the question of protection or free trade in the abstract, this seemed like and *is* rank injustice to Oregon, hence these votes.

. . . Heard the case of ex parte Morrill on habeas corpus on Saturday. Morril[l] was a special deputy Marshal on Monday and was arrested on process from the police court for the crime of assault and battery committed in the arrest of the complaining witness, W F Matthews, for aiding and counseling a person to vote illegally. The weathe[r] has been moist and cool most of the week. Called at the Hall in the evening and had a set to with Miss Clem on the Catalog of the B S Academy which she likened to a patent medicine almanac on account of the numerous testimonials in it from the parents and guardians of its pupils.

*16 (Sat)* . . . Friday, Pioneer day attended the meeting and heard the speeches. Condon delivered an interesting thoughtful address but marred it by the adoption of the Whitman Myth. Elisha Applegate delivered the occasional address. He labored a good deal but did not bring forth much. There was some coarse gold however in his sluices. Attended the pioneer ball in the evening a while where I found Mrs Joseph Watt and Mrs Morgan nee Flint[16] the latter of whom I had not seen for many years. . . .

*30 (Sat)* . . . Thursday [21] went with Mrs Deady or rather started for Baker city, to view the ditches on Pine creek in connection with the suits in the C C involving a controversy between the farmers on the creek and the Nelson Mine as to the right to the water of the creek. Got to Baker city early in the morning and were driven at once to the mine a distance of 8 miles southeast. After a good breakfast at the Superintendents Mr Blasdell, where Mrs Deady remained, Judges [L B] Ison, [Martin] Olmstead, Blasdell, [Calvin] Hyde and others started on the view.[17] We spent the day driving and walking about the side of the mountain and the plain below, examining the creek and tracing ditches old and new, and then came back to the mine and saw the monitor (7 inch one) playing on the bank of gravel and earth and then drove to town. About the time we were ready to return on Saturday afternoon I was taken with a violent vomiting which lasted some time. I got on the train however and got home the next morning quite recovered but weak. Altogether the trip was a very enjoyable one. . . .

. . . On Wednesday evening [27] went to Eugene to attend the commencement and the annual meeting of the Regents and returned on Friday at noon. The address by Miss [Etta] Moore and the one by Gilbert McGinn, the first "The language we speak" and the latter "The two Pitts" were splendid specimens of composition as well as eloquence and forcible delivery. The treatment of the subjects was also excellent. . . . Justice Field arrived with Mrs Field this morning and took rooms at the Holton House where I called on them. They came up to the Chambers about 11 and after a while I took Mrs Field a walk through town to the library &c. At Henrichsens I gave her a silver pin costing $2. Left her at the H H and came up here where I found the Judge hovering over the embers of a dying fire. We chatted away or rather he did for an hour or so and then I went to work and he down town. Have not read much the past fortnight except the *Oregonian* and that has been enough on account of the Convention at Chicago. I am pleased that Blaine was not nominated and am well pleased with Harrison.

*July 7 (Sat)* . . . Wednesday, the Fourth, I acted as chairman of the day. Took Field in a carriage with myself and Williams the Orator of the day. Had a good and a fine procession. I made a few introductory remarks and Williams made a good popular speech well out of the beaten track. In the evening we had fire works at our house and saw the illumination of Mt Hood at 11 oclock and a few minutes. The red light was large and plain and was very distinct and plain in the surrounding darkness.[18] . .

. . . I had a pleasant time with Justice Field while here. He has a new grievance—the nomination of Fuller for Chief Justice instead of himself—and I don't blame him.[19] . . .

*14 (Sat)* . . . Got $120 for my lectures in the school of law this year on yesterday. Every little helps—a poor man. Twelve lectures on constitutional law. The compensation is light. It rained again on Thursday night and Friday and the clouds are still floating or rather hanging over us. I am concerned for the grain and grass crop. Got $5000 for the Library building from S G Reed yesterday and he behaved very well about it too. Tackled D P Thompson today without any result. I talked strong and plain and fancy I made some impression on him. He said if he sells his Albina land he would do it.

*28 (Sat)* Sunday . . . afternoon [15] called at Cedar Hill with Elsie and Emma Failing. Met Reed and his wife Margaret, and Lee Eaton and the baby John Silas, my godson. Had a pleasant call. Called at Woods as we came home . . . Wednesday delivered an opinion in U S v Clapox & Dick overruling demurrer to information charging the defendants with a rescue in violations of § 5491 R S by taking an Indian woman out of the Indian jail on the Umatilla reservation where she had been committed by the Indian police on the charge of adultery. Friday left with Bernard Goldsmith for Wardner, Idaho on the O R & N train at 10:50. Reached Spokane early in the morning and thence by a local train to Fort Sherman on Coeur D'Alene lake, by 9 oclock. Staid there until Monday as the guest of Gen [W P] Carlin, the commander of the Post.[20]

Sunday, July 22. Troubled with diarehea and kept my room most of the day. . . . In the evening sat on the porch and witnessed the total eclipse of the moon. The Post is a beautiful place but hot during the day and cool in the evening. Saturday and Sunday thermometer stood at 99 & 98. . . .

Monday, July 23 took the boat for the Mission, a distance of about 60 miles up the lake and river where we arrived at ½ past 12 after a delightful ride. Gen Carlin was with us as also a clever big boy from New York, James Goldsmith, a son of Bernards. At the landing I met Joset the Jesuit Missionary who has been among the Indians since 1844.[21] He is an old man, with a large head and features, a Swiss German, and quite Teutonic in appearance. There we took the narrow gauge road at the south fork of the Coeur D'Alene to Wardner Junction a distance of [omitted] miles, where we took a wagon for Wardner. Passed through the town, consisting of one street running up a Canyon to Reeds concentrat[i]on [mill] where we witnessed the process of crushing and washing the silver bearing galena from the Sullivan and Bunker Hill mines, the output of which came down the side of the mountain in a shoot to the mill. Stopped that night at Mrs Thompsons in Wardner and next day—Tuesday—visited in the afternoon at the Nelly, Alma and Hawkeye gold miles and saw very rich ore as we supposed and as the washing of a pan showed. In the afternoon we drove to the silver mine Sierra Nevada, which we thoroughly explored, going in a distance of about 450 feet on one tunnel and coming out on another and going back and forth in the drifts in the meantime as much farther. Saw a large amount of valuable ore in the mine—principally galena and copper bearing silver. The mill is a simple affair, but they turn out about 20 tons of concentrates a day, which is supposed to be worth $100 a ton. But this depends largely on the price of lead and this again depends on the tariff. And hence the Mills bill is not in favor in this region.

Wednesday morning started home. Gen Carlin, James G and myself, Bernard remaining behind for a few days. At the Mission landing we met some ladies and gentlemen from the post among [whom] was my admiration Miss Fitch.[22] They returned with us and although she was accompanied by a young officer with apparently serious intentions, I found opportunity to improve my acquaintance with her and enjoyed her society. At Coeur D'Alene we parted with Gen Carlin for whom I have acquired a high regard, and for whose hospitality I have a very pleasant remembrance. . . . We reached Spokane at 10 P M and boarded the overland train at ½ past 11 on which we reached Portland at 4:20 P M. My impression is that the Wardner district as it is called on the head waters of the Coeur D'Alene is very rich in precious metals. . . .

*August 4 (Sat)*. . . Wrote opinion in U S v Trainer which I delivered this morning. It contains a growl against slovenly and bungling legislation of Congress as contained in § 5511 of R S. Wrote a statement concerning my knowledge or information of Scotts conduct in the bribery practice at the Congressional election in 1873, or rather the want of. The occasion was a long rehash in the *Daily News* of the 2 inst, of the oft repeated story that I said I would send Scott to the penitentiary for his part in the matter etc. I gave it to Scott and asked him to publish it if he had no objections, which he did in the mornings paper.[23] . . .

*18 (Sat)*. . . Saturday [11] Mrs Deady took me out to the Riverside horse hop. Hot and rather stupid. Went out on the Narrow Gauge and came back on the *Sel[l]wood*.

Sunday (Aug 12) . . . In the afternoon went over to Sunnyside with Emma & Rhoda Failing. From 5th street East Portland, rode in an open car behind the motor. The car was overcrowded and the smoke and soot from the motor swept through it occasionally. But the "people" enjoyed [it] and it only cost 5 cents from the west end of the Morrison St Bridge. . . .

*25 (Sat)*. . . Worked during the week on the *Nith* case, DeHart libellants. These British shipmasters or hired skippers are the most reckless liars I know of on a question involving the liability or misconduct of one of their kind. Wednesday evening went with the other folk of the Hill House to Sells Circus. It was a great performance but too much at once. The racing, however, was very good. While a woman barebacked rider was performing in each of the two rings I was puzzled which one to look at and felt like Capt Macheath in the "Beggars Opera."

> "How happy I could be with either
> Were t'other dear charmer away."

Friday evening went on an excursion to Astoria in the *Potter* on the invitation of [W H] Holcomb with Mr [Charles Francis] Adams of the U P and his companion, Mr [C R] Codman,[24] a pleasant old lawyer and railway man of Boston and the Oregon directors of the O R & N Messrs Failing, Lewis, Corbett, & Dolph and Mr Scott. We had a good supper on board and a pleasant scattered conversation until 11 oclock. Got up at 7 when found we were on our way home. Breakfast at 8, and more talk till we reached Portland at 15 min past 11. Found a letter here from Miss Fitch with a photograph of the Coeur d'Alene Mission church with herself in the foreground.

*September 1 (Sat)* . . . Worked on the *Nith* case which I finished Wednesday evening and delivered the opinion the next morning. A tedious job, but I found I must decide it in favor of Edward, and I did not feel I could afford to do it and leave any argument of the claimant unanswered.

. . . Tuesday evening dined at Montgomerys where I met the board of engineers including Col [Geo] Mendell considering the feasibility of a portage of some kind at Celilo.[25] An excellent dinner and a pleasant party. Mrs M sat at the table and I sat at her right. I came away as soon as we rose from the table . . . Told Mendell that the nominal problem involved in the improvement of the river at Celilo was how best to carry the crop of eastern Oregon, but the real problem was how best to carry the *vote* of that region. . . .

*8 (Sat)* . . . Thursday came here [Grimes House, Clatsop Beach] on the *Potter* to Tansey [*sic*] point and in the Grimes wagon from there on. Left Portland at 8 oclock and reached here at 20 minutes to 6. Had a very pleasant trip. Mrs Deady and Mrs Edward Deady came with me. Mr & Mrs [B B] Tuttle and Miss Adams[26] from the Hill House were also of the party. Friday worked on 2d volume of Bancrofts *Oregon.* He furnished me a copy with pages pasted on large blank leaves with margins for notes, and asked me to read and revise it for errors of fact. Bathed in the afternoon. Strong tide—the effect of a blow outside. . . .

*9 (Sun)* Another glorious day and bath. Worked on 2 *Oregon.* Ran a race on beach in my bathing clothes with Mrs Wait, and while going at the top of my speed stuck my toe in the sand and fell prone. Wrenched the big toe of my right foot so that I am lame yet and bruised my left side just under the nipple so that it is very sore yet. [Rev] Mr Short had service in the afternoon in the Grimes parlor. The only prayer book in the congregation besides the ministers was ours and that was an English one and did not contain the Canticles the minister read. . . .

*10 (Mon)* Tommy Strowbridge started to the mountains today on a hunt. Another glorious day and bath. Took Mrs Deady in and she enjoyed it. Worked on 2 *Oregon* and finished it. Have made many corrections of fact and might have made many of opinion, but I did not care to. Wrote to Bancroft on the subject and cautioned him a little against Mrs Victors prejudices and predelictions.

*11 (Tue)* . . . Revised Ladd & Corbetts lives for Bancrofts "Chronicles of the Kings." Made some alterations and additions. They are both pitched on high key and contain all the good that can be said of the subjects with their faults left out.[27] . .

*12 (Wed)* Revised Henry Failings life for Bancroft. Made some alterations and additions, particularly in the paragraph relating to Edward Failing and Olivia, his wife. Another glorious day and bath. Mrs Deady gets more venturesome and fond of it. In the morning we had a little rain. It is a pity it was not a large one.

*13 (Thu)* The Woods left this forenoon, and quiet reigns in Warsaw, comparatively. . . . In the afternoon bathed with Mrs Deady and then took a long walk through the woods with her and Catherine. Today has been a beautiful one, but the wind has been pretty strong and cool since noon.

*14 (Fri)* The [W H] Dunckleys,[28] Mrs Tuttle and Miss Adams left this morning.

Commenced to work on my dictation for Bancrofts "Chronicles of the Kings." It puzzles me what to say and what to leave out. However when in doubt I will put in and let Bancroft select and weed out. The morning was very warm with a hot air from the southeast. At 10 oclock the thermometer stood on the porch at 84, but at 4 in the evening it was 64 on the beach and the water was 57. We had a glorious bath—the surf rather light. . . .

*15 (Sat)* Worked on my dictation. Walked up to Cluchers at noon. Mail came at 2 P M and brought the *Oregonian* and Edward. Read the papers and bathed at 5 oclock. Day cloudy. Water 53 degrees.

*16 (Sun)* Rained some about daylight and laid the dust. Bathed at ½ past 9 A M. Cloudy and strong south wind, and swift tide.

. . . All went up to Mrs [Sam] Stanleys this afternoon in Monroes wagon but found no one at home except the daughter, Laura, and we came back.[29] Encountered a severe wind from the south, and clouds of dust. Soon after we got home it rained quite hard for an hour or so which is a great blessing to the country. There has been no rain in western Oregon except the little shower this morning since the 8th or 9th of July. I see by this diary that it rained hard here this day one year ago with much thunder and lightning.

*17 (Mon)* A beautiful day. Bathed at 10 oclock A M. The water was delightful. The wind from the south on Sunday seems to have warmed the water. . . .

*19 (Wed)* Day opened pleasant and cool. In the evening turned cloudy. Worked on dictation. Had a good bath, but have lumbago pretty bad. . . .

*20 (Thu)* Commen[ced] raining in the night, and continued until 11 oclock. [At] ½ past 11 went in the breakers. I was the solitary bather. The waves strong but the water very pleasant. Worked on dictation. Working it over now and there is no end of changes and additions to be made. It will be a pretty complete biography before I get through. . . .

*21 (Fri)* A glorious day after the rain. Walked with Mrs Deady on the beach in the morning and bathed at ½ past 11. Sky and air glorious but tide strong and fierce. After lunch we and the [W J] Van Schuyvers went over to Ebermons,[30] a distance of about a mile for butter and buttermilk. In the evening walked on the beach to the Seaside and back and sat on the bank at our bathhouse and saw the sunset at exactly six oclock. It was a beautiful sight. A bank of clouds in serrated and fantastic shapes rested on the ocean extending above the horizon about 15 degrees. When the sun got behind this the place just in front of it looked like an illuminated alterpiece [*sic*] or reredos. When the sun got down about the water, there was a rift in the base of the cloud through which the sun glowed, until the place suggested the mouth of [a] Cyclopian furnace. . . .

*22 (Sat)* Another glorious day. Mrs Deady and I walked up the beach in the morning and up the creek and round home through the woods about three miles in all. Bathed at noon. The water very swift and strong. In the afternoon, Mrs Deady, Mrs Sutherlin and I walked up to the Seaside by the road and back on beach and saw the sunset. Not as grand as the night before. Walked three miles, making six miles in the day. Read *Makers of Venice*.

*23 (Sun)* A beautiful day with a pretty strong northwest wind . . . Got a horse and cart from [J P] Austin[31] and took Mrs D to drive on the beach. Settled with Mr Grimes, charged us $10 a week for 2½ weeks each—$50 which includes transportation. Going home in the morning.

*24 (Mon)* A pleasant day with a wind from the Northeast, which made it somewhat warm. At 15 minutes after 9 we got away for Astoria in Monroe Grimes four-in-hand, the Sutherlins, and Van Schuyvers, eight in all. Got to Skipenon [*sic*] at 12 and had a pleasant ride over the bay in the *Electric*. Got to Astoria at 20 minutes to 1. Lunched at the Occidental. Took the street railway and rode to the upper town and called at the Shorts and Taylors as we came back. Read the Sunday and Monday *Oregonian*. Dined at 6 P M and went on the *S G Reed* at 7 where we turned in in room 18 and got here at 5 oclock.

*25 (Tue)* and home to breakfast and glad to be at Sister Hills table for breakfast. . . .

*29 (Sat)* Sat in the C C and read affidavits and opinion in petition of Terry for revocation of sentence. Terry certainly appears in a bad light in this phase of the matter, and Heydenfeldt not much better.[32] . . .

*October 6 (Sat)* . . . [Sunday] at Trinity as usual. The Rev Mr Nash in the chancel and pulpit. Mr Foote was in the chancel also having just returned from California, where he has been resting for five months on account of his eyes without getting any relief. Spent the afternoon in my chambers on my accounts for the quarter. Judge Sawyer called having arrived in the morning overland. He is rather sad and serious. This Terry outrage worries him a good deal. David and Sarah ought to have their offending hands chopped off . . . [Sawyer] went to Seattle on Tuesday night and returned on Friday morning and sat in the C C and heard the case of the *Nith*, I sat with him in this case to see how Edward did who was counsel for the libellants and appellees.[33] . . . Got some pamphlets containing the evidence in the Terry contempt and the opinion of Justice Field refusing to revoke the sentence. Some rain and more beautiful weather this week. The Mechanics fair opened on Thursday evening, and I attended with Judge Sawyer this evening.

*13 (Sat)* Sunday . . . at Trinity as usual. Mr Foote officiated and got along very well for a blind man. He professed to use the prayer book. Spent the afternoon in my chambers and with Judge Sawyer in his, where we went over the old Mitchel[l] scandal. Sat in the C C & D C during the week. On Tuesday Sawyer sat in the former and announcing [*sic*] his decision in the case of the *Nith* and the *Director*[34] taken by appeal from my decision in the district court. He affirmed me in both instances, adopting my findings of fact and law & for the reasons given in my opinions, to which he said he could add nothing. I wrote his opinions in brief, in each case and gave them to the *Oregonian*. Wednesday heard a habeas corpus sued out by a young Chinese woman born in San Francisco whom the collector refused to land. Discharged her. Wrote an opinion since of which I read the proof last night for the *Oregonian*. It contains some plain talk on the late exclusion act. The Republicans had a torch light procession which I saw from my chambers window. It was a brilliant affair. The morning *Oregonian* says 3000 persons in the procession but from [all] I can learn there was about 2000. . . . Sawyer went home on Tuesday. He is getting old. His catarrh is still at work and his voice and hearing are getting weak. The week has been pretty evenly compounded of rain and sunshine. L L Robinson of Cal called to see me on Wednesday on his way East via the Canadian Pacific. He is very corpulent but cheery. Says he lost $500,000 by our decision in the Debris case. I am sorry, but could not help it.

*20 (Sat)* . . . Revised the sketch of Mr Lewis for C[hronicles of the] K[ings] and sent it off the first of this week or the last of last. Have gone over my own since it was put into typewriting and it is ready to go now.

Got two copies from Bancroft of the steel engraving of myself. They are well done I think, but the head is too narrow, and I am going to try and have it altered. . . .

. . . Visited the fat cattle show yesterday and saw the usual number of such horses and cattle. A useful affair but not a very refined place of amusement. Called at the Hall in the evening and took Miss Lydia to the [Mechanics] Fair.

*27 (Sat)* . . . Bought 8 seats for the Abbot[t] Opera which commences Monday for 3 nights Thursday, Friday & Saturday, cost $12. Took Blanche Catlin to the first [Eugene] Coursen concert last night. It was excellent. Mrs Reed & Lownsdale were superb and she looked too utterly lovely in her aesthetic Oscar Wilde dress.[35]

Still dipping into Milmans *Latin Christianity*.[36] Am in the third year of our Lords ministry now. His idea of the Sonship will not stand the test of the Nicene creed; and for that matter neither will mine. There ought to be no creed in the prayer book and/or the churches except the Apostles. How Jesus became or is the son of God no man knoweth, and therefore should not undertake dogmatically to declare. . . .

*November 3 (Sat)* Sunday . . . Called on Senator Dolph in the afternoon at Cyrus Dolphs, and took an early dinner with them. Had a pleasant call. The Senator looked well. . . . Wednesday evening attended a fancy dress ball at Academy Hall with Mrs Deady. Henderson was costumed as a Roman youth in white tights, toga and sandals, after the picture in the *Queen* of St Valentines Day in Rome and looked splendid—in fact was the best male character there. Mrs Deady wore her black velvet with powder in her hair and looked very distingué.

The Emma Abbott Opera troupe have been at the Park Theatre this week. Had 3 seats ($1.50 each) for Thursday (Faust) and Friday (Norma). Abbott acts well but is in poor voice. Her support is very good. The Molsons came down on Thursday and are our guests at Mrs Hills. They went with us to see "Norma" last night. Drew the last of Mrs Deadys money from Yamhill on the first inst—$1297.64. The last five years we have drawn in all from this source $2697.64, besides $50 I gave John Henderson for attending to the loaning of the money. . . . Went this evening with Mrs Deady to hear Abbott in "the Good Devil." No pretty airs in it and Abbott who was the Devil had no voice; add to this the uncomfortable seats and the matter might be considered a severe penance.

*10 (Sat)* . . . Voted for Harrison & Morton on Tuesday and am pleased with their election. Cleveland made a fair president the first two years of his term and particularly on the subject of the civil service. Notwithstanding the pressure from the ravenous host of spoilsmen and office seekers in his own party and the jeers and sneers of the same kind in the Republican party he did more in that time to advance the cause of civil service reform than any or all of his predecessors. But after he made up his mind to run the second time he gradually surrendered everything into the hands of the "workers." No man ought to be a candidate for a second term. The temptation to abuse the power and patronage of his office to secure his election is too great for any ordinary man to withstand. And I very much dislike his late action on the Chinese question, and in regard to Canada and the British minister. But I suppose in these matters, he was in the hands of his friends, for the purposes of the election. And now if Harrison leaves Blaine out of his cabinet, as I think he will, all will be well.[37] . . .

*24 (Sat)* . . . Mrs D has been quite unwell the last 2 weeks, but is better now. Had a long characteristic and interesting letter this morning from Benj Stark. Bush and Miss Sally called at my chambers yesterday and then on Mrs D at the house. B is very distressed at the result of the election. Sally is a very nice girl and I think her father is very fond of her. He ought to be . . . Gave $10 to Dodd yesterday for the Foote fund which he ought to be better able to give me than me him. . . .

*December 1 (Sat)* Sunday . . . at Trinity as usual. Bishop Morris was in the chancel and preached. I fear I have lost my interest. His manner is excellent but the matter is only so so. . . . We called last evening at the Rectory but the inmates were out (the Footes). This was our last chance before they vamoosed the ranch. When Mr Foote took the parish I expected to enjoy him and his ministry, so to speak. But I have been altogether disappointed. I don't think he fancied me. I tried to have him, but made no impression, and I can't fancy people that don't fancy me—or at least pretend to. . . . Got copies of the amended engraving of myself for the C of K and am quite well satisfied with them. Made up my accounts this morning and drew my check for $512.95 leaving less than $50 to my credit in the bank. Paid Goldsmith $100 for Lucy Murch for 100 shares of Alma [mine]. Called at the Hall in the evening, where I met Mr [D E] Loveridge, now officiating at Trinity.[38]

*8 (Sat)* . . . Got a letter from Lewis this morning enclosing correspondence with Bancroft about his Biography, asking my advice. I immediately wrote Bancroft asking him to release Mr Lewis from the contract on the payment of the expense incurred, which I hope he will do on my account as he ought to.

I got a proof of my own biography from Bancroft this week with which I am not at all pleased, and so wrote him. Can't say what will become of it.

*15 (Sat)* . . . [Sunday] Heard [Dwight] Moody in the evening at the Tabernacle. Spoke from the words "As ye sow so shall ye reap." He did very well indeed. Was full of apt and pertinent illustrations, told in plain language and way. Heard him again on Monday evening. Did not like him. To many nursery stories. Sat in the C C & D C during the week . . .

In the closing address to the Jury in U S v [Tom] Jordan & [Joe] Taylor,[39] McArthur done remarkably well. He was eloquent and forcible, and if he could only put the facts of the case in detail in his speeches they would be admirable.

As it is he is a little too general, too near the abstract. . . .

*22 (Sat)*. . . On Thursday evening took Mrs Deady to hear the Carleton Troupe in "Myneer Jahn," and was disappointed in the piece and the players. The choruses were pretty and the legs of the Amazons were uniformly beautiful. . . .

. . . Read some articles in the *Political Science Quarterly,* one on the progress of Socialism in England is very interesting and confirms my impression that as population multiplies on a given territory paternalism in government becomes necessary to the preservation of the people and if the government is a popular one the majority will favor paternalism as a means of controlling and taxing the rich. An article on Trusts by Timothy Dwight demonstrates their legality by any standard of legal ethics known to the world.[40]. . .

*29 (Sat)* . . . Tuesday, Xmas, went to the Hall at early service and staid to breakfast and the tree as usual and to M prayer at Trinity at 11 oclock, where I heard an excellent sermon from Mr Loveridge. Worked all the afternoon, and visited the family trees in the evening. Christmas was pleasant this year. I left the making of presents to Mrs Deady this year. Sam Lowenstein presented her with a beautiful lamp costing I believe between $20 & 25. Heard Moody twice this week. I don't think he is doing much here. The people flock to the tabernacle and listened gladly but go away without making any sign. With the greater number I think it is a mere cheap entertainment. . . .

# NOTES

1. R. F. Maconnaughy had purchased land alleged to be swampland from C. N. Felton, assignee of Hen Owens. J. M. Willey and others settled on the land, some of which was on the border of Lake Warner, and farmed it. Maconnaughy sued Willey and his associates, alleging them to be squatters, and demanding recompense for 200 ton of hay which they had removed from the site. Deady found that Willey and his associates were not squatters, and that they were settlers in due form proving up with a view to filing donation land claims. At the same time, Governor Pennoyer, operating on the supposition that the swampland claims were fraudulent, which they undoubtedly were, had sold the land out from under Maconnaughy for the benefit of the School Land Board. Maconnaughy sued. In this case Deady found that Pennoyer had acted illegally, and he was eventually sustained by the U. S. Supreme Court.

U. S. v Barnhart was an action brought against Barnhart as a result of a fraudulent affidavit which Barnhart had prepared some years earlier in connection with a swampland claim. Barnhart demurred to the complaint on various grounds and his demurrer was sustained.

Washington Irving Bishop (c.1848–89), noted mind-reader. His death was macabre. On May 13, 1889, he was invited to the Lambs' Club in New York City as a guest of one of the members. Very late that night he gave an impromptu performance, after which he fell into a cataleptic fit from which he shortly recovered. The members of the Lambs' Club were not convinced of the validity of Bishop's performance and they felt that the cataleptic fit was simply an extension of his act. Bishop eventually was persuaded to perform a second, and much more complicated feat of mind-reading. This he also did successfully and shortly afterward fell into a second and deeper cataleptic fit. A physician who was present thought at first that the fit would pass, but eventually it grew so deep that all the viable signs disappeared. Other physicians were called and certified that Bishop was dead. The body was taken to a mortuary and straightway post mortemed by a team of doctors bent upon finding both a cause of death and determining whether Bishop's mind-reading gift could be explained by some abnormal development of his brain. Neither cause of death nor abnormality was discovered. What was discovered, however, after the autopsy was completed and Bishop indubitably dead, was a note in his billfold warning that he was subject to such seizures and should be allowed to rest quietly. It subsequently developed that he had once lain in such a state for 12 hours and been pronounced dead by a doctor.

2. Thomas Nast (1840–1902), celebrated cartoonist.

3. The Rodney sisters may have become incensed at learning that in seven years Ruskin had never got around to consummating his marriage.

4. F. A. McDonald, register of the U. S. Land Office at The Dalles. Paul's illness was of an enduring nature.

5. Lansing B. Mizner; Benecia attorney. Meizner in original.

6. During the gold mining in what is now Malheur County during the late 1860s and early 1870s the Eldorado Ditch was constructed to bring water from tributaries along the south side of the upper reaches of Burnt River and carried them southeast to the Willow

Creek drainage, where the water was sold to miners engaged in placer mining. One hundred thirty-five miles in length, it was a very considerable engineering job for that day. The Gist case arose out of conflicting claims as ownership of the Ditch. Zera Snow (1858–1922), Portland attorney.

7. Kaiser William I (1797–1888), king of Prussia and German emperor, had died March 9.

8. Augustus H. Garland (1832–99), Arkansas lawyer and Confederate congressman and senator; governor, 1874–77; senator, 1877–85; attorney-general under Cleveland, 1885–89. The telephone cases established Alexander Graham Bell as the inventor of that instrument against the claims of Elisha Grey and others.

9. Capt. S. T. Hamilton of the 2nd Cavalry.

10. Julia Ward Howe (1819–1910), poet, reformer, feminist; best remembered for her "Battle Hymn of the Republic."

11. John Hanover was Canadian-born. His grave is unmarked and the date of his birth unknown.

12. Lewis L. Lehman had accompanied Mrs. Deady and her party to Alaska.

13. The Reverend Mr. Costelle had come from Green Bay, Wisconsin to serve as supply pastor.

14. Thomas M. Anderson, Colonel commanding 14th Regiment of Infantry; rose from the ranks; in retirement in 1900 he was a major-general of volunteers and a brigadier-general in the regular army.

15. Newton McCoy (1855–1939), Portland attorney. Roger Q. Mills, Texas congressman, following President Cleveland's plea of reduced tariffs, had produced a tariff reform bill. It passed in the Democrat-controlled House, but was defeated in the Republican-controlled Senate.

16. In the winter of 1842–43 Marcus Whitman hurried East. He went in a desperate attempt to save his mission, critical reports of which had been sent to the American Board of Commissioners for Foreign Missions by his own associates. He was successful in this and returned the following year. Some time after his death a number of the zealous, among them W. H. Gray and Henry H. Spalding, both of whom had been members of the mission and both of whom had differed bitterly with Whitman, circulated the story that Whitman had gone East to prevent Daniel Webster, then secretary of state, from bargaining away the Oregon Country for New England fishing rights. As it happens, the Webster-Ashburton Treaty, whose terms Whitman is supposed to have influenced, was signed two months before he left Waiilatpu. Sarah Flint Morgan, born in Connecticut in 1844, came around the horn in 1847–48, married Edward S. Morgan of Douglas County in 1861.

17. L. B. Ison (1841–89), Baker lawyer, jurist, rancher and miner. T. Calvin Hyde (1847–96), Baker lawyer. Martin L. Olmstead; Baker lawyer and jurist.

18. The practice of illuminating Mount Hood on occasion with flares and fireworks was continued until well into the present century.

19. Melville W. Fuller (1833–1910), Illinois lawyer; a strict constructionist. Field had reason to be hurt by Cleveland's failure to elevate him. He had been longer on the supreme bench than any justice save Samuel Miller, who had been appointed earlier in the same year, 1863, and Miller was a Republican. And Field was a jurist of marked ability. It is not impossible he was passed over because Cleveland was irritated by the judge's presidential aspirations.

20. It has not been possible to identify Lee Eaton. It is one of the ironies of history that John Silas Reed should be the godson of Matthew Paul Deady. William P. Carlin (Carlan in original), MA, class of 1846; served as a brigade commander in the Army of the Cumberland; retired 1893.

21. Joseph Joset, S.J. (c. 1811–1900), Roman Catholic missionary; first came west in 1845. Jozette in original.

22. Deady had met Miss Fitch, a young lady from Indiana, a few days earlier at Fort Sherman.

23. Deady's statement is a plain piece of disingenuity. He was not aware of Scott's involvement in the vote frauds nor of Scott's efforts to unseat him, until long after the event. It was therefore not Deady who threatened to jail Scott, it was Scott who wrote to Mitchell expressing the fear that Deady would jail him.

24. William H. Holcomb; then general-manager, O.R. & N. Co. Charles R. Codman (1829–1918), Boston attorney.

25. George H. Mendell (Mendal in original), MA, class of 1848; engineer officer; died 1912.

26. Miss Adams was apparently a daughter of Edward R. Adams, an insurance man and a resident at The Hill.

27. "Chronicles of the Kings," the original title for the biographical sketches published by Bancroft under the more democratic style of *Chronicles of the Builders*. Deady remained unreconstructed and always used the monarchial form.

28. William H. Dunckley (1860–1936) and Fannie W. Dunckley (1857–1926); he was with Ladd & Tilton. Dunkley in original.

29. Samuel K. Stanley, hotelman and rancher and formerly manager of the Seaside House; died 1900. His second wife was Mary Grimes (1846–1928). Laura was a daughter by his first wife.

30. N. A. Ebermon; Clatsop County farmer. Everman in original.

31. James P. Austin, Seaside grocer, saloon-keeper and stage operator.

32. On Sept. 3, 1888, Justice Field was reading a circuit court opinion in the case of Sharon vs Hill, a judgment adverse to Sarah Althea, who by then was married to Terry, when she jumped to her feet and demanded to know how much he had been paid to decide against her. Field ordered her removed and Terry intervened forcibly, it requiring the efforts of a number of court attendants and bystanders to subdue him. The next day Terry was given six months for contempt and his wife 30 days. According to witnesses, Terry vowed to get even with Field when Field returned to California and after Terry was out of jail.

Solomon Heydenfeldt was guilty of a more involved legal sin. As a justice of the California supreme court in the 1850s he had written an opinion upholding the validity of a non-solemnized marriage contract similar but not identical to that purported to exist between Sarah Althea and William Sharon. If Heydenfeldt had not so decided, Sarah would never have got into court.

33. The *Nith* case was a libel action against the shipper's agent for cargo damage.

34. The *Director* case, a libel action alleging damage resulting from unseaworthiness of the vessel.

35. Eugene E. Coursen, violinist, organist, teacher and conductor, until his death in 1933, aged 72, he was an important figure in Portland music circles. Rose Coursen Reed was his sister. Millard O. Lownsdale (1851–1911), popular Portland baritone and subsequently an orchardist.

36. Henry H. Milman (1791–1868), Anglican divine.

37. Deady was dissatisfied with Cleveland because Cleveland had recently signed into law the Scott Chinese Exclusion Act, and a year previous had signed into law an act prohibiting Canadian fishing vessels from entering American ports and making possible an interdiction on the importation of Canadian fish and fish products. The English minister to the U.S., Sackville-West, had been the victim of Republican trickery. He replied to a letter from a Californian who called himself Murchison that Cleveland's election would be pleasing to Great Britain. His letter was given wide publication, and Cleveland promptly demanded his resignation.

38. D. E. Loveridge was a Eugene pastor.

39. Thomas A. Jordan, sheriff of Multnomah County, and Joe Taylor, a well-known political shoulder-hitter, were charged with taking a prisoner charged with a voting violation from the custody of a deputy U. S. marshal, by use of strong persuasion.

40. Deady was guilty of a curious error. The article in question was written not by

Timothy Dwight, president of Yale University and a Congregational clergyman, but by Theodore W. Dwight (1822–92), lawyer and educator; cousin to Timothy; professor of law, Hamilton College, 1846–58; first professor at Columbia Law School, 1858, and its warden, 1878–91.

# 1889

*January 5 (Sat)*. . . New year day, spent in my chambers and the evening at home. Mrs Deady received and had some excellent eggnogg for her particular friends of a certain age of which I was one. In the evening we attended a dinner given at the Academy Hall, by Bishop Morris, to the news and messenger boys of the city at which I presided. The room and tables looked very inviting, and the dinner was excellent. Rev Mr Eliot, Judge Williams and the Bishop addressed the boys, and did well, except the latter two were too long. There were about 150 boys present. . . . Am engaged in drafting an act for H[enry] F[ailing] to enable the water committee to issue bonds and bring us the Bull run water to Portland.

*12 (Sat)*. . . [*Sunday*] engaged on draft of act for bringing in the Bull run water. Had a consultation with H F on the draft in the evening and it was settled. Had a typewriter copy of it made next day and sent to him. I see that the water committee have since adopted the act with one amendment—striking out the clause authorizing the interest on the new bonds to be paid in New York, which was right. People that don't want their interest payable in Portland can let the bonds alone. . . .

Called at the Hall . . . [*this*] evening and had a chaff with Miss Clem about Moody and lay preachers. She was very much astonished when I told her they were quite common in the early church.

*19 (Sat)*. . . Wednesday, went with Mrs Deady to a Japanese Tea at the Academy Hall given by the women folk of the Unitarian church, with dancing. It might better have been called Dancing, with Japanese Tea. However it was a jolly joyous affair. . . .

*26 (Sat)*. . . Have been more or less ill all the week, with sore throat and cold in head. Got a pleasant letter yesterday from Mrs Person after a long silence and also one from Miss Buckingham. Have acceded to Mr Stones request and am going on again with my biography for the "C of K," and hope we will get along with it satisfactorily.

I find that Whalley is the author of a communication in the *Oregonian* signed "Advocates" denouncing the practice of the Federal Judges, instructing the jury on the facts, meaning myself and a case he lost before me not long [ago] as much on account of his ignorance of the facts and law as anything else. Poor fellow, he is another "viper that I have warmed" &c; but I think he will find that "he is gnawing a file."[1] . . .

*February 2 (Sat)*. . . Wednesday wrote a letter to Seymour Condon on the subject

FEBRUARY 1889

of the exemption of the Bull run water bonds from taxation, at the request of
Mr Corbett who shewed me a letter from Will Ladd urging that I do so. Got a
letter from Condon[2] next day saying that it was all right as he had a bill he had
just got through the house exempting $50,000 of sewer bonds for Eugene from
taxation.

Heard the Rev Mr [Ross] Houghton[3] deliver a lecture last night at Grace
church on Count Tolstoi the novelist and reformer. It was very interesting and
handsomely delivered. Sent the second copy of my dictation for my life to the
History Co today and have promised to write a character sketch of Pratt and a
statement of the location controversy for the Bancroft His. The weather has been
fine this week and today is perfectly lovely. I am about well of my cold that has
been with me about two weeks, first in my throat, then in my head and then all
over me.

*16 (Sat)*. . . Saturday morning Mrs Deady and I went to Salem to visit the Bushs.
Spent Saturday and Sunday at the house and in driving about. Went to St Pauls
to church, the Rev Mr Post officiated. Small, but devout congregation, mostly
women. The minister lead the singing, and did the praying, preaching and reading with all the most advanced genuflexions, and did them well. Monday I was
at the State house most of the day and sat in the hall of the Representatives during
the debate and vote on the University and Water bill[s]. A very respectable body
of men. Mrs Deady and the Misses Bush were also present. Sunday evening I
called at James Waltons. Saw him and his brother John and their wives, that of
the latter being the mother of the former.[4] James has two very handsome boys
and their mother, a young German is a very decent attractive looking woman.

We came home on the morning train on Tuesday after a very pleasant visit
to the Bushs. Miss Sally is an excellent young woman, and the relations between
her and her father are delightful. Eugenie, is an erratic genius, and full of wit
and sarcasm. . . . Friday evening went to the third Coursen concert with Mrs
Deady and Philura Murch. Ed Brooke and his wife went with us. The concert was
good and some things excellent. Miss Kathy Coursen made her debut in an
aesthetic gown and looked charming, besides singing fairly well.[5] The boy [Al-
fred] Holt, played the violin wonderfully well. Mrs Deady got her new dress home
from San Francisco yesterday and a bill for $95. . . .

*23 (Sat)* Sunday . . . at Trinity as usual. Mr Loveridge is falling off as a preacher—
getting diffuse and somewhat "repetitious." His reading is simply execrable.
Called on grandpa and ma Henderson. The latter is in bed with a cold. Mr
Henderson although 80 on the 14th inst looks very well and does not appear to
have a gray hair in his head. . . .

Thursday went with Mrs Deady to a party at Mr Lewis' given to Sallie on her
debut. A splendid affair. Plenty of pretty girls, supper and champagne. . . .

Mrs Deady went to McMinnville yesterday evening to see her brother Harvey
who is dangerously ill with pneumonia. Had a telegram from her this morning
to the effect that he was better and she hoped the crisis was past. I am glad of
it. The legislature adjourned last night after having done some good and not
much harm—the defeat of the Bull Run water bill, was the worse thing that

*550*

happened. But Pennoyer is more to blame for that than the legislature. They passed it three times, and came within one vote of passing it over his veto.[6] In view of his impracticable cranky nature and conduct he ought to be called Silpester Annoyer. A good rain fell last night for the first time for some weeks.

Yesterday wrote a sketch of the location controversy in Oregon (1850–2) for Bancrofts 2 *Oregon* which is to be reversed in this particular. Judge Pratt was much displeased with the account of the matter so far as he is concerned, and as he has concluded to go into the "Kings," Mr Stone requested me to write a sketch of the affair for the corrected edition. Mailed in type writer today.

*March 2 (Sat)* . . . Mrs Deady has been at McMinnville with her sick brother Harvey all the week. He may live, but it is thought the chances are against him. Got a corrected copy of 2 *Oregon* from Bancroft yesterday, in which I see that there is a new account of the trial of the alleged Whitman murderers before Judge Pratt, said to have been dictated by Gen Lucius Allen of Allen & Lewis who was in Oregon at the time, and which treats the subject in a much more dignified and complimentary way than the original. My biographical note is also corrected. The sketch which I sent them of the location question for the same volume could not have reached them in time. . . .

*9 (Sat)* Sunday . . . at Trinity as usual. The Rev Mr Adams who is out here from N Y inspecting us with a view of coming here if we suit, officiated, assisted by the Bishop. He made the impression of commonplaceness and feebleness. I don't think *we* will suit him. . . .

Had a letter from Mrs Deady last evening. Harvey is hanging between life and death. Inauguration day was a lovely one here, though it rained in Washington. A troop of German marchers paraded the streets—A very common lot. Looked like the vomit of the beer saloons. Well the cabinet is passed from the region of speculation to the [?] hardpan of fact. I am sorry that Blaine heads it. [J W] Noble was counsel for the Whiskey thieves at St Louis in Grants reign.[7] . . .

*16 (Sat)* . . . Sat in the C C & D C during the week. Tried "the Pirates of Astoria" the Grants, Sullivan and McCormick Sailor Boarding House Keepers for preventing some sailors from appearing as witnesses before the U S Commissioner and fined 4 of them $50 apiece. . . . Got a kit of mackerel yesterday from Ben Stark via Ladd. They are very nice. Commenced on Thursday the 14th to diet myself with a view to reducing my weight. I say I have started a "Reduction Works" on this side of the river.[8] It consist[s] in reducing the quantity of food nearly one half and substituting tea for milk and hope to reduce myself from 244 to 220 in six months. . . .

*23 (Sat)* Sunday . . . Rained all day more or less and the San Pat procession and corner stone laying of Paddy Gibeny Irish church got well wetted. . . . Read [Geo] Grotes *Alexander* from the death of Philip to the capture of Halikarnassus —including the battle of the Granikus which latter I always had an interest in from seeing Sylvestre Genins painting of the same in the parlor of the old house near St Clairsville.[9] Attended afternoon lenten service at Trinity during the week.

*30 (Sat)* Sunday . . . In the afternoon Mrs Deady and I crossed the Morrison St Bridge into East Portland and went to see her lots in McMillens addition. Called at McMillens[10] as we came back and rested, then crossed on the Ry bridge and took the cars to 20th & S and walked to 24th, where I have two lots then back to 20th and home on the third street line. A lovely afternoon, and a long jaunt. In the evening went to Trinity where I heard George H Williams lecture ¾ of an hour on the "Divinity of Christ." The church was packed and apparently much interested. The lecture from a popular stand point was a very good one. He assumed the truth of the Gospels and made no mention of how Christ was divine, except that he was "God manifest in the flesh"—"a divine being." Nothing was said either about the atonement or the redemption, but that Chirst came into the world to elevate man spiritually and thus reconcile him or bring him to God— nearer to God. . . .

Finished Grotes *Life of Alexander* and the last volume of his *History of Greece*. His portrayal of Alexander is not by a friendly hand. I remember reading many years ago, when the volume first appeared, in one of the English reviews, that the authors Democratic predilictions qualified him to write the History of the Greek communities like the Athenians but not that of Alexander.

*April 6 (Sat)* . . . Sat in the C C & D C during the week. Have not done much of any one thing but a good many little things including the writing of numerous letters. Settled my quarters accounts and was compelled to overdraw my bank account $112 of which I repaid $60 the next day. Spent most of the day Monday and Friday looking over my lectures at the law School for those days. . . .

At the vestry meeting on Monday on my motion we extended a call to Mr [T L] Cole of Staatsburg for Trinity.[11] If anybody can be believed in such matters, of which I have some doubt, he ought to be the man for the place.

Commenced Taines *History of the French Revolution* (Origin of Modern France). The grouping of the facts is wonderful, and what a brutal people the French were and how directly the popular discontent and outbreak appears to have been caused by hunger and distrust and dislike of the higher classes. Weighed this afternoon and kicked the beam at 236½ a loss of 6½ pds since I commenced to diet myself on the 14 ult. Mrs D and I called at S G Reeds in the evening.

*13 (Sat)* . . . Wrote a sketch of my friend Asahel Bush this week for some History of Oregon that is being prepared [by] the N W History Co. It is contained in 5 fool[s] cap pages of type writer and though I say it, who as Sam Slick says, "hadn't ought to," it is a pretty good piece of work. Sent it to him yesterday. I was to his faults a little blind, of course. Such a thing is understood to be in some sense a eulogy. But as far as I went, I hewed to the line and let the chips fall where they would. Took my 14th & last massage last evening from Dr Weiss. [If] I was able, I would have one every evening as long as I lived.[12]

*20 (Sat)* . . . [*Sunday*] night at half past 11 oclock my daughter-in-law Mrs Edward N Deady was delivered of her first child and my first grandson, both doing well. On Tuesday evening I called to see the newcomer and was duly presented by the nurse, Miss Kean. . . .

. . . Have been at work during the week on my address for the Washington celebration on April 30th. Lectured twice at the law school and devoted the better part of a day to each of the lectures. Good Friday was a beautiful day notwithstanding. Court did not sit and I attended morning prayer at Trinity. Sunday evening dined at Mrs Montgomerys where I met Mr & Mrs Stott. Mrs Deady was invited but she went to the "borning." Had a letter from Bush Thursday suggesting another modification of the paragraph in the Sketch anent his relations with the Union party in 1861 which I accepted, except the phrase "war between the States" for which I substituted "the war of the Rebellion." . . .

Benj Stark arrived Tuesday and called Wednesday at my chambers and at the house. Age is marking him some but he is as bland and blithe as ever. . . . *27 (Sat)* . . . Sat in the C C & D C during the week and worked all the time in my chambers on an Oration I am to deliver tomorrow at the celebration of the Centennial of Washingtons Inauguration. George H Williams is to speak also, and I am curious to see how near or far apart our treatment of the subject is. I have done an immense amount of work on mine. Just finished it last night about half past 9 oclock. Have had a very bad throat and cold in my head for the last ten days. The throat is better this morning and I am in hopes I will be able to read my address on Tuesday tolerably well.

Read the April magazines in the last 2 weeks and the first volume of Taines *History of the French Revolution* and commenced the second one. His analysis of a Jacobean in the Second volume is a pretty good portrait of Pennoyer. . . . Bush objects to the phrase War of the Rebellion in his sketch, and offers to compromise on simple "war" leaving the reader to mental[ly] prefix "Civil" or add "of the Rebellion" as he may wish.

*May 4 (Sat)* . . . Tuesday the Centennial of Washingtons Inauguration, was a beautiful day. Went to church at Trinity at ½ past 9 where we had a special service conducted by the Bishop and a large Congregation. Came back to my chambers and read the proof of my speech for the *Oregonian,* to which I sent a copy the evening before. At one oclock got in a carriage with the Rev [A J] Brown, George H Williams & Donald Macleay, and got into procession and was hauled about town for a couple of hours. Got to the tabernacle about 3 oclock. The house was packed and many went away. After getting about ⅓ of the way through my speech I was taken with a vertigo and had to ask John McCracken to finish for me, which he did very well. When he got within five minutes of the end I felt better and took the matter in hand and finished it. I[t] was I think a very fair [thing] and fairly delivered. Williams followed with a speech longer in delivery, but which did not occupy so much space in print. He is a slow and solemn speaker. At 6 oclock went to a collation at Freimanns[13] given to Gen Gibbon & Staff and others, 80 in all, where I staid until 8 oclock. The entertainment consisted mainly of speeches and champagne of which I was a part. From Freimanns I drove to the exposition building where I witnessed the drill of the militia a little while and came home well worn out. The celebration on the whole was a great success—the procession being the finest ever in the Northwest. . . .

*11 (Sat)* Sunday May 5. Attended . . . Trinity as usual. Called to see Harvey [Henderson] in the evening. Found him better than I expected. From Alices went to Edwards to see my grandson, where I spent a pleasant half hour with the mother and the nurse, Miss Kean. The nurse said the baby was hungry and I bantered the mother to satisfy it but she would not do it in my presence. . . .

Thursday sold the north ½ of block 128 in Caruthers addition for $8000 plus $250 commissions to West & Stevens who made the sale. In April 1881 I paid $2500 for the property. Since then I have paid $450 for street improvements and about $350 taxes—$900. And interest on the purchase price for eight years at 8 per centum is $2000—in all $2800 plus $2500 = $5300 making a profit over all not counting interest on taxes and improvements of $2700—a little more than double the first cost. Got $6000 in cash and a note and mortgage for $2000 payable in 3 years with interest at 8 per centum and taxes.

Today paid note to the 1st National Bank on which I was surety for Edward for $500 and $8.68 interest which I intended to give less the interest to his baby.

. . . Last evening went to Miss Ladds to hear Mrs Kate Douglas Wiggin[14] read one of her own stories for the benefit of the Kindergarten. She did well but few in attendance. The dollar at the door must have kept them away. I was sorry for the reader and the hostess but the latter bore herself beautifully and was very agreeable. . . .

*18 (Sat)* Sunday (May 12) My 65th birthday . . . Barnhart called at my chambers in the afternoon and regaled me with the status of the controversy over the guardianship of the Ben Holladay children, and read me a protest which he had prepared against the appointment of George H Williams, which appeared imminent, on the theory that he would be a mere figurehead or stalking horse for Rufus Ingal[l]s and Aunt Kate. In [it] he gave a graphic and unvarnished account of seeing a stage driver copulate with A K in 1866 on the stage going out from Umatilla landing. It occurred at night. He was a passenger inside, and she was outside with the driver, and the operation was performed while the coach was moving slowly through the sand.[15] . . .

. . . Monday evening called at Mrs Jones with Mrs Deady and thence to the Unitarian meeting house to hear Mrs Kate Douglas Wiggin lecture on the Kindergarten and read "Patsy" one of her stories about to be published. A pleasant bright woman, full of her subject and herself. . . . Thursday attended Mr Rosenbergs funeral at the chapel. A great crowd notwithstanding the rain, particularly women. A good many clergy in the chancel. Miss Clem had to chant the Nicene Creed. I think she will have it chanted at her wedding, "if so be" she ever has one.

Still plodding through Taine. There never was such a ferocious, mendacious, cruel collection as the Paris mob. The Celtic blood I suppose has something to do with it. Had letters from Judge Hoffman & Sawyer complimenting me very much on my Washington speech. The former said I need not fear comparison with Depews much lauded performance.[16]

*25 (Sat)* Sunday . . . afternoon went to the Christening of my first grand child by the Rev Orth at St Lawrences church. I got to the house at 1 oclock where I found a good company of the relatives of the parents, Edward N and Kate Hanover Deady. The church was next door. Mr Memly was Godfather and the cousin Henrietta Failing held the youngster. The ceremony was long and generally in Latin. Preliminary to the actual baptism which was done by pouring, the child was salted and greased, but why I cannot say unless to magnify the proceeding and give it a thaumaturgic air. Of course it did the child no harm. It was named Matthew Edward after myself and its father, whom I pray it may resemble in some particulars and not in others. On returning to the house we had refreshments— strawberries and ice cream and coffee and cake. From there I went to the exposition building to see the German singing birds, taking Henderson and Emma Failing with me. The birds did not sing, and were not worth looking at. . . . Wednesday went down the Columbia on the *S G Reed* with members of the Senate Judiciary Committee, Messrs [Geo] Hoar, [J L] Pugh & [W B] Allison[17] and the Com of the board of trade and other guests, to visit the works at the mouth of the Stream &c, &c. Went out on the jetty on a very narrow gauge railway one and a half miles. A very interesting work indeed. Wandered over the grassy slopes and fields of Ft Stevens. It looked more idyllic than warlike.

In the evening Mrs [John M] Thurston of Nebraska and I played whist with Mr Thurston[18] and Mrs Hoar, and although they are experts and Mrs T and I not, we beat them 5 straight games and the next day we beat Mr Thurston and Mr S G Reed 4 straight games. This verifies the old saying that luck usually accompanies innocence at cards.

On our way up the river on Friday at the request of Senator Hoar I gave the company a little talk on the explorations of Vancouver in Oregon and the origin and nature of the Chinook language. At Kalama we waited 2½ hours for the train from Portland, on which the Senatorial party were going to Tacoma. During this time we had luncheon, and at the close of it, with some few remarks I called on Allison, Hoar, Pugh, Governor Pennoyer, Thurston and Dolph in the order named for a talk, in response to which some very good little speeches were made. I was then called to close up the Symposium which I did. The next mornings *Oregonian,* had a brief report of the affair all through. Got home, all well at 6 oclock on Thursday evening. . . . Drove out this afternoon with Maurice McKim to see a tract of land near Mt Tabor, south of Hawthorne Avenue, and selected block 3 for a deal. . . .

*June 1 (Sat)* . . . Got 50 copies of the engraving of myself prepared for the "C of K." The same plate of which I received impressions some time since. I finally wrote that I was dissatisfied with it, and it has been worked over and much improved. I don't like to think that Bancroft was willing to put me off with that cheap thing. . . .

*8 (Sat)* . . . Have been at work when I could night and morning on an opinion in the Salem Mills case. An immense amount of chaff for a few grains of wheat in the evidence. It seems to me that William (Scotch) Reid has a talent for confusing and obscuring everything he puts his hand to or in.[19] . . .

Mrs Deady has completed the furnishing of the room at the G S Hospital. It has cost $145.53—some more than she expected but it is well invested where moth nor rust doth not consume, nor thieves break in and steal. . . .

*15 (Sat)* . . . Attended the closing exercises at St Helens Hall on [*omitted*] afternoon when two bright, clever Jewesses Ella Hirsch and May Goldsmith graduated and read excellent essays. There is a time for all things, but graduating exercises are not the time for chanting and Nicene creed—if there is any time that it ought to be. . . .

*22 (Sat)* . . . On Wednesday Mrs Deady and I went up to Eugene at attend Commencement. . . . Thursday was a busy pleasant day. Had a meeting of the Regents as ½ past 8. Attended Commencement exercises from 10 A M to ½ past 1 P M. . . . McArthur delivered the diplomas with some well chosen words of advice and commendation. In the afternoon 4 essays were read by the graduates of the law school. I presented the diplomas with a few [remarks] which [I] wrote out and amplified a little yesterday. They are published in this mornings *Oregonian*. In the evening the Alumni gave a dinner to which the Regents and Faculty were invited to attend. I made a speech in response to the toast—The Regents—did not say much and omitted a compliment which I intended to pay Mr [Thomas] Hendricks—that he had borne this University on his shoulders and carried it in his heart from the beginning.

Got on the north bound train at 4 oclock Friday morning and came home.

Found "Me," Edwards baby sick with Cholera Infantum and Mrs Deady went there at once and is there still.

The weather has been pleasant during the week, but is cloudy today. Went last evening to the exercises at the High School, where I saw of class of 20 girls and one boy launched on a suffering world. . . .

*29 (Sat)* . . . Attended the dedication ceremonies of the Jewish Synagogue on 10th street yesterday at 4:30 by special invitation. Some good music, and a good oration by Solis Cohen—besides some stupid old ceremonies. Edwards baby (ME) is better and will probably get well. . . .

Called at the Hall in the evening and discussed the binding effect of vow of celibacy by a person who takes holy orders with Miss Clem. I maintaining that it was nothing more than any other promise or resolution which a person makes to himself concerning his future conduct—as for instance to abstain from the use of spiritous liquors. If the promisor should afterwards become convinced that he made the promise under a mistaken notion of duty or expediency he might disregard it.

*July 6 (Sat)* . . . Thursday, July 4th made the Oration at Vancouver. Rode in the procession with Gen Gibbon whose guest I was. Prepared my address principally on Wednesday and finished it about 12 oclock that night. It was published in yesterdays *Oregonian* and is well spoken of. . . .

Sent 30 copies of the *Oregonian* away yesterday with my address in it. . . .

Called at the Hall in the evening, and had a set to with Miss Clem over a letter which the Bishop wrote to the Rev Mr Cole telling [him] not to have the Congregation join in the general Thanksgiving at M & E prayer as he did the Sunday before. I accused her jocosely of being the real author of the missive and said the Bishop had better prohibit her from singing the Nicene Creed at St Helens Chapel and thus prevent the people from participating in the declaration of belief contrary to the rubric which says it must be "said" by the minister and the people. . . .

*13 (Sat)*. . . Tuesday loaned Edward $150 payable Dec 9, 1889 with legal interest to enable him to send Kate & the baby to Astoria. Philura E Murch, Mrs Deadys niece, started for Paris via the Short Line to New York on Wednesday evening. Mrs Deady accompanied her to Huntington and got back this morning at 6 oclock. At the Dalles the passengers had to take a boat to the Cascades, on account of the burning of a bridge. . . .

. . . Got a letter this morning from Henry Kennon, Princeton, Illinois acknowledging the receipt of a draft I sent him for $50 on account of an indefinite obligation I was under to him for $37 office rent in 1848–9. He was much pleased and said he had no remembrance of anything of the kind and preferred to accept it as a gift from an old friend, rather than as a debt.

. . . Still reading Taines *French Revolution.* The Jacobins and Sans Culottes grow worse and worse. The horrid crimes they daily commit in the name of liberty and equality are fast preparing the country for the reign of the first Napoleon. . . .

*20 (Sat)* . . . Sunday met Mr Rodney and his sister Louisa of Germantown, Pa at Trinity. They informed us that Mrs McSherry and her sister Miss Coombs came in that morning on the train with them. Called with Mrs Deady on Mrs McS & her sister at Mrs Stotts in the afternoon. Found them both genteel pleasant women. Mrs McS is very bright and attractive with a great deal of good manner.

Called with Mrs Deady at the Hall on Wednesday evening on the Germantown Rodneys, and on Thursday morning on Mr & Mrs Oliver Landreth . . . The Landreths gave us a dinner when we were in Phil in 1881 on the strength of a letter from Miss Rodney, who is his cousin and taught in his family years ago. I sent the party a basket of peaches from Vancouver which made them open their eyes. Sent a basket (20 pds $1.75) of the same to Mrs McSherry this morning. Not much miscellaneous reading this week. Still in third Taine. The Bastil[l]e and its abuses was an evil, but comparatively a very limited one, but the movement that demolished it and those who represented it were a worse one, and without limit. . . .

*27 (Sat)* . . . Wednesday evening Justice Strong of Washington City and his two daughters Miss S & Mary Darling Strong arrived from San Francisco. At the request of Justice Field we had procured them rooms at Comstocks to which James conducted them from the train. Thursday morning Mrs Deady took them out to drive. Yesterday morning I had him in the C C on the Bench with me. A large number of the bar were in attendance to meet him, and after transacting some business I took a recess and we went down on the floor and I presented the gentlemen of the bar to him. Judge [C C] Cole, formerly of the Iowa supreme court was in the room.[20] After a while Strong and myself retired to my chambers to which I invited Judge Cole and the District Attorney where we passed an hour in pleasant conversation. Mr George H Williams came in and joined in the conversation. Strong is an interesting old man but objects to being called "aged" and well he may for although in his 82d year he might well pass for not more than 60. . . .

*August 3 (Sat)* Sunday . . . Rev Mr Page a missionary to Japan for 5 years preached in the morning and talked tons about the Japs in the evening. I liked the "talk" better than the "preach." . . . Friday evening I dined at [Zera] Snows where I met Senator & Mrs [Chas] Manderson of Nebraska. Had an excellent dinner and a very pleasant evening. The Mandersons are worth meeting, both of them. Met young Snow of the Navy, and saw a lot of curios that he brought from Samoa with him.[21] He is a splendid looking fellow. Suey the Chinese cook that has been with Mrs Hill for 10 years started for China this morning as "a merchant." I started a subscription among the boarders yesterday to buy him a silver watch which was done, much to his satisfaction. He is a good man whom the law of this country prohibits from returning here, while thousands of his inferiors in every respect are admitted at Castle Garden without question. The explanation lies in the fact that the one [is] "Ilish" and the other not. The temperature is delightful but the air is smoky and the mountains are veiled from sight.

*10 (Sat).* . . Yesterday Chee Gong was hanged for the murder of Lee Yick. Great efforts were made to have his sentence commuted to imprisonment for life, but Governor Pennoyer refused. Judging from his actions in other cases he would not have hesitated if Chee Gong had been a white man. An intelligent, virtuous fanatic is a dangerous depository of power. Pennoyer is a Jacobin.

*17 (Sat).* . . Monday denied a motion for preliminary injunction to the Washburn & Moen Man[ufacturing] Co against Knapp Burrell & Co for selling Glidden Barbed Wire. Read up on the subject pretty well. Barbed wire is a great thing and several people have had a hand in what may be called its invention, but finally the successful wire was produced by Glidden combining his barb with other inventions for which he got a patent Nov 25, 1874, which the courts have held void for want of novelty. Have been at work on the case of the *City of Carlyle* during the week. . . . Wednesday morning we got the news of Terrys assault on Justice Field and the deputy Marshalls [*sic*] killing him. There was a general rejoicing at Fields escape and Terrys death. I telegraphed Field on Thursday morning, "I congratulate you on your escape and your admirable demeanor." Got a telegram from Sawyer on the 14th. Wrote both he and Field today. This lets me off on going to San Fran as I expected to try Terry on the indictment pending against him in the U S District court growing out of his assault on the U S Marshal in the court room a year ago. Wednesday evening Mrs Deady and I called on Sol Hirsch and his wife our new minister to Turkey and had a pleasant and interesting visit. Saw some beautiful specimens of needlework and embroidery that he bought in Constantinople and Carlsbad, Germany. Monday evening we called on Mrs Ladd on her return from Europe. She was looking well. Has lost some flesh in her journey. She says it is the result of much walking and no luncheon. . . . Henderson and Victor Smith[22] got off yesterday in their sailboat for a cruise and a hunt down the Columbia river, to be gone, maybe 4 weeks. Vics mother put two bottles of whiskey on board as medicine, which surprises me. However, Henderson don't drink. I gave him $30 for expenses of outfit and infit. Got a letter this morning from Meek the last link in a correspondence that extends over 43 years. At first it was mostly on my side, but in latter days it has been on his.

*24 (Sat)* Sunday . . . at Trinity as usual. Mr Lund officiated. With his weak voice and North of England accent or dialect I could not understand what he said. It wouldn't take him long to depopulate Trinity. Worked on my opinion in the *City of Carlyle* case in the afternoon and evening. Sat in the C C & D C during the week. . . . Congratulated Carrie [Ladd] on her engagement which had just been announced. Called with Mrs Deady on Wednesday evening on Mrs McSherry and her sister Miss Nannie Coombs at Mrs Stotts. . . . Friday night took Mrs. McSherry, Miss Coombs, Mr & Mrs Stott and Mrs Deady to see "Macbeth." Had Box B. Miss [Margaret] Mather was lady Mac, and she is thought to be somewhat. But she is too girlish, gushing and romantic for the character. I liked [J B] Studleys[23] Macbeth much better and indeed liked it well. . . . Got measured today for a suit of broadcloth, the first for some years. To cost $80.

Heard [Thomas De W] Talmage at the Park theatre this evening on "Big Blunders"—a melange of story wit and rant that was much enjoyed by his audience, but I doubt if the impression made will be lasting or particularly beneficial.[24] Forty years ago today I left Fort Bridger in the morning on my way to Oregon. What things have happened to the world and me in that 40 years.

*September 17 (Tue)* . . . On Friday the 30th [*of August*] Dr [Arthur] Bevan inserted a catheter in my ureth[r]a to draw off the residual urine. For some years, since 1880, I had been annoyed with frequent and scant discharge of urine, and this was a kind of an impromptu experiment to ascertain how much urine was habitually left in the bladder. That evening I went out and about and about 10 oclock at night I was taken with a severe pain across the small of my back. Dr Bevan could not be found until 2 A M when he gave me anodyne which soon reduced the pain. However it soon manifested itself in the muscles of my stomach which another anodyne relieved. The next day, Saturday, I remained in the house and made my water as usual without the use of the catheter, the Dr thinking it dangerous to insert it for the present as the ureth[r]a may have been irritated by the introduction of it.[A]

Sunday, September 1, I remained in the house about the same, but walked down to my chambers in the evening where I remained an hour or two looking over the cases I intended to decide in the morning. Monday morning went to my chambers and sat in the C C . . . By this time my urine began to be very high colored with some brick dust like deposit in it, and the discharge was attended with much pain. Came home in the evening where I have since remained. Dr Strong came into the case and my water was drawn off a few times during the next three or four days. But during all this time I voided a spoonful or two of urine every five, fifteen or twenty minutes in the utmost agony. The anodynes nauseated me so that I could eat nothing and between the pain and the starvation I became very weak. Dr Bevan told me Monday that my kidneys had been so shocked by the introduction of the catheter that they failed to secrete water and only secreted urides which made my water almost pure uric acid, high colored and acrid. He gave me solutions of alkali which restored the urine to its normal condition in this respect in a day or two.

However I continued to suffer such pain in voiding my urine or attempting to that on the night I think it was of Thursday, Henderson being with me alone, I got up in desperation and went to the bath room and inserted the catheter myself and drew off the contents of the bladder to my great relief, the which I have been doing ever since at intervals of from 3 to 4 hours.

Sunday the 15 I dressed myself and went out and drove through the Park, though I had been out in the yard the Friday and Saturday before. Yesterday I walked round the south half of the block just north of the one on which we live. Dr Strong examined my water on Monday and found it all right—neither albumen or sugar in it. . . .

People have been very kind in calling to see me and sending to enquire for me, and in sending me many and beautiful flowers. . . .

27 (Fri) I am still in my room and have suffered much since writing the above from another cause. On Thursday (19th) night I was up and down quite often and in getting out of bed bruised my testicles, so that by Friday night they were very much swollen and very painful. This put me on my back where I have been most of the time since. The doctor gave me a lotion of opium and [?] acetate of lead in which I have kept my testicles bathed and swathed ever since. They are much better now and last evening I rode over to the exposition building and witnessed the opening of the exposition. It was beautiful and the music of Liberatis band was ravishing. On Wednesday (the 18th) the Fields arrived from San Francisco on their way to Washington and left on Thursday. Mr Jones (Neagle) accompanied them.[25]

The Justice came twice each day to see me and told me the story [of] the Terry tragedy with great interest. [Geo C] Gor[h]am was with him twice.[26] I have not seen him before since he was "silting up" the Republican primaries for the Governorship of Cal in the spring of 1867. . . . I felt quite well this day and if the accident to my testicles had not occurred I would have been out some time since.

A few days ago I got two books of William MacKenzie, a History of Scotland, by his father and of America by his uncle. While lying here on my back I have been much entertained reading the former. It is a very attractive story. Oh, the blood that was spilt, the throats cut and the tourneys in the making of modern Scotland. . . .

. . . General Miles called also. Had a pleasant chat with him. He looks very well and is in my judgment a growing man.[27] Mrs Green sent me a box of delicious grapes from her conservatory.

29 (Sun) Saturday read a great deal in the afternoon and evening. In the morn[ing] went to the court room and disposed of some criminal cases and examined the accounts of the officers of the court for the past quarter. Then I went through the mass of papers and documents that had accumulated on my desk during my illness. Worked on my accounts for the quarter ending with this month. Maxwell came in and brought me my tickets for my trip east.[28] Came home at 2 oclock none the worse for the wear.

. . . In the evening went with Mrs Deady to the Exposition. It commenced raining about dusk and rained all night. Got home from the exposition about 10 oclock and slept well.

Mrs Deady has gone to church and I am trying to do a little writing with very poor success. Had quite a levee in the evening that kept me up late. I put on the suspensory today for the first time and it feels quite comfortable. Made up my accounts and filled my checks for over $600.

*30 (Mon)* Sat in the C C today . . . Heard sundry motions and left the court for Sawyer who arrived soon after in the morning. Have settled my Quarters accounts and drew $250 for my expenses. Had a pleasant dinner and tried a bottle of McKees Zinvandel which was good. I left $1760 to my account in bank. 7 oclock I am all packed and ready to go at 9 oclock. . . . Busy all this day getting ready to start for New York. Left Mrs Hills at 9 oclock, first bidding all the people in the House good bye. Paul & Henderson met me at the depot and helped me aboard to lower berth No 2 in car for which I then paid $13 to Council Bluffs. Did not sleep any during the night. The newness of the situation and the motion of the car disturbed me. Had to urinate often in the night and use the catheter, on which account and the swelling of my testicles I had been on my back most of the time for 3 or 4 weeks before starting.

*October 1 (Tue)* Breakfast in the dining car for .75 which I did not relish a bit. . . . Supper in the D[ining] C[ar] which I enjoyed. I do not eat the midday meal but have some fruit in my berth. Passed Huntington about sun down and for 30 or 40 miles back of it coming down the narrow comparatively dry bed of Burnt river passed through the hilliest, not little hills either—country I ever saw. Yet it all seemed to be claimed and enclosed with barbed wire fence as if it had some value. I think it is used as a sheep walk. We then passed into Idaho and had a pleasant run along the bank of the Snake R by moonlight which seems quite a large stream. And no one who has not experienced it can tell how refreshing it is to look upon such a body of pure flowing water in such a dreary, dry country.

*2 (Wed)* Still in Idaho. Got good breakfast .75, and slept well the night before. Today went through Wyoming, passed along Bear river and Hams fork. Passed a place called Idana where the famous military water is bottled, which is nothing but the old Soda Springs on Bear R which the emigrants of 1849 used for [Y]East powder. Began to be afraid of the diareha in the afternoon and got a bottle of Pain Killer just this side of Green river for which I gave $1, and of which I took an over dose which bound me up until I got to Chicago. . . . I forgot to say that on the evening before I sat at the same table with a Mr Brassey and his wife who were returning from an Elk Hunt in Wyoming.[29] He was a son of Lord Brassey the husband of the authoress whose father had been a successful railway contractor, then Lord of the Admiralty and left money in the family. She was a poor Nevil[l] with many generations of blue blood in her veins. She was a little red faced, shy thing. How she had shot an Elk running with her rifle and killed him. . . . He is a plain clever Saxon looking fellow, a graduate of Oxford, and a native of Hastings, from whence his father is regularly returned to parliament. It seems he comes out to hunt every year. What I thought remarkable was they had neither man nor maid with them.

*3 (Thu)* Slept well last night and feel quite well. Passed Fort Sidney, Nebraska. . . . Breakfast on the car at .75. The run through Nebraska was smooth and easy. Endless cornfields on either side of the road and a beautiful dreamy day. The dinner and servant $1. . . . Arrived at C Bluffs at 10 P M and at 11 P M started for Chicago on the C & N W road . . .

*4 (Fri)* A beautiful day in Iowa. Breakfast & servant $1, and very good indeed. Some excellent corn bread, and where should I find it if not here in Iowa. Lightning rods everywhere since we entered Nebraska. In Iowa houses small and low for fear of being blown over. Arrived at Chicago at ½ past 12 and was transferred by 'bus to the depot of the Michigan Central. Paid porter .50. Telegraphed to Mrs Deady (.75) bought a syringe ($1). Been plugged up two days. Got . . . on 3:10 train to Buffalo ($3). Dinner $1. Took injection, no particular effect.

*5 (Sat)* An uncomfortable night. Saw the Falls of Niag[a]ra at 5 oclock, the car stopping a few moments for that purpose. The point of observation is some distance above the falls and they appear insignificant as compared with the view from below. Got a poor breakfast, the worst I ever had, and was transferred by the conductor to Berth 2 on Sleeper Sheridan for N Y. Paid porter $1, a good fellow. Reached dep[o]t at N Y at 10 oclock and got to the Everett House at 11. Had the diareha all the way from Buffalo and I thought I would never get through.

*6 (Sun)* In bed all day and alone, and so lonesome. Sent for Mr [Clarence] Seward and he came around and spent an hour with me in the evening. . . .

*7 (Mon)* Got out and went down to the Convention and took my seat. Met Stark who is an active member of the diocese of Oregon. Was admitted after some delay by captious opposition from Rev [D R] Goodwin of Phil.[30]

*8 (Tue)* Cast my first vote in the Convention to confirm the election of [Wm A] Leonard and [Thomas] Davies[31] as Bishops and signed their testimonials. Dined en famille in the evening at Sewards. An elegant dinner and a lovely company.

*9 (Wed)* Attended the Convention and spent the evening in my room. . . .

*10 (Thu)* Dined at [Andrew W] Kents in the evening . . . The dinner was delicious, a fat goose forming the piece de resistance. Had a delightful evening. I think Mr Kent is the handsomest man I ever saw.[32]

*11 (Fri)* Went down in the morning with Mr Seward to see his office on Nassau street. An interesting place and great library. Went from there to Mr Kents . . . He took me through Wall Street which seems to be a row of magnificent new buildings. Went to the rooms of the Bar club in the Equitable [Building]. It is a beautiful palace. Had a good lunch with Mr Kent, and came up to the Convention. . . .

*12 (Sat)* Remained at my room in the morning and then went to the Convention. Came home early and took to my bed. In the evening went to Sewards to a dinner given me. A round table with 12 at it. I took Mrs Seward in and was seated at her [right]. On her left was Chauncey Depew and at my right was ex Sec [Benj H] Bristow. . . .

Sat down at ½ past 7 and got home at ½ past 11. The dinner and service was simply superb. Depew told his English [stories] and look of the English[man] trying to talk on his feet inimitably.

*13 (Sun)* Went to Old Trinity . . . The *performance* was first rate of its kind, all choral. One boy warbled like a bird. The sermon was by Dr [R A] Holland of

St Louis, very good, a little theatrical and much ornamented with figures, tropes and adjectives.[33]

In the afternoon went to a dinner at The Hoffman given me by Mr Chauncey B Ripley. There were present Dr [John] Ripley, Messrs [A E] Pearsall a genius and a newspaper man, [Edward] Jordan, and [Frank] Loomis.[34] I staid until 7 oclock. I was not well, and ate nothing scarcely, but drank some wine and Appolinaris water. Ripley opens out very differently from what I expected. For an elder in the Presbyterian church he indulges in some very broad stories.

Forgot to say that the seats in Trinity church are the most uncomfortable I ever saw and those in St Georges next.

*14 (Mon)* Went in the afternoon to Fifth Ave to return call of Montgomerys, and thence to Mamaroneck (21 miles up the Sound) to spend the night with D D Field. He is stopping with Friends, Mr & Mrs [Geo] Bliss, 2 charming people on the downgrade of life, the former more than the latter, but well provided with airbrakes and other comforts & conveniences that make the descent safe, easy and almost as slow as you please.[35]

*15 (Tue)* Returned in the morning with Mr Bliss. He quoted poetry all the way and particularly a poem of Mrs Hemans on Spring which I do not remember to have seen or heard before. . . . dined with the Montgomerys at the F[ifth] Avenue [Hotel] in the evening in a room where 300 others were playing the game of Knife& fork. Met Mr [Amos R] Eno and his daughter Mrs Wood at the table and sat between them. They are both pleasant people. Mrs Mont[gomery] was joyous and excited. Mr M was cool and critical. Visited Mrs Tom Platts[36] room with Mrs M & W and Mr Eno. She is a large, plain benevolent looking woman who I found was largely engaged in the business of raising and educating cats. Called at Mr Sewards 143 Fifth Ave and Mr Eno was kind enough to accompany me from the hotel and help me find the house, where I found Mr & Mrs Seward and bade them good by.

*16 (Wed)* To the Convention in the morning and then went out to purchase overcoat at Rogers Peet & Co uptown store, Broadway & 32 street. Bought a Chumley for $20. The[n] got tickets and chairs on the Penn Line for Washington for Mont and self cost $8.85 each of which I think the chairs were $2.30 each. At 2 oclock went to Mrs [Clem] Meyers, Broadway & 55th street, the Auston, who at 3 took me to drive in the Park. She has an elegant turn out. We drove up Riverside Park past Grants grave, and then through Central Park and home by 5. The throng we met as we came home was simply gorgeous. At 7 we had an excellent dinner. . . . Mrs Meyer played the hostess admirably. Her husband (Oscar) is a very bright clever man.

*17 (Thu)* Attended the convention in the morning, where I remained until 12 oclock when I left for good. My impression of the House of deputies is not very favorable. There are a number of intelligent earnest men in the body pretty well divided between the lay and clerical deputies. Besides these there are a number of old, small minded cranks with a large amount of material which simply represents the inertia of the church and stands in the way of all progress and improvement. The cry of anti rubrical went far to defeat any proposition against which it was raised. As if the Convention hadn't as much right to unmake rubrics as to make them.

In the afternoon went to Mr [James] Ruthven[s], who drove me through the Parks, where I saw Grants tomb again which looks like a country ice or milkhouse. Staid to dinner but could take nothing and left the table and went upstairs and laid down on the sofa, with a burning head and cold feet and hands. Mrs Ruthven was urgent for me to go to bed, but I told her it was out of the question, as I had my ticket purchased for Washington the next day. I asked her to give me a wet towel to put on my head which she did, when a good looking woman who had waited on the table—a widow named Mrs Mowbray—came up and took me in hand and rubbed my hands and then my feet until they felt delicious. About ½ past 9 oclock I left for my hotel, where with the aid of Nellie, the chambermaid, I packed my trunk.

*18 (Fri)* Had no appetite and could eat no breakfast, but brought away a big red apple which I ate on the car with good zest. Paid my bill at the Everett and turned my back on the inhospitable hole, where I finally compelled some politeness from the boorish impudent clerks and employees of the House. Montgomery called for me in the F[ifth] Ave Buss [*sic*] and took me to the ferry. We got into a Pen[n] Line Parlor Car and were comfortable. I had bought the tickets for both of us and presented him with his in acknowledgement of many small favors from himself and wife. We reached Washington a little after 4 and soon found myself comfortably housed at Wormleys in room 64 which means a bed room, parlor and bath room on the first floor at $4 per day with board. Soon after I arrived Justice Field came to see me with Dr [Saml C] Busey who commenced to treat me for a disordered stomach. But the fact is as soon as I got into this hospitable social city after being in N Y two weeks I began to feel better at once. Got to bed in good time but woke up about 12 drenched in sweat.

*19 (Sat)* Got up feeling better and ate some porridge for brea[k]fast. Mr Justice Field came early to see me and in the evening drove me out in his carriage to the Soldiers Home, where I called on Capt Robert Catlin, but found him and his wife out. It was a lovely drive a beautiful evening and a grand sight. Dr. Busey called in the morning and evening. About midday I had a drawing sweat. It came on me all at once, commencing in the head from which the sweat rolled down in great drops.

The medicine which I took last night has not operated and Dr Busey ordered me another powder.

*20 (Sun)* . . . In the evening Justice Field called and took me to his house to dinner. Mrs Field was looking very well and as charming and agreeable as could be. At the table was Justice [John] Harlan, Gen [H M] Frisbie, and young Richard McCreery. The dinner was delightful and comprised a number of dishes of which I could only swallow a few, the particular one of which was broiled quail. The claret was delicious and the champagne tempted me as far as one glass which I wished the next morning I had omitted. I escorted Mrs Field to the table and sat at her right. Got home ¼ to ten. Forgot to say that I was much interested in Gen Frisbie. He came to Cal as Capt of a company in the famous 7 Regiment of 1847. He told me that our [J H] Lappeus was in his company.[37] Harlan has grown some older and heavier and has at times a melancholy look. He was very cordial and kind.

*21 (Mon)* Had rather an unpleasant night of it, but it wore off after breakfast, for which I had a fair relish. Justice [Saml F] Miller & [Lucius Q] Lamar called in the forenoon. I never would have known the latter. Since I saw him in 1859–60, leading the little band of Americans (Southern Know Nothings) in the H of R at Washington in the three cornered fight for the speakership, which resulted by means of their votes in the election of [William] Pennington of N J and the defeat of [John] Sherman and [Thomas] Bobcock. Miller has aged some but retains much of his old animation. Shortly before noon rode up to the capitol in a horse car and was taken into the robing room of the judges by Justice Harlan and introduced to them, all of whom I had met save [Saml] Blatchford.[38] Brother Gray as he lets me call [him] was very cordial and looks splendidly. The Chief Justice [Fuller] I had met at the Convention in N Y. His robes size him up and improve him. Had a seat furnished me within the bar and saw the August 9 file in and take their seats, and heard the crier solemnly say—"God save the United States and this honorable court." Came home after one after hearing Justice Bradl[e]y deliver an opinion to the effect that the "district" was a municipal corporation, and within the operation of the statute of limitations, as any natural person, and hearing sundry lawyers make certain motions in which they seemed to be lacking in knowledge of the practice of the court or first principles. . . .

*22 (Tue)* Dr called and practically gave me up—not to die, but as well. This does not include my water works, which remain about so. I must use the catheter at [least] twice a day to keep my bladder clean and healthy, and trust to natural means for the rest. It is not a pleasant thing to contemplate, the use of a catheter all my life, but I am getting used to it, and there are many things worse. Was driven out to Arlington in the afternoon by Senator Dolph. . . . A pleasant trip and an interesting place. The day was dark however and the run down the Potomac was obscured. The old mansion is I suppose a good type of the old Anglo-Virginia country gentlemans residence. In the evening called at Justice Strongs and spent an hour pleasantly with him and his daughters. . . .

*23 (Wed)* . . . Justice Field called in the morning and left another bottle of port, and a great bundle of San Francisco papers from Judge Sawyer, which I certainly will never read. Went out in the rain and purchased some socks and a pair of gaiters. In the afternoon, called at Mrs Kellys . . . Dined there in the evening where I met beside the family, Capt & Mrs Barnett, and Senator Dolph. The dinner was good and the conversation fair. Dolph occupied the right and I the left of the hostess. Mrs Barnett wore her usual radiant honest smile. She sat next me and I enjoyed her. After dinner played a rubber of whist with Miss Nannie for a partner. Barnett & Dolph won the rubber by a point. Mrs Kelly said that Miss Morris' friends to whom she addressed begging letters for Pere Hyacinth [*Charles Loyson*], simply ignored them. I told her that I understood she had obtained $12,000 for him in that way.[39] Got home at 10 oclock and finished a long letter to Mrs Deady.

*24 (Thu)* Capt Robert & Mrs Catlin called in their one horse shay. He looks very well and she is a nice, sensible motherly woman. She drove me down to D & 10th streets where I was going to see the manager of the *Post* about an interview with myself that was published in the edition of the 22d inst.

The *Post* this morning contains an editorial correction of the interview, insofar as I was made to say, that I thought she [*Sarah Althea Hill*] would kill Field, Sawyer & myself. I only asked a correction as to myself and it was so written by the manager (Wilkins) and read to me before I left the office. Well, let it go. Called at Gor[h]ams and on Mrs Field with whom I had a very pleasant visit and a delicious luncheon. She is comme il faut. In the afternoon returned Gen Dandys call, but found no one at home. Called also on Mrs Cox (L Bs mother) and her daughters. Nice people. . . . Mr Cox was there also. I think he will return to Portland with me. He came to attend the funeral of his father who died not long since. He showed me the grounds of Commodore Decaturs which is quite near his house . . . It is being cut up into lots, and all I saw was the porters lodge and the hill covered with handsome forest trees. Dropped in at [Leo] Knotts as I came home where I was invited to take "pot luck," but found they had gone to Baltimore. . . . When I returned to my hotel found Justice Field had been there twice in the afternoon. Called there after dinner, thinking his visits might import something, but found they were only *cultus.* Met a son of Gen [Geo] Wright there who was drowned on the *Brother Jonathan* in 1865.[40] He lives in Louisville and is Marshal of the Supreme Court. The *Post* of this morning contained an editorial correction of the interview contained in the issue of the 22 inst insofar as I was made to say that I thought Sara Althea would kill Field, Sawyer and myself at the first favorable opportunity. I only asked a correction as to myself, and it was so written by the manager of the paper (Wilkins) in my presence, before I left the office. Field writes me a note this afternoon in which he says he is much displeased that I should be made to say that I never heard she threatened his life and wants me to contradict. But I don't want to meddle with it any more. So let it go. . . . Called with Justice Field in his carriage in the afternoon on the Chief Justice, who was not at home and Justices Harlan and Lamar with whom we had pleasant calls, particularly the former, who compounded the best whiskey toddy I ever drank. Field dropped me at Knotts where I took "a pot-luck" dinner as it is called, but which was a[s] toothsome a repast as I ever sat down to. From there I went to Senator Dolphs . . . Dolph walked home with me, and talked a little about the appointments in Oregon. Got a very good letter from Henderson which I answered before going to bed. A wonderful boy when he will.

*26 (Sat)* . . . Montgomery called and said he had made an arrangement for me to call on Secretary [James G] Blaine on Monday at ½ past 10, at the Normandie. Capt John Mullan called and I promised to take tea there tomorrow. He asked me to dinner at 2 oclock, but I was engaged to Capt Catlin. Justice Field called this evening and took me in his coupe to call on Atty Gen [W H H] Miller[41] and Justice Miller. The A G is a very affable sensible man, and read me some of the recommendations he had prepared for his report based on the answer I made to his circular last summer. Justice Miller was kind and communicative, and said he was going to make one more effort this winter to have Congress increase the salaries of the district Judges. I hope he will succeed.

27 (Sun) A rainy blustery day. Went to the Church of the Epiphany where I heard the service decently and reverently read, some good singing and one of the best sermons I ever listened to . . . As I came out of the church I fell in with Mr [John] Goode of Virginia, and had a pleasant chat with him as he walked up with me to my hotel. At the door I found Miss Little waiting for me. She spoke to me and shook hands with me and said she travelled on the steamer with me from Portland to San Fran. I remembered her sweet, composed face at once but I could not recall the circumstances of our meeting, and left her as I thought somewhat mortified. She said she lived on the Columbia road and invited me to call and see her. At the hotel I found Capt Catlin with his coupe ready to drive me out to his house (the Soldiers Home) to dinner. . . . On my way out to Catlins I remembered all about my meeting with Miss Little in '85, and the pleasant time I had with her, and as he drove me down to town we went by her house and I called on her.

Had an elegant supper at Mullans and a very pleasant time. Her two daughters were present. The eldest is a very pretty girl, and has a model arm and fine conversational powers. I staid until nearly 10 oclock and we discussed everybody and everything.

28 (Mon) Went up to the Supreme court with Justice Strong in his carriage. He invited me to a breakfast at 10 A M on Wednesday next. . . . Dined at Knotts. 12 persons present. Cardinal Gibbon and Monsieur Chappel[le] among others. The latter is the brains of the Cardinalate and always accompanies it. You would have thought the dinner was given to the Cardinal instead of me. The guests were all introduced to him first and as he went away he said to the Chief Justice, who was present, that he was invited to meet him. The dinner was elegant, but these things made me feel uncomfortable. . . .

29 (Tue) . . . At 11 Senator Dolph called and we called on the President. Saw him in the Cabinet room 10 or 15 minutes and talked about one thing or another not including the weather, and of which Alaska was a large part. The President looked tired. He has a weak eye and altogether does not impress one as a great man. But I suppose he is a good average, and is quite affable and agreeable. . . .

30 (Wed) Went to a breakfast at ex Justice Strongs at 10 oclock where I met Justices Field and Harlan, Governor [Geo S] Boutwell[42] and Mr [name omitted]. The Justice took the head of the table and said grace like a man and Miss Julia occupied the other end and poured the tea & coffee. The breakfast was good and the company agreeable. Saw something of Gov Boutwell, and took occasion to revise my former opinion of him in his favor. He called on me this afternoon. . . .

. . . After dinner made my call at Mullans and Knotts. Had a charming time with Mrs M and did not get to Knotts until ½ past 9. Mrs K had just fallen and hurt the fingers of her hand pretty badly and was lying down upstairs. Knott came down and we discussed C Gibbon of the Scarlet robe. I told him of his rudeness to me at Portland in not returning my call, and that brought up the usurping of my place and receiving the guests at the dinner given by Mr Knott. He was very sorry for it and much provoked. That he came very early and seated himself in the chair intended for me, and as the guests came in he rose up to receive them and there was nothing left for Knott but to present them, unless he steered them across to one side of the room to which I had retired, as I did not think it polite to stand before, and I would not stand beside the old rascal and play second fiddle to him. . . .

*31 (Thu)* Was not so well this morning. Think I walked too much last evening. Hurt about the ureth[r]a. Drove down to the Washington monument and went up in the elevator 500 feet. It was cloudy and misty and the view was limited, but I could see that I was away up. The dome of the Capitol was far beneath us. Took a view of the Panorama of Bull Run. Like all the rest of them. Everything terribly exaggerated and disgustingly real. . . . Got a dispatch from Mrs Deady proposing to go to Europe. Bless her heart what is she thinking about. Got a letter from her also.

*November 1 (Fri)* Took breakfast at Justice Harlans at 9:30 with the family. . . . brought away a Md biscuit as a memento or souvenir of the affair. Drove with the Justice thence to the Capitol where I heard a case argued on behalf of the plaintiff in error. From there I called on Mrs [H H] Gilfrey and Mrs [J H] Beatty up in that region. Mrs Beatty I knew in St Clairsville 40 years ago when she was the belle of the village. She called on me first. Her husband (second one) is chief of a division in the treasury dept, this 15 years. In the afternoon drove with Miss Julia Strong and her sister in the suburbs from ½ past 3 until 5. Took dinner at Justice Fields and went with Mrs Field to the theatre to see Rhea in "Josephine."[43] She can't speak English as she is spoken in the U S and I did not understand a word she said. She is a Belgian I believe but hails from Paris. . . . From the comments I heard I think the spectators are quite as much interested in the costumes as the acting.

*2 (Sat)* . . . Got away from Wormleys 5 min after 7 [*this evening*] and from Washington at 7:40. A letter was handed me at the depot from Henderson of the 2 inst, which I enjoyed very much indeed.

*3 (Sun)* Reached Pittsburg in the rain about breakfast time, which we [*Deady and L B Cox*] took at the Buffet. The day soon cleared off and was lovely and in the ride through Ohio saw the best average looking country for that distance I ever passed over. Got to Chicago at ½ past 4, and drove to the Richelieu where we took No 11, a pair of rooms with a bath and water closet attached. Got some stewed oysters and beer before retiring and then turned into the best bed I have been in since I left home and slept well.

*4 (Mon)* . . . Went to the Ry ticket office and secured my sleeper for Omaha. In the afternoon got a cab and drove to Agnes Flemings . . . where I spent between 2 & 3 hours. Mr Fleming and Frank Knott[44] came in. Agnes has grown stout and homely. Frank is quite a bright good looking fellow. Fleming is a big fat fellow, not bad looking, a glib talker as his business of traveling implies. Altogether my visit was not a very pleasant one. They are good sensible people but their thoughts do not run in the same channels as mine. . . .

*5 (Tue)* Not very well, did not get up until 10. Drove to the Tribune Building to see Mr [William Demarest] Lloyd. Not in. Called on Gov Bross at the Beaurivage Flats. Gone to vote (election day) but soon came in. Looked [well], but suffering from a paralytic stroke in the right side. Walks pretty well when he is [up] but must be helped up. Was very glad to see me indeed. Staid an hour and a half with [him] during which time we had luncheon. Bade him farewell never expecting to see him again in this world. A worthy old man and a well spent life.

In the afternoon went to the horse show and saw more big fat horses, Clydesdales, and English Shires, than I ever dreamed of. Two of them weighed over 2000 pounds apiece. A riding contest was carried on in a large amphitheatre at which prizes were given. The horse I favored did not secure a ribbon. I think as Jim Bybee once said when he lost a quarter [horse] race in Oregon—"They *outjudged* me.". . . I am off tonight for Council Bluffs, and will leave in the course of an hour.

Got off at 10:30 on the C & N W Ry from Chicago, Cox going on the Burlington.

*6 (Wed)* A beautiful day through Iowa. Got another excellent breakfast on this train. News coming in along the road that Iowa had elected a Dem Gov the day before. The prohibition collar has chafed the people until they determined to get rid of it or show their dislike of it. Reached C Bluffs about 6:30 and left at 7:45 with Cox who joined me there. Got supper at C Bluffs, and was served by girls.

*7 (Thu)* Reached Sidney [Nebraska] about 9 A M where Mr & Mrs Park[e] accompanied by Gen Morrow called to see us. And pretty little Genevieve [Parke] came also and sent her love to her Grandpa Brooke. Crossed the summit late in the evening, the snow being about 6 inches deep. Saw the monument to [Oakes] Ames which looks like a last years Hay stack, fresh thatched.

*8 (Fri)* A lovely day passing through the Bear river country and the Port Neuf Canyon.

*9 (Sat)* Reached Portland about 9:45 P M. . . .

Edward & Paul and Mr Brooke met me at the depot and I was soon at home where I longed to be. I spent on the trip $355 which did not include my transportation east to N Y and from Chicago west. In this was a doctor bill of $30 and $38 for clothes.

I am better than when I left home but not well yet. . . .

*26 (Wed)* [sic] Reached home from the east on Saturday evening the 9th inst about 10 oclock on the Oregon Short line. . . .

I went into court the Monday following and have been on the bench every judicial day since. Called a grand jury on the 19th inst which is still in session—ignoring bills for the most part. On Saturday the 23d inst I called at the Hall, the first time in three months. On Sunday the 17th went to church at Trinity, the first time since early in September. I really felt glad to get back and as I bowed my head on the pew in front I felt the tears come into my eyes. On the 15th commenced to move upstairs in the rooms lately occupied by the DeHarts and we have just about got comfortably fixed in them. We have three rooms instead of two, and the middle one I am going to use as a library. I have not been to my chambers at night since I came home and do not intend to do any more night work except in my library at home. Cost of furniture $200—additional furniture.

My health has been slowly improving, but I am not well about the bladder yet, and am concerned about the outcome of it. Our monthly charges for room rent and board will now be for ourselves $148 and for Henderson $40 in all $188. The weather has been mild since my return and somewhat moist.

*30 (Sat)* Thursday (Nov 27) [*sic*] Thanksgiving Day. Went to Church at Trinity in the morning. A good congregation and a good sermon in favor of "civil service reform." The music was labored but not as good as average. Too much solo in the "Te Deum." Held a session of the district court in the afternoon or rather as district Judge. . . . This evening Dr [Anton] Sonnefeld washed out my bladder after having determined from the examination of my urine that I had catarrh of the bladder. I think he is very expert in his profession.[45] I ought to have had him sooner.

Got weighed today and reached 224 pounds, the least I have weighed for many years.

*December 7 (Sat)* Sat in the D C & C C during the week. The trial jury came on Tuesday the third inst, but I made no use of them during the week. Monday decided two cases, one on a garnishment process against the Oregon Pacific railway company for about $1000. Heard the application of the Oregon Short Line for an injunction against the Northern Pacific to compel it to haul the formers cars over its road from Portland to the Sound. . . .

Dr Sonnefeld has been attending me for catarrh of the bladder, since Sunday evening the first inst. . . . He is a very skilful man and his treatment has changed my urine to a normal condition. Still spend my evenings at home, whence I do some official work and some miscellaneous reading.

Weighed today and turned the scale at 225½, a gain of a pound and a half in a week.

*21 (Sat)* . . . Sunday Dec 15 went to Grace church with Mrs Deady to the dedication of the new building. Dr Houghton preached an elegant and interesting sermon of an hour in length. I gave them $5 on the debt, and told the minister that the sermon was well worth that sum at least. . . .

. . . Dr Sonnefeld is still treating me for Catarrh of the bladder. The water is getting clear and sweet, and I hope to be well again some day. . . .

# NOTES

1. The breach with Whalley was complete.
2. Seymour Condon; Eugene lawyer.
3. Ross C. Houghton, Methodist minister; pastor at Grace M.E. Church, 1888–93.
4. James Walton (1822–1911), Roseburg and Salem farmer and public official; married Mary Elizabeth Barzert. His younger brother, John, married her mother.
5. Presumably Kathy Coursen was a sister to Eugene Coursen. Alfred Holt is not further identified in the newspaper notices.
6. Pennoyer objected to the fact that the water bonds were to be tax exempt.
7. James W. Noble (1831–1912), Missouri lawyer and Union soldier; as secretary of the interior, 1889–93, he performed more ably than Deady had feared.
8. John and Pete Grant, Larry Sullivan and Henry McCormick were sailors' boarding house keepers and professional crimps, engaged in "shanghaiing" crews for ships departing from Portland and Astoria. The Grant brothers, rather more proficient than most of their contemporaries in the uses of bungstarters, knockout drops, and other devices of persuasion, prospered and retired. Larry Sullivan, who was also a notably unsuccessful professional pugilist, eventually became a bank president—of a bank set up by the redoubtable "Yellow Kid" Weil in connection with one of the con games Weil was conducting. There was a reduction works in East Portland.
9. Father Gibeny was first parish priest of St. Patrick's Church. George Grote (1794–1871), English historian, businessman and MP. Sylvester Genin (1822–50), St. Clairsville painter; died at Jamaica of tuberculosis.
10. James H. McMillen (1823–1913), married, as his second wife, Tirzah Barton (1832–1903).
11. Thomas L. Cole, Episcopal minister; rector of Trinity, 1890–97.
12. Deady was suffering the first twinges of bilateral sciatica, an ominous sign, though he could not know it.
13. Arthur J. Brown; pastor of First Presbyterian Church. Freimann's (Freeman's in original) was a popular restaurant.
14. Kate Douglas Wiggin (1856–1923), author and pioneer kindergarten worker. Wiggins and Kintergarten in original.
15. Esther Campbell Holladay died April 5, 1889, leaving two minor children, Ben Campbell and Linda Holladay, and a will which named General Rufus Ingalls as the children's guardian. The following day her sisters, Maria Smith and Mrs. Barnhart, and Joseph Holladay petitioned for the appointment of Mrs. Harriet Campbell, Esther's mother, as guardian. The general, conscious that his stewardship of Holladay affairs would shortly be subject to the unpleasantly close scrutiny of the courts—he was executor of Ben Holladay's estate—fought strenuously to retain custody of the children. He was able to point out that Harriet herself petitioned for Ingalls' appointment, although she subsequently withdrew her support of him, and he alleged that she was unfit to be the guardian of young children by reason of her advanced age. This last argument had obvious merit, and on May 7 another petition was before the court, this one requesting the appointment of Maria Smith. In the end, Mrs. Harriet Campbell was appointed guardian. Unfortunately

she was quite as unfitted for that task as would have been the general.

The incident to which Barnhart referred occurred, if it occurred at all, before the Williams were married.

16. Chauncey M. Depew (1834–1928), New York lawyer, railroad president and public speaker; his oration at the Washington Inauguration Centennial was much admired.

17. Bertram Orth. Mr. Memly has not been identified. George F. Hoar (1826–1904), Massachusetts lawyer and legislator; Republican congressman, 1869–77, and senator, 1877–1904. James L. Pugh (1820–1907), Alabama lawyer and Confederate congressman; Democratic senator, 1890–97. William B. Allison (1829–1908), Iowa lawyer and politician; Republican senator, 1872–1908.

18. John M. Thurston (1847–1916), Nebraska lawyer and Republican politician; *post* 1888, general counsel for the U.P.R.R. Co.; U. S. senator, 1895–1901.

19. Reid was trained as a lawyer, which may account for this talent for obfuscation.

20. Martha Comstock operated a boarding house on Alder Street. Chester C. Cole (1824–1913), Iowa lawyer and jurist; justice of the state supreme court, 1864–76; taught law at Drake University.

21. Charles F. Manderson (1837–1911), Nebraska lawyer; Republican senator, 1883–95. The "Naval" Snow may have been Eliot Snow, assistant naval constructor.

22. The Glidden patents, or the most important of them, were eventually upheld by the supreme court.

Because both Terry and Sarah Althea had repeatedly threatened to take Field's life, deputy U. S. Marshal David Neagle was assigned as the judge's bodyguard. On August 13 Field, then traveling in his official capacity, was eating in a Stockton, California restaurant when Terry approached, passed a few remarks, and made a threatening gesture. Neagle promptly shot and killed him. California authorities arrested Neagle for murder but his counsel applied to the federal circuit court for a writ of habeas corpus on the ground that Neagle was being held in custody "for an act done in pursuance of the law of the United States." The U. S. Supreme Court upheld the writ.

Barlsbad in original. Victor H. Smith, a son of W. K. Smith, and afterward a Portland physician; died 1915.

23. William Lund, Episcopal pastor at Salem and Roseburg; acted as supply pastor until Mr. Cole's arrival. Margaret Mather, American dramatic actress; made her New York debut in 1885 in "Romeo and Juliet." J. B. Studley played second male leads in numerous New York productions in the 1880s and 1890s.

24. Thomas De Witt Talmage (1832–1902), Dutch Reformed clergyman and popular lecturer; noted for his sensational style of preaching.

25. Epididymitis was then relatively common in cases of prostatic obstruction. Neagle was traveling as "Jones" because the supreme court had not yet acted on his case.

26. George C. Gorham, California lawyer and politician; secretary of the U. S. Senate, 1869–79.

27. Nelson A. Miles eventually became commander-in-chief of the army, 1895, and directed the organization and training of the troops which fought in the Spanish-American War.

28. A. L. Maxwell; general passenger agent, O.R. & N. Co.

29. Thomas A. Brassey (1868–1919), later the 2nd Earl of Brassey; he married Lady Idina Nevill in 1889, and they were apparently on their honeymoon. De Brassey in original.

30. Daniel R. Goodwin (1811–90), Episcopal clergyman. Deady would have said that Stark was a resident of Connecticut but a citizen of Oregon.

31. Thomas Davies (1831–1905), made Episcopal bishop of Michigan.

32. Andrew W. Kent, New York attorney.

33. Robert A. Holland (1844–1909), clergyman; originally a Methodist he became an Episcopalian in 1872; he was rector of Christ Church, St. Louis.

34. Chauncey B. Ripley (1835–93), prominent New York attorney. Dr. John H. Ripley was his brother. Alfred S. Pearsall (c.1846–1919), journalist and economist; commodity

reporter for Associated Press and founder of Pearsall's News Bureau. Edward Jordan, New York attorney and former solicitor, U. S. Treasury. Frank Loomis, New York lawyer; counsel for New York Central Railroad.

35. George Bliss (1816–96), banker and merchant.

36. Felicia Hemans (1793–1835), English poet best known for her "Casabianca." Amos R. Eno (1810–98), New York merchant and financier, and owner of the Fifth Avenue Hotel. Reno in original after the first appearance. Ellen Lucy Platt, wife of the New York politician and Republican party boss, "Me too" Tom Platt, so-called because when his friend Conkling resigned from the senate in a fit of pique, Platt resigned also. Mrs. Platt died in 1901.

37. Henry M. Frisbie (d. 1897) rose from captain of the Illinois Volunteers to brevet major-general during the Civil War. James H. Lappeus (1828–94), Portland saloon-keeper, police chief and businessman.

38. William Pennington (1796–1862), New Jersey politician. Thomas S. Bobcock (1815–91), Virginia lawyer and politician; Democratic congressman, 1847–61, and speaker of the Confederate House of Representatives. Samuel Blatchford (1820–91), New York lawyer and authority of patent and maritime law; justice of the U. S. Supreme Court, 1882–93.

39. Charles Loyson (1827–1912), an extremely popular French Roman Catholic priest, protested against the doctrine of papal infallibility and was excommunicated, 1870. He later married, and founded the Old Catholic Church in France. Rachel Wells Morris was apparently an admirer.

40. Lewis B. Cox (c.1846–1901), Portland attorney. George Wright (1803–65), soldier; MA, class of 1822; served in Florida and Mexican wars and *post* 1852 on the Pacific Coast; drowned in the sinking of the *Brother Jonathan* off Crescent City, California, July 31, 1865.

41. William H. H. Miller (1840–1917), Indiana law partner of Benjamin Harrison; Harrison's attorney-general, 1889–93.

42. George S. Boutwell (1818–1905), Massachusetts lawyer and Democratic governor, 1851–52; radical Republican congressman, 1863–69; secretary of treasury, 1873–77.

43. Hortense Rhea made her New York debut in 1881. A European favorite in heavy dramatic roles, she never achieved great success in the United States.

44. Frank Knott was Agnes Fleming's brother, thus Deady's nephew.

45. Anton Sonnefeld, physician, practiced only briefly in Portland. Sonnenfeld in original.

# APPENDIX  A

### DEADY'S ILLNESS

Though neither Arthur Bevan nor any of the many other doctors who treated Deady seems to have diagnosed it, the judge's illness was clearly prostatic in origin. The symptoms—urine retention, hematuria, bladder and renal infection—are characteristic. The violent pain he suffered after catherization was certainly acute pyelitis; the "bruising" of which he complained, epididymitis, relatively common in prostate sufferers of that day. The nausea, vertigo and coma of his final days are typical symptoms of uraemia.

It is, of course, impossible to determine beyond question whether Deady was afflicted by benign hypertrophy of the prostate, or from cancer, but the bilateral sciatica which caused him so much distress suggests malignancy.

John W. Whalley (above), lawyer, hunter, dog lover, Odd Fellow.

Right, Rev. John Rosenberg, Rector of St. Stephens Episcopal Church, Portland.

Judge O. C. Pratt, Oregon Territory politician, was among old acquaintances the Deadys met in San Francisco, 1890.

Presbyterian elder Ripley surprised Deady at the Hoffman House dinner in New York. (Deady Collection.)

*Dinner given to*

HON. MATTHEW P. DEADY,
BY
CHAUNCEY B. RIPLEY, LL. D.

### MENU

HUITRES

VARIES   HORS D'ŒUVRES   VARIES

POTAGE
Tortue Verte

POISSON
Filet de Sole au gratin

ENTREES
Côtelettes d'Agneau à la Maison d'Or
Piments farcis
Pommes sautés quartier
Bouchées de Ris de Veau
Petits Pois

SORBETS AU RHUM

ROTI
Dindonneau au Cresson
Salade Céléri

ENTREMET SUCRE
Omelette au Rhum

DESSERT
Petits fours                    Gateaux assortis
Fromage                        Fruits
Café

VINS
Hochheimer              Pommery Sec
Pontet Canet Superior

HOFFMAN HOUSE.                    OCTOBER 13, 1889.

Picnic at City Park (Washington Park), 1889. Seated from left: Hamilton Brooke (straw hat), Sanderson Reed, L. Hawley Hoffman, W. J. Burns, Dr. Holt C. Wilson (with plate), Clementine Wilson, Mrs. George B. Wallace (nee Burns), Miss Dede Page, Phillips Beck, Dr. R. B. Wilson, Virginia Wilson, Mary Pope, Dr. Eaton, Rodney L. Glisan, Erskine Wood (boy standing right end).

The Holladay children, Ben Campbell and Linda, with their guardian, Quartermaster General Rufus Ingalls, who had gone on to greater things from his AQM post at Fort Vancouver in the 1850s, and nurse.

Views of the Portland public library for which Judge Deady was active in collecting building funds. It was located on S.W. Stark Street, between 7th (Broadway) and Park (8th).

Portland Marine Band played at the Washington's Inauguration Centennial on April 30, 1889. They stand at S.W. 5th in front of the U. S. courthouse and post office, with the partially built Portland Hotel visible beyond. The procession was "the finest ever in the Northwest."

# 1890

*January 7 (Tue)* . . . Sunday, Jan 5. Did not go to church in the morning. In the afternoon called at Edwards to see the baby. I gave it a silver cup on Xmas, which pleased its mother very much. I made no presents this Xmas worth mentioning. Sent 8 copies of photographic Portland to persons in the east who were polite to me when I was there this fall. Gave Mrs Hill a copy of Prangs *Babies and Their Nurses*. I told her she had everything but a family and so I gave her this.

*11 (Sat)* Tuesday (Jan 7th) Mrs Deady and I left Portland at ½ past 4 in the drawing room of the Pul[l]man car, the Klamath, for San Francisco. Took supper on the car and were up for breakfast at Ashland where we were well cared for. The snow was about 6 inches deep from Portland to Ashland. The night before we left was the coldest of the season, the thermometer being 10 degrees above zero. From Ashland to the head waters of the Sacramento we had a grand ride by daylight, the sun shining brightly, the depth of the snow ranging from two to four feet on the line of the road. While crossing the Siski[y]ou we had a splendid view of Mt Shasta to the southeast of us. The passage down the mountain height from Sissons to the Sacramento is a wonderful piece of engineering. The track doubles on itself twice in making the descent. From Delta we travelled in the night and reached here [*SF*] on Thursday morning about 8 oclock where we found no snow but plenty of white frost.

*9 (Thu)* Stopped at the Occidental, in rooms 35 on the first floor, where we got an excellent breakfast. During the day got our tickets on the Steamship *Alameda* to Honolulu and back for $125—half rate. Sent cards to sundry persons and staid in the house all day except going to the Bank of Cal where I deposited $920 and took a letter of credit from the bank for the amount.

We left home with $1205—In the afternoon Judge Sawyer called and he and Mrs Deady went out to ride. Bought a syringe for $2.50 with which to treat my bladder with a solution of manganese.[1]

*10 (Fri)* . . . had a number of callers including Judge & Mrs Pratt, nee Lizzie Jones. By the way she is a very handsome attractive woman, and I am not surprised that she won the heart of O C away from the Old Wisconsin tavern keepers daughter.[2] Called at the P[acific] U[nion] Club to which I had been introduced by William Alvord who called Thursday. It is a splendid place. . . .

Today we went out to the [*Golden Gate*] park and back in the cable [car] and while there were driven about in a dirty old hack for $1. The monument to [Francis Scott] Keys [*sic*] built with the Lick legacy pleased me more than anything

I saw. Maryland, and particularly Baltimore, ought to be ashamed of itself that it had not honored his memory in some such way long since. Gen Miles called today and invited us to dinner on Monday which we were compelled to decline. Had a letter from Paul and another from Mrs Catlin this morning. All right in Portland. . . .

*12 (Sun)* A cold wet day. Mrs Deady not well, Neuralgia. I went to Trinity church and heard an admirable sermon from the new Rector, Mr [J Sanderson] Reed, on the words—"Wist ye not that I must be about my fathers business.". . .Judge Hoffman called in the evening or rather afternoon and spent an hour with me. Shows the flight of time. Dr G[h]iselin gave Mrs Deady a hypodermic injection of morphine which allayed her pain.

*13 (Mon)* Mr & Mrs Southard Hoffman called. Judge Pratt was in and out. Mrs Deady still unwell. Had another hypo. A pleasant day.

*14 (Tue)* Went aboard the S S *Alameda* at 4 oclock. Major Hooper of the Hotel sent Mrs Deady a basket of fruit and flowers. . . .

Got in to our room "G" on the starboard side of the deck in good condition, where we found a case of wine and a box of oranges sent us by Mr Eugene Meyer.[3]

*15 (Wed)* Lay in the stream all night waiting for the English mails, which came on board this morning, when we steamed away out of the Golden Gate into the fog and cold winds of the California Coast.

*23 (Thu)* The voyage was what people of experience called an unusually rough one. We reached Honolulu at 11 A M of Jan the 22. Mrs Deady was more or less sick all the way, but after the [second day] I was on deck and at the table regularly. We made the acquaintance of some very pleasant people on the ship. The master, Capt [H G] Morse, was confined to his room with la grippe. Mr Godfrey Brown was a passenger and was both agreeable and serviceable to us. We knew him years ago in Portland. Ex Gov [Frederick W M] Holliday of Va was also on board, making I believe his third voyage around the world.[4] He is a very interesting, attractive man and we became very good friends—particularly Mrs D and he. She says it is a pity there are not more men like him in this world.

Yesterday afternoon we took a ride on the railway up the coast about 15 miles and back at the invitation of Mr [Benj F] Dillingham, one of our fellow passengers.[5] About 25 passengers went along. The trip was an interesting one. We saw rice fields submerged in water—the young plant growing in it, and banana trees laden with fruit. The oleander was in full bloom.

We are quartered at [the] Hawaiian Hotel in room 17 on the first floor. There is a parlor and a large bedroom and a large porch at the back end facing a handsome yard full of hotel cottages and the healthy north east trade wind for which we pay $8 per day.

Chief Justice [A Francis] Judd and Justice [Lawrence] McCully called today; also Mrs [Alexander] Macintosh and Mr Robert B[r]enham.[6] The latter is to be married this evening to a Miss Dowsett, and he came to invite us to the wedding at St Andrews Cathedral and reception at the house of the brides parents. We are going. Mr Macintosh called last evening and dined with us. He celebrates the marriage this evening. Finished *Looking Backward* today. The dream of a Utopian.

Yet what a pity it cannot be realized. It might and is being realized to some extent by the growth of cooperation and the discouragement of destruction and expensive competition. Wrote a long letter to Henderson today, which goes out on a sailing vessel.

My health is pretty good. Still use the catheter once a day, but have not washed my bladder since I left S F. Will commence again now. I write this on the porch in the balmy out of door air. The day has been a lovely one. Yesterday and last night it rained in showers, short, wet and quick. And so indeed the first lesson in Hawaiian life.

*24 (Fri)* This was a phenomenal day. The sun shone bright, the wind blew in strong gusts carrying with it blocks of fine rain or mist in a cloudless sky apparently from the mountain range back of the town. By invitation of the Chief Justice, Judd, I sat in the Supreme Court with himself and three associates, McCully, [Sanford] Dole and [Richard F] Bickerton. I heard two cases argued on appeal (in equity) and very well argued. The government building is a handsome one in the center of a large plot of ground. The courtroom is on the lower floor. It is commodious and airy. The walls are covered with the portraits of former members of the court, and the royal family past and present. The judges wore black silk gowns fastened at the neck with red strings. They are all pleasant respectable looking men, and constitute I have no doubt a capable trustworthy court. In the evening the U S consul Mr [H W] Severance and his wife called and also Mr Irving [*W G Irwin*] & wife. The former is a fine looking man and converses well. Irwin is a partner of [Claus] Spreckels and the agent of the Company. His wife is a handsome, showy young woman and was the widow of young Ben Holladay from whom she was divorced a few years ago.[7]

*25 (Sat)* This was a lovely day without a sprinkle. In the afternoon we drove out to Macintoshes at Sunnyslope. Found them all at home except Marie [von Holt] who was off on the Island of Hawaii with her sister [*Bertha*].[8] We staid about half an hour and had a very pleasant call. The drive was about a mile towards the mountain, in which we passed many handsome places and residences. Came back in the horse car and went on down to the wharf. Mrs Deady returned to the Hotel and I made some business calls down town.

Godfrey Brown called in the evening and we went through the town a little and the inhabitants thereof. . . .

*26 (Sun)*. . . Today we attended service at St Andrews (Church of England). The service was conducted by the Rev Macintosh. In the afternoon we were driven to Waikiki about 5 miles down the coast, to the park and bathing place by Mr & Mrs Irwin.[9] They have a beautiful summer residence there on the seashore. The whole drive was enchanting. Palm trees, cocoa trees, banyan trees, Banana orchards and other tropical growths I cannot recall, lined the road and filled the grounds. Ten years ago Irwins place was a piece of white sand. Now it is covered with grass and luxuriant trees. He has about 2½ acres in the enclosure. The day has been a lovely one indeed. Thermometer about 75 degrees.

*27 (Mon)* This was a lovely day. At 10 oclock we took the tramway on King St opposite the Palace and rode to the beach, called Waikiki, a distance of about two miles, through a beautiful country to the bathing house kept by Johnson. Here we obtained bathing suits and went into the sea and had a delicious bath for which we paid 25 cents apiece, after which we sat in the open house or covered verandah and watched the native girls disporting in the water like young seals. Occasionally they plucked a handful of sea grass which they ate. Came home on the cars by ½ past 12. The whole ride only cost 40 cents. The car was full of natives each way, most of them well dressed and respectable looking. As a rule they have handsome dark eyes, smallish well shaped hands and feet. But in cases of old people who have never worn a shoe the foot is often quite large and sometimes ill shaped—the toes being large and long. The ride was delightful.

In the afternoon Mr [Alfred S] Hartwell called and drove us out to his place about a mile and a half up the valley and just outside of town.[10] He has a lovely home. The house is roomy and airy and all on the ground, and commands a full view of the harbor and the wide sea beyond. It is a place of all others to realize the idea of the Italians *dolce far niente.* In the evening we dined en famille with the Macintoshes. Had an excellent dinner and a pleasant evening.

*28 (Tue)* This day comes in bright and warm, the thermometer being now (10 A M) at 74. Took some soda with my claret last night and I was passing water all night. Went to Waikiki in the morning and had a sea bath. . . . Visited a district school by the wayside kept by a half caste young woman named Miss Markham. She said her mother was a native and her father an Irishman. When I told her that her father might have been a native of Ireland, but the name Marquam or Markham was pure English and that an Englishwoman of that name had written some celebrated school histories, she seemed pleased. She said, she was educated by the "English Sisters," meaning Sister Albertina and her Associates at St Andrews Cathedral.[11] There were about 40 scholars in the school of both sexes ranging from 4 years to 14 years of age, probably. A class of two boys and girls read a lesson in one of Swintons readers for me about George Washington and the cherry tree, and did very well, particularly when we consider that they were reading in a foreign tongue.

In the afternoon Mr [Chas R] Bishop[12] drove us around and on the punch bowl and over the grounds of the "Old Peoples Home." It is a beautiful drive and the view of the valley, town harbor and shipping was very fine. The day was lovely. The Home is a handsome building situated on a large plot of ground, which is beautifully laid out and ornamented. It was built and is maintained from a legacy left by the late King [*?Kamehameha IV*] for that purpose and will accommodate about 70 persons. At present there are near 40 inmates.

In the evening Judge & Mrs Judd, Mr & Mrs [Lorrin] Thurston and Mr [Archibald S] Cleghorn called. The latter is a fine looking old Scotchman. Has been in the country since he was a boy. We called at the Severances where I met Cap [Jos B] Coghlan,[13] the commander of the *Mohican,* and drank a cup of delicious Russian tea. Pleasant good people.

*29 (Wed)* Called on the American minister, Mr [John L] Stevens, in company with Consul Severance. Found him an intelligent, interesting old man. Promised to get us permits to visit the Palace. He called in the afternoon. In the afternoon went with Mrs D to Mr Cogswells studio in the Spreckels Building, to sit for her picture. Called at the banking house of Mr Bishop. Got some blank checks and left my signature. In the evening went to dinner at Mr Irwins. A pleasant company and an elegant dinner. I took Mrs I to the table & Mr I took Mrs Deady. Mrs [Jas H] Woodhouse, the wife of the British Commissioner sat on my right and her husband on that of Mrs Deady.[14] They are an interesting couple, particularly "She."

Capt Coghlan of the *Mohican* & Capt Sinclair of the H M S *Champion* were present. A young married couple Mr & Mrs [Francis M] Hatch.[15] She was very pretty and had a very handsome neck and arm—particularly the latter.

The hosts sister Mrs [Z S] Spalding[16] and a Miss Kauffman completed the party. The hostess was elegantly dressed. Her diamonds were large and lustrous, but after all she bears the marks in her manner of her early association with the Holladays.

*30 (Thu)* Today I did not feel well and remained at home—at the hotel—Mrs Deady went to luncheon at Mrs Thurstons, wife of the minister of the Interior, and she and I went to dinner at Judge McCullys in the evening, where we met Dr & Mrs [Ezra] Derr[17] of the *Nipsic* and a Miss Waugh, a part caste who appears to be an inmate of the family. She is bright and genteel and has a beautiful hand. The dinner was a good plain one without wine. There was an attempt at Roman punch which was not a success. Mrs McCully is a large fine looking woman from Maine, with a handsome, striking head and face and pronounced opinions on current topics. She is a Republican, a missionary and don't like the English nor their church, and thinks poorly of the natives. The Judge is a very pleasant man, positive and firm enough I imagine when the pinch comes, but ordinarily illustrates well the suaviter in modo.

*31 (Fri)*. . . Visited the English Sisters school, Albertina, Phoebe, and Beatrice. They are rather good looking English-women of the order called the "Davenport Sisters." The school is for boarders and day scholars. There were about 40 of the former present and but few of the latter. The schoolrooms are large and airy and the scholars were generally well clad and fairly good looking. Most or many of the smaller ones wore but one gown and were bare legged and footed. The school is connected with St Andrews Cathedral and is within the Cathedral close. Thence I went to the Royal School for boys under the charge of the Rev Mr Macintosh and several assistants at the head of Emma Street. A large number of boys are in attendance [*space left*] generally natives or part caste. As I approached the school they were all on the large playground and as merry [a] crowd as I ever met. Playing marbles was the principal amusement. I was in Mr Macintoshs room a half hour at least. A class wrote some sentences from dictation on the blackboard. They were beautifully written and correctly spelled. The natives seem to have the gift of what phrenologists used to call "Form" in a large degree. The sentences were then analyzed or "parsed" quite well. Then while the teacher prepared a music less[on] in harmony on the blackboard, I heard a class read in Swintons 4th reader and another in the 5th reader. They all pronounced the words well, but were inclined to let the voice fall at the comma and semicolon.

I believe there was only one boy perfect in this respect. His name was Jonah, in the native, Eona. He was a lightish brown with curly, not Kinky hair. The teacher said he was a pure native so far as known. The lesson in the Fifth reader was the apocryphal and meritricious speech of Robert Emmet when sentenced to death for treason in the Irish insurrection of 1798. I was surprised to find it in such a book, though pruned of some of the most extravagant passages.

*February 1 (Sat)* By the procurement of the American Minister, Mr Stevens, I was this morning at 11 oclock presented to the King [*Kalakaua*].[18] Mr Justice McCully presented me. The Chief Justice was to have done so, but unfortunately he got down with "la grippe." I had met His Majesty before at the Dowsett wedding. The King after shaking hands sat down and the Judge and myself did the same on either side of [him] where we talked commonplace[s] for 15 minutes the bulk of the conversation being furnished by myself. The palace is a handsome building and the interior is beautifully finished. The floor is Oregon fir.

In the afternoon Mrs Deady and I made sundry calls, return ones. In doing so we drove 2½ hours for which we paid $3. In the evening we called at the Irwins where we spent a pleasant half hour. Got acquainted with a pretty N H girl, Miss Spaulding, a niece of Mr Irwin.

Today [2] we went to the Native church in the morning and St Andrews in the evening. The former was built many years ago of blocks of coral cut out of the reef by the natives. We went before church time, while S S was going on. The services were conducted by the Rev Mr Parker in the Hawaii[a]n language. He is an American by race but a native of the country. In preaching he spoke apparently very fluently with much graceful gesticulation. The choir was large and sang well. The Organ was played by a white man. In walking about the building during the school hour we came in contact with a party of Old men and women from the Home. Each one of them rose up and greeted us with a shake of the hand and a kind "aloha." One of the women kissed my hand repeatedly which is a mark of great respect. Judge Dole of the Supreme Court had a class of girls in a separate room in which the exercises were conducted in English. The congregation were nearly all natives, many of them were very genteely dressed and appeared very respectable. In the S S was a small class of natives of the Gilbert Islands, under the direction of Mr & Mrs [Hiram] Bingham who had been missionaries on these Islands for 34 years.[19] Mr B was an invalid. In the evening we went to St Andrews . . . The music was fair. The first hymn was a stupid one both as to words and music. The second was "Abide with me" and made us feel perfectly at home.

*3 (Mon)* Went shopping in the morning and purchased James Jackson Jarves *Hawaiian Islands* for the modest sum of $4.50, the same being a cheap 4th edition published here by Henry M Whitney, and also a copy of Miss Birds book on the Islands Putnams Sons publication for $2.75—pretty steep reading.[20] Then I bought a straw hat for $3.50, when I felt I had shopped enough for one morning.

At 3 P M we sailed (and steamed) away on a coaster for Waianae, a plantation about 35 miles northwest around the coast. Mr Irwin accompanied us. Judge [H A] Widemann, to whom the place belongs went ahead of us by land. When within 10 miles of the landing we had a squall with a shower, and the sea got quite rough.

*580*

Mrs Deady was quite seasick all the way. We went ashore in the ships boat about 7 oclock rowing about ¼ of a mile to a substantial pier which projected into the water probably 100 yards. There we were met by Mr Wideman[n][21] and escorted to the house, a distance of near a mile, where we met the manager and his wife, a Mr & Mrs Ahrnes, who treated us most kindly. He is a young German from Hamburg, who was brought up in the beet sugar business. He is a tall robust fellow and a fine specimen of humanity—besides which he concocts an excellent cocktail. His wife is the daughter of a former manager and part owner of the property. She is one half American and the other half Chinese and native. She looks more Chinese than either. She presided at the table with grace and dignity, speaks English, and looks like a lady. Our bedroom was large and airy and contained one of the largest and best beds I ever slept on. The house is one story, covers a deal of land, is surrounded by large verandahs and well and tastily furnished.

*4 (Tue)* After a good breakfast we (Mrs D, Widemann,[22] Irwin, Ahrnes and self) walked down to the mill, distance about a mile, going through a large grove of coconut trees, loaded with fruit which Mr Widemann says he thinks are not less than five or six hundred years old. The mill is a very interesting place and complicated piece of machinery which I will not undertake to describe in detail. Long trains of cars were constantly arriving from the cane fields laden with the cut cane from 6 to 8 feet in length and 1 to 2 inches in diameter. These were cut up and run through successive powerful rollers until they were thoroughly mangled and squeezed as dry as shavings, during which they were carried along on revolving bands until they were dropped in front of the furnace where they were pitchforked into the fire and furnished the heat to make the steam for the mill—no other fuel being used. The juice runs into a vat and is pumped up into the third story, where it is subject to clarifying crystallizing process until it is sacked as sugar—at the rate of 20 tons a day—daylight. In the meantime a considerable quantity of molasses has been drained off by the way which is heated over again and the final residuum is used as a fertilizer.

After "doing" the mill we boarded some cane cars and travelled through the southern part of the valley northerly out towards the mountain in which there were hundreds of acres of cane at different stages of growth. Then we returned to the mill and went up the valley to the mountains in a north-east direction, where several hundred acres had been prepared for planting, but for want of lumber for fluming, the water was not forthcoming; and now they were digging an artesian well on the ground. It is now between five and six hundred feet deep and the water is within 20 feet of the surface, but they are still boring in the hope of getting an overflow. Our ride through and to and from the plantations was about 16 miles which we "did" on an excellent narrow gauge railway at the rate of from 10 to 15 miles an hour. On our return to the house, which is much my idea of an East India Bungalow, we sat down to an excellent luncheon, including fresh coconut in the soft and hard state and the milk of the same. These nuts were pulled for our benefit as the white people here seldom use them and they are allowed to go to waste.

Mrs Ahrnes has 4 children. The two eldest, a boy and girl, were at the table and appeared well. She has a niece with her from Wahaii who is the same caste as herself only less so. She spent 9 years at school in Philadelphia and is a very attractive pleasant woman.

Between 2 & 3 oclock we bade our kind host and hostess good by and started for Honolulu. Mrs Deady took the carriage that Mr Widemann[23] came up in, to avoid the sickness, and he came down with Irwin and myself in a coast steamer that was in the bay taking on sugar. I got home about 7 oclock and found Mrs D at dinner after a pleasant ride. And so ends a very pleasant and interesting excursion. Judge Widemann is a character. He came to the Islands 40 years ago from Hamburg. He married a native. Has a large family of girls, 6 of whom he has educated at an Ursuline convent in Germany, and some of whom are well married here. He is a Romist by tradition, hates Bismarck and don't like the missionaries. He is an intelligent, interesting man however, whom everyone seems to respect notwithstanding his stubborn and unreasoning prejudices. He is very wealthy.

*5 (Wed)* This is election day. A House of Representatives and Nobles is elected throughout the Islands. The affair is passed off very quietly. The opposition has carried the day on this Island with the exception of one representative. Cecil Brown, Marie von Holts uncle was elected on the government ticket. The opposition was supported by the natives and old settlers with native families and relations. The government party represented the intelligence and property of the country and the missionary people and their descendents.

*6 (Thu)* Kept my room all day. Have not had a stool since Saturday. Took some syrup of figs in the morning and had an operation in the afternoon. Called at Dr [Geo] Tro[u]sseaus in the evening and he agreed with me that the difficulty was in the smaller intestines.[24] Said they lacked vermicular motion and gave me a pill of belladonna and nux vomica which he said, by reason of the former would give the desired motion to the bowel, while the latter would act as a tonic on both the bowels and the bladder. Took one of the pills at night and rested quite well. Only got up once and then not to urinate, but to get a drink.

*7 (Fri)* Today felt better. A cool breeze blowing. About 12 oclock the steamer arrived from S F. We were all expectation to hear from home, but got nothing later than a letter from Henderson of the 16th ult, which came to S F just after we left. California has been snowed in on the east and north since the 15th ult. The train got through from the east on the 31st, but were not through from Oregon. The mails might have been sent by steamer from Portland but the department higgled over the cost of $500 a trip. We are so disappointed.

Of course the steamer brought a lot of new passengers to the Hotel. A Mrs Dutton and three children from San Francisco are at our table.[25] She is what they call joly [*sic*]—not in the French sense, but the American. We had a grand concert by the Royal band at the house in the evening. . . .

*8 (Sat)* This is a lovely day, went down town in the morning and bought some late magazines and S F papers. Of course there are no Oregon ones to buy. Bought a copy of Thrums *Hawaiian Annual* for 1890—a very interesting and useful publication for 50 cts. When I got home I found Mrs Harris[26] had sent Mrs D 4 copies of the *Oregonian*—the 20th to the 23 inclusive. . . . and just then the boy came in with copies of the 16 & 17th sent me by mail. . . . We fell to reading the *Oregonians* and never stopped until six numbers were gone through page by page, including editorials, locals and telegrams. It was a great treat, but like to have ruined my eyes—the print is so pale. Why are the publishers so niggardly of their ink. In the evening we rode to Waikiki and back in the cars. The steamer from Australia for San Fran had not arrived at bedtime. I wrote a long letter to Henderson before going to bed. Took another belladonna pill last night which operated on me like a charm today. More than all I did not get up once last night, a thing which has not occurred, lo these 10 years.

*9 (Sun)* The day is cool and cloudy. We went to St Andrews at the morning service and heard Mr Macintosh read his declaration of belief on accepting the appointment of pastor of the Second (the White) Congregation. The singing was hearty and largely congregational—"The Churchs one foundation" being one of the hymns. The sermon was good and related to the speaker and his mission here from his English home. Reading all the afternoon. John Dillon the Irish agitator and his companion Lord St Esmonde[27] arrived this morning on the *Zelandia* from Australia, where they have been "taking toll" for the support of the Irish patriots, that they may live without work. D[illon] is rather a fine looking man, tall and spare, with a dark complexion, black beard and hair and a long well shaped head. Esmonde is a small, modish, genteel looking man with nothing to indicate his rank or position.

In the evening we went to the Fort St church (Congregational) where we heard rather an ingenius and eloquent sermon by the Rev [E G] Beckwith on the importance of the study of the Bible and some of the poorest, trashiest music imaginable.

*10 (Mon)* This morning Mrs D was sick and remained in bed. She was so dizzy she couldn't rise. Sent for Dr Trousseau but he could not come until 12 oclock. Gave her a couple of anti-febrine pills, and told her to take one then and the other in the morning and she would be well. In the afternoon, she had a good sleep and awoke refreshed and better. . . . Called at Cogswells studio and inspected Mrs Deadys picture. It will be I think a good picture, but not perfect by any means.

The people of the house and the men of wars men had a dance in the hotel last evening. We were invited to be present. Mrs Deady made an effort and dressed herself and we went in and staid until after 11. . . .

*11 (Tue)* Mrs Deady is better this morning and able to be up and about. It has been raining softly since early this morning, but now (20 min after 11) it has stopped and the sun is coming out. . . . The weather was fair and cool in the afternoon. The party returned from the volcanoe, wonderfully impressed with the sight and full of the feeling, that the exploit involved great hardship and danger—how much no one knows. [Chas] Lombard has been in all evening giving us the details in a serio-comic vein.[28]

*12 (Wed)* In the morning went down to Waikiki with Mrs Deady and party of ladies from the Hotel to attend a pic nic given by Mrs Joseph Carter. The pic nic was given at the [Saml M] Damon place but I went on to the Hotel place to take my bath. At the end of the tramway Lombard met me with a carriage and drove me to the place, where I had a splendid bath and swim. The bottom is excellent and you can go from a pier at once into the water up [*incomplete*]. After the bath . . . I came up to the pic nic ground which was at the Damons summer house on the beach. There were between 30 & 40 persons present, mostly ladies. An excellent lunch was served on pretty wooden platters under the shade of four gnarled trees whose branches interlaced together made an ample and comfortable shade for the party. Met Gen [Jas F B] & Mrs Marshal[l][29] with the former of whom I had a long and interesting talk of early times in the Islands including the appointment and removal of T J Dryer of Portland as U S Commissioner here.

*13 (Thu)* Today. Dined at the Stevens, the American Minister where I met Mr [Jonathan] Austin,[30] the Minister of Foreign Affairs, and his daughter also Dr & Mrs Derr of the *Nipsic.* Mr & Mrs Stevens are nice old people from Augusta, Maine, who have taken a good deal of finish on to[o] plain but strong foundations. They have two cultivated and charming daughters. The dinner was elegant, but it was of the tropics and not satisfying. There was no wine, and singularly enough I did not notice the omission until we got home. Mr Austin is a New Yorker, plain, strong and full of good sense. Mrs Derr is a woman of fine cultivation and excellent speech. She and her husband are from Md, and show it. Had a sea bath in the morning, and called at Mrs Carters and on the Marshal[l]s in the afternoon.

*14 (Fri)* It rained last night and this morning in torrents. I heard that from 12 M until 10 today when it practically cleared up the fall was 5½ inches. The *Australia* was to sail this morning at 10, but it was postponed until 12, then 3 and lastly until 10 tomorrow. Waiting for bananas coming in from the country I understand. In the meantime there has been a running to and fro in the hotel and a shaking of hands and bidding good by to those who are going away. Early in the morning the steps of the hotel were covered with native men and women, mostly the latter, with baskets and armfuls of flower garlands which you are expected to buy at 25 cents apiece and hang around the necks and on the arms of your going friends. . . . In the evening went to dinner at the Macintoshes, where we met Gen Marshall besides the family. Had an excellent dinner. Marie [von Holt] was present and sat beside [me] and was very entertaining. Marshal[l], Mrs Mac and Marie sang a song with solos and did it quite well. He [*Genl Marshall*] is 72 years of age and was here 51 years ago and remained here about 31 years in business since which he has lived in Boston.

*15 (Sat)* At 12 oclock the *Australia* got off with our friends leaving a lot of strangers in their place. Early in the morning the *Mariposa* came in from S F and we got letters from home, but not later than the 27th ult, and *Oregonians* to the 26th. . . . Also clipping from the *Alta* [*California*] containing a dispatch from Portland via Chicago, to the effect that the melted snow had sent the Wallamet river out of its banks all along the valley and out onto 2d street in Portland, and almost destroyed the railway in southern Oregon. Spent the day in reading the *Oregonian* and visiting the fish market in the afternoon. Haven't felt so well today. Passed some blood through the ureth[r]a last night.

*16 (Sun)* Remained at home today. Was feeling quite unwell. My urine was thick and clouded. Mrs Deady went to church in the morning. I put in my time mostly on my back reading the *Oregonian.* The day was lovely though a little warm. Consul Severance called in the evening, and gave me the S F *Bulletin* containing Justice Fields remarks at the Justice Centenary in New York and the burning of Secretary [of Navy B F] Tracys house in Washington and the death of his wife and daughter. A terrible calamity indeed. Fields speech has a good deal of "states rights" in it and rather irrelevantly brought forward I think.[31]

*17 (Mon)* Drove to the Palis this morning. Took Marie von Holt with us. The dinner was perfect and the drive charming, except the shaking gave me a pain in the groin. Finally (in about 1½ hours) we arrived at the summit and looked down the precipice, a distance of 800 feet, and over the beautiful valley and sea beyond. There is a road cut in the side of the mountain, down to the valley over which the natives were passing to and fro on shoeless horses and driving pack trains laden with rice in sacks and other things. After feasting our eyes on the sublime and picturesque spectacle a reasonable time we came home. I spent the rest of the day on my back reading . . . Judge Judd has presented me with a copy of his mothers reminiscences of her island life.[32] She came here in 18[28] and the book was written in 1860. I will commence reading it today. Last night was a very uncomfortable one. Was up 4 times. Did not sleep well. A pain in my groin.

*18 (Tue)* . . . In the morning Mr Bishop called as per previous arrangement and drove us out behind his noble bays to the Kamehameha Schools. The visit was an interesting one. The schools are industrial as well as scholastic. The boys are charged $40 a year which includes instruction, board and lodging. They spend an 1½ [hour] each day in the shops under the charge of a foreman or instructor, engaged in carpentering, wood turning, tinning, shoemaking and blacksmithing—the latter was the only shop in which the boys were at work. The place was a primitive one with one stationary and two little portable forges. The principal workman engaged in bending a piece of iron about an inch wide and ⅝ of an inch thick so as to make a right angle. It was done tolerably well after a great deal of pottering. The hammers were light and the peen end was round and pointed instead of being wide and sharp. They worked in their bare feet and occasionally caught a cinder. They don't weld much or else they would have to wear shoes.

A lot of boys were on the ground playing ball, and a number were in school at their lessons. The latter manifested the usual extraordinary ability to write and spell sentences from dictation. The school buildings are all new and of first class. The dormitories contain a room for each boy, wash rooms & bath rooms. The water is furnished by an artesian well about [*omitted*] feet deep with an overflow of 25 feet from which it is pumped into separate tanks in the top of large towers, from which it flows all over the grounds and buildings. The schools and grounds are the gift of Mr Bishops late wife, the last of the Kamehameha dynasty and the inheritor of much of their wealth.[33] The grounds contain about [*omitted*] acres. Mr B has supplemented his wifes generosity by building a handsome school house for small boys—where they are prepared for the higher one. Also a large handsome stone building for a museum in which he intends to deposit his fine collection of Hawaiian curios. He is also building an assembly house of stone which must cost a deal of money. . . .

*19 (Wed)* This Ash Wednesday. I was not able to be out. Pain in the region of the bladder. Have taken too much exercise. Mrs Deady went to church in the morning. In the afternoon, half past 1, we took breakfast at the Irwins where we met "Sam" Parker, a large handsome half caste who keeps cattle on Mauna Loas sides, about 4000 feet above the level of the sea. He speaks English very well. The breakfast was simple but delicious and the hostess was charming. With it all we had a glass of hock from the Rhine that has not left its superior behind it. Met Mrs Irwins charming little girl, Helen, after dinner. She is about two years old. Talks French like a Parisienne, and sings a pretty little native song and understands English. Her mother and nurse speak French to her altogether.

As we walked home went into the Cathedral grounds where we heard or saw a young Chinam[an] teaching a class of 12 Chinese children to sing church hymns while he plaid [*sic*] a reed organ. They sang in their own language and did very well. I think the children range from 5 to 8 years of age, the sexes being about evenly divided. We then turned into the Church where we witnessed the funeral services of an aged Hawaiian woman. A good many respectable people of her race were in attendance. The services were in the Hawaiian tongue throughout and were conducted by the Bishop [*Alfred Willis*], Mr Macintosh & another clergyman whose name I don't know.

Judging from the time it took Mr Mac to read the Epistle to the Corinthians it must take more words or sounds to express an idea than it does in English. One of the hymns that was sung was Troytes Chant—"My God my Father while I stay"—I could accompany the congregation very well in English, so there must have been no more sounds than in the English version. In the evening called on Dr Day, a homeopathic physician about my bladder trouble. Talked the matter over and made an appointment for 9 oclock in the morning.[34]

*20 (Thu)* Had an acute pain in the bladder region during the latter part of the night and urinated frequently. Called on Dr Day as per appointment. He examined my water under the microscope and said the turbidity resulted from mucous and pus thrown off the walls of the bladder, but he saw no evidence of crystalene formation in it, indicating the presence or probability of gravel. Nor did he see any sign of albumen or sugar. Approved of the wash I am using, hypermangan and proposed to administer it to me tomorrow morning. Gave [me] a bottle of half pellets that look like split peas and taste like brandy sauce with directions to take one every half hour. I am very much pleased with the doctors conversation and manner. He don't slop over. Been on my back since 10 oclock reading Mrs Judd, part of the time with a hot water bag on my bladder, but the pain has ceased some time since.

In the evening we went to a reception at Mr Bishops given to Gen & Mrs Marshal[l]. The house is a large place built by one of the old Princesses who died without issue and left it to Mr Bishops wife, who is also dead. The company consisted I imagine of the elite foreign and native of Honolulu. The dining room

is very large and the refreshments were excellent. We went at ½ past 8 and
returned at 10 and were among the last that went.

*21 (Fri)* Got up with a sharp pain in my left testicle from which I have suffered
all day. Only made water twice last night but have done so every 10 minutes today.
Called on Dr Day this morning and he washed my bladder out with a solution
of boric acid. Voided a good deal of pus. Put a flannel cloth saturated with pain
killer on my testicle, and it is easier now. The epedidymus has got bruised
somehow. Finished Mrs Judds book today. It is a model book of the kind. Also
read Dr [Joseph] Holts[35] address on the race problem delivered Jan 15th in the
Unitarian church at Portland. He takes my ground that the slave trade and Negro
slavery were the means providential or otherwise by which the negro was educated and prepared for his present career of self dependence. . . .

*22 (Sat)* This is the anniversary of Washingtons birthday. I remember or noted
it more particularly by an incident personal to myself. On this day 22 years ago
on the old steamship [*Ajax*] on the bar of the Columbia river I threw away the
pipe and have never smoked since. A good riddance. Today is a lovely one and
the Americans are calling on the American minister, Mr Stevens. I am sorry I was
unable to go, and Mrs Deady did not like to go alone. Went over the February
magazines again, and read several articles theretofor [*sic*] omitted. Among these
are Gladstone and Blaines tariff articles. Both right and both wrong. Blaine
certainly makes a good point against the "old man," when he says that if free
trade is good for England, it does not follow, that it is good for the U S.

. . . I was on my back nearly all day nursing my poor cods, but had to get
up to make water nearly every hour. Only voided a small quantity and that often
with much pain. The cause was apparent when I came to draw my water in the
evening—I had difficulty in passing the catheter under the prostate gland. Well
how this is going to end I don't know, and it may be best for me that I don't. . . .

*23 (Sun)* Dr Day had trouble in inserting the catheter this morning but succeeded.
Says it is too large. How doctors differ. Sonnefeld said the one furnished by Bevan
was too large and now Day says that the one furnished by the former is too large.
I am inclined to think they are all right. Spent the day on my back reading and
meditating and wishing I was at home. Tried to insert the catheter before going
to bed but failed, and for the first time. Felt despondent.

*24 (Mon)* Dr Day used a smaller catheter this morning and inserted it without
any trouble. Had a pretty good rest last night. Was up 4 times and made my water
without difficulty and it looked healthy. My testicle is getting better, but the
swelling or thickening of the skin recedes very slowly. Had a better appetite today
than for some time past. It has rained much of the time yesterday and today. The
temperature is delightful—about 74. The time of the arrival of the mail and our
departure for home draws nigh or nigher and I am very anxious for both to
come. . . .

*25 (Tue)* On my back all day, reading one thing or another. In the evening went
to dinner at Mr Godfrey Browns . . . The dinner was not elaborate but excellent
—particularly the fish.

*26 (Wed)* This is Mrs Deadys 55th birthday. The doctor washed my bladder with a solution of manganese this morning and from the time I came home until I went to bed I was driven to make water at least every half hour which was attended with a good deal of pain, and this although I was on my back most of the time. Put on a suspensory this morning and find it quite agreeable. Read the January number of *19th Century* through today, and Huxleys article on Rousseauism twice. He demolishes the "born free and equal" proposition which lies at the bottom of it, and which Jefferson with his congenial Gallic mind worked into our Declaration of Independence—"More's the pity."

*27 (Thu)* Up every hour last night until towards morning when I got a couple of hours sleep. The doctor washed my bladder this morning with warm water only. After I came home got down on the sofa about ½ past 10 and slept sweetly until nearly 1. . . .

. . . Begin to count the time it will take to reach home where I wish I was now. . . .

*March 1 (Sat)* Rained hard this morning. Was washed out as usual. Water improving. Spent the day mostly on my back. . . . Took a hot bath in the afternoon.

*2 (Sun)* Went to church at 11:15 at St Andrews and stayed to Communion. Macintosh had a short plain sermon. Spent the rest of the day on my back. . . . This evening the mosquitos were very bad and we burnt buhach which silenced [them] but in the morning they commenced to rise from the floor where they had dropped when stupified.[36]

*3 (Mon)* After returning from Dr Days I drove to the Spreckels building where I visited Mr Cogswells studio and made my last criticism on Mrs Deadys picture—to the effect that the face is too short and I thought it was in the chin. On comparison with a photograph he agreed with me and said he would alter it. I walked back to the hotel and soon passed some blood through the ureth[r]a, whether from the ride or walk I can't say, but think the former. Kept on my back the rest of the day and felt better by evening. . . .

*4 (Thu)* Went to Dillinghams to lunch at 1 P M. A lovely place about 2 miles from the Hotel a short ways off the Waikiki road. The grounds include about 10 acres. The house is a one story frame covering a good deal of ground with a large lanai and conservatory. The inside is beautifully and curiously furnished. The lunch was elegant and palatable. Had fresh grapes, the first I have seen on the islands. They were the Concord and were very good. I was hungry for grapes and enjoyed them. Met Mrs Dillinghams father, Mr [Lowell] Smith an old missionary who has been on the Islands since sometime in the thirties. Mrs D was born here. She and her husband were fellow passengers with us from San Francisco. She was returning from the east from which she brought a copy of the first Bible printed in the Hawaiian language in 1838. It was sent to her grandfather, Dr Moses Smith, Springfield, Mass in 1840 by his son, her father. Mechanically considered it is a great curiosity. The print is good, but the form is so small that it is almost as thick as it is long. We met here Mr & Mrs Frank Damon, Chinese teachers and missionaries.[37] He is the son of the missionary known as Father, for long the pastor of the Seamens Bethel here and the publisher and editor of *The Friend.* He is a very bright intelligent man, both well read and travelled. Mrs Damon is of the third generation of Chinese Missionaries. Her maiden name is Haffen and she was born near Pittsburg and was taken to China at 6 months old where she grew up with the exception of 3 or 4 years spent in . . . school at Steubenville, Ohio. She is one of the loveliest women I ever saw, and has the face of a Madon[n]a. I enjoyed her very much indeed. She has two pretty little girls, the youngest one still in arms, called Viola and Vera. Felt no ill effects from my ride but passed a little blood.

*5 (Wed)* Visited Dr Day who washed me out, the first time since Monday. My water in good condition. Visited Mr Damons Chinese school situate near Dr Days office. Heard a class recite a lesson in Physical and Historical geography of the Islands. They were I think from 8 to 10 years of age and did very well. Visited a room under charge of a good looking young Chinese woman, and another under charge of two young white women. Mr Damon speaks the language, but the instruction is all in English as it ought to be. He is very enthusiastic in his work and I think very disinterested.

At 1 oclock we went to a lunch given us at Mr Bishops . . . After lunch we visited Mr Bishops curio room, where there is a superb collection of native Kahilis and other relics of the past.[38]

In the evening the Royal band played at the Hotel and we had a call from Mr & Mrs Irwin and Mr Godfrey Brown. Mr I left me the *Call* of the 14 & 15 ult from which I learned that the road between Portland & San Francisco would be open throughout in about a week and that the President had nominated Mr Hanford for the district judgeship of Washington, with which I am pleased or think I am.[39]

*6 (Thu)* Rained all night and all the forenoon. Called on Dr Trousseau and settled my bill—$10 for two visits and medicines and got a bottle of the belladonna pills and the prescription for the same. An interesting old man. He is of the opinion that there is some encrustation on the wall of the bladder, which causes the bleeding after exercise. Went to Mr Bishops bank and took up my checks amounting to $535.55 for which I gave a draft, in duplicate, on the bank of California. He charged me nothing for the exchange and has been very polite to us since we have been here.

Yesterday I gave Cogswell $30 for Mrs Deadys picture. He wanted to paint it in discharge of some obligation he considered himself under to me and probably in part as an advertisement. He said [he] would not take but $25—the cost of material. A great many of the leading people in the town have been to see it, and it has proved a good advertisement for his studio.

Miss Mary [*sic*] von Holt dined with us last evening. She couldn't stay and spend the evening with us, she was so busy. Organ to play at church at 7 oclock and then choir practice. She will wear herself out before she has lived out half her days. It still rains and pours down. Sent cards to some persons in the house, who were not in.

*7 (Fri)* It rained and blew hard nearly all night and is still at it. Everything in the house is getting damp. No word of the *Australia* yet but she is not expected until the afternoon.

12 oclock the *Alameda* was sighted 5 miles offshore. She came to the bar but the pilot could not go out and she stood off. The bar is very rough and unless there is a lull in the storm she will not come in and we will be left here for a week to go on the *Australia.* Well we will see, but must submit and make the best of it. The rain ceased about one oclock, and the wind has abated some. I believe I never saw it rain as it did between 10 & 12 oclock. Between 1 & 2 I went to Dr Days and he pumped and washed me out. Paid him my bill of $30—about $2 a treatment, I think he is a good physician and a gentleman. My water was in good condition. He made a siphon contrivance to use in washing my bladder such as he used, which is much better than the syringe. Rode down town at 2 oclock and got consular certificate for Mrs Deadys picture. Bought 7 Samoan photoes, a model of a native boat and a little tortoise plaque. Got the Koa (Ko) bowl as I came home, made to order, for which I paid $3.50. In the evening went to a dinner at the Hamilton House given by Chief Justice Judd to the Bench & Bar. About 35 persons present, members of the bar nearly all of them, which included several good looking natives and half breeds and one Chinese. I sat at the Chief Justices right and Judge Widemann at his left. Judges Bickerton and McCully sat at the cork ends of the horseshoe table while we sat at the toe end. The dinner was elaborate and each guest [ *?furnished*] with an elegant menu, in cover, containing the names of the guests and the music played by the Royal band. There was no wine, the Chief Justice being a teetotaller. Towards the end of the course glasses of soda and ginger ale were passed around and I took two of the latter. Speeches were made by several of the guests on subjects connected with the profession of law and the administration of justice, previously suggested by the host. I was unexpectedly called up as number 3 and made a little speech in which I ran a parallel between the settlement of Oregon and the Islands by missionaries and the secular element in which I characterized the first traders here as a cross between the pirate and mercantile adventurer, and paid the missionaries a compliment as having been the devoted teachers and leaders in every good work tending to the elevation and improvement of the native race spiritually and economically. I also complimented the Supreme Court, and said that so long as it was composed of judges holding office during good behavior and in the assured receipt of a comfortable compensation, they might expect a fair and impartial administration of Justice. In the report of the affair in this mornings *Advertiser,* favorable notice was made of my speech—the only fault, it was too short.

*8 (Sat)* Day came in clear. The Steamer *Australia* arrived off Diamond head in the night. The bar too rough to cross. Wind wearing round to the west. At ½ past 1 the *Alameda* crossed in and the *Australia* is now (4:15) coming in. Have just had word from the agent Irving, that there was a room reserved on deck for us but that we could have the bridal room downstairs, the best cabin in the ship and advised us to take it, which I did. Went down to the office and got my ticket and room 1 on the main deck, a bridal chamber. Got my passport also. Bought another Samoa fan from a man who just brought up a lot on the *Alameda.* At 4 oclock called at Bishop Willis', and had a delightful visit with him and his pleasant wife, besides a cup of tea and a piece of bread and butter made on the spot. She loaned me [Annie] Besants, *All Sorts and Conditions of Men* to read on the voyage home.[40]

The *Australia* came in and in the evening we had a deluge of letters and some papers from home.

*9 (Sun)* Slept none last night. The effect—I suppose of the letters and papers I read last night the former up to the 22 ult and the latter up to the 9th. Got up at 7 and made this entry and closed the book until we reach San Francisco. Weather quiet and fair.

San Francisco. Got away from Honolulu at ½ past 10 in room No 1 on the dining room floor, which we enjoyed much more than the room on deck because of the abundance of room. Seasick the first two days, but regularly at table after that. The last four days of the voyage were lovely. The fare was excellent. The master—Capt Morse—was kind and entertaining and the passengers agreeable.

*16 (Sun)* We reached Farallone Islands on Saturday at ½ past 2 and were taken in charge by a S F pilot. Got to the dock and got ashore at 5 oclock and drove to the Occidental with our hand baggage leaving the trunks with the customs house officers. Got comfortable rooms on the second floor (No 108). Here we met letters and papers from home which occupied [us] until bedtime. Nothing unusual except that Mr Henderson is still quite sick. Sent a telegram to Paul in the evening. Got an answer this morning that Mr Henderson was "Comfortable. No radical change." Went to Trinity church, Mrs Deady staid in. Met Mrs Hatch as we came out and she gushed over me a good deal while I was waiting for the car. Judge Sawyer called this afternoon. He has lost his daughter, Mrs Adams, since we were here and looks sad. Dr & Mrs Derr of the *Nipsic* were fellow passengers with us from Honolulu and are stopping at the house. We have become quite friends. She is a very agreeable and interesting person to me. . . .

*17 (Mon)* San Pats day. The Irish are getting modest in S F and celebrate this day in doors, omitting the usual shirt parade. Went up to Vails in the morning and arranged for the framing of Mrs Deadys picture . . . Went to the U S court rooms where I saw Sawyer & Hoffman. Saw Mr Collector [Timothy] Phelps and got an order for the delivery of two pieces of dress goods that were taken from Mrs Deadys trunk on the impression that they were imported, when in fact she bought them in Portland and took them with her instead of leaving them here. The Collector behaved very well about it. . . . Got the *Oregonian* of the 14th inst in which I see that Scott pays his respects to Judge Thayer.[41]

*18 (Tue)* The day came in cool and wet and has continued so. Did not get up last night until ½ past 4 and not again until ½ past 6. I have remained at home. . . I intended to work on the revision of my biography today, a copy of which was sent from Bancroft last evening. But I have been so much occupied with company that I did not have time. Will try it tonight.

*19 (Wed)* A beautiful day. Remained in the house until 4 oclock looking over [David] Sessions draft of my biography. Leaving out what he copies from my dictation—my early life, prior to taking my seat in the legislature in the fall of 1850, and Mr [C E S] Woods analysis of my judicial character and career, there is but little of it, and that is loose and undiscriminating. I will give him one more chance at it, and [if] he don't do better—inform himself—I'll draw out of the enterprise. Went to the P[acific] U[nion] club in the afternoon and saw a few of the old faces in the card room . . . Judge Pratt made Mrs Deady a present of $100 wherewith to buy a present for herself. Today we purchased at Shreves a 2 stoned diamond ring with the money. I contributed a sketch of his judicial career in Oregon, to the Bancroft biography for which he feels kindly, and on this and other accounts growing out of a 40 years acquaintance and friendship—hence this present I suppose. . . .

20 (Thu) A beautiful day. Dined with Mrs Walter Smith at the Pleasanton.[42] Mrs Foster was invited but could not leave her mother. However she came after dinner and spent the evening. Both Mrs S & F were agreeable but the former is so ingenuous and natural. Called at Pratts about ½ past 8 and got home after 10. The Pratt parlor is beautifully furnished. Mrs P was sumptuously dressed and agreeable. The Judge took Mrs D upstairs and showed her the boy and his mothers bath room.

21 (Fri) Another beautiful day. . . . Went to S[anborn] & V[ails] and paid for the picture frame ($30) and had the package sent to Wells Fargo & Co. Called on John Valentine and had a pleasant chat with him and then home and on the lounge. . . .

In the evening Harry Toomy called. Had not seen him for a long time and enjoyed him.

Got a telegram from Paul this evening that Grandpa much better.

22 (Sat) Went to the Matinee at Baldwins with Mrs H H Bancroft to see the Kendals [William and Dame Margaret] in the "Maitre de Forge"—the Iron Master, and enjoyed it very much.[43] The acting was excellent. Unlike most plays—the action commenced with the marriage and ended with the reconciliation of the parties. Rained in the afternoon. In the evening we dined at Mr Eugene Meyers w[h]ere we met an interesting and intelligent family of a mother and eight children—3 boys and 5 girls, the 3 eldest being of the latter. The second one Elise was my company at table and most of the evening, and contributed not a little to the pleasure of the same. The father is a French Jew, and the family hope to see France recover Elsas [sic] again, while I hope the contrary. The dinner was good and the wine excellent.

23 (Sun) A beautiful day. We went to Trinity church in the morning. Walked down to Montgomery with Mr & Mrs Alvord. I dined in the evening with the Pratts. Mrs Deady did not go on account of her fathers condition. . . . The dinner was good—a saddle of mutton was the piece de resistance. Mrs P is quite interesting and agreeable. O C was very kind and happy. He has got himself beautifully surrounded in his old age. Got telegrams and letters during the past few days as to Mr Hendersons condition. Will probably not live long. I hope we will get home before he dies.

24 (Mon) Another beautiful day. A through train starts for Portland today. Have engaged our passage for Wednesday. In the purchase of tickets from Coles to Ashland the clerk laid down $2.80 change on the counter which I forgot to pick up and when I went back for it, it was gone. In the evening dined with Mrs

Ashburner at the Pleasanton. . . .

*25 (Tue)* Got a telegram from Ed Failing last evening saying that Father Henderson was worse. On the strength of this I tried to get our transportation changed [to] today, but could not. . . . Mr & Mrs [B B] Tuttle called this morning. Just arrived from Portland on the steamer. They are very [happy] have received since we left $60,000 for a portion of his interest in the land on which the new town of Anacortes is being built on the Sound. I am rejoiced at their good fortune.

*26 (Wed)* Another beautiful day but it rained last night. We leave for Portland today and this journal will be closed until we reach there. Will get home with a few dollars and no debts.

*April 3 (Thu)* We left San Francisco on the evening of the 26 in the drawing room of the car Santa Barbara. At ½ past 9 on Thursday morning we were detained by a slide between tunnels 9 & 10 on the upper Sacramento for 5 hours. We reached Ashland in the evening at ½ past 9 and Glendale some time before day on Friday morning where we waited until 9 oclock before starting through Cow Creek Canyon. We travelled at a snails pace through this canyon on account of the condition of the road. We left Roseburg at ½ past 1 and reached home at ½ past 11. Stopped at Edward Failings, driving first to Catlins to see Mr Henderson whom we found better than we thought.

Saturday [*March 29*] I remained in doors all day. On Sunday afternoon was in my chambers a short time. Monday we went into our rooms at Mrs Hills. . . . Spent the day in my chambers and was glad to get home once more where I could get a good meal, bath and bed. Tuesday & Wednesday sat in the district court. Wrote up my accounts and paid my bills for the past quarter. Wrote a number of letters and replied to many that I found here on my return. Sat in the D C today. Wrote a letter to Capt Ellicott in reply to his announcing the death of Mrs E. Ought to have done it before but could not. The weather has been quite pleasant since our return. Dr Sonnefeld called to see me today and we had a long talk about my case. He thinks from the occasional discharge of blood that there is some encrustation about the neck of the bladder. He is going to examine me on Tuesday evening, but if there is any encrustation there he does not wish to operate for it, as he is out of practice, and thinks I had better go to New York. Oh dear me!

*5 (Sat)* Yesterday—Good Friday—I went to church and heard rather an interesting sermon from Mr Cole from the 2 chap of Phillippians 4–9 verses. The congregation I thought was large for the day, but as usual mostly women.

This is a rainy day, a drizzly day. I have been doing chores yesterday and today. I have felt better than usual. Last night took up *Mr Isaacs* by Marion Crawford and worked through about ¼ of it and then looked at the closing chapter.[44] It is a queer thing and nothing like what I anticipated. I was rather pleased with some philosophical suggestions in the first chapter on the rise of adventurers and favorites in Democracies and despotisms, but I soon tired of the story which is highly artifical and altogether unreal and improbable. . . .

*12 (Sat)* Sunday (April 6) Attended morning prayer at Trinity as usual. The first time for 3 months. It was Easter day. Attended the S S festival at Trinity at 4 P

M. Brother Dodd was at the fore as usual. . . .

. . . Friday evening commenced my lectures on Constitutional law before the senior class of the school of law in my chambers. It snowed a little yesterday and is cool today. Read *Mr Isaacs* by Marion Crawford. It is hash plus a little Bud[d]hism.

*19 (Sat)*. . . Judge Hanford of the Washington district has been assigned to hold court in this district. He appeared and took his seat at the opening of the court. We have arranged that he will hold the Circuit court and I the district court between now and June. . . .

. . . Col Kelly and his wife put in an appearance at our hostelry on Thursday. They are going to Europe with the Fields in June. . . .

*26 (Sat)* Sunday [*last*] . . . Met Bellinger at my chambers at 2 oclock and talked over an injunction that he has applied for to restrain the land commissioners from selling his clients swamp land as forfeited to the State. Made the order to show cause on Monday. Called on Kate and the baby and to see Mr Henderson whom I fear is near deaths door. . . .

Have suffered a good deal during the week . . . Better now. Mr Henderson is still alive but daily grows weaker. Weighed today and turned the scale at 232 pounds.

*May 3 (Sat)* Sunday (April 27) Attended morning prayer at Trinity. Mr [Wm] Lund officiated. A clever sensible man from the north of England but unfortunately he can't speak United States. In the afternoon took Edward Failing on the Cable railway on to the heights. Pleasant ride and a grand sight. Came home by Mr Catlins and called to see Mr Henderson. The old man is gradually sinking and may not last long. . . . Am reading the report of the Parnell Commission. It will gradually settle the hash for the Fenian & Land League respondents, including Parnell. It is a d——d tale of unprincipled demagoguery and agrarian outrage by "the finest *pisantry* in the world." When their blood is up or their ignorant and bitter prejudices are aroused, assassination or a stab in the back or a blow in the dark is their natural gait.[45]

The weather has been charming during the week. Called on Camilla Urso on Thursday afternoon. She has aged some since she was here 12 years ago. . . . Got a letter from Justice Field enclosing some certificates of stock in the mines at Wardner [Idaho] which Goldsmith is to redeem or take back at 40 cents on the dollar. Poor Barney, his friends all come back on him when the mine fails. This evening went to the Camilla Urso concert at the Grand. . . . Enjoyed Urso, particularly the last piece, the "Reverie," and [Mrs E H] Palmer[46] and [Mrs Rose] Reed. Urso told me that their voices were phenomenal.

*10 (Sat)*. . . [*Last*] Monday evening partook of wine and biscuit with the officers of the 9th Regiment of the O[regon] N[ational] G[uard] and their military guests from Vancouver barracks Gen Gibbon, Col Sumner et al at which a good many crude little speeches were made, of which I did some. Mr Corbett and myself were the only civilians present and he made himself solid with the warriors by agreeing or rather proposing to furnish a prize of $100 to be competed for in a drill between the O N G and the Regulars. . . . The week has been cool and sometimes cloudy. The river is 17 feet above low water mark with the Snake well out and the Columbia coming. My health I think is still improving, and also my special ailment. Sonnefeld comes to see me once a week now. Mrs Deady and I called at the DeHarts this evening. We went all over their new house. It is a gem indeed. Our new choir is going very well. [Fred] Gilmore is bass now. He has a good deal of skill and taste but not many good notes. Mrs Palmer is superb.

*17 (Sat)* . . . Monday was my 66th birthday. Took Box "C" at the Marquam to hear [Edw H] Sothern[47] in "Lord Chumley" and invited Mrs Deady, Mr Brooke, Lucy Failing and Blanche Catlin to sit with me. The play was well done. . . .

Lectured to the senior class law school on Friday night. Commenced reading Leas *History of the Inquisition.* What a picture of the corruption and degradation of the church in the tenth, eleventh and twelfth centuries, he draws. Tuesday evening attended Dr Houghtons lecture on Browning, very interesting, but too long. He is a very clever lecturer indeed. The weather has been very cool for the past two days, for the time of year. . . .

*24 (Sat)* . . . Sat in the C C & D C during the week. Wrote and delivered opinion in the habeas corpus case of Wong Hams wife and child in which I held that a Chinese merchant entitled to enter the U S might bring his wife and minor child with him, without a certificate. . . .

. . . . The weather has been delightful this week. My general health about the same. My water works not so good. Dr Sonnefeld seems to be at his wits end. Prof Thornton has prepared my annual report as president of the Regents. Lectured to the law class on Monday evening. Will finish next week, I hope. Attended Mrs W[alter] Smiths grand party at the Palace [*Portland Hotel*] on Tuesday evening. A beautiful affair. Went home at ½ past 12.

*31 (Sat)* . . . Monday sold the 4th Presbyterian church note & mortgage for $2000, interest paid until May 9 belonging to Mrs Deady to Mr Ladd at par and bought a certificate (one 15th) on the Palatine Hill property for her for $2700. The certificate represents an undivided 9 acres. Bought of Robert Bell[48] who acted for the owner [*omitted*] Jones. This is Mrs Deadys speculation not mine. I loaned her $700.

Sat in the C C & D C during the week. Have appointed and commissioned about 75 inspectors of election in this town and county. My annual report for 1888–9 as president of the Regents was published in the *Oregonian* of the 29th. Prof Thornton helped me prepare it. It ought to have been done last fall, but I got sick and could not do it.

On Monday & Tuesday nights heard Locke Richardson read Dickens *Xmas Carol* and "Macbeth."[49] Took Mrs Deady and Henderson. It was a great treat. Dined with he and his wife at Montgomerys on Sunday evening. I was better of my bleeding the first of the week but relapsed again on Thursday and Friday. We have had a gracious and welcome rain this week with a promise of more for which the country is and will be thankful. Father Henderson has been better this week. Swore in 41 dep marshals today.

*June 7 (Sat)* . . . Monday a general election. I did not vote for governor. Voted for Catlin, Snow & Couch [Flanders] on the Dem legislative ticket and for the treasurer & commissioner on the same. . . .

Tuesday wrote a little critique or eulogy on Mr Richardsons Recitations for Miss [Ella] Sabin, which was published in the *Oregonian*. He called on me on Thursday and gave me circular in which my essay was printed in full. . . .

On Tuesday Dr Rodney Glisan, Rector, Warden and vestryman of Trinity church died of appoplexy. He was buried on Wednesday from Trinity church and the vestry were the pall bearers. I did not feel able to go to the grave yard and therefore dropped out of the procession at the church. He did well for himself and his own in this world, and further than that this deponenth sayeth not.

*14 (Sat)* Sunday . . . evening [*June 8*] the Bishop preached the Baccalaureate sermon for the Bishop Scott Academy to a very full house but a very poor one in a pecuniary sense. . . .

Monday evening attended the laying of the cornerstone of the new St Helens Hall at 5 oclock. Mr Loveridge made the address. Did not amount to much, was archaic and out of touch with the age and the surroundings. Mr Cole ought to have made the address. He would have had something to say that people would have listened to. . . .

Mrs Deady went to Yamhill with her father yesterday. Got a note from John in the evening saying that they got him on his bed in the parlor on the old place by 12 oclock and that he stood the trip well, but broke down when he found himself at home on the old place where he had lived 40 years. . . . Had a letter from Judge Sawyer today concerning his son Prescotts difficulty. He acted in self defense.[50] Weighed today, drew 230 a loss of 2 pounds since last time.

*21 (Sat)* . . . Saturday evening June 14th attended a delivery of the "Merchant of Venice" by Mr Locke Richardson at the hall of the High school. Barring the everlasting climb to the Hall, it was a most delightful and interesting entertainment. I call it "delivery" for want of a better word. Neither "reading" nor "recital" are adequate, as they do not express the dramatic action involved in his performance. Besides which is his introductory exposition of the play and casual comments in the progress of it. Sat in the C C & D C during the week, except Thursday and Friday when I was at Eugene attending a meeting of the Regents and the commencement. . . .

The Regents employed Philura E Murch as tutor at a salary of $1000 a year, and voted $1000 to the school of medicine. The country about Eugene and as far north as Harrisburg looks very dry and the crops are short. The late rain has improved them some and may more. There was no rain of any consequence fell in April or May. Got home from Eugene last evening. Left Mrs Deady there. She was going over to Murchs and will be back on Monday. Still reading Leas *His of the Inquisition.* Near the end of the 2d volume. Read the *murder* according to the canon law of Huss and Jerome of Prague last evening. A black page in the history of the church, indeed. The weather has been showery and cool during the week and this has prolonged the life of the strawberry, for which I am duly thank [f]ul. . . .

*28 (Sat)* . . . Friday evening went with Mrs Deady to hear "The Senator" at the M[arquam] G[rand] and enjoyed it much. A good genteel American comedy, full of hearty honest fun and hits and here and there a bit of good, natural pathos. . . .

Attended the Convention yesterday of the Episcopal church of this Diocese. Prepared two Resolutions creating two boards of trustees, one for the schools and the other for the Hospital, which passed today. The trustees hold at the pleasure of the Convention. This morning there was an attempt led by Dodd to have one of the trustees elected every four years. I opposed it, the vote stood 12 to 12 and the Bishop gave the casting vote against it. Called with Mrs D at the Hall in the evening, and tried to console Miss Lydia over the appointment of the School trustees. She said sadly she felt as if she was deposed. . . .

*July 5 (Sat)* Sunday (June 29th) . . . Bishop [Ethelbert] Talbot preached on good works from the Epistle of St James.[51] Said he treated Christianity from the stand point of action or works while St Paul in his "preaching" spoke from the Contemplative point of view or that of faith. He is very voluble, speaks with ease from manuscript. Has some Methodism in his manner. While [he was] speaking I likened in my mind the general effect to that of "a sonorous, monotonous drum beat."

. . . Friday the 4th was a lovely day. The sky was just sufficiently overcast to make the temperature pleasant—about 65 in the shade. I did not ride in the procession, for fear of the jolting, but sat on the stand and heard Mr Cole, the Rector of Trinity deliver one of the best orations I ever heard on such occasions, and also deliver it well without note or memorandum. In the evening attended the exhibition of fire works on the river, as the guest of the Committee on the *Potter*. They were very good, and the fleet of small boats and canoes illuminated with Chinese lanterns, as they moved over the water in long lines and circles, gave a fairy like appearance to the scene. . . . Thursday obtained a certificate for Mrs Deadys 50 shares in the Com[mercial] Nat Bank and on Tuesday paid the balance ($2062.42) due on my note that I gave for it in 1887. The stock is now paying a dividend on the par value ($5000) of 8 per centum per annum, with a reserve of more than as much more. . . .

Mail[ed] a large number of catalogs of 1890 of the University on Thursday.

Still reading the 3 vol of *His of the Inquisition*. On the schism in Franciscans concerning poverty—as usual poverty lost and the good things of this world prevailed.

Weighed today and turned the scale at 235 pounds, a gain of 5 pounds in a few weeks. I must diet again. . . .

*12 (Sat)* . . . Tuesday afternoon attended a special meeting of the directors of the Library, where action was finally taken to commence the erection of the building. Got my copy of the *History of Portland—the Book of Beauty* this week and paid the balance due on my subscription $115—the $15 being for the copy of the book, and the $100 the balance due on my picture and biography. This was $200 being a deduction of $150 from the prescribed rate. My biography was to have been written by the editor H W Scott, but it is made up largely of a sketch written by Whalley some years ago. The picture is good except the hair is too smooth.

*19 (Sat)*. . . Monday commenced to discharge blood from the ureth[r]a and kept it up all week. On Friday afternoon went home early and got on my back where I laid most of the time the rest of the week. Sat in the C C & D C during the week except Saturday. Read the *History of the Inquisition* while lying on my back, the third and last volume including the suppression and martyrdom of the Templars and the murder of Joan D'Arc (Jeanne Darc). Oh religion (the faith) what crimes have been committed in thy name. . . .

*26 (Sat)* . . . The circus here last night and I staid at home—for the first time in my life. Whether it was want of will or ability I won't say.

*August 2 (Sat)* Sunday (July 21) . . . In the afternoon Mrs Deady & Mr Brooke and I went down to Alki, Mr Catlins country place near St Johns, on the electric and steam cars and got home by 6 oclock. It is a delightful summer place and we had a very pleasant time, indeed. The electric car stalled on this side of the steel bridge with us, and we had to wait some time—½ an hour for an increase of power. . . .

Am reading Leas *His of Sacerdotal Celibacy,* an interesting book. Celibacy has made the Roman Church a strong *machine,* but grossly immoral. . . .

*9 (Sat)* Sunday (Aug 3) . . . After dinner called in company with Mr Brooke on Miss Blackler at Capt Flanders. She called on us the evening before with Mrs F. She is looking remarkably well—even 10 years younger. Is on her way to Mills Seminary where she is teaching. Mr Brooke as we came away said in his way that he was surprised that they (M S) allowed the Methodists to take Dr [C C] Stratton away from them. Miss [B] replied, positively, "I am very certain that Mrs Mills is very glad to get rid of him."

. . . On Thursday evening sent off the draft of my biography to the History Co, directed to Stone. I worked on [it] 4 day[s] and some nights mostly in correcting Sessions draft, striking out extravagant or improbable expressions and/or passages, and adding extract[s] from my addresses, lectures, charges and after dinner speeches. The first part of it, until my entry into the Legislature at Oregon City in the fall of 1850, is told autobiographically. As it would be evident that I furnished this information, I thought it better to speak in the first person. I never intended to meddle with the rest of it, and refused over and over again to do so. But at last I was compelled to do so much against my will. Dr Sessions, the writer who had charge of my life, is a bright clever man, but not qualified to write my life because he is not a lawyer and has little or no familiarity with the office and labors of a judge.

If I had known what I do now, I would have employed some competent Oregonian who knows me in the country, with my aid, to write the biography and been done with it. As it is, it's a hotc[h]pot[ch] of many hands rather disorderly arranged, but with a good many of my good thing[s], if I may say so, scattered through. The next I expect to hear is that the Company will want to cut it down.

Mrs Deady went to Yamhill Thursday to see her father. I expect her home this evening. On the same day I had a violent fit of vomiting which in time did me good. Dr Sonnefeld called in the evening, for the first time since July 1. Drew off my water and was much pleased at its good quality. Called also last night and reported the examination of some water that I sent him in the morning as very good. Dr John M Brooke called on Thursday to say good bye. He started for N Y on the evening train. His name is John McCarty Brooke and has always been known as a boy as Mac. I gave him $5 as a fee for some attention he gave me in New York last fall. He did not want to take it, but I insisted on having the pleasure of paying him his first fee. Still reading, when I can, Leas *His of Sacerdotal Celibacy*. Hildebrand has just appeared on the stage as the power behind "the Pontiff," and the priests wife who is now common, is soon to be doomed, to be replaced in time by the convenient concubine. Rode to the heights yesterday afternoon on the Cable Car, and walked around about a mile. . . . Felt well this morning.

*16 (Sat)* Sunday (Aug 10th) Attended morning prayer at Trinity as usual. The Rev Chumley Lund officiated in a dialect unknown to me.[52]. . .

There have been three hot days this week but it is pleasant today. The thermometer was at 78 in my chambers on Wednesday afternoon, and once in the week at 83 in our rooms at 6 P M. Sent a letter last Sunday to Miss [Marye] Thompson of S F—Pauls lady love, and at his request. Was a little [*word undecipherable*] but kind. She may be my daughter. Lotta Stout wrote Mrs Deady and myself as a profound secret that she is engaged to Mr Laidlaw, and we were very glad to hear it. The next evening or the next but one, Thursday, George Durham leaned over and whispered the same fact to me in strict confidence. I believe Mary blabbed it, and everybody knows it now. Still reading *Sacerdotal Celibacy* slowly. Hildebrand has passed off the stage but the priests wife is with him yet and sticketh closer than a brother. Now, however, the close of the 13th century, she is being replaced by the focare or concubine. The wife is heresy but the concubine only a sin . . .

*23 (Sat)* Sunday (Aug 17th) . . . Did some work writing letters at my chambers in the afternoon and then called with Mr Brooke at Benj I Cohens and the G S Hospital. At the latter place met Mrs [Emma] Wakeman and Miss [Emily] Loveridge.[53] The latter is rather an attractive and agreeable woman. At Cohen[s] we were shown some of the old family silver, seals and a gold snuff box which B I had lately gotten out from Baltimore, and some Ginger ale with which we quenched our thirst. Before leaving Mrs C and I ran into some pretty broad talk anent the probability of her yet becoming a mother. . . .

Wednesday heard the case of Case v Loftus, suit for injunction, and on Thursday at the request of counsel went to Newport (Yaquina Bay) to *view* the premises—a strip of tide land in front of Cases tavern (Ocean House) along which the defendant has constructed a tramway on which stone are carried out to the north jetty. Took Mrs Deady, Edward and Lucy Failing & James [Fullilove]. McArthur went along. At Derry Mrs Mc[Arthur] and Clifford McA and his cousin John Ankeny joined us with a good lunch which we disposed of at the depot in Corvallis. W[e] reached Newport in the evening. Found the place full of people from the interior. However we were comfortably stowed about and took our meals at the tavern. Examined the premises in the afternoon with Mr [Saml] Case and [Jas] Polhemus.[54] The rest of the party drove to the light house. In the afternoon went out over the bar in the Tug *Mischief,* and floated round a couple of hours whilst a lot of men fished with hook & line. They caught some rock cod, a grub[b]er, some bass and a salmon. A party of young people mostly girls did some good singing until the mal de mer overcame them. . . .

We came in with the steamer, *Wallamet Vall[e]y,* from S F. Came home today via Albany and on the whole had a pleasant time. . . .

*30 (Sat)* . . . Finished the proof of my biography and made some additions thereto selected from [C E S] Woods sketch of my judicial labors and character, and two extracts from my Washington Centennial and Vancouver 4th of July Oration. Mailed the package on Wednesday the 27. . . . Still reading *Sacerdotal Celibacy* by Henry C Lea. It appears that after the Celibacy was thoroughly established the fornication commenced. . . .

*September 6 (Sat)* . . . Got a subscription of $100 each from S G Reed and Henry Failing for Mrs Victor to aid her in the publication of her book on Oregon & Washington, and gave her their checks last evening.

Gen Miles called on me yesterday on his way to his new command at Chicago. . . .

*13 (Sat)* . . . Monday sat in the C C and got ready for Clatsop. Drew $400 for Henderson to pay his transportation to New York, buy clothes and pay his ordinary expenses as a medical student for the first quarter. During the day Mr Maxwell presented me with a ticket for him to Chicago which he said was equal to $60, which amount Henderson returned to me.

In the evening got off on the *R R Thompson* in room 9 at a cost of $1.50. Got off at Astoria Tuesday morning at 7 oclock. Breakfasted at the Occident ($1) and then took the *Electric* for the end of the Ry bridge in Youngs bay (.50). From there on the railway to Grimes ($1.28) where we arrived at ½ past 10. We had Alice Strong with us all the way. The prices given above do not include her, but only Mrs Deady and myself. Got our old room at Grimes on the ground floor leading out of the parlor. I miss the old man Grimes, who died on the 22 ult. I used to love to sit around the fire after all others had retired and hear him talk of his eventful life, and give me all of the gossip of the neighborhood for the past year.

Wednesday went in bathing, the first time in two years. At first the water was cold but the reaction soon came and all was right. Bathed every day since. Mrs Deady went in Friday and today and seemed to enjoy it. The weather has been cloudy one day & sunshiny the next. Mrs W K Smith is here and sits at our table. She is as active and enthusiastic as a girl.

Have read *Wanda* (Ouida) and found nothing objectionable in it. It is the only one of Ouidas that I ever read. An interesting story with a great deal of fine writing in it, and some philosophy. Have also read *The Courting of Dinah Shadd and Other Stories* by Kipling. Rather coarse and somewhat extravagant but interesting and marked with original sayings and turns of thought. I am surprised however at the fuss that has been made over him . . .

*20 (Sat)* Sunday (Sept 14) A cold day, went in bathing alone. Monday came to Astoria in the afternoon. Staid at the Occident. Tuesday went to the north beach and up to Sealand, the terminus of the railway, and back to Astoria. It rained lightly all day. In Astoria Wednesday visited at Flavels, and rode over the town in the horse cars and on the motor. Nellie Flavel accompanied us and proved a very pleasant companion. Called also at the Rodney cottage. Found Miss Lydia at home and glad to see us. In the evening went aboard the *R R Thompson* and reached home in the morning. Today we start to the Sound to be gone 7 or 8 days. Weighed yesterday 233 pounds a gain of 2 pounds for Clatsop. Got the proof of my biography this morning.

*27 (Sat)* Left Portland with Mrs Deady at 12 M for Tacoma and a trip on the Sound and to Victoria. Staid two days at Tacoma. Went to St Lukes church on Sunday and saw and heard the most churchly man officiate and preach I ever did see or hear. The choir consisted of 5 or 6 young men who made excellent music in which the congregation joined heartily. Dined with Schulze who also drove us about the town. Met Prof [James] Bryce and his young wife at the Tacoma. Did not strike me as a great man, but bright and agreeable.[55]

At Seattle stopped at the Rainier. Alfred Holman showed us around and I lunched with him at the club, where I drank the best champagne cocktail I ever tasted in my life. Went to Washington Lake and back on the cable railway passing up a trestle said to be over 300 feet high and not less than 40 degrees in ascent. Was interviewed by the reporter of the *P[ost] & I[ntelligencer]* and said my say about changing the name of Rainier to Tacoma.

In going from Tacoma to Seattle passed through the hop fields of Puyallup and White rivers. The planters assisted by Indians were busy gathering the hops and altogether it was a pretty and picturesque sight.

Went to Victoria in the N P steamer the *Kingston.* A fine boat and poor table. Stopped at the Driard. A fair table excellently served. Room cold and no way of warming it. House dreary and dingy. Sir Joseph & Lady Trutch drove us out in the afternoon about 10 miles and had us to dinner at 7 where we met Sir Matthew B Begbie, the Chief Justice. Altogether we enjoyed the Trutchs, and Lady Julia was very kind. The next day Mr Marvin, the American vice consul drove us about 8 miles in the course of which we visited the dry dock at Esquimalt. It is a splendid piece of work.

Left Victoria Friday night on the *Kingston,* made Tacoma by morning and thence to Olympia in the *Multnomah.* Stopped at the Olympia, where we got more comfort for less money than any place we saw or was. Went to St Johns church on Sunday the 28th and met . . . Lizzie Ferry. Monday morning called on Gov Ferry with whom I spent a few moments very agreeably. Got home on the Railway via Tenino about half past 7 of the same evening. This entry though dated on the 27 is actually made on the 30th which accounts for the mention of Sunday and Monday of this week.

On the whole we had a very pleasant journey at a cost of $101.25. Our trip to the Sound and Clatsop cost us according to my account just $144.39—probably $150 in all.

*October 4 (Sat)* Tuesday (Sept 30) Got to work again in the courts after 19 days vacation. Sat in the C C & D C during the week. Henderson writes to Mr [Herbert] Folger[56] under date of Sept 25 that he had been admitted to the college of

P[hysicians] & S[urgeons] in New York and matriculated that day. But we hear nothing from him. I don't understand it.

I am still at *Sacerdotal Celibacy,* or rather I have resumed it. I find the confessional has been a convenient contrivance for the seduction of female penitents. The fall rain has commenced this week in a mild way. It is very much needed. I am receiving complimentary acknowledgements from many persons to whom I sent a pamphlet a few weeks ago containing my Washington Inauguration, and Vancouver 4th of July addresses.

Congress has adjourned without passing the salary bill, and I shall be agreeably disappointed if it is passed at the next session. . . .

*11 (Sat)* . . . [*During the week*] Prepared a substitution for an endowment of $50,000 for the Library for current expenses. Got $25,000 subscribed yesterday by four persons. Mrs Deady went up to the farm yesterday to see her father who is very low. She writes this morning that she will not be home until Monday. . . .

Have not been so well for the past few days. Sent Henderson $300 by draft last Monday for school expenses. Attended the Organ Concert ([Frederick] Archer) at the new Pres church last evening.[57] Was bored with too much organ and gymnastic music, although well done. Mrs Reed sang a solo and encore divinely which was worth the whole performance. . . .

*18 (Sat)* . . . Sat in the C C & D C during the week.

*25 (Sat)* . . . On Thursday morning I was taken with a copious bleeding from the bladder, or neck of it. Sat in court awhile and remained in my chambers, passing black blood and clotted blood until late in the afternoon when I went (came) home and went to bed, whence, practically I have been until now . . . Dr Sonnefeld attended me. Gave me styptics, ergot, solution of iron internally, morphine suppositories . . . and ice bags . . .

*November 1 (Sat)* Sunday Oct 26. Home in bed all day. Still bleeding from the bladder, but not so much. By Wednesday the bleeding was stopped practically. I continued in bed until Friday when I got up, dressed and laid on the lounge during the day. Today made up my accounts for October and drew my check for $252.40 for board, Mrs Deadys allowance of $50 and incidental expenses. We heard today that Mr Henderson, Mrs Deadys father, was drawing near his end after being bed ridden near a year, and she and her sisters Mrs Failing and Mrs Strong started up to the farm in the evening.

I forgot to say in the proper place that on Wednesday evening the 22 of October Mrs Deady and I attended the wedding of Miss [Jessie] Gill and John Hartman at Grace Church where we had the pleasure of seeing Dr Houghton make the nuptial knot according to the ritual set forth in the Prayer Book. From thence we went to the Exposition building for the first and only time.[58] The music was excellent. Did not see much of the exhibit except the art gallery. Of that what was not obscene and coarse was generally common. My bleeding came on the next morning and may have been caused by the exercise, including stair climbing of the evening before. But I think not. I think there has been a congestion . . . for some time which was painful to me when I sat down and I think it has ended in this rupture and hem[h]or[r]age.

*2 (Sun)* A telegram came from Harvey Henderson this morning, that Mr Henderson died yesterday evening at 6 oclock, and will be buried on Tuesday morning at McMinnville at ½ past 10 oclock. A good man and true has gone to his rest and I hope reward. He never wronged anyone nor failed in his duty, as he saw it—and his standard was high and generous.

I want to go to the funeral and must if I can stand it. I am going into court in the morning or try to. The writing of these memoranda, commencing with October 18 is the first thing I have done, except drawing my check yesterday since the 23 ult. . . . Talked with . . . [*Bishop Morris*] about the urgency of incorporating the School & Hospital Coms of the church, and said I would not serve on a dummy Com. . . .

*8 (Sat)* The doctor would not hear of my going to Mr Hendersons funeral. I was very sorry I could not go. Mrs Deady came home on Tuesday evening tired and sad. I have not had any discharge of blood since about the 26th ult, and feel today quite well. I am going down town this afternoon for the first time since I was taken sick. . . .

*15 (Sat)* Sunday (Nov 9) At home in the forenoon on my back. Walked too much Saturday. The first time I was down town since the 23 inst when I was taken sick. In the afternoon went to my chambers and prepared notes for the decision of Joseph Kelleys Habeas Corpus case in the Circuit Court on Monday.

Sat in the C C & D C during the week. Monday gave decision in the C C discharging Kelley from imprisonment on the ground that no crime having been committed in Clatsop county by the petitioner, the justice of Astoria had no authority to commit him. The decision was published in Tuesdays *Oregonian* as reported by Sholes. I have since revised it, and it will probably be published in pamphlet form by the board of trade.[59] . . .

Had a pamphlet during the week from Mr James C Carter of New York on the nature and growth of the law—an address delivered before the Bar Association.[60] I read it with great pleasure. Coincides with much that I said in my lecture on Law & Lawyers, in 1866. . . .

*22 (Sat)* . . . I think I am improving in condition gradually. Have had no discharge of blood in this month. The weather has been beautiful, cool foggy mornings, and warm balmy days. But the farmers are still suffering for rain. The ground is too dry for the plough. Did some magazine reading this week. Notably on Sir W Scotts diary just published. The publication appears to have enhanced the estimate in which he was held as a man. Mazarin and his nieces is an interesting sketch. What a smart, unscrupulous race the Italians of the 14 to 17 centuries were, particularly those who wore the clerical dress. I have been going over our expenses for the years 1889 & 1890 and find we have spent in that time at least $1500 of our capital more than our income. We must set our stakes to keep inside of $5000 next year. This year I have paid $895.18 for taxes and assessments for street improvements.

*29 (Sat)* Sunday (Nov 23) Attended . . . Trinity as usual and heard an excellent sermon by Mr Cole on the text—"Be not drunken with wine &c." Called to see Mrs Henderson in the afternoon. She is looking well under the circumstances.

. . . Thursday, Thanksgiving day went to Trinity at 11 service. The Congregation was large, the music splendid, the sermon excellent, both original and instructive, and the collection for the G S H $190.

Friday evening I attended a reception given at Dr Eliots, the 25 anniversary of his wedding. A large number of people called, and altogether the affair was a pleasant one, and must have been very gratifying to Mr & Mrs Eliot, and their charming daughter Dorothea.

My health or rather ailment is getting perceptibly better. No issue of blood in this month.

. . . The weather still keeps clear and warm for the time of year. The land is so dry that the plough will not enter. The city people and builders are jubilant over the beautiful weather little thinking that there is a promise of a wheat famine in it. . . .

*December 6 (Sat)* . . . Have been reading this week of the Mazarin family and particularly the nieces, in the *Atlantic*. A sweet scented lot. Have had some rain this week, but not much. Paul went to San Francisco last Sunday to see his sweetheart. A letter came to his mother from him this morning. I took the liberty of reading it, as I would have been allowed to, anyhow, after she perused it. He is very much smitten and is very happy. Hope he will always be so. . . .

*13 (Sat)* . . . On Monday the 8th received 100 bound copies of my biography from the "Chronicles of the Kings" with engraving, and the quotation of four lines from Socrates about a Judge, with which the copy commenced was left out. I sent a postal for $25 for the last 50 the first 50 being a present, and said I was chagrined and sorry the quotation was left out.[61] It was taken from Woods contribution to the life. Thursday the History Company telegraphed me to send the books back, and expect letter today.

Am rereading the life of Madame Recamier. Have not seen it for 20 years. It reads as well as new. She is another conspicuous instance of Napoleons low estimate and vulgar, harsh treatment of women. . . . Yesterday got a new cushion for my desk chair with a hole in the centre of it that I may sit without pressure on the region of the prostate gland. I think it will be a success, and if so a great comfort.

*20 (Sat)* . . . The weather has been warm and moist with an occasional hard rain at night. Wrote a letter to Joseph N Dolph telling him that all I wanted was my salary increased, and he might give any circuit judgeship that came within his control to Cyrus, or if he would get a law passed allowing me to resign, I would do so and he could get Cyrus appointed.

My cushion with a "hole" in it does very well and I can sit for hours without inconvenience. . . . Xmas is drawing nigh and I am making no preparations for it—no gifts this year. Trying to economize.

Weighed this afternoon. Drew 233½ a gain of ½ pounds in 2 weeks which I attribute to a new pair of pantaloons. . . .

*27 (Sat)* . . . Sat in the C C & D C during the week, except Thursday which was Christmas. Attended M prayer & Communion at Trinity. A large congregation, good choral music and a sensible sermon on the Origin and Significance. Gave

Mrs Deady an engraving of myself (the Bancroft plate) handsomely framed. . . . Got 5 copies of my biography from the History Company with the Socratic quotation in place. But they write me that the two boxes which were returned to them by the Southern Pacific have either been side tracked or mislaid.

The weather has been warm and cloudy with fair days particularly Xmas, which was lovely. Mr Fred V Holmans choice roses in bud. . . .

Sent a copy of my biography to Miss L R as a Christmas present today. Issued a warrant in an extradition case under the treaty of 1842 with G B for one William Stuart Crook calling himself McDonald. Arrested on Friday and hearing continued until Monday. Charged with forging a will.

*28 (Sun)* Attended . . . Trinity as usual. The Rev Mr Cole of the House of Clafin [*sic*] & Co preached.[62] Has an elegant voice. Spent the afternoon in my chambers, and called on Mrs Henderson, taking in the Catlins and Strongs on my way home. Commenced . . . to take honey and Honeyaden water, half a tumbler before breakfast, a dose of Vitalized Phosphates after breakfast and dinner, and also a half tumbler of Bests tonic after the same. . . .

# NOTES

1. Probably a solution of potassium permanganate.

2. Judge Pratt married his first wife, Ann, in Wisconsin. They had one child, a son, Samuel Stevens Pratt, who died in 1852 at the age of 14 months. His second wife was Elizabeth E. Greene Pratt (1840–1911). By her he also had a son, Orville C. Pratt, Jr., born December 19, 1882, just four months before the Judge's 64th birthday.

3. Eugene Meyer, San Francisco banker and Los Angeles merchant; resident partner, Lazard Frères.

4. Godfrey Brown, British-Hawaiian merchant; sometime minister of foreign affairs under the monarchy and minister of finance, 1890; he had previously lived in both Victoria and Portland. Frederick W. M. Holliday; governor of Virginia, 1878–82.

5. Benjamin F. Dillingham; merchant, planter, railroad promoter and politician.

6. A. Francis Judd; chief justice, Hawaiian Supreme Court. Lawrence McCully; associate justice, Hawaiian Supreme Court. Robert Brenham was a son of Charles and Betty Adair Brenham of Oregon.

7. Sanford B. Dole (1844–1926), lawyer and jurist; was a leader in the revolution of 1887 which forced King Kalakaua to grant a new constitution and was appointed to the supreme court that same year; in 1893 was a leader of the revolution which overthrew the monarchy and was first president of the Hawaiian Republic, 1894–1900, and first territorial governor, 1900–1903, after which he became federal district judge. Richard F. Bickerton, Hawaiian attorney; associate justice of the supreme court. William G. Irwin (Irving in original), merchant and shipping master; his wife, formerly a Miss Ives of San Francisco, married Ben Holladay, Jr. in 1873, but shortly after divorced him. Spreckles in original.

8. Marie Rosalie von Holt (1865–1952), daughter of Hermann J. F. and Alice Brown von Holt Macintosh, and stepdaughter of the Rev. Alex Macintosh. She never married, but until 1942, when blindness overtook her, she devoted the whole of her life to church and charitable work in Hawaii and Great Britain. Her sister, Bertha Louise von Holt (1866–1942), afterwards became Mrs. Frederick W. Glade of Honolulu.

9. Irving in original.

10. Alfred S. Hartwell, Hawaiian lawyer; sometime attorney-general and justice of the supreme court.

11. The Devonport Sisters (Deady makes it Davenport in a later entry), otherwise Sisters of the Holy Trinity, an Anglican order founded about 1849.

12. Charles R. Bishop (1822–1915), banker and philanthropist.

13. Lorrin A. Thurston (1858–1931), lawyer and journalist; attorney for Claus Spreckels; drafted the 1893 proclamation of the Provisional Government and labored for annexation by the United States; owner-editor of the Honolulu *Advertiser*. Archibald S. Cleghorn, English-born merchant and husband of Princess Likelike, Liliuokalani's only sister; served as collector of customs and governor of Oahu; a strong supporter of the monarchy. Capt. J. B. Coghlan (1844–1908), naval officer; his ship, the *Raleigh,* first returned Spanish fire at Manila Bay.

14. John L. Stevens (1820–95), journalist and diplomat; successively U. S. minister

to Paraguay, Uruguay, Sweden and Norway, 1870–83. Resident minister and later ambassador extraordinary to Hawaii, 1889–93, he took a large part in the revolutionary overthrow of Queen Liliuokalani. Spreckles in original. Major James H. Woodhouse, British commissioner. Woodehouse in original.

15. Francis M. Hatch, Hawaiian businessman; minister to Washington from the Provisional Government.

16. Mrs. Spalding was the wife of a prominent sugar planter.

17. Ezra Derr; naval surgeon.

18. David Kalakaua (1836–91), reigned 1874–91.

19. Hiram Bingham (1831–1908), Congregationalist minister and missionary.

20. James Jackson Jarves (1818–88), author, editor and world traveler. Henry M. Whitney; Hawaiian journalist and publisher. Isabella L. Bird (1832–1904), travel writer.

21. Hermann A. Widemann, planter and lawyer, sometime minister of the interior and associate justice of the supreme court; during the revolutionary troubles a close advisor to Queen Liliuokalani.

22. Widerman in original.

23. Widerman in original.

24. George Trousseau, Honolulu physician; sympathizer of the queen's at the time of the Revolution.

25. Mrs. Dutton cannot be positively identified.

26. Mrs. Harris was perhaps the wife of Charles C. Harris, Honolulu lawyer and holder of a number of offices under the monarchy *post* 1850.

27. Thomas Henry Gratton Esmonde, Bart. was less close to Dillon than Deady indicates. When the Kitty O'Shea scandal split the Irish party in Parliament, Esmonde joined with Timothy Healy and John Redmond in opposing Dillon's bid for leadership.

28. Charles Lombard, Portland businessman; he resided at The Hill.

29. Joseph O. Carter, Honolulu businessman; very active in government circles, he was a supporter of the Queen at the time of the Revolution. Samuel M. Damon, managing partner of Bishop & Co.; a strong friend of the Hawaiians, he was briefly finance minister under both Kalakaua and Liliuokalani. James F. B. Marshall (1818–91), Hawaiian merchant and educator; during the Civil War he served as a Union officer.

30. Jonathan Austin, New York attorney; moved to Hawaii about 1877, became minister of foreign affairs, 1887.

31. Field's speech celebrated the centenary of the first session of the U. S. Supreme Court.

32. Laura Fish Judd, wife of Gerrit P. Judd (1803–73), medical missionary and Hawaiian official.

33. Bernice Pauahi Paki Bishop, Hawaiian princess; last of her line, she gave most of her estate to the people of Hawaii; died in 1884.

34. Homeopathy was a system of medicine based upon three theories: first, that a disorder was cured by drugs which produced symptoms similar to those produced by the disorder; second, that the smaller the dosage, the greater the effect; and third, that all illnesses were the manifestation of a suppressed itch.

35. Epididimus in original. Joseph Holt, Portland physician; a Virginian, he was a Confederate military surgeon during the Civil War, and afterward practiced medicine and served as a sanitary commissioner in New Orleans.

36. Buhach; pyrethrum.

37. Frank Damon was the son of Samuel C. Damon, who went to Honolulu in 1843 as a missionary.

38. Kahilis; ceremonial plumes.

39. Cornelius Hanford (1849–1926), lawyer and jurist. Hanaford in original.

40. Annie Besant (1847–1933), English theosophist, free-thinker, and India home rule agitator; J. Krishnamurti was for a time her protege.

41. A. J. Cody was a runner (i.e., one employed to frequent stage lines and railroad

terminals and steamship wharfs and persuade incoming passengers to lodge at a particular hotel, not infrequently by simply picking up the victim's luggage and storing it away on the hotel's private omnibus, or running ahead with it to the hotel itself) for Portland's Holton House. Joseph Morin was the hotel porter. Cody accused Morin of beating the bellboy and when Morin denied it, attacked him and proceeded to bite off a chunk of Morin's upper lip, chewed a thumb and one finger into a ragged state, and mangled Morin's cheek. The altercation took place in the lobby of what was then one of the city's most respectable hotels, in full view of a number of visitors and local citizenry, none of whom felt impelled to intervene, though a few had a sufficient sense of responsibility to arrange for the making of a ring so that Cody could proceed with his work of demolition without fear of obstruction. Morin eventually was able to escape from his assailant, ran off and shortly returned with a revolver, took five shots at Cody, none of which was effective, and surrendered to the police.

At that time the Oregon Criminal Code said, in part, "If any person shall purposely and maliciously . . . cut or tear out or disable the tongue, put out or destroy the eye, cut or slit or mutilate the nose or lip . . . of another, such person, upon conviction thereof, shall be punished by imprisonment in the penitentiary for not less than one or more than twenty years." Cody was charged with mutilation of Morin's lip by biting off a portion thereof, and was convicted in the lower court. He appealed, and the supreme court of the state reversed the conviction, with Judge Thayer writing the majority opinion. It was Thayer's contention that the portion of the statutes quoted above was aimed at those who might, using a knife or some other weapon, and with malice aforethought, inflict the injuries described. To justify this position he wrote: "It was a contest for mastery, in which each of the combatants relied upon his own courage, skill and prowess. It was not conducted in accordance with the conventional rules recognized by popular pugilists, but in a primitive style—a manner which Western people vulgarly term a 'ground squabble,' wherein nice honor as to the mode in which parties hurt each other is not observed.

"Such occurrences are not respectable, but are disgraceful and demoralizing; yet it is better they be indulged in occasionally than that men lose their grit and become dudes and poltroons." Scott's editorial objected to this portion of the opinion. For details, see 18 *Or. Rep.*, pp. 507 ff.

42. Edith Carter Smith, wife of Walter D. Smith, son of Joseph S. Smith and a Portland business executive and lumberman.

43. William H. Kendal (1843–1917) and Margaret Robertson Kendal (1849–1935), English actors; "The Iron Master" was one of their great successes.

44. F. Marion Crawford (1864–1909), American novelist; his first novel, *Mr. Isaacs: A Tale of Modern India,* was enormously popular.

45. Parnell was charged with complicity in Irish terrorist activities beginning with the assassination of the Chief Secretary for Ireland, Lord Frederick Cavendish, and Under-Secretary Thomas Burke in Dublin's Phoenix Park, May 6, 1882. The Parnell Commission sat for nearly 18 months before issuing its report in February, 1890. Three specific charges were brought against Parnell. The commission found the first not proved and judged Parnell innocent of the other two. Deady was consulting his prejudices.

46. Mrs. Palmer was the wife of E. H. Palmer, manager of Palmer & Rey, typefounders. The Palmers lived for a time at The Hill.

47. Fred N. Gilmore was employed by James Laidlaw. Edward H. Sothern (1859–1933), light comedian and romantic actor and son of E. A. Sothern; Rudolf in "The Prisoner of Zenda" was one of his most successful roles.

48. Robert Bell, Portland real estate and loan man.

49. Locke Richardson (c.1844–99), was one of the most remarkable performers of his time; his repertoire was incredibly large and varied.

50. Prescott Sawyer was charged with assault. The jury found he had acted in self-defense.

51. Ethelbert Talbot (1848–1928), Episcopal clergyman; missionary bishop of

Wyoming and Idaho, 1887–97, and thereafter bishop in Pennsylvania; residing bishop, 1924–26.

52. Chumley Lund; because of the accent.

53. Benjamin I. Cohen, Portland banker; died 1910. Emma A. Wakeman, superintendent of Good Samaritan Hospital; died 1907 at age 55. Emily Loveridge (1860–1941), for many years matron and superintendent, Good Samaritan Hospital.

54. Samuel Case, proprietor of the Ocean House, Newport. James E. Polhemus, rivers and harbors engineer for the Army Corps of Engineers; died 1930 at age 78.

55. James Bryce 1838–1922), British statesman, jurist and author; his *American Commonwealth* is a classic. A many-facetted man, enthusiastic traveler, Liberal MP and diplomat, he was created viscount after serving seven years as ambassador to Washington. Deady's assessment is ungenerous.

56. Herbert Folger, Portland manager of the New Zealand Insurance Co.; he lived at The Hill.

57. Frederick Archer (1838–1901), British-American organist and composer.

58. Jessie Gill married John L. Hartman (1856–1925), Portland merchant and banker. The three-story Exposition Building fronted on Burnside almost due north of the present Stadium.

59. Joseph "Bunco" Kelley (he also spelled it variously as Bunko and Buncko) was a notable Portland character. One of the most successful crimps on the coast, he was sentenced in 1895 for the murder of a man named Sears and imprisoned in the Oregon State Penitentiary. The result of that imprisonment was a little book, now become rather rare, called *Thirteen Years in the Oregon Penitentiary*, in which Kelley laid bare the vile conditions which existed in that institution. In 1890 Kelley was accused of having shanghaiied a man at Astoria. He was then in Portland, and the sheriff of Clatsop County, realizing that the Multnomah County authorities would be unlikely to act on a Clatsop County warrant, however properly issued, came to Portland, arrested Kelley and carried him off to Astoria. Kelley promptly applied to Deady's court for a writ of habeas corpus on the ground of illegal arrest. Both sides tried openly to influence the judge. Edward was one of Kelley's attorneys; Paul was one of those retained by the sheriff. In fact, Deady had no choice but to issue the writ. The Board of Trade interest in the affair was commercial rather than legal. Crimps, by seeing to it that departing ships had adequate crews, helped keep the traffic of commerce flowing. They must therefore be kept safe from harassment by officials from competing ports.

60. James C. Carter (1827–1905), New York lawyer and reformer; opposed codification of the common law as proposed by D. D. Field. Deady had great affection for the common law.

61. The missing lines read:
Four things belong to a judge—to hear
Courteously, to answer wisely, to consider
Soberly, and to decide impartially.—Socrates

62. Deady apparently means Claflin for Victoria Claflin Woodhull and her sister, Tennessee Celeste Claflin, clairvoyants, journalists, advocates of free love and women's rights; as "proteges" of Cornelius Vanderbilt, they made a great deal of money in stock speculation and used some of it to float *Woodhull & Claflin's Weekly* in 1870. Victoria was the presidential nominee of the Equal Rights party in 1872. In that same year, the *Weekly* published the alleged seduction of Theodore Tilton's wife by his friend, the Rev. Henry Ward Beecher. *Post* 1877 the sisters lived in England, where they married respectably and lived on well into the present century. It is not possible to determine why Deady would apply this epithet—or so he would consider it—to the Reverend Mr. Cole.

Locke Richardson, "a great treat." (Courtesy New York Public Library.)

Dr. Rodney Glisan died in June, 1890.

Saturday melodrama at Cordray's Theater, 1890.

Chinatown, Portland, 1890. Second St., south from Washington.

Duck shoot at the Crystal Palace. The flood of February, 1890, S.W. 1st, between Washington and Stark. (B. C. Towne p

Mass transit circa 1890, at the uphill end of the line. Note elegant colored glass "skylights."

Front and Morrison, February, 1890. The Esmond Hotel—awash.

The completed Portland Hotel, with cab in front.

Kamehameha I's statue, made in commemoration of the centennial of the Islands' discovery by Captain Cook, was placed in front of the Judiciary Building in 1883. (Dye Collection, OHS.)

Hawaii: the Avenue of Royal Palms, Honolulu. (Dye Collection, OHS.)

Deady conversed with King Kalakaua, shown here on Iolani Palace steps with his officials. The king died in San Francisco early in 1891. (Courtesy Bishop Museum, Baker Collection.) The palace floor was Oregon fir, Deady noted.

". . . with baskets and armfuls of flower garlands . . ."

Since Chief Justice Hudd had "la grippe," Justice McCully presented Deady to the king.

Perhaps Bunco Kelley (see note 59) used this underground passage under the Press Tavern, Front and Morrison in Portland, to transport shanghied sailors to ships in the Wallamet.

Stark Street Ferry crossing to the west side about 1890.

The music was excellent, but the art exhibit was common or worse. Exposition Building, on the south side of Washington St. between 19th and 20th, built in 1888 and burned in 1910.

eet scene at S.W. 1st and Oak, Portland, circa 1890. That year the Union Station was built. (Hazeltine Collection, OHS.)

# 1891

*January 3 (Sat)*. . . Heard the application for the extradition of McDonald alleged
to be Crook and discharged him for want of identification. Nothing to hold him
on but a whiskered photograph and [he is] smooth shaven except a mustache.
. . . Distributed 26 copies of my Biography as Xmas presents. Paid my bills
yesterday for the quarter ending Dec 31 and sent Henderson by telegraph $285,
the $85 to pay for his dress suit and the rest his current expenses for the coming
quarter. The week has been warm and generally moist. My balance in bank after
paying my bills was only $143. Has not been so low for a long time. I have over
$300 owing to me, however.

*10 (Sat)*. . . Last night went to Grace church and heard the Canadian evangelists
[J E] Hunter & [H T] Crossley. They can both talk and the latter sing. They
angled adroitly for Sinners, but got nobili, ni[h]il after a while.

*17 (Sat)* Sunday (Jan 11) Attended M prayer at Trinity church as usual. Mr Cole
discoursed on the Old Epiphany "story" as he called it of the visit of the wise
men, the Magi, to the child Jesus. The moral was the duty of giving gold, ones
havings, frankincense, ones time and myrrh, making a sacrifice. Altogether it was
the most interesting and effective sermon I ever heard on the subject. . . .

Today heard an application for a habeas corpus in re McDonald on the
ground that the Commissioner had lost jurisdiction by adjourning the examination for more than 6 days, namely 11 to await the arrival of a witness from
England.

*24 (Sat)*. . . Wednesday evening attended the marriage of Ada McCracken and
Mr [Charles] Hurley of Tacoma at Trinity and the reception at the house.[1] It was
the most picturesque wedding I ever saw. Both the church and house were filled
to overflowing. Mrs Palmer sang a lovely solo [*words omitted*] and the chorus a
charming carol. The night was beautiful. A ful[l] moon, a clear sky with the
temperature of spring. . . . Attended a library meeting this evening and called
at the Hall. Miss Rodney is confined to her bed. I don't know what the school
would do without her. The weather has been bright and balmy during the week.

*31 (Sat)*. . . Wednesday tried [*two cases*] . . . for disposing of spiritous liquors
to Peter Dowd an Indian on the G[rande] R[onde] reservation, whose mother
was a ½ breed and father an Irishman. Verdict in the first case guilty and in the
second not guilty on the same evidence for the prosecution and the testimony
of the deft in each case. The first one was a saloonkeeper and the other a druggist
who sold alcohol in quantities not less than a quart. They were equally guilty,
but differently situated. . . .

This evening called at the Hall and had a stormy interview with Miss Clem Rodney in the presence of Miss Lydia, commencing with an insult she put on Miss Jessie Murch and extending generally to her misconduct as a teacher at the Hall and her general unfitness for the place and the injury she had been and was to the school. Of course she boasted of her blood. But I told her that had nothing to do with the case. That if she condescended to teach school, she must be subject to the obligations and perform the duties of one, that here she was a teacher in a public school and Miss Murch was the same and on the same level.

*February 7 (Sat)* . . . [Received a letter] this morning giving me the news of the death of Col Benjamin Mackall of Barnesville, Ohio, on the 31 ult. He was an early and good friend of mine. On the 21 ult, also died another good friend of mine, Henry Kennon at Princeton, Illinois. . . .

*14 (Sat)* Sunday (Feb 8) . . . at Trinity as usual. Sermon on Indians and Negroes, the offertory being for them. Good of its kind. Mr Lewis asked me at the vestry meeting on Monday evening what I thought of it. I answered "It was very good" —but omitted to say "of its kind."

Sat in the C C & D C during the week. Tried two civil cases with a jury, and discharged the jury on Thursday evening finally. Tom Strong was counsel for the plaintiff in the last case, and I caught him in 2 whopping lies in his argument to the jury—palpable misrepresentations of writings in the case and one of which he held in his hand and pretended to be quoting from it at the time.

Went to the bal costume at the Elks last night as a spectator. Was invited and 2 tickets sent me. Took Mrs Dunckley with me. It was a failure. Got home at ½ past 10. The report in this mornings *Oregonian* makes a great affair of it.

Snow fell yesterday morning 1 or 2 inches deep and disappeared during the day. Fell again this morning about the same depth. The sun is out and it is disappearing gradually. . . .

*21 (Sat)* Sunday (Feb 15) . . . at Trinity as usual. Mr Cole gave us an excellent sermon on the denunciation of the Pharisees who would neither let anyone enter into the Kingdom nor enter themselves by applying it to *us*. In the afternoon attended the christening of Edwards baby—William Hanover, at St Lawrences church, next door to the residence. It seems the baptism—the water part of the ceremony—was administered some time ago when the child was thought to be in danger of death. What I witnessed was a lot of prayers and ceremonies, in which greasing and salting the infant occurred. Bishop Gross officiated and he regaled us with a preliminary talk of ten minutes in which he informed us that these ceremonies as he called them had constituted a part of the Sacrament of baptism from the earliest days of Christianity. He forgot the case of Philip and the Eunuch in which baptism consisted of the use of water by the roadside only. How a man can have the cheek to talk to intelligent people in this way, I can't conceive, but he don't often talk to that kind of people. . . .

Tuesday mailed a draft of $50 to Agnes Fleming at Chicago to aid her on the death of her husband. Poor girl!

Wednesday evening Mrs Deady started southward with Mrs Catlin who is not well. They will go to San Francisco, and thence after a few days to Pasadena, and will probably be gone 2 months. Had a telegram yesterday announcing their arrival that morning at San Francisco.

. . . When I went home to dinner today found two telegrams on my table, one from Senator Dolph and the other from Mr [Binger] Herman M C announcing that the salary bill had passed that day, making my salary $5000. I telegraphed thanks in reply and to Mrs Deady in San Francisco. Well it has come at last, and it is a great shame that it did not come 20 years ago. But it is welcome and better late than never. Now I am waiting patiently for my seventieth birthday so that I may retire and take it easy thenceforth. . . .

*28 (Sat)* . . . Commenced this week to read Bryces *Commonwealth of America.* Interesting and accurate generally, but somewhat tedious in places to one who necessarily knows as much about the Constitution and the workings of the departments of the government under it, as a Federal Judge for 40 years standing ought to. . . .

There has been all kinds of weather during the week except the very cold. Yesterday was [a] lovely day and this is overcast and cool, foreboding snow. Sent a 25 pound Chinook Salmon to Mr Justice Harlan, by express on Thursday, the 26, and telegraphed him today. Weighed this afternoon and drew 233½ pounds.

*March 7 (Sat)* Sunday (March 1) . . . Trinity as usual. Had an excellent sermon from Mr Cole on "Society," in which he said, referring to the Sunday reports of society doings, that dancing and drive whist had their proper place in society, but he thought it was rather a poor society that could afford no other amusement. . . .

. . . Had two or three letters from Mrs Deady this week. She is still at S F but expected to leave this morning. Will get a telegram from her if she does. Had a letter yesterday from Maria H von Holt and a copy of a paper containing an account of the Hookupu[2] at Honolulu given to Admiral Brown of the *Charleston,* by the native women. Reading Bryce slowly. It is well and intelligently written, and shows in theory at least, many imperfections in our scheme of government, which in practice have never been developed or made manifest.

*14 (Sat)* . . . The weather has been clear and mild most of the week except one night and day it rained lightly. Got a letter yesterday from Mrs Deady at Los Angeles. She is well and happy. Got a letter from Ben Stark acknowledging the receipt of my biography and saying that the *auto* part of it reminded him in "the straightforward candor and unaf[f]ectedness of its style of the autobiography of an American patriot and philosopher, Dr Franklin" but that the other part of it "does not do full justice to the later career and the present and sometimes past social position and influence of its subject." Miss [Marie] Wainwright is billed for "12th Night" at the Marquam next week and I am strongly tempted, "lent" though it be, to see her.[3] As Old Ritchie used to say *Nous verrons.* . . .

*21 (Sat)* Sunday (March 15) . . . Called to see grandmother Henderson in the afternoon and called at the Hall also. Miss Lydia was sick in bed and sent her regrets. The others were at dinner. After a while Miss Rodney came in. She was quite chilly at first but tried to be polite and warmed up a little at the last. Miss Clem did not come in and her name was not mentioned. I met her on the street the other day. She was heavily veiled and I did not recognize her until I was close to her—just in the act of passing her. She managed to speak and I replied in the same way. . . .

. . . Thursday dined at Mr Walter Burns . . . An excellent dinner, Mrs Burns was charming and her wine was excellent. She has a family of four sweet little girls. The oldest one puts me in mind of her when she was [an] S S scholar of mine, and a very interesting one. . . . Got several letters from Mrs Deady this week. Telegraphed her at Rodondo [sic] yesterday, where she arrived on Wednesday from Pasadena. Delivered my first lecture to the law class last night.

28 (Sat) . . . Sat in the C C & D C during the week except on Good Friday when I went to church in the morning, and heard a good sermon on self sacrifice, and made a contribution with others, "for the conversion of the Jews.". . .

Still reading Bryce. Read the chapter on the State Courts last night. In theory they are badly designed and constituted, but work better in practice than might be inferred, owing to a somewhat healthy public opinion, and the good example of the better environed Federal Judges. . . . Got a letter from Sarah McMillan nee Norris this week acknowledging the receipt of my biography. It takes me back 40 years and more, to the Sunday evening we spent in the orchard on the hill under the apple tree, when I first felt the effect of her handsome eyes.

29 (Sun) Easter Day . . . at Trinity as usual. A very large congregation. Many turned away. Chorus singing very fair. Sermon by Mr Cole on the resurrection excellent. A spiritual resurrection. As we sow so shall we reap. I told him it [was] in effect the teaching of my old Quaker Sermon—

Our entry into this world is naked and bare.
Our passage through it trouble and care.
Our exit from it no knows where.
If you do well here, you will do well there,
I could tell you no more if I was to preach a year. . . .

April 4 (Sat) . . . Settled my accounts on Wednesday. Paid out $1040, including $483 for taxes, $200 to H B and $100 to Mrs D.

11 (Sat) . . . Thursday evening had the Murch girls, Philura, Lucy & Jessie to dinner. The same evening attended a libra[r]y meeting when we authorized the architect to proceed with the construction of the building upon the basis of a cost of $135,000. We estimated our resources in property and money at $154,000 and I think we will add to our estimate $5000 making the cost $140,000, leaving us a margin of $14,000.

Last night I went to the theatre to see "Kajanka," w[h]ere I saw some excellent acrobatic performances and ballet dances by a little girl as well as the Sailors hornpipe admirably done by the same. Have dipped into Bryce a little this week . . . He is now talking about the place and work of parties in the Commonwealth and is more interesting than he was. . . . I see Judge Hoffman is going to die. Poor man. What will San Francisco be without him?

18 (Sat) . . . Sawyer called in the afternoon but stupid George reported me as out when I was simply upstairs.[4] I met him Monday morning in my chambers. Just over from Seattle where he has been holding court. Looks much better than

he did before he was taken sick. I think he is on short ration now also. At least much fairer than he did. He has been sitting in the C C all week. . . .

Thursday evening dined at Mr C E S Woods . . . The dinner was elegant and his house and furnishings are delightfully picturesque. Enjoyed a Caviare Salad, the first time I ever did relish the stuff. . . .

*25 (Sat)* . . . Judge Sawyer got through on Thursday evening. He was 7 days hearing the Terwilliger case[5] and 2 the case of the *Oregon*—the latter on appeal. He left for Boise on Friday morning. The evening before we dined at Ladds. Had an elegant dinner and a pleasant evening. The Woods were there. The Madame is near her time and did not look as if she had room for any dinner.

Had letters regularly from Mrs Deady during the week. She left S F on Thursday evening and arrived at Eugene this morning and drove over to Coburg where I had a telegram from her. All well. Had a letter from Justice Field dated the 18th in reply to my telegram announcing the sending of the 36 pound salmon. Said they were prepared to give the Leviathan a hearty welcome with champagne to the health of the sender or words to that effect.[6] . . .

*May 2 (Sat)* . . . Sat in the C C & D C during the week. Mrs Deady came home on Wednesday looking very well but with a cold in her throat so that she could not much more than speak audibly. Col Ben Stark called at my chambers on Thursday and at our rooms in the evening. He is the same old Benjamin softened and moderated a little by age.

. . . The weather has cleared and is now perfect—such days as are to be found in no part of the world except Oregon, and not always here. News reached here from Washington that the Supreme Court has affirmed me in the Maconnaughy case and the Bybee case.[7] The ruling in the former settles the question that "Bro Pennoyer" is *not* the State of Oregon. This will chafe him, and we may expect another tirade anent National Courts at the first favorable opportunity or even unfavorable one.

*May 9 (Sat)* . . . Friday evening "Kate," Mrs Edward N Deady, started for home in Canada via the Sound & Canadian Pacific with her two babies. Mrs Deady went with her as far as Tacoma. I furnished the money for her transportation and section $132 and $50 for incidental expenses, in all $182. I hope to get some of it back from the sale of their household effects. She had involved Edward so in debt by her extravagances that he was driven to drink, and there was nothing left but to send her home. I don't know what will be the result but I feel now as if I never wanted to see her again. E was in court this morning and looked pretty well. It seems my nose is to be kept on the grindstone (pecuniarily speaking) all the days of my life. Mrs Ladd & Mrs Holbrook called today and spent an hour speaking with me concerning the Presbyterian Chinese Home for women, and other things. What a sweet, wholesome, handsome looking woman Mrs Ladd has grown to be, and the (Angel of Mercy) Mrs H is all life and enthusiasm in the good cause of Chinese Women who stand on slippery places. The President [*Benjamin Harrison*] was received here in the rain—a light rain on Tuesday. I was hauled in the procession and in the evening sat on the platform in the exposition building, where 15,000 people gave the President as hearty a welcome as a man ever had, which he acknowledged in one of the best speeches for such an occasion, that I ever heard. I had a little conversation with the President in which I conveyed to him Judge Sawyers message and told him I wished Congress would change the retiring law so that he might have the opportunity to appoint my successor.

*16 (Sat)* . . . Tuesday the 12 inst was my 67 birthday. I had many handsome flowers sent me and with one basket there was an elegant and eulogistic Acrostic, which was published in the *Oregonian* of the 13th. The author is unknown to me[8]. . .

*23 (Sat)* Sunday (May 17) Attended Trinity . . . Mr Cole gave us an admirable sermon, Whitsunday-sermon on the theory that the church was guided by the Holy Spirit during the progress of the ages and still was as against the depontum theory—that Christ gave definite instructions to the Apostles during the forty days on earth between the resur[r]ection and the ascencion. He said by way of illustration that the Spirit was as much promised and was doubtless as much present at the Convention which lately elected Phil[l]ip[s] Brooks Bishop of Massachuset[t]s as at the Council of Nice[a].

. . . Early in the week accepted an invitation to the Banquet of the B B Society on the Queens birthday, and withdrew it last evening. I don't feel equal to the occasion. . . . I was to respond to the toast—The U S, which I have done once or twice. The weather has been delightful this week, only a little warm in the sun in the middle of the day.

Thursday attended the entertainment at the Trinity Parish House, where I heard some good music, ate some Strawberries & ice cream, and had a good time generally. Sorry to say not many society people present. Afraid of meeting some of the [h]oi polloi I suppose. . . .

*30 (Sat)* . . . The case of Rauh v The Southern Pacific Ry Co, was on trial all the week, and adjourned last night until Monday next. It is one of the Lake La Biche cases.[9] Mr [W H] Doolittle of Tacoma is one of the counsel for the pltf. He takes up a great deal of unnecessary time in cross examining a witness on trivial matters. This is Memorial Day and the "veterans" will strew flowers over the graves of their dead comrades. A pretty custom and one that does more for the living than the dead. . . .

*June 6 (Sat)* Sat in the C C & D C during the week. The trial of Rauh v The Southern Pacific Co was continued until Wednesday evening when I gave the case to the jury. The next morning they came in with a sealed verdict in favor of the plaintiff for $10,000. Another case against the Southern Pacific growing out of the Lake La Biche disaster was settled on Wednesday at noon and so we had no case for the rest of the week, and I have been taking it easy after my long siege. Engaged to take a set of Britan[n]ica from Mr Hardcastle for $65, to contain 25 volumes including the index, and to be in all respects like the English original save it is bound in cloth. I couldn't resist the temptation.

*13 (Sat)* . . . Justice Field arrived on Tuesday evening, and sat in the C C on Wednesday and heard the case of the [Oregon] Short line & Utah Northern v the Northern Pacific, a suit to compel the latter to interchange traffic at Portland by the carload. . . .

I am undergoing a massage treatment twice a week. Took it the 6th time last night at a dollar and a half a time, and an hour and a half a time. . . .

I concluded today my subscription for $40,000 for the endowment of the library. I stood at $35,000 for a long time and began to be afraid I was going to fail. I went to Mr Simeon Reed as a last resort and asked him to take another $5000 which he did without a word and paid me the compliment to say that he did it on my account more than otherwise. I felt happy you may rest assured.

*July 11 (Sat)* . . . Wednesday went to Eugene with Mrs Deady to attend commencement and annual meeting of the Regents. Thursday night at 12:40 boarded the overland train for San Francisco in the drawing room. Reached the Occidental, S F, Saturday morning at 10 oclock.

. . . Monday [*June 22*] Sat in the Circuit Court of Appeals with Justice Field & Sawyer, in robes, which Justice Field brought out from Washington. Sat in the district court for Hoffman the rest of the week and in the circuit court of appeals on Thursday. Saturday, June 27, went to del monte, stopping over at Palo Alto on an invitation from Governor Stanford.[10] We visited the School buildings and had luncheon at the house. The whole affair is superb. Reached del monte in the evening. Remained there until the afternoon of July 4th when we came back to San Francisco, took dinner at the Occidental, crossed the bay and started for home on the 9 oclock train. At Del Monte I bathed in the tank every day and twice in the ocean. *Sunday* we took a 17 mile drive in a coach and four by a Mr Taylor. . . .

*18 (Sat)* . . . [*During the week*] Wrote an argument or some suggestions for Justice Field in support of the injunction in the case of the Short Line and Utah Northern v the Northern Pacific on the 3 section of the Interstate Commerce act and the 5 section of the act organizing the defendant and forwarding it today. The weather has been clear and warm and my health has been tolerable. . . .

*25 (Sat)* . . . Thursday morning, Mr Whitney and his daughters Anita & Stephany arrived from Alaska and went on to San Francisco on Friday evening. Henderson took the girls to a water pic nic on Thursday evening and Mrs Deady took the party for a drive on Friday morning. The girls are a sweet interesting couple. Thursday, the Signal Service thermometer marked 102 in the shade, the highest since the service was instituted—17 years ago. I *think* I remember that sometime in the early sixties that the thermometer stood at 108 in [Saml] Smith & [Tom] Davis back yard in the shade, and that in 1859 it stood in the post office at Salem at 110 and that by 4 oclock in the afternoon the valley was bathed in a cool sea breeze from the Yamhill gap in the coast mountains. I *think* this was on the 27th of June, and that in northern California it stood at 117 degrees and the heat killed the crows. The apples in the Wallamet vall[e]y were cooked on the side exposed to the sun. Last night was cool and so was this morning. Weighed on Failings scales and marked only 226½, three and a half pounds less than I have weighed for many a year. The cause of [it] is loss of appetite which I am satisfied was produced by taking Oregon Kidney tea before breakfast.[11]

*August 1 (Sat)* . . . Wednesday evening [*July 29*] went out 2d street Electric Road with Mrs Deady to the cemetery. A picturesque ride—it was indeed grand in places. A meeting of some members of the Oregon Bar Association to take steps to receive Chief Justice Fuller was held in my court room. He will be here on Monday and will make his appearance in my court in the morning and then will go to drive. . . .

*8 (Sat)* Sunday (Aug 2) . . . Called at Bellingers in the afternoon in East Portland. He has a beautiful house on a whole block of ground on Holliday Avenue. We had lunch seasoned with a bottle of Champagne.

Sat in the C C & D C during the week. Monday had Ch Justice Fuller in court in the morning, when after deciding a couple of cases, we adjourned and the members of the bar and their friends were presented to the Ch Justice and also Judge [Moses] Hallett,[12] who happened to be present on his way to Alaska. This over we proceeded to the Portland and met Mrs Fuller and her daughter . . . A committee of ladies consisting of Mrs Deady, Dolph, Good, Corbett & Miss Failing were in attendance. We drove around town until 1 oclock and then had lunch, after which we went on the Heights in the cable car, and out to the cemetery on the Second street electric car. The male committee consisted of Mr Cyrus A Dolph, George H Williams, L B Cox, W B Gilbert, L L McArthur and myself. Altogether it was a pleasant day and the Ch Justice and his wife and daughter proved themselves very agreeable people. . . .

*22 (Sat)* . . . [Last] Saturday morning went to Salem with Mrs Deady to visit the Bushs. Sunday, Aug 16 staid at Bushs all day and left Monday at 1 oclock. Had a very pleasant time. Mr Bush and Sally were very kind and she is a charming girl. Simple, natural and sensible. . . . Decided a habeas corpus [case] yesterday in which I held that the Collector of Customs at Vancouver, British Columbia was a proper person to give a certificate to a Chinese merchant, a citizen of that country, and about to visit this. The Collector of this port had refused to allow him to land. . . . Bush has a grandson, Asahels son, whom I am glad to see he is fond of. He is a very attractive boy.

I see Pauls name among the list of passengers this morning that passed Medford northward bound on the Southern Pacific, but nothing of the Fields who were expected by the same train. . . .

*September 5 (Sat)* . . . [*Today*] came on the *Potter* and Astoria Railway to Gearhart Park, reaching there by 9 oclock and were lodged in room 5 on the office floor. The warrant for my monthly salary for August came this morning $400 and some cents.

*12 (Sat)* Spent this week at Gearhart Park. Went in the surf bathing every day. It was fine. Commenced raining on Tuesday and rained every other day of the week, clearing off in the afternoon to allow us to bathe. Most of the people at the Hotel went away during the week. . . . The living is pretty good except the fresh meat. We have a good room on the second floor at $5 per day. . . . We get the morning *Oregonian* in the evening of the day of its publication. I have read *Lorna Doone* here with as much zest and pleasure as when I read it or galloped through it 4 or 5 years ago. We got the news of Judge Sawyers death on Tuesday. It makes a great gap in my personal relations which never can be filled. . . .

*19 (Sat)* Spent the week until Friday evening at Gearhart Park. Bathed every day except when on account of a hard southwest wind on Wednesday and the night following the sea was rough and angry. Friday evening we left for Astoria. . . . remained until Monday morning. Saturday we rode to the upper end of the town on the horse cars, and Sunday afternoon we rode on the motor around Smiths Point. Our bill at Gearhart was $75 and at Astoria was $10.50. The whole cost of the excursion was $100.65. I think I feel the better for it. Mrs Deady and I walked up to Dodds place one afternoon. It is about ¾ of a mile from the Park. It is a lovely place. The first Monday, the 7th—we were there Mrs Deady and I went up to Grimes and had a choice lunch. Philura Murch was with us. The lunch cost $1.50 which added to [$]100.65 makes the whole expense $102.15 or $6.38 a day for both of us for 16 days there and going and coming.

*26 (Sat)* Sunday (Sept 18) At the Occident in Astoria. Went to Grace church and heard a good rat[t]ling sermon from Mr Short on "Judge" Samuel. Went on board the *R R Thompson* at night, and reached home the next evening. Sat in the district court during the week . . .

*October 3 (Sat)* Sunday (Sept 27) . . . Mr Cole preached on Angels. A little foggy. Sat in the C C & D C during the week and did some business. Do not consider my vacation over until Monday. Received a telegram from the clerk of the C[ourt] of A[ppeals] informing me that he had been directed by Justice Field to inform me that my services were required in said court at the October term. I telegraphed back that I could not come and that said term had better be allowed to lapse, and that by the January term there would be two circuit Judges appointed. Senator [W F] Sanders of Montana called on me yesterday, and in the evening Mrs Deady and I met him and his wife at the Exposition.[13] We saw the Indian War dance, and it amounted to nothing.

. . . This morning the Indian chiefs, Joseph, Moses, Lot and a Umatilla whose name I cannot make on hearing it once, called on me.[14] I showed Joseph his picture I had on the wall and he seemed to be pleased with it. He is a fine looking man, and so is Moses. . . .

*10 (Sat)* . . . Spent [*Sunday*] afternoon in my chambers cogitating my "remarks" on the death of Judge Sawyer Monday. Judge Williams presented resolutions on his death, prepared and passed at a meeting of the bar. McArthur secon[d]ed them. Ws address was lengthy and not equal to what I have heard him do. Mcs was extempore and also fell below his average. The Resolutions were short and to the point. I understand they were drawn by Bellinger. I feel the loss of Sawyer very much . . .

I have had what I suppose is lumbago since Thursday morning. Slept with a window in my bedroom partly open, and I suppose this was the cause. I have suffered from it exceedingly and I can walk with difficulty. . . . I telegraphed Henderson yesterday $350 of which I expect him to keep house until January first including $200 for tuition, and $50 for a suit of clothes. Gen [A V] Kautz called yesterday to see me. I had not met him since 1854 when we walked from Coos Bay on the beach to the mouth of the Umpqua river. He bears his years well.[15]

*17 (Sat)* . . . My lumbago is quite well. Bentzon sprayed my back with hot water Friday and Saturday nights of last week and rubbed me.[16] Did the same last Thursday. The week has been cool. Rained some mostly at night. This day is beautiful. The State Bar Association held its annual meeting in my court room today. The retiring President [*Cy Dolph*] made an admirable address. Cox was elected president to succeed him . . .

*24 (Sat)* . . . On Thursday the 22d, sold Mrs Deadys 1/15th interest in the Palatine Hill property for $3500—$300 cash and 16 notes of $200 each payable in one to 16 months with 8 per cent to A E Durand. Bought in May of 1890 for $2700. Dr Brooke (Mac) called to see me Thursday and bade me good bye. He goes to Vienna . . .

*31 (Sat)* . . . Wednesday [Sol] Hirsch, minister to Constantinople . . . made a long and pleasant call, and brought me a cane headed with a strange old piece of silver, which he got in Con the stick being malaga [ *?Malacca*] wood which he got in London. Mrs Deady and I called on him and his family last night at the Portland. We had a very pleasant call and a bottle of champagne. . . .

*November 7 (Sat)* . . . Tuesday evening met Mr & Mrs Villard by appointment at the library and afterward drove with them to the new building. Called with Paul at their reception at the Portland in the evening. Not many there I am sorry to say. Wrote a paragraph calling attention to Villards gift of $50,000 to the University and predicting that he would be remembered for it when the fame of his financial and railway exploits shall become a thing of the past. Gave it to the *Oregonian* in which it appeared on Wednesday morning. . . .

*21 (Sat)* . . . Friday evening went with Mrs Deady to Trinity Guild fair at the Exposition building. Spent $6.35 including $1 for tickets. Bought a boy doll for Katy Story, cost $2.50. The affair was a pleasant one and reasonably well attended. At the request of a Mrs [F L] Richmond I made "a few remarks" and unveiled a picture of Bishop Morris, which is to be presented to the hospital. The artists name is [L H] Roethe.[17] Miss Morris said it was an "*awful* likeness"—emphasis on the first word—and I think she is quite right. . . .

*28 (Sat)* . . . Sat in the C C & D C during the week except Thursday, Thanksgiving day, when I went to church in the morning and sat to Mr Couse[18] in the afternoon for an oil painting which the members of the bar are having done for my court room. It will have to hang in my or the circuit Judges chambers until I retire . . .

*29 (Sun)* Attended . . . Trinity as usual. Mr Cole officiated. I went partially to sleep—the first time under his ministrations. . . .

*December 12 (Sat)* . . . Wednesday we moved to Mrs Hills new house, and bid farewell to the old house where we have lived more than 6 years.[19] Have suffered a great deal this week from inf[l]ammation or irritation of the neck of the bladder. . . .

*19 (Sat)* . . . Attended Mrs Goldsmiths funeral yesterday at the House. It was packed with people—particularly Jewish women. The Rabbi made rather a good address—a little hifalutin here and there. She was a good woman and will be sadly missed. . . .

# NOTES

1. Charles B. Hurley; Tacoma contractor.

2. Hookupu; demonstration of paying tribute to.

3. Marie Wainwright (1853–1923), American actress.

4. Apparently George C. Stout (1869–1903), then crier of Deady's court; Lansing Stout's son, he was admitted to the Bar in 1893 and practiced with his step-father.

5. The heirs of Philinda Green Terwilliger alleged that a will prepared by her, and excluding her sons and heirs at law, was forged. The property involved was 150 acres of land having an estimated value of $500,000. Sawyer died before completing the opinion. After a second trial, the will was declared forged.

6. The salmon had continued to grow while in transit.

7. Bybee v the O.C.R.R. Co. was an early court test of the legality of the O. & C. land grants. Title to much of the O. & C. land reverted to the government years later.

8. The author of the acrostic was Frank V. Drake, Portland lawyer and businessman.

9. On November 11, 1890, the railroad trestle crossing the Lake La Biche area north of Salem collapsed under the weight of a passenger train. Five persons were killed outright and 83 injured, a number of them critically. The tragedy resulted in a series of law suits based upon the allegation, eventually accepted, that the trestle was improperly constructed.

10. The wearing of robes by the judges was not universally approved. "Old Judge Field, who has the brains of a Webster, the malice of a monkey and the vanity of a woman all packed in his handsome head, came out to reorganize the Court of Appeals, which consists of himself and a judicial man named Lorenzo Sawyer and an Oregon person called Deady. Field and Sawyer opened the court on Thursday morning in the presence of a gang of toadying lawyers, and they both wore black silk robes from their shoulders to the ground. . . . If a man cannot decide the law and listen to testimony in the ordinary garb of a gentleman I have some doubts of his honesty of purpose and no doubts of his incompetence." (Attributed to the Stockton *Mail*, OHS scrapbook 211, p. 113.) Standford in original.

11. Oregon Kidney Tea was a proprietary remedy which, according to its advertisers, prevented Bright's disease, diabetes, bladder stone; was a specific for ulceration of the kidneys, cured inflammation of the bladder and urinary organs, incontinency of urine, painful and suppressed menstruation, leucorrhoea and catarrh of the bladder.

12. Moses Hallett (1834–1913), Colorado lawyer; federal district judge for Colorado, 1877–1906.

13. Wilbur F. Sanders (1834–1905), Montana lawyer; Republican senator, 1890–93.

14. Chief Joseph the Younger (c.1840–1904); Moses was a Sinkiuse (Salish) and Lot a member of the Lower Spokane tribe.

15. August V. Kautz (1828–95), soldier; during the Civil War served as a cavalry brigade and division commander; *post* 1864 served in West and Southwest.

16. Harry Bentzon was the local masseur.

17. Nothing can be learned of Roethe beyond his name and the fact that he returned to California.

18. Eanger Irving Couse, American painter; specialized in painting Indians.

19. The new Hill House, the last over which Mrs. Hill would preside, was on 14th & Jefferson. It subsequently became the Jeanne D'Arc and is now the Marabba West, an apartment house catering largely to college students. It is one of Portland's more impressive Victorian piles.

When Chiefs Joseph, Moses, Lot and a Umatilla called on Deady in 1891, the judge pointed out Joseph's picture on his wall. He thought Joseph and Moses fine looking men. (Olin L. Warner bas relief, OHS.)

From left, standing: Miss Min Couch, Walter J. Burns, Virginia Wilson, Elizabeth R. Glisan, Clementine Wilson and Holt Wilson. From left, sitting: Louise Wilson (Linthicum), Kathleen Burns and her mother, Mrs. W. J. (Mary Carrie Wilson) Burns, Caroline Couch Wilson (widow of Dr. R. with baby Anita Burns, Georgina Burns (Wallace), Fan W son (Dr. Holt's wife) with Caroline Burns (Hoffman).

Southern Pacific track near New Era (just above Oregon City on the Wallamet), 1890.

The Glorious Fourth in Butteville, with band, dignitaries, pioneers, children and the community. Veteran of such occasions, Deady's most notable "procession" in 1891 was that welcoming President Benjamin Harrison to Portland in May.

# 1892

*January 9 (Sat)* . . . Thursday evening started for San Francisco to sit on the court of appeals and reached here this morning with Mrs Deady after a pleasant trip and at an incidental expense of $8.75. . . .

*16 (Sat)* Sunday (Jan 10) Attended church at Trinity and heard a good sermon. . . . Took a car ride in the afternoon. Staid at home (in my hotel) during Monday and rested. Tuesday sat in the Court of Appeals . . . Heard a patent case on Wednesday in which my old Salem friend [John] Boone appeared as counsel. Heard two of Judge Hanfords cases on Thursday and I am afraid we will have to reverse them both. . . . Saturday evening we went to a wedding reception at John D Sp[r]eckels. Mrs Donahue and Mrs Martin called for us. It was a splendid affair. A fine house superbly furnished and beautifully decorated for the occasion. The whole party were seated at tables for refreshments . . . We had oysters, terrapin, tongue, ham and salad, and ice cream and champagne galore. . . .

*30 (Sat)* . . . Sunday, Jan 24. Went to dinner at Whitneys. Called at McGraws on the way. Met Garber at Whitneys. Had a good dinner and a pleasant time. . . . Since we have been here we have been entertained very much. . . . Saturday, Jan 30th we went to Col George Hoopers in Sonoma county and staid until Sunday afternoon. Had a delightful time. The Col and Mrs Hooper are two genial, hospitable interesting people, particularly the Madam.

*February 6 (Sat)* Monday . . . Settled my account with the marshal and drew $235 for travel and expenses attending the Court of Appeals 28 days. . . . Tuesday went to the wedding of Paul and Miss Mary[e] N Thompson at Redwood. It was a lovely [ *?affair*]. The wedding took place at High Noon. The company consisted of Maryes relatives—a nice lot by the way—Bishop [Wm] Nichols[1] performed the ceremony assisted by the Rector of the Parish. Altogether it was a very nice affair. Mrs Deady gave the young people $100 worth of silver and I gave Paul a check for $500. They had many nice presents. We returned to S F on the three oclock train and left for Portland that evening where we arrived at ½ past 7 Thursday evening. Sat in court that day and since.

*13 (Sat)* . . . Paul and Mary[e] arrived Tuesday evening from San Francisco and took possession of their room which had been handsomely decorated by Mrs Deady and Folger and the girl cousins. A rush of nice presents have been coming in all week.

Got a letter from John L Stevens, American minister to Honolulu with a copy of his life of Adolphus Augustus, which I am now reading and much interested in. . . .

Wednesday evening there was a pleasant gathering of the "relations" to welcome Mary[e] to her new house. Weighed today and drew 226½ pounds.
*20 (Sat)* Sunday . . . at Trinity as usual. Mr Cole officiated and preached on the sermon on the mount, a good portion of which was devoted to the refutation of an article in the morning *Oregonian* in praise or defense of war. . . . Paid Mrs Ds and my city taxes on the 17th—San Pats day—amounting to $261 just $112 more than last year. Stated the account between Mrs D and [myself] for the year 1891. She is a little over $3000 in my debt. Was a little over $4000 last year. . . .
*21 (Sun)* . . . at Trinity church as usual. Mr Cole officiated. Preached from the words "Seek first God and his righteousness and all things else shall be added unto you," and explained the paradox after a fashion.
*27 (Sat)* Monday announced a decision in Gilbert v New Zealand Ins Co holding that the clause in Sec 1 of act of 1888 permitting a suit between citizens of differing states to be brought in the district where either resides, did not apply to a suit between a citizen of a state of the Union and a foreign subject or corporation. Got an opinion yesterday from Justice Harlan, holding that a foreign corporation or domestic corporation is an inhabitant of a district in which it has an agency and does business. . . .
*March 5 (Sat)* . . . Tuesday evening with Mrs Deady heard Joe Jefferson and a first class troupe in "The Rivals." It was splendid. Mrs Drew as Mrs Malaprop was delicious.[2] Wednesday evening was what we call Ash Wednesday. I generally go to church on that day but I had a case to hear and couldn't go this time. Thursday evening delivered a lecture before the graduating class in the School of medicine and will deliver another on next Tuesday. On next Wednesday commence my lectures before the graduating class of the School of Law. Yesterday was Hendersons 23d birthday. Telegraphed him $25.
Attended a dinner given by Mr Corbett last night at his residence to commemorate the 41 anniversary of his arrival in Oregon. There were 16 persons present all but one who came before he did. The dinner was elegant, and the wines choice and abundant. Mr Corbett welcomed his guests in a well worded address which on account of his health Col McCracken read for him. I made a few impromptu remarks. Mr Corbett referred particularly to 4 merchants present, including himself, Mr Lewis, Mr Ladd & Henry Failing. . . .
*12 (Sat)* . . . The weather has been delightful during the week. Perfect springtime. Paul & Mary[e] went down to San Francisco I believe on Thursday evening. . . .
*19 (Sat)* Sunday . . . Mr Cole officiated and preached a pretty good sermon, but did not quit when he got through. Monday allowed a motion for a new trial in the case of Isaacs v Southern Pacific Company on the ground of an error in admitting the plaintiff to show that the defendant in reconstructing the bridge which was the subject of the action, used longitudinal braces where none were used before. . . . Have been reading in odd hours at my chambers Robertsons *Charles V.* What a lifelong duel was waged between he and Francis I of France, and what a corrupt and scurvy lot of rascals, except Adrian, were in the Papacy during the time. Delivered my second lecture in the law course on Wednesday evening, and the first on the Wednesday before. Delivered the last of three

lectures to the Medical class on Thursday. Slim attendance after the first one. That lets me out. Large attendance in the law class—22 in number I believe. . . .

*26 (Sat)* Sunday . . . Called at the Storys in the afternoon and congratulated Katy on her engagement to Dr Jones. She looked charming and behaved well. Monday delivered opinion in the C C in Gilbert v New Zealand Ins Co holding that a foreign insurance company which does business in this state pursuant to the laws thereof is an "inhabitant" of the same within the first section of the judiciary act, and also that when it created an attorney in the state with power to receive service of process for it, it thereby consented in advance to be sued therein.[3]

. . . Read Goldsmith during the week—"She Stoops to Conquer" especially. It don't amount to much. "The Traveller," "Deserted Village" and "Retaliation" are his fame. Lectured to the law class Wednesday evening. . . .

*April 2 (Sat)* . . . Wednesday swore Mr [William B] Gilbert in as circuit judge. The clerk administered the oath and I introduced him to the bar, when there was a general handshake and congratulation.

Left home on Friday evenings train for this place (San Francisco) accompanied by Mrs Deady where we arrived this morning and are stopping at the Occidental.

*9 (Sat)* Monday Judges Gilbert, [W W] Morrow and myself opened the court of appeals and heard some motions and adjourned the court until Monday the 11th to await the arrival of [Joseph] McKenna. Wednesday Mrs Deady and I went to Santa Rosa where we remained until Friday evening the guests of Mr Robert A Thompson. We had a very pleasant time and enjoyed his two charming daughters Virginia and Betty immensely. Visited a winery where 400,000 gallons were stored in process of curing. Visited some stables and saw some very fine horses. Called at the public library and made the acquaintance of the Librarian, Miss Kumli and told her she ought to spell her name Comely. She is a Swiss German and a handsome interesting woman. Friday we lunched at Mr Thomas Thompsons, the editor and publisher of the Santa Rosa *Democrat*.[4] . . .

*16 (Sat)* . . . Sat in the circuit court of appeals during the week except Good Friday and Saturday. . . . Wrote an opinion in U S v Gee Lee, maintaining the right of a merchant Chinese to return to the U S after a temporary absence without producing certificate required by Sec 6 of the restriction acts.

*17 (Sun)* Easter Day, and a beautiful one. We went to Trinity church and staid to communion. The church was beautifully decorated, the music was elaborate and the sermon good. Went to Mrs Donahues to dinner, where we met Mrs Lilly Coit the same person I used to know in the Sixties at the Occidental.

Sat in the court of appeals during the week . . . Friday called with Mrs Deady on Miss [Minnie] Lake at her Seminary. Met her sister Mrs Thompson there. The School was receiving and we had a pleasant time. . . .

The new Circuit Judge McKenna sat in the court the past week. He is a smooth pleasant man, but I do not know what to say of him yet.

In the evening went with Judge Gilbert to the Baldwin to hear "Beau Brummell." Sprightly little thing, with a large house, mostly Jewish.

Start home tomorrow afternoon.

*30 (Sat)* . . . [*Sunday*] Went on board the train in the evening and started for Portland where we arrived on Tuesday morning. Sat in the C C & D C during the rest of the week. It has been showery during the week. My legs have been weaker than usual. Commenced the massage again. Mrs Deady has been confined to her bed since our arrival with rheumatism and sore throat. . . .

*May 7 (Sat)* . . . The weather has been charming most of the week. Rained a little this morning. Getting ready for the Columbia River Centennial, as I supposed it rained on the 12th of May, 1792, when Capt Gray crossed the bar. . . .

*14 (Sat)* Sunday . . . Mr Cole gave us a Screed on the expulsion of the Chinese, saying it (the Geary bill) was a disgrace to the country.[5] . . . Heard [John] Fiskes lecture on Jackson as a backwoodsman and a general on Thursday night and am going to the second one tonight on his career as a politician and President. Monday went to Astoria on the *Potter* to attend the Centennial of the discovery of the Columbia river by Robert Gray. Came back in the same boat Thursday morning and lived on her in the meantime. The celebration was a success. The war steamers *Baltimore* and *Charleston* were in the harbor and will be in this port this morning. Fiske was the Orator of the day and did well with the exception of the adoption of the Whitman myth as to the acquisition of this country. . . .

*21 (Sat)* Sunday . . . Mr Cole gave us a talk on Presbyterianism, seeing the General Assembly was about to meet here. It was very well done and interesting. The assembly met on Thursday the 19th and the town has been full of black coats ever since. . . .

Attended a Banquet given at the Portland last evening by the chamber of commerce to the officers of the cruisers *Baltimore* and *Charleston*. Made a response to the toast "the President of the U S" in which I talked about the Presidency saying the President ought to be elected for 10 years and not re-eligible. Got home at ½ past 3.

*28 (Sat)* . . . On Wednesday and Thursday attended the [*Presbyterian*] Assembly meeting on the former day in the evening and on the latter in the morning when I heard the famous Dr [C A] Briggs for 1½ hours in opposition to the Assembly entertaining the appeal from the N Y Presbytery in his case.[6] It was a technical question and a very technical argument, weakened somewhat by the multiplicity of points, many of which seemed frivolous to me. He had one good point I thought and that was that the appeal should have been taken to the Synod of N Y. . . .

*June 11 (Sat)* . . . The state election was held on Monday. The Republicans won in the state, but lost some county offices in this county to the citizens ticket.

The week has been an anxious one on account of the doings of the Republican convention at Minneapolis. To our great relief on Friday the trickster Blaine was thrown overboard and Harrison nominated by a large vote. . . .

*18 (Sat)* . . . The weather has been dryer and warmer this week than last. Strawberries have been and are very plenty. Cherries are good but somewhat scarce. We go to Eugene next week to attend commencement. Weighed 223 pounds light.

*25 (Sat)* . . . Tuesday went to Eugene to attend Commencement at the University. Returned Friday evening. Took Mrs Deady and Elsie Failing with me and had a grand time generally. Stopped at Hoffman House. Had good rooms but bad fare. It cost $21 for the three of us 2 3/4 days each. I paid Elsies. Drew $15 from the University on expense account which included $7 for Mrs Deadys tavern bill for which I charged so much of my railroad fare.

Three members of the law Class, [Dan J] Malarkey, [Rodney L] Glisan and [Russell E] Sewall delivered first class orations on Wednesday.[7] A class of eight from the School of letters delivered good orations on Thursday. The regents increased the pay of the professors and the teachers 10 per cent. The weather was delightful and the country beautiful. . . .

*July 9 (Sat)* . . . Wednesday [*June 29*] Mrs Deady, Lucy Failing and I went to Coburg to attend Lucy Murchs wedding with Mr [F P] Chamberlain[8] which took place on Thursday afternoon. It was a very pleasant affair. Elsie Failing was there. The minister, Mr Bates was a pleasant fellow and performed the ceremony after the Episcopal form admirably. Got home on Friday. Went up and back on the Coburg road. . . .

*16 (Sat)* . . . Have been reading a volume of Essays of Huxleys, entitled *Controverted Questions.* Very interesting. Wrote to Judge Morrow agreeing that the Court of Appeals could not review the action of the trial court in refusing to grant a new trial on the ground of excessive damages.

*23 (Sat)* . . . Weather has been pleasant during the week. At times a little cool. Finished Huxley and he had finished Gladstone therein . . .

*30 (Sat)* Sat in the C C & D C during the week. . . . The weather has been very pleasant a little cool and cloudy in the morning and tolerably warm the latter part of the day. Weighed 220 pounds this afternoon.

*September 10 (Sat)* On Wednesday [*August 18*] evening Mrs Deady and I started for Castle Crag Tavern on the Sacramento river [*near Shi-lo-th Springs*] 4 miles below Dunsmuir and returned on Wednesday morning September 7. We found it a pleasant place in a little vall[e]y in the mountains on a small stream that puts into the Sacramento. The tavern is a handsome commodious building that will accommodate about 100 persons. The spring is about 3/4 of a mile up the vall[e]y from the tavern. The water is heavily charged with carbonic acid gas and is delightful drinking—almost equal to champagne. Made some pleasant acquaintances from California—principally from San Francisco. My legs got weaker on the journey there and have not got better. I commenced massage with Miss Keene again on Thursday night and am going to continue it every other night. Weighed this afternoon 219 lbs, the lowest for many years.

*17 (Sat)* . . . Sat in the D C during the week. Dr Strong attended me. Gave me a purgative that acts like a charm. Also gave me mixture for my legs. Can't say that it has helped them. Though I am inclined sometimes to think it has. Mrs Deady went up to McMinnville last night. I and Henderson went out to the graduation of the class of nurses from the Good S Hospital. It took place at the new medical school building of the Oregon University just across the street from the Hospital and was in every way a success.

*November 4 (Sat)* On Friday evening the 26th day of September, I started to

Baltimore to attend the General Convention of the Episcopal church at Baltimore. Mrs Deady accompanied me. . . . Henderson was with us going to New York to attend the medical school. At Chicago we separated and we remained there a day at the Grand Pacific, and proceeded the next day on our Journey via the Baltimore & Ohio. We reached Baltimore the next Sunday the 2 Oct and stopped at St James.

On Wednesday 5 Oct the Convention [met] in Emmanuel church. We remained at Baltimore until Tuesday the 11th when we went to Washingto[n] City where we put up at Wormley[s] where we staid until Friday the 21st. While there we were entertained . . . and had a pleasant time generally. We reached Chicago on the evening of the 22 and proceed[ed] to Portland which we reached on the morning of the 26th. While at Baltimore we had a visit from Gov Holliday of Winchester, Va for a day and a night which we enjoyed very much. At Washingto[n] I was at a dinner given by the Chief Justice to the newly appointed Judge [Geo] Shiras.[9] All the Judges of the Supreme Court were there except Field besides other judges of the court of claims and the district. Justice Gray took me to dinner and I sat on the right of Shiras the guest of the occasion.

Deady Collection, OHS.

# L'Envoi

He was desperately ill when he arrived back at Portland. The doctors diagnosed a stroke and prescribed rest, but the habit of work was ingrained. Before the end of October he had left his bed and was dragging himself painfully to his chambers.

Somehow he managed to hold court regularly throughout the remainder of that year and into the early months of the next. It was during this time he made the final entry in the diary, describing his trip East and the dinner for Shiras. The writing is a sick man's writing, crabbed and marred by errors, and laboring over it must have cost him terrible effort, but he was determined to see it recorded that in such distinguished company he was seated well above the salt.

On March 6, 1893, he opened the new term but a week later took to his bed for the last time, passing into a coma broken only by occasional moments of lucidity. Bush came. Deady recognized and greeted him, but slipped back into unconsciousness almost immediately. On March 24, with the family gathered in the room to await the end, he roused himself and asked for a drink of water. A little dribbled onto his wrist and he flicked it away irritably before sinking back onto the pillows. Dr. Strong, who was in attendance, leaned over the bed and asked if there was anything more he wished to say.

"Nothing," the old man murmured wearily. "Nothing."

# NOTES

1. Bishop William Nichols (1849–1924), assistant bishop of California, 1890; succeeded as bishop in 1893 and continued until 1919.

2. Joseph Jefferson (1829–1905), actor. Bob Acres in "The Rivals" was among his most famous parts. Louisa Lane Drew (1820–1897), actress and theatrical manager; she was a grandmother to Ethel, John and Lionel Barrymore.

3. Justice Harlan's decision forced Deady to reverse himself with embarrassing haste.

4. William W. Morrow (1843-1929), California attorney and jurist; Republican Congressman, 1885–91; federal district judge, 1891–97; *post* 1897, federal circuit judge. Joseph McKenna (1843–1926), California attorney and jurist; Republican congressman, 1885–92; federal circuit judge, 1892–97; succeeded Field as associate justice of the supreme court in 1897. Robert A. Thompson, Santa Rosa editor, publisher and historian, died 1903. Thomas L. Thompson (1838–98), California editor, congressman and diplomat; owner-editor of the Sonoma *Democrat.*

5. The Geary Act of 1892 was named for its sponsor, Thomas J. Geary (1854–1929), a California congressman. Intended to replace the expiring Scott Act, it suspended Chinese immigration for ten years and required non-resident Chinese to get yearly certificates of residence, providing that any who failed to do so could be expelled from the United States.

6. Charles A. Briggs (1841–1913), clergyman, Hebrew scholar and theologian; *post* 1890, professor of biblical theology at Union Seminary; tried and acquitted of heresy by the New York Presbytery, 1892; his prosecution appealed to the General Assembly which condemned him and suspended him from the ministry. The Seminary refused to remove him from his position and broke its connection with the Presbyterian church. Briggs later became an Episcopalian.

7. Dan J. Malarkey (1870–1939), Rodney Glisan (1869–1934), and Russell E. Sewall (1870–1948) all practiced law in Portland.

8. F. P. Chamberlain was later a Portland attorney.

9. George Shiras (1832–1924), jurist; associate justice of the United States Supreme Court, 1892–1903.

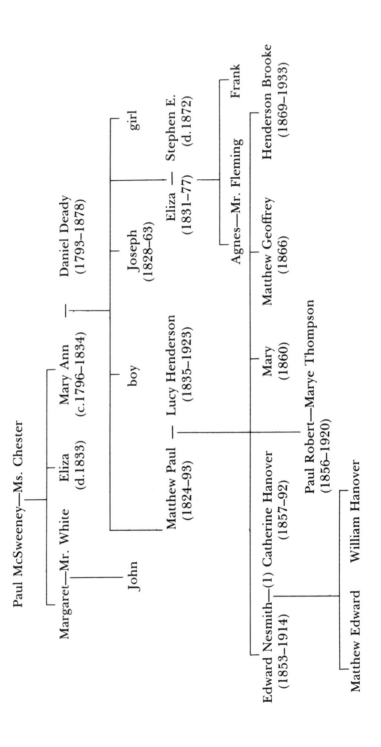

*Deady Family Genealogy*

GOOD CITIZENS ARE THE
RICHES OF A CITY

Skidmore Fountain, Portland, by Olin Warner. It was unveiled in 1888.
1975 view toward "Wallamet" and east side. (Hodge photo.)

Skidmore Fountain, about mid-1930s. The New Market Theatre ("Garage") still remains today, but the two-story building at right has vanished. (Boychuk Collection, OHS.)

# INDEX

Arnold, B. L., 466, 483
Arnold, Frederick K., 156, 223, 391, 395, 414, 462, 479, 492
Arnold, Mary Tower, 213, 223
Arrigoni, Elizabeth Lacey, 31, 50
Arrigoni, S. N., 31, 50
Arthur, Chester A., 306, 384: descr., 371
Ash, John, 310
Ashburner, Emilia Field, *xxi*, 428, 593
Ashburner, Sallie, *xxi*, 195–96
Ashland, Ore., 444, 516
Askew, Ann, 367, 381
Aspinwall, William H., 26, 49
Astoria, Ore., 31, 32, 89–90, 240, 286, 399, 479
Atkinson, George H., 184, 204, 306
Atkinson, Josiah L., 336, 376
Atwood, Abigail W. T., 129, 146, 519
Aurora (Dutchtown), Ore., 21, 31, 48, 136, 159, 193, 214: dissolution, 340, 377; gift to MPD, 342
Austin, Jonathan, 584, 607
Avery, Benjamin, 12, 45
Avery, J. C., 34, 50, 204
Avery, Martha M., 188, 204, 466

Babbitt, Edwin B., 85, 109, 183
Babbitt, Sarah Sprague, 109, 300
Bache, Charles M., 360, 361, 380
Bachelder, R. M., 143, 148
Back, Seid, *see* Seid Back
Bacon, Hattie, 132, 146
Bailey, Mark, 216, 224, 431
Baker, Dorsey S., 322, 332
Baker, Edward D. (I), 341, 378
Baker, Edward D. (II), 397
Baker, Ore., 536
Balch claim, 19, 47, 400, 407, 441, 449, 503
Baldwin, Charles H., 385, 406
Baldwin, E. S. (Lucky), 474, 484
Ball, M. D., 311, 330
Ballou, Mrs. A. Z., 263, 273
Baltimore, Md., 361–65
Bancroft, A. L. (and Co.), 16, 90, 117, 165, 166, 474, 489: and *Deady's Reports*, 3, 10, 14, 21, 23, 64, 67, 96, 100–101, 104; *Fifth Reader*, 137; *Oregon Code*, 163, 212; school book case, 280, 293
Bancroft, Hubert H. (and Co.), 396, 403, 414: *Chronicles of the Kings (Builders)*, 539–604 *passim; History of Oregon*, 424, 502, 539, 551
Bancroft, Mrs. H. H., 592
Bank of British Columbia, *xxvii*, 173, 178
Bank of California, suspension, 197, 205
Barker, A. H., 189

Barker, Laura Adair, 32, 50, 130, 169, 171, 282
Barker, William M., 139, 147, 384
Barnes, William H. L., 471, 474, 476, 477, 502
Barnesville, O., *xxxiii*, 368–69
Barnhart, Henry, 469
Barnhart, Mary De L. Campbell, *xviii*, 83
Barnhart, William H., *xviii*, 469: Holladay biog. planned, 83; Holladay-Campbell scandal, 96; Holladay custody fight, 554; Holladay buys off, 103–104, 105; Williams scandal, 554
Barrett, Charles, 140, 147
Barrett, Lawrence, 294: MPD meets, 281–82; plays Boston, 348, New York, 346, Portland, 282
Barstow, A. C., 220, 224
Bartsch, Albert, 333
Bassett, Elisha, 350, 379
Bastian, Adolph, 305, 330
Bayard, T. F., 369, 381
Beardslee, Lester A., 311, 331
Beaver, Herbert, 85, 109
Beck, Helena J., 193, 205
Beck, James B., 386, 406
Beebe, Charles F., 514, 527
Beecher, Henry Ward, 420, 433, 609
Beekman, B. B., 447, 459
Beekman, C. C., 444, 446, 458, 459
Beers, Hiram W., 425, 434, 474
Begbie, Matthew, 313, 314, 315, 331, 601
Belcher, John L., 346, 378
Belcher, William C., 425, 427, 434
Bell, Joseph, 389, 406
Bell, Robert, 595, 608
Bell, Sam, 359, 360
Bell, William H., 12, 45
Bell, Will N., 277, 293
Bellaire, O., 369
Bellinger, Charles B., 97, 110, 121, 128, 140, 233, 270, 294, 304, 492, 594, 617, 618
Belt, A. M., 329
Bemis, B. B., 285, 294
Bentley, Robert, 188, 204
Bentzon, Harry, 618, 620
Berry, M. P., 312, 331
Besser, Luzerne, 425, 426, 434
Bevan, Arthur, 559, 560, 574
Bickerton, Richard F., 577, 590, 606
Bierstadt, Albert, 354, 379
Biles, John D., 168
Billings, Frederick, 95, 110, 421, 439
Bills, Cincinnati, 16, 47
Bingham, Mr. and Mrs. Hiram, 580, 607

632

Bingham, John A., 28, 149
Bishop, Bernice Pauahi Paki, 607
Bishop, Charles R., 578, 579, 585, 589, 606
Bishop, Washington Irving, 530: Deady meets, 530–31; death, 545
Bishop Scott Grammar School (later Bishop Scott Academy): building fund, 1, 15, 16, 85, 92; endowment fund, 22, 27; exams and closing exercises, 3–4, 25, 84, 129, 192, 305, 306, 396, 446, 517, 535; financial condition, 1, 27; fire destroys, 242; headmasters, *xvii–xviii*, 1, 9, 160, 186, 190, 257, 270; rebuilt, 258, 270
*The Black Crook,* 29, 54–55
Black, John C., 498, 506
Blackler, Lydia H., *xvii*, 23, 66, 76, 135, 167, 168, 244, 290, 319, 331, 598
Blacks, 82, 587; *see also* individuals, *e.g.,* J. H. Butler, James Fullilove
Blaine, James G., 307, 371, 455, 536, 543, 551, 625
Blair, Montgomery, 386, 406
Blake, Lillie Devereaux, 471, 484
Blanchet, Francis Norbert (Archbishop), *xvii,* 11, 123, 142, 194, 195, 264, 335, 395
Blanding, Gordon, 398, 407, 427
Bliss, Duane L., 266, 273
Bliss, George, 563, 573
Blodgett, Henry W., 344, 378
Bloomfield, Nathaniel, 397, 407
Blum, Lehman, 278, 293
Bogus Charley, 150
Boise, Elizabeth Theresa (Lizzie), *xvii,* 34, 86, 124, 128, 129, 138, 157, 192, 199, 236, 240, 255, 261, 270, 281
Boise, Reuben P., *xvii,* 12, 167, 219, 269, 392: legal tactics, 210; 4th of July address, 193
Bolles, Frederick, 454, 459
Bond, Hugh L., 364, 380
Bonham, B. F., 53
Bonnell, C. R., 83, 86, 91, 102, 109, 360
Bonnell, Mrs. C. R., 31
Bonney, Charles C., 344, 378
Boone, John L., 67, 106, 622
Booth, Newton, 30, 49
Boruck, Marcus D., 475, 484
Bosco, Carl, 87, 109, 171
Boston Charley, 150
Boston, Mass., 348–50
Boston Bar, B. C., 316
Bourne, Jonathan, 395, 407
Boutwell, George F., 567, 573
Bowen, Charles, 421, 423, 433
Bowen, John D., 71, 107
Bowie, August J., 64, 106, 425

Bowlby, John Q. A., 90, 109
Bowlby, Wilson, 69, 107, 235
Bowles, Samuel (II), 8, 44, 350
Bowles, Mrs. Samuel (II), 350–51
Bowles, Samuel (III), 44, 350–51, 402, 403, 472
Bowne, Mrs. S. R., 514, 527
Boyd, Hamilton, 187
Boyd, Ida, 80, 86, 87, 136, 158, 161, 323, 332
Boyd, James T., 423, 434, 473
Boynton, H. V., 422, 433
Bradford, Amory H., 166, 167, 177
Bradford, Daniel, 58–59
Bradford, Putnam, 59
Bradley, Joseph P., 264, 273, 302, 387, 565
Bradwell, James B., 344, 378
Bradwell, Myra, 344, 378
Bramlette, William, 101, 116
Brasfield, James, 499, 506
Brasfield, Lydia Owens, 499, 506
Brassey, Idrina Nevill, 561, 572
Brassey, Thomas A., 561, 572
Breck, Annie Ashmead, 26, 43, 66, 89, 90, 133
Breck, Gretchen, 499
Breck, J. M., 4, 43, 66, 300
Breck, Mabel, 499
Breck and Ogden, 314
Breckinridge, John C., *xxxvi,* 376
Brenan, D. B., 79, 108
Brenham, Robert, 576, 606
Bretherton, C. E., 280, 285, 293
Brewster, Benjamin H., 385, 386, 406
Bridgman, H. L., 422, 433
Briggs, Charles A., 625, 629
Brigham, A. C., 428
Bristow, Benjamin H., 562
Bristow, Iola, 130, 146
Bristow, William W., 466, 483
Bristow, Mrs. William W., 281
British Benevolent Society, 104, 111, 213, 234–35, 305, 338, 414, 446, 467, 495, 518, 615
Britt, Peter, 445, 458
Brockenbrough, Mrs. J. B., 512, 527
Broetje, John, 502, 506
Bronaugh, Earl C., 88, 92, 109, 202
Brooke, Belle, 165
Brooke, George, 385
Brooke, Lloyd, family of:
    Brooke, Edward (son), 136, 170, 174, 236, 246, 302, 550
    Brooke, Genevieve Hamilton (wife), *xvii,* 3, 4, 18, 19, 27, 35, 62, 88, 92, 122, 123, 136, 166, 169, 170, 184, 189, 196,

633

552; T. H. Huxley, 626; J. Keats, 513; R. Kipling, 600; H. C. Lea, 596–602, *passim;* LeSage, 393; Margaret of Navarre, 80; P. Merimee, 190–91; H. Milman, 542; J. T. Morse, 217, 218, 219, 410; J. Motley, 197; "Ouida," 500, 600; Restoration dramatists, 442; W. Robertson, 623; W. W. Roscoe, 183, 184–85; J. J. Rousseau, 264; W. Scott, 38; *Scottish Songs,* 290; *Secret Museum of the King of Naples,* 90; Shakespeare, 62, 64, 462, 463; L. Stephen, 325; F. Stephens, 467; J. L. Stephens, 622; Suetonius, 389; H. Taine, 230, 552–57 *passim;* A. Tennyson, 195, 231; W. M. Thackeray, 165, 191–92; L. Tolstoi, 522; A. Trollope, 412; Vergil (Dryden trans.), 448, 449; E. Whymper, 310; W. Wycherly, 162; C. M. Yonge, 229, 230; E. Zola, 306, 320, 522

lobbying, 96–97, 324; marriage, *xxxiv–xxxvi,* 24–25, 84–85, 130, 193, 236, 307, 339

opinions on—

    historical figures: J. Q. Adams, 410; Blucher, 399, 400; J. Bunyan, 324; Elizabeth I of England, 122, 124; A. Hamilton, 218; Henry VIII, 119, 494; A. Jackson, 524; T. Jefferson, 217, 218, 416, 472; Marie Antoinette, 230; Mary I of England, 121; Mary Stuart, 122; J. Monroe, 416; Philip II of Spain, 197; A. Pope, 325; J. J. Rousseau, 264; Wellington, 400

    religions and religionists: Baptists, 277, 470; Congregationalists, 277; Episcopalians, 563–64; Jews, 188, 532, 556; Lutherans, 39; Methodists, 135, 157, 188; Presbyterians, 229, 301; Roman Catholics, 301, 472, 531, 554–55, 596–602 *passim,* 611, 623; Spiritualists, 95, 137; Unitarians, 262; *see also* Evangelists

    social, political and moral questions: democracy, 521; European immigration, 339, 354; Indian wars, 241, 262; international tribunal, 1; juvenile delinquency, 8, 9; monarchy, 98; municipal corruption, 506; presidential term, 625; prohibition, 160; reconstruction, 82; secret ballot, 100; slavery, 253, 455, 524, 587; socialism, 544; states' rights, 511

portrait painted, 263, 518, 619; resig-
nation considered, 604, 615; self-estimate, 66, 72; senatorial candidacy, 399, 400; Stanford University trustee, 489

travel—

    Alaska, 310–12; British Columbia, 137–38; 309–18 *passim,* 601; California, 163, 264–68, 342–43, 389–91, 422–29, 473–78, 575–76, 591–93, 616, 625; Connecticut, 347–48; District of Columbia, 365–66, 369–75, 384–88, 564–68, 627; Hawaii, 576–91; Idaho, 537–38; Illinois, 344–45, 569; Maryland, 361–65, 627; Massachusetts, 348–51; Nevada, 265–66; New Mexico, 389; New York, 345–54, 562–64; Ohio, 366–69; Oregon, *see* placenames; overland to Oregon (1849), *xxxiv,* 30, 165, 316, 475; Pennsylvania, 354–61; Rhode Island, 348; Virginia, 371–73, 565; Washington, 137–38, 322–23, 443–44, 449–50; *see also* city and town names

verses, 86, 135, 167–68, 174, 211, 217, 288, 289

Deady, Paul Robert (son): bar exam, 401; conduct, 175–76, 499, 500, 515; court crier, 240, 339; debts, 500, 515, 534; education, 3–4, 25, 118, 125, 129, 160, 235, 290, 299, 302, 304, 325; employed, 244, 289, 304; ill, 531, 532, 533, 545; later career, *xxxvi;* marriage, 622; travels to Calif. and Nevada, 264–68; U. S. Commissioner, 471, 484

Deady, William Hanover (son END), 614; christened, 611

*Deady's Reports,* 3, 10, 14, 21–24 *passim,* 29, 41, 64, 67, 94–98 *passim,* 100–101, 104

Dearborn, Helen Flint, 130, 145

Dearborn, Richard, 124, 145

Debris case, 411, 424–28 *passim,* 437–38, 440, 542

DeHart, Edward J., *xx,* 466, 569, 595

DeHart, Ella, *xx,* 414, 443, 448, 450, 456, 516

DeHart, Elmira Thresher, *xx,* 466, 569, 595

Dekum, Frank, 93, 110, 255, 272, 447, 532, 535

Dekum, Lisa, 400, 407

Delay, Joseph, 45

Delay, Joshua, 45

Dell, Sidney, 230, 235, 246, 275, 278, 281, 287, 446

Delmas, Delphin M., 423, 434, 477

Delorme, B., 194, 205

Dement, Ralph, 327, 332

Henry, J. Q. A., 470

Hermann, Binger, 13, 46, 61

Heth, Henry, 478, 485

Hewett, Frances Piper, *xxvi*, 27, 98, 102, 129, 132: death, 289, 295; marriage, 103

Hewett, Henry, *xxvi*, 98, 198, 340

Hewett, Mary Piper, *xxvi*, 27, 102, 129: marriage, 197–98

Hewett, Robert, *xxvi*, 206

Hewett, Susan Piper, *xxvi*, 27, 102, 132, 282, 284, 414

Heydenfeldt, Solomon, 541, 547

Higby, W. H., 243–44, 251–52

Higgins, Alice S., 193, 205

Higgins, William L., 34, 198, 205

Hilgard, Eugene W., 236, 265, 273

Hill, Jessie Adams, 271, 274

Hill, Joseph, 270, 271, 274, 333, 336, 396, 415, 511

Hill, Mary, 281, 294

Hill, Sarah Althea, *see* Terry, Sarah A. Hill

Hill, Sarah E., 306, 457, 485, 503, 541, 578, 593: Deadys lodge with, 287, 295; new establishments, 455, 479, 619, 621

Hill, W. Lair, *xxii*, 2, 11, 88, 97–99, 128, 162, 169, 195, 204, 218–20: angers MPD, 264; resigns from *Oregonian*, 232; Will-Wall controversy, 171, 187

Hiller, David A., 49, 434

Hiller, Sarah Ladd, 26, 27, 31, 49, 424, 434: and W. S. Ladd, 426

Hills, George, 313–18 *passim,* 331

Hillyer, E. W., 11, 45, 265

Himes, George, 237, 263, 282

Hines, Harvey K., 525, 528

Hinman, Alanson, 34, 50

Hinsdale, George, 17–18, 47

Hipple, *see* Mitchell, John H.

Hirsch, Ella, 555

Hirsch, Solomon, *xxiii*, 11, 12, 30, 36, 97, 163, 212, 402, 532, 619: Dolph election, 403; minister to Turkey, 558; retains MPD, 23; state cases, 291, 300, 337; water bill, 96, 100

Hoadly, George, 498, 506

Hoar, Ebenezer R., 468, 484

Hoar, George F., 555, 572

Hobbs, Sarah, 82, 108

Hobhouse, Arthur, 421, 422, 433

Hobson, Richard, 32, 150

Hodges, Annie Abernethy, 398, 407

Hodges, Henry Clay, 407

Hoffman, Ogden, Jr., *xxiii*, 11, 265, 302, 343, 391, 411, 424, 425, 428, 473–74, 554, 576, 591: last illness, 611; opposes MPD, *xxxvi*

Hoffman, Southard, 477, 484, 576

Hogg, T. Egenton, 72, 100, 107

Holbrook, Annie, *see* Withington, Annie Holbrook

Holbrook, Mary Hooper, *xxiii*, 31, 66, 75, 198, 276, 282, 324, 614

Holbrook, Will, 32, 50

Holcomb, William R., 538, 547

Holgate, Ann Watt, 466, 483

Holladay, Ben, *xxiii*, 12–13, 17, 24, 30–31, 62–104 *passim,* 121–29 *passim,* 170, 171, 185, 199, 218, 300, 375: Barnhart, 96, 102, 103–104; creditors, 496, 506, 525, 526, 533; Elliott case, 26, 45–46, 105; Grant, 189, 287; G. Helm, 199; Ingalls, 189, 204–205, 238; Mitchell, 79, 97, 127, 218; Nesmith, 70, 221; O&C RR Co., 45–46, 67, 162, 180, 186; Portland primaries, 79, 80; Mary Van Camp, 96, 97, 445; Wallamet locks purchase bill, 98

Holladay, Ben, Jr., *xxiii*, 128, 577

Holladay, Ben Campbell, 554, 571

Holladay, Esther Campbell, *xviii, xxiii*, 70, 96, 97, 103–104, 185, 205, 445, 571

Holladay, Joseph, *xxiii*, 496, 503, 506

Holladay, Linda, 554, 571

Holladay, Notley Ann Calvert, *xxiii*, 128

Holladay, Samuel W., 429, 434

Holland, Josiah, 346, 378

Holland, Robert A., 562–63, 572

Holliday, Frederick, 576, 606, 627

Holman, Alfred, 400, 407, 470, 490–91, 514–15, 601

Holman, Emma Rounds, 229, 246, 422

Holman, Frederick V., *xxiii*, 8, 397, 450, 497, 516, 605

Holman, James D., 8, 93, 95, 106, 161, 176, 404, 405

Holman, John, 25, 166, 177

Holman, Katie, 84, 516

Holman, Libbie Buss, 447, 463

Holman, Rachel Summers, 66, 93, 95, 106, 457, 497

Holman, Sprague, 131

Holt, Joseph, 587, 607

Honolulu, Hawaii, 576–80, 582–91

Hooker, Joseph, 109: descr., 87

Hooker Jim, 150

Hooper, George F., 622

Hooper, Mary, 163, 176, 286, 426–27, 622

Hoover, Miss H. R., 75, 108

Hope, B. C., 315

Hopkins, Mary F. Sherwood, 425–27 *passim,* 434

Horton, Dexter, 243, 247

Hosmer, Theodore, 130, 146, 158, 450

36, 63, 78, 89, 92, 130, 242, 309, 449, 494

Lewis, David (son), 398, 410, 499

Lewis, Elizabeth (dtr), *see* Good, Elizabeth Lewis

Lewis, Emma (dtr), 156, 161, 392, 479, 520

Lewis, Eva (dtr), 320, 334, 457

Lewis, Sallie (dtr), 499, 550

Lewis, J. R., 188, 409

Lewis and Clark, 33, 240, 254

Library Assn. of Portland, 1, 2, 5, 9, 16, 68, 69, 76, 79, 81, 90, 117, 119, 120, 128, 158, 159, 166, 173, 182, 185, 188, 210, 229–32, 242, 254, 275, 278, 302, 327, 335, 336, 409, 430, 463, 471, 490, 492, 493, 511, 518, 526, 533: building programs, 75, 76, 156, 162, 185, 410, 466, 526, 531, 532, 533, 537, 597, 613, 616; catalogue subscription, 255, 257, 261; librarian elected, 8; perpetual memberships, 201, 209–12, 270, 328, 481, 510, 526; special collections, 128, 141; special endowment, 602

Lindau, Paul, 423, 433

Linderman, Dell, 99, 106, 111

Linderman, Martha Thompson, 63, 99, 106

Lindsley, Aaron L., 7, 22, 44, 64, 96, 103, 125, 135–36, 158, 168, 172, 196, 221, 229, 257, 269, 334–35, 454, 455

Lindsley, Julia (Mrs. A. L.), 64, 196

Lindsley, Julia, *see* Gilbert, Julia Lindsley

Linn City, Ore., 93

Linthicum, Stewart B., 479, 485, 499, 516, 520

Lippincott, J. P., 360, 380

Little, Sophie, 473, 474, 567

Lloyd, Jessie Bross, 344, 378

Lloyd, William Demarest, 344, 378, 422, 423, 569

Logan, David, 7, 19, 22, 30, 34, 44, 160

Lombard, Charles, 583, 584, 607

Long, John D., 350, 379

Longfellow, Henry W., 349, 393

Loomis, Frank, 563, 573

Lord, Juliette Montague, 304, 321, 330

Lord, William P., 209–10, 223, 392

Loryea, A. M., 13, 47, 125

Loryea, Elizabeth Stephens, 47, 125

Los Angeles, Calif., 390

Loveridge, D. E., 543, 544, 547, 550, 596

Loveridge, Emily L., 599, 609

Lowell, John, 348, 349, 379

Lowenstein, Samuel, 184, 204, 532, 544

Lownsdale, Daniel H., 42–43

Lownsdale, Millard O., 542, 547

Luéres, Frederick, 231, 232, 246

Lund, William (Chumley), 558–59, 594, 599, 609

Luttrell, John King, 200, 206

Lyman, Horace, 235, 246

Lyon, Mrs. S. M., 132, 146

McAllister, Hall, 24–26, 31, 48, 471

McArthur, Clifton (Clifford), 599

McArthur, Hattie Nesmith, *xxiv, xxvi,* 25, 26, 81, 142, 157, 169, 255, 277, 337, 599: marriage, 262

McArthur, Lewis Linn, *xxiv,* 91, 142, 157, 229, 255, 262, 277, 431, 447, 469, 492, 495, 510, 531, 533, 543, 556, 599, 617, 618

McBean, John, 237, 247

McCall, John M., 444, 458

*McCall vs McDowell,* 37, 60

McCartey, John, 135, 146

McClure, A. K., 360, 380

MacConnell, Christine, 396, 407

McCormick, Harry J., 302, 329

McCormick, Patrick J., 242, 247

McCormick, S. J., 26, 44, 199, 262

McCown, Ferdinand O., 143, 148, 446–47

McCoy, Newton, 535, 546

McCracken, Ada, *see* Hurley, Ada McC.

McCracken, Henry, *xxv*

McCracken, John, *xxv,* 33, 34, 63, 75, 86, 99, 102, 118, 167, 190, 192, 195, 215, 216, 281, 325, 338, 339, 443, 454, 503, 524, 553, 623: amateur actor, 28, 156, 256, 301, 391–92, 395, 396; BSGS, 1, 15, 85; TrCh, 17, 161, 188

McCracken, Minnie Pixley, *xxv,* 256

McCreary, Belle Swearingen, *xxi,* 372, 375, 387

McCreary, Richard, 564

McCully, Lawrence, 576–79 *passim,* 590, 606

McDonald, Angus, 65, 69, 106

McDonald, F. A., 531, 545

McDougal, John, 171, 177

MacElroy, Ebenezer, B., 447, 459

McFadden, Obadiah, *xxxv,* 98, 111, 138

McFarland, Mrs. A. R., 310, 330

MacFeely, Robert, 365, 380

McGibeny, Mrs. J. B., 26, 49

McGibeny family, 503, 506

McGinn, Henry E., 523, 528

McGraw, Edward W., 98, 100, 110, 121, 138, 221, 229, 299, 424, 426, 622

Mack, Mary, 129, 146

Mackall, Benjamin, 368, 369, 381, 611

McKay, Alex, 70, 115

Snow, Zera, 532, 546, 558, 595

Sonnefeld, Anton, 570, 573, 593, 595, 598–99, 602

South Portland Real Estate Co., *see* Caruthers case

Sox, Weltha Young, 34, 50

Spalding, Mrs. Z. S., 579, 607

Sparks, William A. J., 525, 529

Spiller, Mary Boise, *xvii*, 216, 281, 340, 397

Spores Ferry, 261

Sprague, John W., 12, 45, 136, 283, 318

Sprague, Robert B., 481, 485

Sprague, William, 348, 379

Spreckels, Claus, 577

Spreckels, John D., 622

Springfield, Mass., 350–51

Spuhn, Carl, 311, 313, 330, 419

Squires, Watson C., 303, 305, 330, 480

Stanford, Leland, 267, 273, 476, 502, 616

Stanley, Laura, 540, 547

Stark, Benjamin, family of:
    Stark, Benjamin, *xxviii*, 2, 94, 134, 135, 171, 335, 347–48, 443, 446, 543, 551, 612: descr., 345, 553, 614; TrCh, 98, 123–26 *passim*, 562
    Stark, Benjamin, Jr. (son), 134, 347, 443, 446
    Stark, Genevieve (dtr), 345
    Stark, Grace (dtr), 345, 347
    Stark, Will (son), 347

*Stark vs Starr*, 2, 21, 42–43

State political conventions: Democrat, 74, 159, 302; Republican, 72, 82–83, 218, 303, 394

Stearns, Loyal B., 492, 505

Stebbins, Horatio, 281, 294

Steel, George, 333, 376

Steel, James, 85, 109, 131

Steele, Alden H., 138, 147, 319

Steffen, John H., 514, 527

Stephens, Ann Sophia, 344, 378

Stephens, Elizabeth Walker, 78, 108

Stephens, James, 78, 108

Stevens, Hazard, *xxviii*, 220, 224

Stevens, John L., 577, 580, 584, 587, 606, 622

Stevens, Kate, *xxviii*, 10, 137, 157, 158, 286, 349, 350, 379

Stevens, Margaret Hazard, *xxviii*, 10, 137, 138, 286

Stevens, Oliver, 350, 379

Stevens, Robert J., 341, 378

Stevens, Ward, 520, 528

Stevens, William B., 358, 359, 380

Stevenson, John, 35, 51

Stewart, Cornelia C., 354, 379

Stewart, Katie, 203, 207

Stewart, William, 187, 204

Stewart, William M., 424, 425, 434, 474–75, 477

Stickeen Glacier, Alaska, 312

Stickney, William, 220, 224

Stirling, Frederick H., 317, 331

Stone, Fred P., 14, 47, 67, 100, 162, 549, 551, 598

Stone, Mary, *see* Strong, Mary Stone

Story, George L., *xxviii*, 29, 86, 531

Story, Elizabeth, *see* Hamilton, Elizabeth Story

Story, Kate, *xxviii*, 203, 237, 275, 319, 412, 452, 512, 516, 531–32, 619: engaged, 624

Story, Sarah E., 66, 216

Stott, Raleigh, *xxix*, 124, 219, 260, 262, 320, 396, 410, 443, 464, 498, 499, 535, 553, 559: marriage, 217

Stott, Susan Plowden Stout, *xxix*, 2, 7, 8, 12, 62, 75, 91, 123, 127, 131, 140, 143, 157, 161, 168, 172, 174, 182–86 *passim*, 191, 200, 202, 213, 219, 235, 258, 262, 320, 396, 408, 443, 498, 553, 559: descr., 169; epithalamia, 217; financial troubles, 15, 20, 33, 88; ill, 105

Stout, Charlotte (Lottie), *xxix*, 84, 327, 418, 419, 422, 443, 446: engaged, 599

Stout, George, 613, 620

Stout, Lansing, *xxix*, 4, 7, 8, 10: death and funeral, 11; financial difficulties, 8–9, 14

Stout, Mary, 516, 599

Stout, Susan Plowden, *see* Stott, Susan Stout

Stoy, W. H., 2–7 *passim*, 16, 89, 304, 427: resignation, 3–6 *passim*, 17

Stratton, Charles Carroll, 518, 519, 528, 598

Stratton, Sallie Dearborn, *see* Kearney, Sallie Stratton

Straub, John, 340, 377, 515

Strong, Alice Henderson, *xxii*, *xxix*, 2, 4, 8, 13, 16, 17, 18, 25–26, 33, 38, 62, 73, 83, 84, 86, 93, 100–104 *passim*, 117–21 *passim*, 128–31 *passim*, 135, 136, 139, 158, 161, 165, 167, 172, 174, 193, 236, 241, 260, 271, 291, 308, 327, 340, 342, 453, 456, 466, 471, 490, 498, 503, 517, 600: anniversary verse, 288; child christened, 299; marriage, 169; M. Rodney, 66, 73

Strong, Curtis C., *xxii*, *xxix*, 84, 109, 165, 169, 172, 174, 183, 228, 230, 238, 288, 443, 471, 497, 510, 535, 560, 629: child dies, 405; chloral overdose, 403, 404

Strong, Fred, 142, 169, 498

Strong, Julia, 557, 567, 568

233–34, 249–50; B. Holladay, 63; J. H. Mitchell, 96, 211, 223, 503; *Oregonian* ownership, 232
Scott, Irving M., 478, 485
Scott, Lemuel, 264, 273
Scott, Thomas Fielding, 159, 175
Scott, Winfield, 341, 377
Seamen, legal status, 6, 15, 68, 69, 126, 128, 141, 172, 210, 212–13, 287, 299, 489, 491, 500–501, 538, 539
Sears, Alfred F., 338, 376
Seattle, Wn., 138, 243, 341, 396, 601
Sebree, Uriel, 506, 514
Sebree, Mrs. Uriel, 502
*Seeley vs Reed*, 464, 465, 486, 495
Seeleye, Nellie, *see* Evans, Nellie Seeleye
Seely, Jonas, 265, 266, 273
Seghers, Charles Jean, 300, 301, 329
Seid Back, 526, 529
Seller, Moses, 38, 73
Sellwood, James, 6, 44, 134, 137
Sellwood, John, 44, 157, 342
Sellwood, John W., 44, 199, 305
Semple, Eugene, 132, 143, 146, 159, 162, 163
Sessions, David R., 591, 598
Severance, H. W., 577, 578, 585
Sewall, Russell E., 626, 629
Seward, Clarence A., 409, 432, 562, 563
Seymour, S. A., 160, 176
Shakespeare Club, 396, 409, 411, 412, 479–80
Shannon, Davis, 411, 432
Shannon, Milton, 161, 176
Shannon, Wesley, 431, 434
Shapleigh, Elisha B., 357, 379
Shapleigh, Mrs. Elisha B., 355, 379
Sharon, William, 265, 273, 480, 487, 488
*Sharon vs Hill*, 465, 471, 473, 474–78 *passim*, 480–81, 487–88, 489, 491, 494, 502, 541, 547, 558
Sharpless, Abram, 340, 377, 415
Shattuck, Erastus D., 235, 270, 401
Shaw, A. C. R. (Sheep), 408, 432
Shelby, Annie Blanche, 287, 295
Sheldon, Lionel L., 389, 406
Sheridan, Philip H., 197, 206
Sherlock, Dorothea, 132, 146
Sherlock, William, 20, 48
Sherman, Frank, 468, 484
Sherman, John, 468, 484
Sherman, Rachel: descr., 323
Sherman, William Tecumseh, 321–23 *passim*, 386, 419: descr., 323
Shiel, George, 71, 72, 107, 157
Shillaber, Cynthia Hoff, 267, 273

Shiras, George, 627, 629
Shiras, Oliver P., 455, 459
Shively, John M., 32, 50
Shofner, Alice Jackson, 287, 295
Shofner, James C., 287, 295
Shorb, Mrs. J. Campbell, 6, 44
Shorb, James de Barth, 494, 505
Shuck, Andrew, 284, 294
Sillitoe, Acton Windeyer, 317, 331, 463
Silver, C. S., 81, 108
Silverton, Ore., 411
Simon, Joseph, 442
Simpson, Ben, *xxviii*, 63, 72, 94, 97, 100, 102, 125, 134
Simpson, Samuel Leonidas, *xxviii*, 2, 185, 215
Simpson, Sylvester Confucius, *xxviii*, 2, 3, 8, 67, 75, 92, 97, 99, 119, 136, 137
Sinnott, Nicholas B., 62, 106
Sister Joseph, 242, 247
Sister Mary Theresa, 242, 247
Sitka, Alaska, 311–12
Sitton, Charles, 535
Sitton, Nathan (Doc), 402, 407
Skidmore, J. H., 394, 406
Skidmore, Stephen G., 328, 332
Sladen, Joseph A., 352, 379
Slater, James H., *xxviii*, 17, 366, 369, 386, 387
Slavery, 253, 455, 524, 587
Sloan, Sarah A., 415, 432
Smalley, E. V., 422, 433
Smith, Andrew J., 166, 176
Smith, Debbie Harker, 32, 50, 558, 600
Smith, Edith Carter, 592, 595, 608
Smith, Elijah, 470, 486
Smith, George Venable, 75, 107, 125
Smith, Hiram, 137, 147
Smith, John, 71, 107
Smith, John Mott, 402, 407
Smith, Joseph S., 71, 107, 126, 127
Smith, Louise Humphrey, 455, 459, 470
Smith, Maria Campbell, *xviii, xxviii*, 76, 103, 120
Smith, Milton W., 270, 274, 281, 282, 290, 299, 302: admitted to bar, 335
Smith, N. R. (Barnesville, O.), 368
Smith, Samuel M., *xviii, xxviii*, 96, 103
Smith, Seneca, 210, 223, 492
Smith, Silas B., 240 247
Smith, Solomon, 32–33, 50, 254
Smith, Tom, 444, 458
Smith, Victor, 558, 572
Smith, William K., 50, 85, 127
Snead, Mrs. (Mrs. Grundy), 386, 406
Snow, Eliot, 558, 572

657

Tilden, Samuel J., 220, 225, 227, 229, 307

Tilton, Charles E., 81, 136, 211, 222, 230, 268, 426

Tilton, James, 28, 49, 137

Tolmie, William L., 94, 110, 129, 137, 212, 215, 271, 313, 314

Toomey, Harry, 170, 171, 172, 177, 592

Towler, Reginald H., 103, 111, 127

Townsend, C. W., 448, 459

Townsend, Frederick, 235, 246, 456, 517

Townsend, George Alfred, 523, 528

Townsend, Luther T., 195, 205

Tracy, Bessie, 271, 274

Travers, William R., 345, 378

Travis, Martin V. B., 409, 432

Trevett, Kate, 496, 505

Trevett, Lou, 524

Trevett, T. B., 97, 110, 256, 402, 530, 534

Trimble, W. F., 11, 45

Trinity Episcopal Church (TrCh): building, 66, 73, 78, 79, 89, 99, 102, 123; consecration, 135; convocations, 134–35, 165, 338–39, 468–69; finances, 29, 131–32, 334; fire, 172; general convention, 165, 501, 562–64 *passim*, 627; Mens' Guild, 100, 102; organ loft, 304, 305; organization, 91, 121, 124, 157, 161, 263, 597; parsonage, 160, 165, 167; pastors called, 40, 65, 68, 70, 119, 123, 201, 447, 552; pastors resigned, 3, 4, 6, 17, 123, 129, 447; Women's Guild, 201, 218, 301, 409, 429, 441, 512

Tripp, Bartlett, 497, 506

Troll, Emma Steenrod, 367

Troupe, James W., 322, 332

Trousseau, George, 582, 583, 589, 607

Truckee, Calif., 266

Trusdell, George, 473, 474, 484

Trumbull, Lyman, 344, 378

Trutch, Mrs. John, 315, 317

Trutch, Joseph, 216, 224, 309, 313–18 *passim*, 399, 601

Turner, Creed, 255, 272

Tuttle, B. B., 210, 223, 539, 593

Tuttle, Daniel, 354, 379, 415

T'Vault, Rhoda Boone, 445, 459

T'Vault, William, 79, 108, 312, 331, 494

Tyler, George, 475–76, 484

Tyler, Robert O., 31, 49

Tyson, Jesse, 362, 380, 385

Tyson, Julia, 361, 362, 380

Underwood, J. B., 203, 207

Underwood, Margaret J., 447, 469

U. S. Courthouse, Portland, 126, 168, 170, 184, 199–200, 221, 479: investigation, 198; stone contract, 3, 5, 103

University of California, *xxiii*, 265

University of Oregon, 219, 256, 298, 301, 396, 412, 419: Board of Regents, 216, 220, 229, 240, 255, 258, 261, 270, 280, 281, 320, 340, 342, 397, 415, 431, 447, 469, 492, 536, 556, 596, 616, 625–26; buildings, 212, 464, 469, 492; commencements, 261, 281, 397, 415, 447, 495, 517–18, 536, 556, 596, 616, 626; faculty, 212, 216, 236, 240, 255, 270, 281, 340, 431, 447, 523, 596, 626; finances, 239, 240, 341, 400, 409; law school, 447, 453, 494, 495, 516, 534, 537, 552, 556, 595, 624, 626; medical school, 596; observatory, 533; student voting, 280, 293; H. Villard, 341, 342, 398, 400, 409, 413, 420, 492

University of Washington, 243, 396

Upton, W. W., 10, 11, 45, 74, 118, 127, 159, 160, 373, 382, 384

Urso, Camilla, 230, 231, 232, 246, 594

Valentine, John J., 218, 224, 231, 370, 592

Valentine, J. Townsend, 499, 506

Vancouver, Wash., 30, 323, 397, 556

Vanderbilt, John M., 311, 330

Vanderbilt, Lena Bancroft, 311, 330

Van Fridagh, Elizabeth Rumpen, 106, 167, 193

Van Fridagh, Hortense, *see* Taylor, Hortense Van Fridagh

Van Fridagh, Prosper, 106, 167, 193

Van Horn, Thomas B., 191, 205

Van Schyver, William J., 15, 47, 540, 541

Vernon, George W. H., 66, 68, 69, 106, 120

Vest, George G., 369, 381

Victor, Frances Fuller, 76, 108, 341, 424, 446, 539, 600

Victoria, B. C., 137–38, 309–10, 313–15, 317–18, 601

Victoria Boys School, 138

Vigilantes, 430

Villard, Henry, *xxix*, 213, 214, 280, 303, 336, 343, 387, 392, 403, 413, 417, 422, 426, 496, 619: accused, 452; Board of Trade address, 412–13; failure, 439, 458; Ore. Imp. stock, 334, 335; OSN Co., 281, 293–94; transcontinental spike driving, 420; U. of O., 341, 398, 493

Vinton, Francis, 276, 292

Virginia City, Nev., 266

von Holt, Bertha, 432, 577

von Holt, Harry, 412, 432

von Holt, Marie R., 432, 577, 584, 585, 589, 612

Wadhams, William 218, 221, 224, 481
Waianae, Hawaii, 580–82
Waikiki, Hawaii, 577–78, 588–89
Waite, Louise Breyman, 124, 145, 159, 229
Waite, Morrison R., 374, 382, 387, 497, 498: death, 533
Wakefield, Leland H., 5, 19, 43
Wakeman, Emma A., 599, 609
Waldo, Daniel, 160, 176
Waldo, John B., 169, 220, 304, 447, 517
Waldron, D. V., 390
Walker, John S., 85, 106
Walker, Mrs. John S., 65, 83, 106
Wallace, Ada, 429
Wallace, Lucien W., 131
Wallace, William T., 66, 106, 265, 267
Wallace, Mrs. William T., 428–29
Wallamet Falls Canal & Lock Co., 10, 15, 30, 45, 93, 98, 211, 278, 279
Wallamet Society, 13, 14, 21, 22, 70, 75, 80
Wallamet Transportation & Locks Co., 211
Wallamet University, 157, 212, 214, 216
Wallamet University Medical School: building, 532, 626; commencement, 442; MPD, prof. of Med. Juris., 255, 279, 280, 290, 291, 298, 304, 333, 334, 338, 394, 532, 623–24; dissection, 394; Oregon Med. College disbanded, 211; reformed, 254–55; Wall. U. Med. Dept. & Ore. Med. Col. combine, 260
Walla Walla, Wash., 322–23
Walton, James, 550, 571
Walton, John, 550, 571
Walton, Joshua J., 118, 145, 236, 281, 399
Wantland, Charles E., 401, 407
Ward, John P., 285, 294
Ward, Robert, 138, 147
Wardner, Idaho, 537
Warren, Henry, 17, 47
Washburn, Edward A., 353, 379
Washburne, Elihu B., 259, 273
Washington, L. Q., 371, 381–82
Washington, D. C., 365–66, 369–75, 384–88, 564–68, 627
Washington Inaugural Centennial, 553
Wasserman, Philip, 93, 110, 503
Waters, W. S., 302, 329
Watkinds, William H., 24, 28, 48, 52–53, 338, 376: attacks Bush and Thayer, 520, 528
Watkins, W. H., 37, 51, 279
Watson, David Lowery, 449, 459

Watson, Edward B., 449, 459
Watson, James F., 97, 110, 285, 303, 393, 441
Watt, Ahio, 120, 145, 170, 198, 219, 228, 260
Watt, Jo, 193, 205, 415
Watt, Levina Lyon, 415, 536
Watt, Mary Elder, 145, 170, 219
Watts, Mrs., 93, 99
Watts, Julia, 3, 4, 22, 27, 28
Waymire, Fred, 28, 49
Weaver, Jonathan, 165, 176
Webster, Gaius, 97, 110
Weeks Reuben, 161, 176, 242
Weidler, George, 146, 526
Weil, Oscar, 232, 246
Welch, James, 32, 50
Welch, Nancy Dickerson, 50, 522
Wells, Lemuel H., 199, 206, 239, 322, 450, 497
Welsh, John, 355, 356, 357, 359, 379
Wentworth, John P. H., 489, 502, 505
West, Henry, 366, 367, 368, 381, 515
West Point, N. Y., 352
Whalley, John W., *xxix,* 13, 41, 302, 410, 495, 496, 497, 510: attacks MPD, 549; biog. of MPD, 403, 597; partnership with PRD, 500
Whalley, Mary, 325, 332
Whalley, Susan, *see* Allison, Susan Whalley
Wheat, J. R., 299, 329
Wheaton, Frank, 125, 145, 149
Wheeler, Mary Mackall, 368
Whidden, William M., 526
Whipple, Henry B., 353, 379
White, Horace, 496, 506
White, John, 364
White, R. C., 215, 224, 339
White, T. Brook, 472, 484
Whiteaker, John, 118, 145, 302
Whitehead, Charles E., 471, 484
Whitehouse, May, 320, 331
Whitman, Marcus, 193: myth, 536, 546, 625; trial of murderers, 551
Whitney, George E., *xxi,* 285, 398, 426, 616, 622
Whitney, Henry M., 580, 607
Whitney, Mollie Swearingen, *xxi,* 398, 426
Whitworth, Richard, 266, 273
Whyte, William P., 364, 380
Widemann, Hermann A., 580–82, 590, 607
Wilbur, James H., 135, 174, 236, 336, 525
Wilbur, Lucretia Stevens, 336
Wilbur, Ore., 236–37
Wilcox, Ralph, 31, 49, 78, 191: death, 233